The publisher gratefully acknowledges the generous contributions to this book provided by the Classical Literature Endowment Fund of the University of California Press Foundation, which is supported by a major gift from Joan Palevsky, and by The Jane K. Sather Professorship in Classical Literature Fund.

SATHER CLASSICAL LECTURES

Volume Sixty-Six

Creationism and Its Critics in Antiquity

Creationism and Its Critics in Antiquity

Creationism and Its Critics in Antiquity

DAVID SEDLEY

University of California Press

BERKELEY   LOS ANGELES   LONDON

University of California Press, one of the most distinguished university presses in the United States, enriches lives around the world by advancing scholarship in the humanities, social sciences, and natural sciences. Its activities are supported by the UC Press Foundation and by philanthropic contributions from individuals and institutions. For more information, visit www.ucpress.edu.

University of California Press
Berkeley and Los Angeles, California

University of California Press, Ltd.
London, England

Library of Congress Cataloging-in-Publication Data

Sedley, D. N.
    Creationism and its critics in antiquity / David Sedley
        p.   cm. — (Sather classical lectures ; 66)
    Includes bibliographical references and index.
    ISBN 978-0-520-25364-3 (cloth : alk. paper)
        1. Intelligent design (Teleology).   2. Philosophy, Ancient.
    I. Title.
    BD581.S377   2007
    213—dc22   2007021528

Manufactured in the United States of America

16   15   14   13   12   11   10   09   08   07
10   9   8   7   6   5   4   3   2   1

This book is printed on New Leaf EcoBook 50, a 100% recycled fiber of which 50% is de-inked post-consumer waste, processed chlorine-free. EcoBook 50 is acid-free and meets the minimum requirements of ANSI/ASTM D5634-01 (Permanence of Paper).

For Bev

Contents

Acknowledgments   xi

Preface   xv

I / ANAXAGORAS

1. The Presocratic agenda   1

2. Anaxagoras's cosmology   8

3. The power of *nous*   11

4. Sun and moon   13

5. Worlds and seeds   14

6. *Nous* as creator   20

7. Scientific creationism   25

Appendix. Anaxagoras's theory of matter   26

II / EMPEDOCLES

1. The cosmic cycle   31

2. The double zoogony   33

3. Creationist discourse   52

4. Design and accident   60

Appendix 1. The double zoogony revisited   62

Appendix 2. The chronology of the cycle   67

Appendix 3. Where in the cycle are we?   70

Appendix 4. A Lucretian testimony for Empedocles' zoogony   72

III / SOCRATES

1. Diogenes of Apollonia   75

2. Socrates in Xenophon   78

3. Socrates in Plato's *Phaedo*   86

4. A historical synthesis   89

IV / PLATO

   1. The *Phaedo* myth   93
   2. Introducing the *Timaeus*   95
   3. An act of creation?   98
   4. Divine craftsmanship   107
   5. Is the world perfect?   113
   6. The origin of species   127

V / THE ATOMISTS

   1. Democritus   133
   2. The Epicurean critique of creationism   139
   3. The Epicurean alternative to creationism   150
   4. Epicurean infinity   155

VI / ARISTOTLE

   1. God as paradigm   167
   2. The craft analogy   173
   3. Necessity   181
   4. Fortuitous outcomes   186
   5. Cosmic teleology   194
   6. Aristotle's Platonism   203

VII / THE STOICS

   1. Stoicism   205
   2. A window on Stoic theology   210
   3. Appropriating Socrates   212
   4. Appropriating Plato   225
   5. Whose benefit?   231

EPILOGUE: A GALENIC PERSPECTIVE   239

Bibliography   245

Index Locorum   257

General Index   267

Acknowledgments

This is the book of the Sather Lectures that I delivered at the University of California, Berkeley, in the fall of 2004. I shall therefore start by expressing my very warm gratitude to the Berkeley Department of Classics, both for taking a chance in inviting me to be the ninety-first Sather Professor of Classical Literature, and for its unfailingly generous hospitality and support during my stay. Although it is invidious to pick out individuals, special mention must be given to Mark Griffith, Leslie Kurke, Tony Long, and Donald Mastronarde for making my wife and me feel so welcome from the start. I shall also take the opportunity here to thank by name my three Sather Assistants, Bridget McClain, Athena Kirk, and Chris Churchill, for all their help, and especially Bridget, who among many other things undertook a major restocking of the Sather Office's library during my tenure.

The material that makes up the book's contents has been brewing for some five years. I have taught various aspects of it in courses at the University of Cambridge; the Central European University, Budapest; Keio University, Tokyo; Berkeley itself, where Plato's *Timaeus* was the subject of my graduate seminar; and the Institute of Continuing Education, Madingley Hall, Cambridge. I have learnt more than I can say from discussion with those who participated in these courses.

In addition, over the years I have presented many papers developing one aspect or another of the book's argument. Although I doubt if the following list will be exhaustive, the venues have included the Institut des Hautes Études de Belgique, Brussels; the Université de Paris X, Nanterre; the University of Pittsburgh (conference in honor of Allan Gotthelf); the University of Edinburgh (A. E. Taylor Lecture); the University of Texas at Austin; the University of Warwick (conference on ancient materialism); the University of Leeds (Leeds International Latin Seminar); Princeton University (annual

Ancient Philosophy colloquium); the University of California at Los Angeles; the Institute of Classical Studies, London; the Collegium for Advanced Studies, Helsinki; the University of Durham (Northern Association for Ancient Philosophy); the University of St Andrews (also Northern Association for Ancient Philosophy); Charles University, Prague; the Università degli Studi di Lecce (conference on Aristotelian causation); and the University of Nottingham. My thanks to the organizers of these events, and to the many participants whose comments helped me sharpen up my argument.

The following have been so generous with their time as to read and comment on all or much of my initial draft: Gabor Betegh, Sarah Broadie, Sophia Connell, Thomas Johansen, Inna Kupreeva, Tony Long, Stephen Menn, Dmitri Panchenko, Gretchen Reydams-Schils, Malcolm Schofield, Liba Taub, Alexander Verlinsky, Robert Wardy, and James Warren. Others who have contributed comments on the original lectures or on parts of the book manuscript include Myles Burnyeat, Victor Caston, Andrew Gregory, Mark Griffith, Charles Griswold, Brad Inwood, and Charles Murgia. Yet others, from whose conversation or correspondence I have benefited in various ways, include Peter Adamson, István Bodnár, Robert Bolton, Jennifer Bryan, Gordon Campbell, Philip van der Eijk, John Ferrari, Gail Fine, Stefania Fortuna, Verity Harte, Anna Ju, Stavros Kouloumentas, Henry Mendell, Ian Mueller, David Norman, Kevin Padian, Diana Quarantotto, Richard Patterson, David Robertson, Bob Sharples, John Van Wyhe, Jula Wildberger, and Emma Woolerton. To all of the above, and to numerous others with whom I have discussed related matters over the years, my profound thanks.

It would be impossible to catalogue all the scholars whose published work has guided and informed me in this project. Some of these debts, but by no means all, will be visible in my footnotes. I would also like to take the opportunity to single out Gordon Campbell, whose recent publications on the ancient antecedents of Darwinism and creationism I have found particularly inspiring.

If my footnotes have grown to excessive length, one reason has been the need, without constantly interrupting the flow of my argument, to deal with the many pressing questions and problems that those thanked above have brought to my attention. Another reason is my concern to pitch the main text of the book so far as possible at the same level as I aimed for in the original lectures, which were designed to be accessible to a broad university audience, classical and non-classical alike. Relegating the more technical argumentative support to footnotes and appendices has been one means of achieving this.

At the University of California Press I have been fortunate to have the expert advice and guidance of Laura Cerruti, Rachel Lockman, Cindy Fulton, and Kate Toll. For the cover design I am grateful to Nola Burger, and to Cayetano Anibal for generous permission to use his engraving "La Creación del mundo" as its basis.

Finally, my warm thanks to my twin Cambridge institutions, Christ's College and the Faculty of Classics, both for providing the hothouse conditions in which the book has sprung to life, and for granting me the leave which enabled me to give the lectures at Berkeley.

I am grateful to the Institute for Philosophical Research, Patras, for kind permission to reproduce in chapter II material that originally appeared in D. Sedley, "Empedocles' life cycles," in A. Pierris (ed.), *The Empedoclean Kosmos: Structure, Process and the Question of Cyclicity* (Patras 2005), pp. 331–71; and to the *Revue de Métaphysique et de Morale* for kind permission to reproduce in chapter VII material that originally appeared, in French, in D. Sedley, "Les Origines des preuves stoïciennes de l'existence de dieu," *Revue de Métaphysique et de Morale* 4 (2005), 461–87.

Preface

The dining hall of my college—Christ's College Cambridge—displays portraits of its most illustrious alumni. One pairing is of unique symbolic value. On the left is William Paley (1743–1805), author of the classic version of the Argument from Design. In his *Natural Theology* (1802), Paley developed his celebrated comparison of the world and its natural contents to a watch, on finding which one could not but infer that "there must have existed, at some time and at some place or other, an artificer or artificers who formed it for the purpose which we find it actually to answer, who comprehended its construction and designed its use." To Paley's right stands Charles Darwin. In his days as a student at Christ's (1827–31) Darwin was immensely proud to occupy what he believed to be the same set of rooms as Paley had before him. Yet within months of leaving Cambridge Darwin had embarked on the research which would, when it reached maturity, radically and irreversibly destabilize Paley's confident arguments for intelligent creation.

In today's Cambridge it would rarely if ever occur to me to check with my colleagues whether any of them believe Paley's arguments to trump Darwin's. Locally at least, whatever residual skirmishes may still divide Darwin's successors, the war is generally perceived as having been won by the evolutionists. But the lectures that form the content of the present book were delivered in a country where the legacy of the 1925 Scopes trial in Tennessee still resonates in battles fought on school boards and elsewhere over the teaching of evolution, and where polls suggest that nearly half the population believes that the human race has been created by God in the last ten thousand years, while at the opposite pole fewer than one tenth believe that evolution occurred without God's intervention. In the United States of all places it would have been a mistake to consign the debate to history.

Indeed, my aim is the very reverse of that: it is to use history in order to shed new light on the debate. However, at no point will I address the issue of biblical authority, which has explicitly or implicitly bulked so large in the modern era but has virtually no counterpart in the ancient pagan debate.[1] My interest is in the arguments for and against divine creation and the appeals that were made to its explanatory power. In classical antiquity, these were formulated and deployed by a series of leading philosophers, nearly all of whom agreed, at least tacitly, that settling the issue is fundamental to establishing a proper relationship with the divine, and hence to the quest for human happiness.

What is the value of conducting such a historical exercise? For my money, it lies precisely in treating both sides of the ancient debate with equal sympathy. The object is not to determine who was right, but to understand each position's rationale from the inside. The potential rewards include new historical perspectives on the pantheon of thinkers who laid the foundations of western philosophy and science, perspectives which are likely to enhance our understanding of their ethics, their physics, and even in some cases their logic. But an equally rich recompense lies in the sheer intellectual exercise of thinking one's way into lines of reasoning with which one may well at the outset have no intuitive sympathy, while establishing a matching critical distance from those one is inclined to favor.

In the first two chapters I explore the creationist tendency of the "Presocratic" thinkers Anaxagoras and Empedocles. My third chapter reconstructs Socrates' radical contribution to creationist thought, both in the pages of Xenophon and Plato and in its historical context. Chapter IV is devoted to Plato, with special reference to his *Timaeus*. And the following three chapters trace reactions to this uniquely seminal text among Plato's successors— first (chapter V) the atomists,[2] who tried to show how creationist arguments can be successfully resisted; then (chapter VI) Plato's pupil Aristotle, whose project was to retain all the explanatory benefits of creationism without the

---

1. In later antiquity Platonist interpretation of Plato's *Timaeus*, although it came to manifest some of the same reverential methodology as biblical exegesis, nevertheless differed in never regarding Plato's say-so as sufficient by itself to establish truth. This Platonist tradition constitutes a fascinating story (on which see especially Baltes 1976–78), but not one that I shall pursue in the present study.

2. Since only the first part of chapter V, on the atomists, deals with early atomism, while the greater part is devoted to the Epicureans, this chapter's placement before the chapter on Aristotle may look chronologically eccentric. My choice rests on the conviction that Aristotle's *via media* between creationism and mechanism is better appreciated in the light of the early atomists' articulation of this latter position, to which indeed he explicitly responds.

need to postulate any controlling intelligence; and finally (chapter VII) the Stoics, who developed the battery of creationist arguments broadly known under the label "The Argument from Design." Finally, in a short epilogue, I look back over the debate from the point of view of its most significant direct heir, Galen. To the best of my knowledge, this is a history that has never hitherto been written in full.[3]

To anticipate any misunderstandings, let me clarify here what for the purposes of this book I mean by "creationism."

Some have assumed me to be referring to the belief that the world was, as the Genesis account is usually understood to say, created by God *out of nothing*. But that issue will play no part in the book. That even a divine creator would, like any craftsman, have to use preexisting materials is an assumption that the ancient Greeks apparently never questioned.

Others have assumed that by creationism I mean the thesis that the world was created *at some past time*, as Plato's *Timaeus* appears to say if taken at face value, rather than having always existed, as many Platonists took to be Plato's real meaning. That topic has been ceaselessly debated among interpreters of the *Timaeus* for two and a half millennia. In this book I give it just ten pages (chapter IV §3, pp. 98–107).

What I intend by creationism is neither of these things, but rather the thesis that the world's structure and contents can be adequately explained only by postulating at least one intelligent designer, a creator god.[4] This is, indeed, the primary issue that divides modern "creationists" from their Darwinian critics.

It also divided the greatest thinkers of antiquity.

3. However Pease 1941 is an article which offers a very judicious outline of the story, indeed one that goes beyond this book in covering late antiquity as well. Partial approaches to the same goal are Theiler 1924, which takes the teleological side of the story down as far as Aristotle (on Theiler's book, cf. p. 75 below), and Hankinson 1998, a valuable synopsis of ancient causal theory which includes a good deal on teleology.

4. Following the practice of the ancients, throughout this book I shall vary without warning or apology between "god" and "the gods." Use of the former does not imply monotheism.

I Anaxagoras

1. THE PRESOCRATIC AGENDA

The earliest western philosophers were the dazzlingly original Greek thinkers conventionally known as the Presocratics—a line-up which included such heterogeneous figures as Thales, Anaximander, Pythagoras, Heraclitus, Parmenides, Zeno of Elea, Anaxagoras, Empedocles, Democritus, and Protagoras. Our label "Presocratics" assumes that Socrates, who lived in the late fifth century B.C., initiated a new direction in philosophical thought sufficiently radical to mark off his predecessors and many of his contemporaries as jointly constituting a distinct group. While such demarcations inevitably oversimplify, for example by conferring spurious homogeneity on the group thus labelled,[1] one of my contentions in this book (chapter III) will be that, at least on the issue of divine creation, Socrates really can be seen to mark a fundamental new beginning in western thought. So I shall stick with the conventional term and speak of a "Presocratic" agenda.

It is a widespread perception that the Presocratics were materialists who did not think teleologically—that with the possible exception of one minor thinker, Diogenes of Apollonia, they simply did not anticipate Plato's insistence on the irreducible presence of purposive structures in the world. Both Plato and Aristotle have done much to foster this impression, even though it in fact rests on a rather selective reading of their works.[2] One reason, no doubt, why the impression has not been as actively resisted as it

1. For warnings about this and other dangers of the term, along with a more nuanced characterization of early Greek philosophy, see Long 1999.
2. Plato *Philebus* 28d5–9, in particular, is a useful antidote to the better-known *Phaedo* 96a5–99d2; cf. also Sedley 2003a, pp. 90–92, for further Platonic evidence. In *Metaphysics* A (esp. 3–4) Aristotle seeks to establish his own originality in iso-

1

might is that many would like to regard materialistic explanation as one of the Presocratics' great merits, contrasting favorably with Plato's turn to theistic teleology, this latter being a regrettable step with long-term damaging consequences for the progress of science.

Setting aside any such historical evaluation, my aim in the opening two chapters is to correct what I believe to be, for better or worse, a serious misperception of the Presocratic agenda. That the world is governed by a divine power is a pervasive assumption of Presocratic thought. The assumption does not always focus specifically on the world's origins, but where it does it is again a widespread view that the world's original creation exhibited that same divine causation.

To see where these assumptions came from, there is much to be gained by making a brief start, around 700 B.C., with Hesiod, one of the earliest two surviving Greek poets, and author of a classic cosmogonic myth in his *Theogony*. Despite its considerable common ground with the mythologies of neighboring cultures, Hesiod's own perspective on the world's formation seems to have been seminal in forming the distinctively Greek tradition of cosmogony that grew up in its wake. The agenda of the Presocratic cosmologists was in effect already largely set by this creation myth's opening:

> The very first thing was that Chaos came to be. Then
> broad-bosomed Earth, a safe seat forever of all the gods . . .
> *Theogony* 116–17

There followed a range of further births, including that of Love—a procreative force, ensuring the emergence of subsequent generations. The initial deities then became the forebears of a variety of further actors on the cosmic stage, including Night, who would become in turn the mother of Day; Heaven, the offspring of Earth; and Ocean. In due course further races were created by the gods, including mankind.

Without going into details, we may usefully note some features of this mythological sketch.

1. The explanatory model used by Hesiod is genealogical. The main structural features of the world as we know it are imagined to have come into being as successive generations of a family—at first a somewhat dysfunctional family, as it turns out, but one which has now settled down into a kind of equilibrium. It is not entirely clear in what relative measures these

---

lating the final cause *as a cause*, but is far from denying a teleological component to the thought of Hesiod, Parmenides, and Empedocles so far as regards the presence in the world of intelligent powers aiming at good outcomes.

protagonists' representation as divinities alludes to their everlastingness, to their power over our lives, and to their purposive functioning, but this last is unlikely to be wholly absent. If so, the presence of some kind of conscious controlling agency was implicit from the outset.

2. The very first deity was Chaos, who has the rare privilege of being grammatically neuter.[3] Being a divinity and therefore immortal, Chaos must be assumed to be still with us, but now transformed by the presence in it of the other divinities. Whether—debatably—Chaos is to be assimilated more closely to our notion of matter or to that of space,[4] its precedence over the rest of the world order already sets the pattern for an enduring feature of ancient cosmology: the world is an orderly structure imposed on a preexisting entity, namely a substrate, matrix, or background which so far as its own nature is concerned is unstructured. Later physicists would vie to identify the true nature of this primeval entity: is it air, fire, or some nameless and indefinite substance or container such as the mysterious "receptacle" described by Plato?[5]

3. The most fundamental feature of the orderly structure, and hence the first named by Hesiod, is the amazing stability of the earth ("broad-bosomed Earth, a safe seat forever of all the gods . . . "). Generations of philosophers would compete to explain how the earth, the heaviest thing known to us, is not at this very moment hurtling downwards. Their various solutions—the earth's floating on water or air; its perfect centrality in the cosmos; its infinite downward extension; its occupying the center of a vortex; and, most daring of all, its eternally orbiting a central fire[6]—came to be emblematic of Presocratic research into the causes of cosmic order.

4. Hesiod recognizes, in the early appearance of Love, the need for a creative force to give direction to the continuing process of cosmogony (a point respectfully acknowledged by Aristotle, *Met.* A 4, 984b23–31).

5. The origin of mankind is itself one of the recognized explananda. While the divine beings who jointly constitute the cosmos are linked by family

---

3. Hesiod's only other neuter divinity seems to be Chaos's offspring Erebos. (Tartarus is referred to by the neuter plural Τάρταρα only, I think, when the name is designating a region rather than a divine individual.)

4. On Chaos in Hesiod, see e.g. Stokes 1962, Podbielski 1986, Miller 2001. The word's basic meaning is undoubtedly something like "space" or "gap," but connotations of material fluidity (via an etymological link to χεῖσθαι, "flow") were being attached to it as early as the sixth century B.C.; see Pherecydes 7 B 1A DK.

5. Cf. p. 97 below. For Plato's "receptacle" as combining features of both space and matter, see Algra 1995, chapter 3.

6. Thales (water), Anaximenes and Anaxagoras (air), Anaximander (centrality), Xenophanes (infinite depth), Empedocles and the atomists (vortex), some Pythagoreans (orbiting).

membership, human beings are not part of that same genealogy, but are its manufactured products. In Hesiod's *Works and Days*, the gods are said to have "made" the series of mortal races that culminated in mankind (110, 128, 144, 158).[7] Hesiod's further myth of the origin of woman, Pandora, supplies the additional information that she was made out of earth and water by the craftsman god Hephaestus (*Works and Days* 47–105), to whom Zeus had delegated the task. By this symbolism it is already made clear in outline that man is not a first-level component of the divine cosmic structure, but somehow a secondary product.[8] Although Hesiod supplies no further information about the divine craftsmanship that generated mankind, we already have here the matrix for later creationist theories of human origins.[9]

All of these issues were to remain high on the cosmologists' agenda. The very word *kosmos*, "order," and hence "world-order" or simply "world," sums up the main task of the early physicists, despite the uncertainty as to how early the actual word came to be used in such a sense.[10] How does the world succeed in possessing and maintaining such orderly features as the fixed arrangement of its four strata, earth, water, air, and fire, the cyclically recurrent motions of the heavenly bodies around a miraculously stable earth, the user-friendly food supply and cycle of seasons, and the enduring presence of stable life forms, ourselves included? All these questions became and remained a focus of debate.

Most of the earliest discussions of which we are aware were concerned with the search for the best type of explanatory model. Hesiod's genealogical model was quickly superseded by a variety of others.[11] Among these, the mechanical model is of particular importance to our story. One very simple explanation of the earth's stability and the motions of the heavenly bodies was that of floating, as even relatively heavy things are seen to do on water or air.[12] A more complex and fruitful mechanical model was that of

---

7. See esp. Clay 2003, pp. 85–86, for the importance of this. I take it that the enigmatic "distinguishing" of humans and gods at Mekone (*Theogony* 535) was, as it were, political or legal, rather than biological (West 1966, *ad loc.*; cf. Clay 2003, pp. 100–101).

8. Cf. Plato's *Timaeus*, where the world and the lesser gods are themselves created by the primary creator, and the creation of mankind is then delegated to those lesser gods themselves, an alternative way of marking off mankind's strictly subordinate status. I see no reason to agree with Solmsen 1963, p. 474, that the making of mankind is not germane to Hesiod's basic conceptual outlook.

9. For the dependent tradition of aetiological fable, see chapter II §3 below.

10. See Kahn 1960, pp. 219–30, who argues for pre-Heraclitean origins.

11. Lloyd 1966 remains the classic study of these models.

12. Earth floats on water (Thales 11 A 14 DK), or on air (Anaximenes 13 A 7(a), 20 DK).

the vortex. In a familiar vortex of water or air, denser stuffs are drawn to the center, finer ones to the periphery. If we imagine the world as a vortex, we can see why the earth would automatically tend to the lower center, with the progressively rarefied stuffs, water, air, and fire, lying outside it. But that would generate a world in which the heavens rotate horizontally around us with their pole of rotation directly overhead (figure 1). We therefore have to imagine the outer part of this vortex tilting to one side while the earth stays upright, and that does then give us a model for a stable flat earth with the heaven rotating at the angle it does (figure 2).[13]

A refinement to this mechanical approach, based on structural equilibrium, is traceable back to Anaximander. Provided that the world is sufficiently symmetrical in structure, its parts, including the earth, will maintain their places simply because they have no more reason to move off in one direction than in another.[14] If, as has been argued,[15] Anaximander was influenced in this appeal to equilibrium by the principles of architecture, the postulation of a cosmic architect is not lagging far behind.

The relevant question for our purposes is whether such paradigms can ever seem *sufficient* to account for cosmic regularity. Certainly they do a fine job of accounting for the world's broad structure and patterns of motion. But how about the emergence of life? This last question is complicated by the fact that biology itself came to provide, not just some of the focal *explananda*, but a second type of explanatory *model* for cosmic structure, one going far beyond Hesiod's simple genealogical model. Thus, to take a very simple example, Anaximander compared the stratification of the cosmic masses to a botanical structure: the layering of a tree, with the bark at the perimeter.[16] Far more ambitiously, and more decisively so far as concerns the eventual direction of cosmology, philosophers would come to assimilate the entire world to a living organism, governed by an immanent deity. Although this conceit found its full expression only much later, particularly in Plato and the Stoics, it had Presocratic antecedents as early as Heraclitus.[17]

13. Cf. Anaxagoras's description of this two-stage process, DL II 9.
14. I am inclined to adhere to this traditional interpretation of Anaximander, founded on Aristotle *DC* 295b10–16, despite the impressive challenge mounted by Furley 1989b. For defense of it, see Bodnár 1992, Panchenko 1994.
15. Hahn 2002.
16. 12 A 10 DK.
17. Cf. n. 25 below. The familiarity of hylozoism in the later fifth century is attested by Melissus's denial that the One, which he equates with the universe, suffers pain or distress (30 B 7 DK).

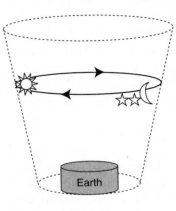

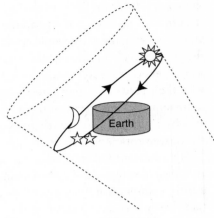

Figure 1   Figure 2

This kind of hylozoism is closely related to a supplementary principle of explanation, which we may call the political model of cosmology. If the world enjoys divine control, its internal regularities can be attributed to a kind of political stability. Such features of the world as the regular cycle of seasons could be presented as exemplifying, on a cosmic scale, that same regulatory factor which in human societies is called justice. Anaximander has been plausibly interpreted[18] here as thinking of the partial victory of cold and wet over hot and dry in winter, followed by the symmetrical reversal of that victory in summer, when he compared cosmic change to the juridical sequence of transgression and retribution (12 B 1 DK).

For reasons like these, the assumption that the cosmos is controlled by one or more divine agents is, far from being Plato's innovation, at least implicitly present in Greek cosmology from a very early date. For most early thinkers such a conception raised no particular problem, because of their starting assumptions about the place of mind in nature. We may put this point in terms of a threefold choice that they faced.

(a) For the majority of these thinkers, the world is inherently animate. Thales, conventionally the earliest of all western philosophers, working in Miletus in the early sixth century B.C., famously remarked that "All things are full of gods" (11 A 22 DK). Most other early thinkers[19] tended to characterize the world's underlying matter as if it were itself divine, if not indeed

18. Esp. Kahn 1960, pp. 178–83.
19. Cf., for Anaximander, Aristotle, *Ph.* 203b11–15, and for Anaximenes, Aetius I 7.13, Cicero *ND* I 26, with discussion by Kirk, Raven, and Schofield 1983, pp. 150–51.

identifiable with god. For thinkers in this pantheist tradition, life and divinity are given as primitive and irreducible properties of things, and there is therefore simply no problem about explaining the world's inclusion of apparently animate features, especially at the level of individual organisms such as ourselves. On the contrary, the problem would be, if anything, to explain why, unlike what we call living beings, some things in the world, such as stones, seem *not* to be animate. But Thales was in fact able to point out pertinently that at least one kind of stone does seem to be animate—namely the magnet, which has visibly motive powers.[20] Hence, no doubt, his celebrated assertion that magnets have souls (11 A 22 DK). In other kinds of stone, then, their animate character could be assumed simply to be too muted to show overtly. How far this panpsychism was exploited by Thales himself in accounting for the details of cosmic functioning is hard to say, given our very meager evidence,[21] but the basis of such an approach was certainly in place.

(b) At the end of the Presocratic period, the exactly contrary thesis was developed, by the atomists, to whom we shall return in chapter V §1. Instead of reducing the inanimate to the animate, they on the contrary systematically reduced the animate to the inanimate. There is nothing but an infinite set of atomic particles, moving in infinite space. These have no properties but basic physical ones. Consciousness is not a basic but a derived or secondary property, an epiphenomenon that occurs when a large number of particularly fine and mobile atoms are arranged in a certain way.

(c) Both these first two approaches are essentially monistic: the reduction either of the inanimate to the animate, or vice versa. Leaving aside the obscure and controversial early Pythagoreans,[22] the one thinker before Plato whom we can confidently regard as an exception to this monism is Anaxago-

---

20. Modern magnets are typically used to move other things, not themselves. In the ancient world, magnets were naturally magnetized pieces of iron ore, and would have been familiarly attracted and repelled by each other, as well as attracting iron.

21. One striking testimonium, overlooked by historians till now, but kindly pointed out to me by Inna Kupreeva, is Philoponus, *In Ar. De anima* 86.29–30, where Thales is reported as having said "that providence (πρόνοια) extends to the extremes and nothing escapes its notice, not even the smallest thing."

22. It seems likely that a Pythagorean doctrine of metempsychosis predated Anaxagoras (cf. Kahn 2001, esp. p. 18). Indeed, Hermotimus, also of Clazomenae and treated by Aristotle as if a forerunner of Anaxagoras (*Met.* A 3, 984b15–22, *Protrepticus* fr. 10c Ross), was both credited with out-of-the-body experiences (e.g. Lucian, *Musc. Enc.* 7) and identified as one of Pythagoras's own previous incarnations (DL VIII 5) in a tradition that can be traced back as early as Empedocles (31 B 129 DK). But whether the transmigrating soul was in this pre-Anaxagorean phase firmly distinguished from matter is harder to establish. In the first surviving version of the doctrine, that of Empedocles, there is no such dualism (see pp. 31–32 and p. 51 n. 62 below).

ras (early to mid fifth century B.C.). Anaxagoras is the first dualist of mind and matter, and he argues that only by making mind and matter two irreducibly different kinds of thing can we explain the power of mind to control matter, as the very existence of a world like ours attests it must do.

Thinkers of group (a), then, did not have a problem with explaining the presence of apparently intelligent structures in the world—any more than there had been such a problem for Hesiod, who treated the main components of the cosmic structure as simply being themselves gods. But *so* unobtrusive was the problem that, to all appearances, these panpsychist thinkers had little to say about it. In other words, in the sixth and early fifth centuries B.C. there is no sign of *debate* about the creative role of such a power. The tradition represented by Hesiod made philosophers slow to realize the need to detail and defend, rather than take for granted, the presence in the world of some superior governing power.[23] The greatest thinker of this early phase, Heraclitus, set out to undermine Hesiod's naïve treatment of the main cosmic players, such as Night and Day, as discrete individual deities;[24] but Hesiod's underlying divinization of the world, far from facing any challenge from him, was taken for granted by Heraclitus.[25] Even Parmenides, who in the second half of his poem outlined a cosmology that he judged, although false, liable to prove congenial to his audience, included in it a role for a creative goddess (28 A 37, B 12–13). In none of these cases is there any sign that divine causation had yet become a subject for philosophical *argument*.

2. ANAXAGORAS'S COSMOLOGY

In this regard, Anaxagoras was the truly revolutionary thinker.[26] He was rightly recognized by Plato[27] as the first overt champion of a creative cos-

---

23. Xenophanes' insistence on god's superhuman nature and powers (21 B 10–16, 23–26) is a partial exception, to this limited extent anticipating Anaxagoras's elevation of the power of *nous* (see below); but there is little sign yet of emphasis on god's creative intelligence.

24. See Mourelatos 1973.

25. In 22 B 30 DK, Heraclitus speaks of the world as an "ever-living fire" which "neither any god nor any man made." The paradoxical addition of "man" makes it unsafe to infer from the fragment that Heraclitus was engaged in speculation or debate about divine creation of the world.

26. I here rely on Aristotle's information that Anaxagoras was older than Empedocles, *Met.* 984a11–13. When he adds that Anaxagoras was τοῖς δὲ ἔργοις ὕστερος, that is a relative evaluation of importance, not a reference to the date at which he wrote: see Kahn 1960, 163–65; an unpublished paper by Stephen Menn has further encouraged me in this direction.

27. Cf. n. 2 above.

mic intelligence, even if Plato found his actual use of that concept to be in the event disappointing. Anaxagoras explains the world as what resulted when *nous*—"mind" or "intelligence"—set out to act upon the preexisting stock of matter.

The interpretation of Anaxagoras's physical theory is something of a minefield.[28] His main tenets are in outline as follows:

1. The world's basic ingredients (whatever these may be) are entirely mixed together and can never be fully separated.

2. Originally, before the world came into being, that mixture was so homogeneous that nothing was distinguishable from anything else.

3. *Nous* has since then created a cosmic vortex, thanks to which the ingredients have increasingly separated out from each other.

4. This separation is, however, only ever a partial one: the proportions in the mixture change, but it remains permanently true that "there is a portion of everything in everything."

5. The way that perceptible stuffs are differentiated from each other is determined by whatever predominates in each part of the mixture: each stuff is named after whatever it has got most of in it.

For present purposes, I shall baldly state what I take this theory to amount to. The original matter on which *nous* set to work was a more or less even mixture of all the pairs of perceptible opposites: hot and cold, wet and dry, bright and dark, light and heavy, sweet and bitter, black and white, and so on. The main manifestation of this even mixture was endless stretches of two bland stuffs with few if any discernible features, stuffs which Anaxagoras calls "air and aether" (59 B 1 DK).[29] But when intelligence decided to set up a cosmic rotation, the vortex began to separate the pairs of opposites, so that some regions had more hot than cold and vice versa, some more rare than dense and vice versa, and so on for all the opposites. It is from this intelligently generated set of imbalances that familiar stuffs like earth and water have been formed. As Anaxagoras says (B 15) when

---

28. This is not the place to offer a systematic bibliography of Anaxagorean interpretation, for which see Sider 2005. My own views have most in common with those of Schofield 1980.

29. By "aether" Anaxagoras means, not fire, as Aristotle thought, but the particularly dry and refined atmosphere of the heavens (see Schofield 1980, p. 71; Kingsley 1995b, pp. 28–29), while his "air" is the familiar atmosphere we inhabit. Air and aether, then, are chosen as the two major component stuffs still evident in the cosmos that are least distinguished by discernible visual, tactile etc. properties.

explaining how the earth formed during the cosmic separation, "Dense, wet, cold and dark came together here, where there is now earth."[30] Earth, that is, is not a basic ingredient in the mix, but is itself a product of the partial separation of opposites that *nous* has engineered.[31] That separative process is in its very nature uncompletable. For example, there neither is nor ever will be an instance of absolute brightness which does not still contain some darkness, that is, which could not in theory become even brighter. Moreover, the bright object will never fail to have in addition some temperature, some degree of density, some color, and so on for all the scales of opposites. And each of these properties similarly admits of further intensification or diminution: no phenomenal object ever stands at the extreme end of any such property scale. In this way, every opposite really is and always will be mixed both with its own opposite and with all the other pairs of opposites. Anaxagoras's celebrated thesis that "There is a portion of everything in everything" (B 11, etc.) does not describe a merely contingent fact about the world, but embodies a basic metaphysical principle.

Now it has to be admitted that the majority of interpreters, following Aristotle's lead, do not restrict the ingredients to pairs of opposites as I have done. They hold that included in Anaxagoras's grand mixture are stuffs such as flesh, bone, and gold. This addition is not only unsupported by the surviving parts of Anaxagoras's text, but in my view introduces almost intolerable problems for the coherence of his doctrine. Nothing that I shall go on to propose is entirely dependent on the simpler interpretation that I favor, the one which limits the ingredients to opposites alone. I shall for present purposes proceed as if it were correct, saving my defense of it for an Appendix to the present chapter.

---

30. τὸ μὲν πυκνὸν καὶ <τὸ> διερὸν καὶ τὸ ψυχρὸν καὶ τὸ ζοφερὸν ἐνθάδε συνεχώρησεν, ἔνθα νῦν γῆ. Here the last word, "earth," is marked in Diels-Kranz 1952 as an editorial supplement, but Sider 2005, p. 149, shows that it in fact has unanimous manuscript attestation. One manuscript also carries the definite article (ἡ) before "earth," and this is often printed too, but Sider gives good reason for omitting it.

31. Anaxagoras probably speaks here of "earth," not "the earth" (see previous note). In doing so, he refers most directly to the *stuff* earth, although he probably thereby implies a reference to the cosmic zone of that same name, just as the second half of the fragment (see p. 13 below) refers to "the far side of the aether," thus designating a cosmic zone (the heaven) by naming the material mass it consists of. Despite this unclarity, there should be no doubt that the material composition of the stuff earth of which the earth consists is his explanandum in the first half of the fragment.

3. THE POWER OF *NOUS*

We must now turn to Anaxagoras's causal principle, *nous,* variously translated "intelligence" and "mind," whose powers he hymns eloquently and at length in fragment B 12. In reading this passage (pp. 11–12 and 20 below), it is important to recognize that the reference of the word *nous* ranges, without clear demarcation, over both intelligence as a power resident in each of us, whose properties we therefore know at first hand, and the great cosmic intelligence which created the world. The ambiguity is permissible because Anaxagoras almost certainly holds that the great cosmic intelligence, having created the world, apportioned at least some of itself into individual living beings, ourselves included (more on this in §6 below).

Anaxagoras's most decisive philosophical innovation is, as I said earlier, his dualism of mind and matter. His great predecessor Parmenides, the ultimate monist, had argued that being is utterly homogeneous, so that its differentiation into a varied world such as we seem to experience must be a mere illusion. In the second half of his poem Parmenides had added, enigmatically, that the necessary price to be paid for vindicating the physical world is a shift from his own monism to some kind of dualism, and had offered, in far from lucid terms, his own suggestion as to what the paired principles of this dualism might be: two stuffs which he calls "fire" and "night."[32] Anaxagoras's own preferred answer as I interpret it is that *nous*—mind, intelligence, or thought—which Parmenides had fully identified with being,[33] must instead be radically separated from the rest of being. Intelligence's power to act on matter, and to differentiate it into the world as we know it, requires that it itself be "unmixed" with the matter. As he says at the beginning of B 12,

> The other things share a portion of each, but intelligence is something infinite and autonomous, and is mixed with no thing, but it alone is by itself. For if it were not by itself, but were mixed with something else, it would share in all things, if it were mixed with any of them—for in each

32. It is at least possible that Parmenides gave Anaxagoras a cue by somehow identifying his fiery element with the creative goddess of whom he also spoke in the Way of Seeming. But the evidence for this is difficult at best, and I shall not pursue it here.

33. This remains the most natural reading of 28 B 3 DK, τὸ γὰρ αὐτὸ νοεῖν ἐστίν τε καὶ εἶναι: "For it is the same to think and to be." If Parmenides is, as most agree, a metaphysical monist, he is in any case committed to denying any distinction between the thinking subject and the object thought. This is argued briefly in Sedley 1999a, and fully in Long 1996b.

thing a portion of each is present, as I have said earlier—and the things mixed with it would prevent it from controlling any thing in such a way as it does in being alone by itself.[34]

This is at first sight curious. *Nous* is for Anaxagoras not merely a cosmogonic cause, but the very same entity which in today's world governs animate beings like ourselves. And he is quite explicit that *nous* is present "in" those beings (B 11). If *nous* is in our bodies, how can it remain altogether unmixed with them?

What Anaxagoras means is, I take it, the following. The stuffs that our bodies are made of either are (on my preferred interpretation), or at least include, pairs of opposite properties like hot and cold, wet and dry. For intelligence to be "mixed" with these would be for it itself to have a certain temperature, a certain degree of moistness, etc. And that would make intelligence subject to physical change, so that it could be acted upon *by* matter, being for example heated and dried in summer, cooled and dampened in winter, when the reality is that it itself controls matter. To say that intelligence is unmixed is thus Anaxagoras's way of saying that, despite being present in living things, it is in itself neither hot nor cold, neither wet nor dry, and so on for all the pairs of perceptible opposites. In short, to call intelligence unmixed is his way of saying that it is free of physical properties.

Anaxagoras is never reported as distinguishing mind or intelligence from body as the "incorporeal" from the corporeal, and indeed he betrays just the opposite assumption when he calls *nous* "the finest and purest of all things," and when, later in B 12, he speaks of it in quantitative terms ("*nous* is all alike, both the larger and the smaller"). He thus treats it as if it were a physical stuff, albeit a very special one. But it seems clear to me that his device of making mind "unmixed" is as close an approximation to the now familiar separation of the incorporeal from the corporeal as was conceptually possible in the first half of the fifth century B.C.[35]

---

34. τὰ μὲν ἄλλα παντὸς μοῖραν μετέχει, νοῦς δέ ἐστιν ἄπειρον καὶ αὐτοκρατὲς καὶ μέμεικται οὐδενὶ χρήματι, ἀλλὰ μόνος αὐτὸς ἐπ' ἑωυτοῦ ἐστιν. εἰ μὴ γὰρ ἐφ' ἑαυτοῦ ἦν, ἀλλά τεῳ ἐμέμεικτο ἄλλῳ, μετεῖχεν ἂν ἁπάντων χρημάτων, εἰ ἐμέμεικτό τεῳ (ἐν παντὶ γὰρ παντὸς μοῖρα ἔνεστιν, ὥσπερ ἐν τοῖς πρόσθεν μοι λέλεκται), καὶ ἂν ἐκώλυεν αὐτὸν τὰ συμμεμειγμένα, ὥστε μηδενὸς χρήματος κρατεῖν ὁμοίως ὡς καὶ μόνον ἐόντα ἐφ' ἑαυτοῦ.

35. Cf. esp. Renehan 1980. He contrasts Plato's clear attributions of incorporeality with their weak anticipations in pre-Platonic thinkers, including (pp. 114–18) Anaxagoras, albeit without any discussion of the mixture theme in B 12.

4. SUN AND MOON

Originally, says Anaxagoras, there was an undifferentiated mixture. *Nous* managed to produce a partial separation of the mixture by stirring it—making it rotate in a vortex which stratified it into the familiar layers of earth, water, air, aether, and fire. Let us revisit and complete our reading of fragment B 15:

> Dense, wet, cold and dark came together here, where there is now earth, while rare, hot and dry travelled out to the far side of the aether.[36]

Earth's distinctive properties have accumulated down here, while the partially separated opposites of those same properties—the light, the rare, the bright etc.—have travelled outwards to the perimeter of the cosmos, at the far edge of the region of aether,[37] to form the fiery outer heavens. But stones, Anaxagoras tells us (B 16), also have a certain tendency to heat up and travel to the cosmic perimeter. Hence the sun, according to him, is itself a vast red-hot rock whose anomalous position, caught up in the celestial rotation near the outer perimeter rather than at rest down here, testifies that the separation engineered by intelligence is never either clean or absolute. The moon, comparably, is an outlying mass of earth, not inherently fiery but irradiated by the sun.[38] That the separation process is still continuing, with some

---

36. τὸ μὲν πυκνὸν καὶ <τὸ> διερὸν καὶ τὸ ψυχρὸν καὶ τὸ ζοφερὸν ἐνθάδε συνεχώρησεν, ἔνθα νῦν γῆ. τὸ δὲ ἀραιὸν καὶ τὸ θερμὸν καὶ τὸ ξηρὸν ἐξεχώρησεν εἰς τὸ πρόσω τοῦ αἰθέρος. When Aristotle writes that for Anaxagoras each of the four elemental masses is a composite (GC 314a24–b1, ἐναντίως δὲ φαίνονται λέγοντες οἱ περὶ Ἀναξαγόραν τοῖς περὶ Ἐμπεδοκλέα· ὁ μὲν γάρ φησι πῦρ καὶ ὕδωρ καὶ ἀέρα καὶ γῆν στοιχεῖα τέσσαρα καὶ ἁπλᾶ εἶναι μᾶλλον ἢ σάρκα καὶ ὀστοῦν καὶ τὰ τοιαῦτα τῶν ὁμοιομερῶν, οἱ δὲ ταῦτα μὲν ἁπλᾶ καὶ στοιχεῖα, γῆν δὲ καὶ πῦρ καὶ ὕδωρ καὶ ἀέρα σύνθετα· πανσπερμίαν γὰρ εἶναι τούτων) I suspect that he is basing himself primarily on this fragment, even though in doing so he is, in line with his usual interpretation, elevating the homoeomerous stuffs to priority over the opposites. His addition of the term πανσπερμία, as DC 302a28–b5 confirms, reflects his belief (which I dispute, see §5 below) that Anaxagoras calls the homoeomerous stuffs σπέρματα. If Anaxagoras did himself somewhere call cosmic masses like earth and air πανσπερμίαι (which is far from clear), he is more likely to have meant that each is a universal seed-bed, in the literal sense of "seed" which I go on to defend below. It is true that fire could hardly be a seed-bed in this sense, but aether could be; and since Aristotle mistakenly believes that Anaxagoras uses "aether" to designate fire (DC 302b4–5, see n. 29 above), he would here have a further reason for assuming that the "seeds" in question were elements, not biological seeds.

37. Note that aether was not generated by this separation, because as B1 indicates it was there all along.

38. Panchenko 2002.

of the celestial rocks gradually returning to earth and cooling, was confirmed, in Anaxagoras's eyes, by the periodic fall of meteorites.[39]

5. WORLDS AND SEEDS

With this brief sketch in mind, let us turn to my key passage, B 4, quoted verbatim by Simplicius from book 1 of Anaxagoras's treatise without giving the slightest clue as to its context there. In the first part of this passage, Anaxagoras seems to argue that there must be other worlds like our own:

> These things being so, one must believe that there are many things of all kinds in all the things that are being aggregated, and seeds of all things, which have all kinds of forms and colors and savors. And that human beings were compounded, and all the other animals that have soul. And that the human beings, for their part, have cities that they have populated and farms that they have constructed, just as where we are. And that they have both sun and moon[40] and so on, just as where we are. And that their earth bears many things of all kinds,[41] of which they harvest the best and bring them to their dwelling to use. So much then for my statement about the separation—that it would not happen only where we are, but elsewhere too.[42]

Anaxagoras here starts by asserting, as an inference from whatever preceded, that in every collection of matter there are not only all kinds of things—meaning either the usual pairs of opposite properties, as on the interpreta-

---

39. This seems the best way to interpret the reports that he had *predicted* the fall of the meteorite at Aegospotami in 467, A 1 (10), 11–12.

40. I translate "sun and moon" not "a sun and a moon," to avoid endorsing Simplicius's inference (*In Ar. Phys.* 157.22–24) that these must be a sun and a moon other than our own. Although that inference would support my interpretation, it is unfortunately groundless. But it is important, as we shall see shortly, to note that Anaxagoras's locution does at least indicate that each other civilization has precisely one sun and one moon.

41. I follow Sider 2005, p. 99, in translating τὴν γῆν αὐτοῖσι as "their earth," with αὐτοῖσι construed as a possessive dative, rather than "the earth bears them many things of all kinds."

42. B 4. τούτων δὲ οὕτως ἐχόντων χρὴ δοκεῖν ἐνεῖναι πολλά τε καὶ παντοῖα ἐν πᾶσι τοῖς συγκρινομένοις καὶ σπέρματα πάντων χρημάτων καὶ ἰδέας παντοίας ἔχοντα καὶ χροιὰς καὶ ἡδονάς. καὶ ἀνθρώπους τε συμπαγῆναι καὶ τὰ ἄλλα ζῷα ὅσα ψυχὴν ἔχει. καὶ τοῖς γε ἀνθρώποισιν εἶναι καὶ πόλεις συνῳκημένας καὶ ἔργα κατεσκευασμένα, ὥσπερ παρ' ἡμῖν, καὶ ἠέλιόν τε αὐτοῖσιν εἶναι καὶ σελήνην καὶ τὰ ἄλλα, ὥσπερ παρ' ἡμῖν, καὶ τὴν γῆν αὐτοῖσι φύειν πολλά τε καὶ παντοῖα, ὧν ἐκεῖνοι τὰ ὀνήστα συνενεγκάμενοι εἰς τὴν οἴκησιν χρῶνται. ταῦτα μὲν οὖν μοι λέλεκται περὶ τῆς ἀποκρίσιος, ὅτι οὐκ ἂν παρ' ἡμῖν μόνον ἀποκριθείη, ἀλλὰ καὶ ἄλλῃ.

tion I favor, or these plus primitive stuffs like flesh and gold—but also what he calls "seeds of all things, which have all kinds of forms and colors and savors." What are these seeds?

Here once more we enter a quagmire of controversy. It has been widely assumed since Aristotle that "seeds" *(spermata)* is Anaxagoras's technical term for his basic physical principles, whether these be the opposites and/or other underlying stuffs, or some kind of constituent particles. Other interpreters,[43] albeit a minority, have taken them to be simply ordinary biological seeds. I am fully convinced of the latter interpretation. The introduction of technical terms such as the former party postulate here was a surprisingly late development in philosophy, the first clear cases being with the atomists, a generation after Anaxagoras. Although Anaxagoras did himself make an important contribution to that development, he did so not by introducing terms with technical senses, but by outlawing ordinary-language usages which he considered misleading. Thus in fragment B 17 he objects to the words "become" and "perish," pointing out that what the Greeks loosely designate with these verbs is in reality nothing but mixture and separation. True to his word, he never once uses either verb in his surviving fragments, and instead sticks to the language of combination and separation. But that key contribution to the Greek philosophical vocabulary lies in a cleaning up of philosophical language by studious *exclusion*. The further move of creating new terms, or redeploying existing words in unfamiliar technical senses, came only later. If "seeds" were being used by Anaxagoras as an innovative technical term, it would be a probably unique exception[44] to the pattern I have described.[45]

It therefore seems to me fairly clear that the "seeds" of B 4, far from being any kind of theorized elements or principles, are ordinary biological seeds, the origins of plants and animals. This is fully confirmed by what follows. For what Anaxagoras immediately goes on to infer is that not only in our part of the universe, but elsewhere too, there are worlds—structures with an earth, a sun, and a moon—in which human beings have come into existence just as in our world. Those human beings, moreover, lead both urban and rural lives, in that they will both have founded cities and have constructed farms. On these farms, he continues, all kinds of things must grow

43. Notably Furley 1976, Schofield 1980.
44. Regarding *logos* in Heraclitus, see p. 226 n. 49 below.
45. Indeed, it is precisely Anaxagoras's failure to supply a technical term for his ingredients, instead simply calling them "things," that lies behind the difficulties every interpreter since Aristotle has had in reconstructing his theory: see Appendix to this chapter.

from the earth, of which they can be assumed to harvest the best and bring them home.

Why does all this follow from the initial assertion about the existence of seeds in the mixture? The reason why Anaxagoras is confident that the same range of life forms, humans included, has occurred in other worlds too is clearly that the "seeds" contained in the universal mixture are assumed to be the very same complete range of biological seeds which, in our own experience, give rise to life. Wherever in the universe the right conditions recur, the same life forms are bound to emerge, Anaxagoras has inferred.[46]

I have spoken of other worlds here, although it is by no means generally agreed that Anaxagoras held there to be other worlds than our own,[47] mainly because the ancient doxographies (catalogues of doctrines) report that he did not.[48] Some have for this reason preferred to see in our passage a reference to merely hypothetical worlds: the same results *would* have ensued anywhere in the universe *if* intelligence had gone to work there. The Greek syntax however favors a reference to actual, not counterfactual, civilizations. Nor is it plausible, as yet others have suggested, that these are civilizations merely in other parts of our own world. As a flat-earth theorist[49] Anaxagoras cannot be postulating people in the antipodes, and if he just means distant civilizations on the same flat surface as we inhabit he hardly had to argue for them, as he does here, since the Greeks were well aware of the existence of distant barbarian races. No, he really has to be referring to other worlds, even if he never developed the doctrine with sufficient clarity to earn it a place in the later doxographies. The reason why the doxographers overlooked the significance of B 4 in this regard is, I imagine, that they had already classified Anaxagoras as a one-world theorist on the evidence of B 8: "The things *in the one world* have not been severed from each other, nor has the hot been chopped apart with an axe from the cold, or the cold from the hot." Here Anaxagoras was probably in fact referring to the world's unity, not its uniqueness, but the expression was no doubt enough to mislead a doxographer scanning the text to find out Anaxagoras's position in the "One world or many?" controversy.

---

46. True, the ability of animal seeds initially to germinate and grow directly from the earth (for which see DL II 19 and n. 51 below) would require some assumptions about, for example, the spontaneous formation of surrogate wombs. For Lucretius's postulation of such "wombs," and possible Presocratic antecedents, see Campbell 2003, pp. 75–77.

47. For recent discussions of the issue which *inter alia* helpfully survey the earlier bibliography, see Schofield 1996, and cf. Louguet 2002.

48. Aetius II 1.2, cf. Simplicius *In Ar. Phys.* 178.25.

49. DL II 8; Hippolytus, *Ref.* I 8.3; 59 A 87 DK.

What Anaxagoras is telling us, then, is that there must be other worlds with the same kind of flora and fauna as ours, including human civilization as we know it. Moreover, the confident prediction is based specifically on the ubiquity, in the universal mixture, of the full range of seeds from which life develops.

This impression is confirmed by what he immediately goes on to say in the remainder of B 4, if I have understood it right:

> Before these things were separated off, all things were together and not even any color was evident. For it was prevented by the mixture of all things—the wet, the dry, the hot, the cold, the bright, and the dark, there also being present in it much earth and seeds infinite in quantity, quite unlike each other. For of other things too, one is quite unlike another. These things being so, one must believe that in the universe all things are present.[50]

This passage has caused a great deal of puzzlement, largely, I believe, because it has been unanimously assumed to describe the original primeval state before intelligence started the cosmic rotation. That this is wrong is, it seems to me, shown by the fact that in the situation described there is already a lot of *earth* present: for, as we have seen in B 15, earth came to be only after the cosmic separation had started, thanks to the heavy, the dense etc. gathering together. Probably then these lines describe not the primeval state of matter before intelligence had even begun work on producing a world, but our world in its drab, uniform state just before life, as described in the immediately previous lines, emerged from it. The introductory words "Before these things were separated off . . . " refer by "these things" to life forms within our world, and not to the world as such.

With this thought in mind, look again at the list of items which Anaxagoras singles out for mention: in this colorless primeval world there was a mixture of the wet and the dry, the hot and the cold, the bright and the dark, a lot of earth, and innumerable seeds of widely differing kinds. Contrary to what appears to be the universal scholarly assumption, what he has set out here is no random list. Ask any farmer or gardener. Anaxagoras has set out the perfect hothouse conditions for the emergence of life: earth, seeds, and a temperate balance of moisture, temperature, and light. It is because the

---

50. πρὶν δὲ ἀποκριθῆναι ταῦτα πάντων ὁμοῦ ἐόντων οὐδὲ χροιὴ ἔνδηλος ἦν οὐδεμία· ἀπεκώλυε γὰρ ἡ σύμμιξις πάντων χρημάτων, τοῦ τε διεροῦ καὶ τοῦ ξηροῦ καὶ τοῦ θερμοῦ καὶ τοῦ ψυχροῦ καὶ τοῦ λαμπροῦ καὶ τοῦ ζοφεροῦ, καὶ γῆς πολλῆς ἐνεούσης καὶ σπερμάτων ἀπείρων πλῆθος οὐδὲν ἐοικότων ἀλλήλοις. οὐδὲ γὰρ τῶν ἄλλων οὐδὲν ἔοικε τὸ ἕτερον τῷ ἑτέρῳ. τούτων δὲ οὕτως ἐχόντων ἐν τῷ σύμπαντι χρὴ δοκεῖν ἐνεῖναι πάντα χρήματα.

world has turned out to possess such amazing biodiversity that we can work out, as Anaxagoras says in the concluding words of the fragment, that the universal stuff from which intelligence made our world must already contain all these necessary ingredients, seeds included. And that is how we can further work out that, as we saw in the earlier part of the fragment, the same diversity of life forms must have emerged *everywhere* in the universe that *nous* has got to work.

This interpretation, if correct, has important implications. Life forms arise, not because intelligence plans, designs, and constructs them, but because the universal stuff is already full of seeds.[51] This may sound like an abnegation of the scientist's responsibility to *explain* life, but on the assumptions available to Anaxagoras it is more than reasonable.

First, there is the familiar empirical fact that almost any portion of earth subjected to moisture, warmth, and light will produce life forms. These life forms may include not only weeds, molds, and other such growths, but also primitive animals—worms, grubs, insects etc.

Second, many small organisms were widely believed, in and well after antiquity—even by Aristotle—to be the product of spontaneous generation,[52] self-formed without seeds. So if Anaxagoras, by making the ubiquitous presence of seeds a primitive fact, is avoiding the alternative of a resort to spontaneous generation, he earns some credit here. Indeed, Theophrastus speaks approvingly of Anaxagoras's doctrine of ubiquitous seeds for precisely this merit—its reduction of the need to postulate spontaneous generation.[53]

---

51. Cf. Anaxagoras A 113: animals first arose from seeds that fell from heaven to earth.

52. For Aristotle's belief in spontaneous generation, see e.g. *HA* 569a29–570a3, *GA* 761b24–763b16, *Met.* 1032a12–b1, and for more references Bonitz 1870 s.v. αὐτόματος 4. For the Epicureans, see Lucretius II 871–73, 898–901, 926–29, III 713–40, V 795–800. Although the doctrine's origins are likely to lie in legends of "earthborn" races, rather than in scientific speculation, cf. Plato, *Phd.* 96b2–3 for evidence of its currency in at least later Presocratic physics, and DL II 16–17 and Hippolytus, *Ref.* I 9.5–6 for its association with Archelaus, the pupil of Anaxagoras and teacher of Socrates. The closely interrelated versions in Diodorus Siculus I 7.3–6, 10.1–7 and Ovid, *Met.* I 416–37 are likely also to be of Presocratic origin or inspiration; they cite the supposed evidence of regions, like the Nile valley, where creatures are said to form in the mud that are half organic, half inorganic. For more discussion, cf. Blundell 1986, pp. 62–65, and esp. Campbell 2003, pp. 61–63, 330–33, where a comprehensive range of parallels is assembled. However, one may question the latter's inclusion of Anaxagoras on the strength of DL II 9, "Animals started coming to be out of what is moist, warm, and earthy, but later from each other." The first part of this, which captures B 4 well, is not meant to exclude the role of seeds.

53. Theophrastus, *CP* I 5.2; cf. *ib.* III 1.4. Theophrastus here refers to seeds borne in the air—an attested part of Anaxagoras's *panspermia* theory; see n. 36 above.

Third, it was widely assumed that the earth in its infancy had been much more fertile than it subsequently became, so that a far wider range of animals could be born from it than would be possible today. Hence Anaxagoras's projection onto a primeval earth of a greatly enhanced power to generate life from these ubiquitous seeds would, in context, seem like a satisfactory explanation of the origin of all life, even human. In fact some individual Greek peoples, the Athenians included, claimed to be "autochthonous"—indigenous to their present lands—and this was sometimes taken to mean that their earliest ancestors had been "earth-born," literally sprung from the local soil.[54] The same idea of "earth-born" races had a widespread currency in myth.

In short, not only does the evidence point to a reading of Anaxagoras whereby the ubiquity of seeds is a primitive fact, not demanding further explanation, but in its cultural context the postulation of such an explanatory principle was at least as satisfactory as its main rival, the theory of spontaneous generation.

Anaxagoras did, we know, theorize about the internal structure of seeds (B 10).[55] An animal seed *(gonē)* already contains minute portions of bone, flesh, hair etc., he maintained, since only on this supposition can we understand its having causal powers sufficient to generate the developed specimen that grows from it. But we have no hint in our sources that he went on to explain the structure of seeds as having been itself planned and imposed by *nous*, and in the absence of such evidence it may be safer to assume that he viewed it as an irreducibly primitive fact about the universe.[56] Whatever *nous* may have done, there is no sign in Anaxagoras's text that it designed life forms. Either the seeds have simply always been there, as *nous* presumably has been too, or else (we might more hazardously speculate) they have spread from previously formed worlds. The latter hypothesis would at best endlessly push back, rather than solve, the question how these seeds originally came into existence.[57]

54. Diodorus and Ovid as cited in note 52 above; Aristotle, *GA* 762b28–30; Philo, *Aet. mundi* 57; more in Campbell 2003, p. 331.

55. Quoted in full, n. 71 below.

56. I suspect, in fact, that the reference in B 1 to things in the original mixture being invisible "because of smallness" is intended at least partly to cater for the presence of seeds.

57. Cf. the surprisingly enduring theory that life reached Earth from outer space, first proposed by Lord Kelvin in lectures of 1864 and 1871 ("life originated on this earth through moss-grown fragments from the ruins of another world," in "seed-bearing meteoritic stones") and subsequently supported by the high levels of amino acids and other organic substances found in meteorite fragments.

6. NOUS AS CREATOR

How much then *did* intelligence contribute to the emergence of life, both
in our world and in the others that it has created?[58] We have already seen
Anaxagoras's insistence on its causal powers, due to its purity. He also, in
the continuation of B 12, has a lot to say about its cognitive powers. When
intelligence started off the cosmogonic rotation in our own world, it knew
exactly what the result would be, he tells us:

> And the entire rotation was controlled by intelligence, so as to make
> it rotate in the first place. And at first it began to rotate in a small way;
> subsequently it has been rotating more; and it will rotate still more. And
> the things which are being mixed, separated, and segregated, intelligence
> knew all of them. And both what they were going to be like and what
> they were like—both the things that are not now and the things that are
> now—and what they will be like, intelligence arranged them all, and also
> this rotation which is now being undergone by the stars, sun, moon, air,
> and aether that are being separated off.[59]

58. I relegate to a footnote the difficult question whether the *nous* which creates
a world is in any sense an individual, and, if so, whether each world is created by a different *nous*. *Nous* was not often used as a count noun at this date (cf. Menn 1995,
p. 16), so one might wonder how easily Anaxagoras could even have formulated the
question. What creates a world, it might be thought, is not *an* intelligence, just intelligence. On the other hand, consider B 14 (on the reading of Diels-Kranz 1952), ὁ δὲ
νοῦς, ὃς ἀεί ἐστι, τὸ κάρτα καὶ νῦν ἐστιν ἵνα καὶ τὰ ἄλλα πάντα, ἐν τῷ πολλῷ
περιέχοντι καὶ ἐν τοῖς προσκριθεῖσι καὶ ἐν τοῖς ἀποκεκριμένοις. "The mind, which
is for ever, certainly is now too, when there are all the other things in the large amount
that surrounds and in the things which were aggregated and those that have been separated." Here ἵνα is usually translated "where," but with the temporal antecedent νῦν
it is more likely to mean "when" (cf. Antiphon 6.9), which also makes the sentence
inferentially more coherent: if νοῦς is *everlasting*, it follows that it exists *now*, whereas
no further inference to *where* it is seems warranted. This, however, would be a pointless inference if ὁ νοῦς just referred to intelligence in general, which *obviously* exists
now, namely in us. It is therefore almost certainly a reference to the cosmogonic *nous*,
which, Anaxagoras holds, is still causally operative, as B 12 also attests in asserting
that *nous* will continue to speed up the rotation. Such a reference would also account
for the addition of the definite article, ὁ . . . νοῦς, "the intelligence," i.e. the intelligence
which created our world. Hence in B 14 it may well be being treated as a distinct intelligence both from our own and from those responsible for other worlds.

59. καὶ τῆς περιχωρήσιος τῆς συμπάσης νοῦς ἐκράτησεν, ὥστε περιχωρῆσαι
τὴν ἀρχήν. καὶ πρῶτον ἀπὸ τοῦ σμικροῦ ἤρξατο περιχωρεῖν, ἔπειτε πλέον περι-
χωρεῖ, καὶ περιχωρήσει ἐπὶ πλέον. καὶ τὰ συμμισγόμενά τε καὶ ἀποκρινόμενα
καὶ διακρινόμενα πάντα ἔγνω νοῦς. καὶ ὁποῖα ἔμελλεν ἔσεσθαι καὶ ὁποῖα ἦν,
ἄσσα νῦν μὴ ἔστι καὶ ὅσα νῦν ἐστι, καὶ ὁποῖα ἔσται, πάντα διεκόσμησε νοῦς
καὶ τὴν περιχώρησιν ταύτην ἣν νῦν περιχωρέει τά τε ἄστρα καὶ ὁ ἥλιος καὶ ἡ
σελήνη καὶ ὁ ἀὴρ καὶ ὁ αἰθὴρ οἱ ἀποκρινόμενοι. In adopting Ritter's ἔπειτε for
the MSS ἐπεὶ δέ, I follow Sider 2005.

Here it is explicit that, in setting off the vortex, *nous* not only was aware of the inevitable outcome, but indeed controlled it. But just how far-reaching was this foresight? There is no mention here of the emergence of life among the things foreseen and controlled by intelligence. All that is explicitly picked out for mention is the cosmic rotation now being undergone by the stars, sun, and moon, as well as by the upper atmosphere: this, at the very least, was planned by *nous*.

Having started to worry about the extent of *nous*'s planning, we have to consider in addition a complaint lodged against Anaxagoras by both Plato and Aristotle.[60] As Socrates protests in Plato's *Phaedo*, although Anaxagoras *said* that everything was caused by intelligence, when it came down to it he hardly made any use of intelligent causation, but fell back on the traditional material causes—air, water, aether, and the like. Now in one sense the criticism is undoubtedly correct. The creationist methodology which Plato advocates, and whose absence from Anaxagoras's treatise he therefore laments, is one of accounting for a cosmic structure by explaining why that was the intelligent, in other words the *best*, way to construct it. There is little doubt that Anaxagoras did not adopt any such methodology. But from his failure to be explicit about the goodness of the world's structures we need not necessarily infer that his account was not even implicitly cast in terms of intelligent planning for the best. As with so many of Anaxagoras's doctrines, we must be prepared to read between the lines. If we do so, the following creationist doctrine emerges.

Nous starts off cosmic rotations both here and elsewhere in the universe fully knowing and fully planning what the outcomes will be. The first outcome is an at least primitively stratified world with earth accumulated in the center, while air and aether circle overhead. In the earth are distributed countless biological seeds, ready to generate life. Moreover, the conditions that obtain are a temperate blend of temperature, moisture, and light, perfectly suited to the seeds' germination.

So far one might nevertheless retain the suspicion that this emergence of life is, as such, a mere accident of the cosmic arrangement, not necessarily an integral part of intelligence's plans. That suspicion will however not survive the following consideration.

The reason why in B 4 Anaxagoras is confident that the human civilizations of other worlds are agricultural is that they too, as we do, have a sun and a moon. That a sun is necessary for agriculture is obvious enough. The relevance of these other civilizations' also having a moon may seem less ob-

60. Aristotle, *Met.* A 4, 985a18–21. For Plato, see chapter III §3 below.

vious, but we have only to recall the importance which Hesiod, in his agricultural poem, the *Works and Days* (especially 765–828), attributes to the farmer's systematic observance of the lunar calendar, with specific properties attached to each day of the month.[61] In the world attested by Hesiod, as indeed throughout antiquity, the moon, and also the stars, which in B 12 Anaxagoras adds alongside sun and moon as features of the world planned by *nous*, provided human civilization with an utterly indispensable agricultural calendar.[62]

But why is Anaxagoras confident that those other worlds have, each of them, a sun and a moon? These celestial objects are, let us recall, lumps of rock or earth stranded up in the rotating aether, far from the location to which a complete cosmic separation would have assigned them. There seems absolutely no reason why accident alone should have ensured that each world had precisely one large fiery rock in its upper atmosphere, and one large non-fiery mass of earth capable of absorbing and reflecting light from the first. If all the other worlds can be conjectured to have a sun and a moon, the only plausible explanation is that *nous* is assumed to have planned and created them that way.[63] And once we appreciate that, we can bring into focus the teleological subtext which eluded Plato. When intelligence creates worlds, it designedly constructs them so as to be hospitable to agricultural civilizations like Anaxagoras's own. It not only sets up the original hothouse conditions in which the ubiquitous seeds will germinate, but also provides the right heavenly bodies to serve the vital agricultural needs of the humans who will emerge from the primeval earth. We may also here remind ourselves that the vortex, once *nous* had created it, had then to be *tilted* to a suitable angle, but for which neither the succession of day and night nor the stellar calendar would have become available to us.[64]

The reason why these assumptions have to be teased out of Anaxagoras's text is that, as I argued at the outset, the presence of personal or quasi-personal control in the world is already the default assumption of nearly all Presocratic thought. The need to spell out what its beneficial effects are does

---

61. Likewise the Derveni Papyrus in col. 24 (on whose problems of interpretation see Jourdan 2003, pp. 98–101, and Betegh 2004, pp. 247–49) identifies the moon's two services to us as enabling farmers to distinguish the seasons and teaching sailors when to sail.

62. On these calendars or *parapēgmata*, see Taub 2003, chapter 2.

63. Or is it that those worlds that *happened* to have just one sun and just one moon generated life, the others not? This does not seem a credible reading of B 4, which rather gives the strong impression of generalizing over all other worlds ("in all the things that are being aggregated").

64. See p. 6 above, with DL II 9, for the two-stage vortex in Anaxagoras.

not occur to Anaxagoras, in the way that it would later occur to Plato, writing in a very different intellectual atmosphere, with the anti-teleological challenge of atomist materialism hanging over him.

When speaking earlier of Hesiod (pp. 3–4), I pointed out that the motif of divine craftsmanship was already at least embryonically present in his account of the origin of mankind. From the fact that it is Hephaestus to whom Hesiod's Zeus delegates the job of creating woman (*Works and Days* 60, quoted p. 54 below), we can infer that the art of the bronzesmith was being to some extent singled out as a model for divine craft. In Anaxagoras's system *nous* takes over the role of divine creator, and we are now in a position to ask what kind of creative expertise *he* has in mind.

The answer should be clear. *Nous* is a farmer. Its creation of worlds is its way of setting up environments which will enable seeds to germinate, with plant and animal life the outcome.

Can we go further? Is Anaxagoras interested in the question what motivates *nous* so to act? Here my comments must become increasingly speculative.

First, according to Anaxagoras, everything that has soul contains some *nous* (B 11, B 12.11–12). At the very least this includes all animals, and it would not be untypical of Greek usage to include plants too as having soul.[65] So either all or at least a great many of the organisms whose seeds *nous* sows will, once grown, be vehicles for the distribution of intelligence around the world. Just why *nous* might prefer this incarnate accommodation to its previous extra-cosmic existence is a separate question, on which I have up to now found no help in the sources.[66]

I think we can nevertheless go a little further. *Nous*, I have said, is a cosmic farmer. How then does Anaxagoras view the nature of farming? Fortunately the very same text, B 4, contains the rudiments of an answer.[67] First of all, as we have seen, farmers are said there to "construct" farms, a verb *(kataskeuazein)* which mirrors accurately enough the purposive construction of the great cosmic farm by *nous*. Secondly, Anaxagoras says

65. Aristotle *DA* II 2, 404b1–5, despite the fact that he himself assigns soul to plants, seems to understand only animals as falling within the scope of Anaxagoras's theory. But Anaxagoras A 116 and 117 provide evidence for plants having soul and *nous*. See further Sider 2005, pp. 97–98.

66. The apparent fact that *nous* does, for whatever reason, prefer incarnate accommodation has the advantage of explaining why, being infinite (B 12), it finds the need to keep on creating further worlds, as argued above.

67. The very special significance of farming in Anaxagoras's worldview tends, I believe, to confirm that in B 4 ἔργα does indeed mean "farms," as translated above (p. 14), and not "manufactured items," as argued most recently by Sider (2005, p. 99).

of farming civilizations that "their earth bears many things of all kinds, of which they harvest the best and bring them to their dwelling to use." What farmers do, then, is orchestrate the intrinsic generative powers of the earth. Under their management, it grows many things, including no doubt brambles, moles, wasps, and other unwanted life forms. The farmers encourage the earth's generative activity, not for the sake of these lesser organisms, but for the sake of the *best* things it produces, namely the crops.[68]

Should we then not assume something similar about the cosmic farm? *Nous*, like human farmers, makes the earth grow all kinds of things, but we may infer that it does so for the sake of the best things to emerge from it. And what are these best products of cosmic farming? Even without specific textual evidence, we might have ventured the guess that Anaxagoras shares in the widespread consensus that nature's best product is man. And that obvious guess gains direct support from Aristotle (*PA* IV 10, 687a8–10), who criticizes Anaxagoras for saying that it is because man has hands that he is the wisest of animals (according to Aristotle it is the other way round: it is because he is the wisest of animals that man has hands). If for Anaxagoras man is the "wisest" of animals, it hardly need be doubted that this already implies "best," especially given the obvious assumption that wisdom is *par excellence* the kind of goodness that *nous* would favor.[69]

It therefore seems ultimately implicit in Anaxagoras's text that *nous* constructs and, as it were, farms worlds primarily in order to generate human beings. The teleology proves to have an anthropocentric bias. Since he further regards humans as, among all living creatures, the best vehicles for *nous* itself to occupy, it is at least a possibility that he thinks of worlds as created by *nous* out of motives of pure self-interest.

In the light of these findings, I submit that Anaxagoras is a creationist in a much stronger sense than Plato was prepared to recognize. When Anaxagoras insists that the world must be the product of intelligence, *nous* is being postulated not merely as the moving cause that first stirred the mix-

---

68. That this is a distinctive way of viewing the farming enterprise can be seen by contrasting it with Plato, *Rep.* 589b1–3, "{ . . . } like a farmer, who nurtures and tames domesticated kinds *but prevents wild kinds from growing.*"

69. For *nous* as good-seeking, see Aristotle, *DA* 404b1–2, "Anaxagoras{ . . . } in many places says that *nous* is the cause of good and correct states of things. . . . " For contemplative knowledge as the human good in Anaxagoras's view, see the anecdotal evidence of Aristotle, *EE* 1216a10–16, and cf. *ib.* 1215b11–14. This, however, even if correct, does not remove practical skills (farming included, no doubt) from the domain of wisdom, as is confirmed by Anaxagoras's reference to hands as making man the best of animals.

ture, but as the planning cause that creates worlds in order to proliferate intelligent beings like itself.[70]

7. SCIENTIFIC CREATIONISM

If he really was, as I have argued, a committed creationist, it may seem paradoxical that Anaxagoras acquired in his own day the reputation of an irreligious thinker. But the reputation was not unjustified. His sun and moon are, after all, not divine beings, just huge inanimate objects, as his critics were said to have pointed out at his Athenian trial on charges of impiety. Even his supreme power, *nous*, is not overtly a divinity. Far from being essentially superhuman, the power he describes is most directly recognizable as familiar human intelligence. Even when he hymns its powers, there is little sense that he is thereby fitting it out with the trappings of traditional divinity, and much more reason to say that he is, on the contrary, replacing the traditional notion of a supreme divinity with a fundamentally naturalistic concept, one best known to us by study of our own human nature and more widely exemplified by the animal kingdom.

The religion-science polarity is an almost unavoidable area of uncertainty when interpreting the rational theology of the Greek philosophers. Rationalization of traditional religion can frequently be understood, at one pole, as endorsing that religion by giving a firm scientific reality to the divine powers it describes, but no less frequently, at the other pole, as undermining it by construing its divinities as popular misrepresentations of what are in reality nothing more than natural entities. Anaxagoras might of course be doing neither of these, because between the two poles lies much intermediate ground, in which theological and scientific explanation can operate in fruitful partnership. Plato's *Timaeus* (chapter IV) would come to be the classic occupant of that middle ground. Nevertheless, in Anaxagoras's case the scientifically reductive style of reading seems to me well suited to capturing the naturalistic tone of his writings. His motivation in advocating a dualism of mind and matter, and in postulating the former of these as supreme cause of matter's organization, is not theological in its essence, but scientific and causal.

70. It is hard to resist the further speculation that Anaxagoras may have supposed *nous* to transmigrate from body to body. The grounds for this speculation are (see n. 22 above) that Hermotimus, an earlier inhabitant of Anaxagoras's native city Clazomenae, (a) was considered a possible forerunner of his theory of *nous*, and (b) was associated with a doctrine of transmigration (see further Betegh 2004, pp. 283–84).

Thus the upshot of my first chapter is something of a surprise. Teleological explanation started life in Anaxagoras's doctrine of creationism, and came, as we shall see in the next three chapters, to promote a religious agenda. Only at a much later stage in the history of thought would Aristotle finally separate the two strands, preserving teleology while abandoning creationism. That subsequent history might have led one to expect teleology to have had an essentially religious origin. But the expectation would be mistaken. For Anaxagoras's creationism itself belongs firmly in the domain of natural science. If it has any theological import, it is not one that we see Anaxagoras himself setting out to advertise. To witness the religious lobby's appropriation of teleology, we will have to wait for the next chapter.

APPENDIX. ANAXAGORAS'S THEORY OF MATTER

Although Aristotle's reading of Anaxagoras has been dominant, we should not be too quick to endorse it. Enough of Anaxagoras's treatise survives to demonstrate that he can be a maddeningly obscure as well as imprecise writer. When he says that there is a portion of everything in everything, he does not in any surviving passage pause to say a portion of *what* in *what*. Aristotle, I suggest, may have been misled into his assumption that the reference is to stuffs like bread and flesh by a single passage where Anaxagoras asks, "How could hair come to be from not-hair, and flesh from not-flesh?"[71] We have explicit evidence that the context of this question was in

---

71. B 10, ὁ δὲ Ἀναξαγόρας παλαιὸν εὑρὼν δόγμα ὅτι οὐδὲν ἐκ τοῦ μηδαμῇ γίνεται, γένεσιν μὲν ἀνῄρει, διάκρισιν δὲ εἰσῆγεν ἀντὶ γενέσεως. ἐλήρει γὰρ ἀλλήλοις μὲν μεμῖχθαι πάντα, διακρίνεσθαι δὲ αὐξανόμενα. καὶ γὰρ ἐν τῇ αὐτῇ γονῇ καὶ τρίχας εἶναι καὶ ὄνυχας καὶ φλέβας καὶ ἀρτηρίας καὶ νεῦρα καὶ ὀστᾶ καὶ τυγχάνειν μὲν ἀφανῆ διὰ μικρομέρειαν, αὐξανόμενα δὲ κατὰ μικρὸν διακρίνεσθαι. "πῶς γὰρ ἄν, φησίν, ἐκ μὴ τριχὸς γένοιτο θρὶξ καὶ σὰρξ ἐκ μὴ σαρκός ;" οὐ μόνον δὲ τῶν σωμάτων ἀλλὰ καὶ τῶν χρωμάτων ταῦτα κατηγόρει. καὶ γὰρ ἐνεῖναι τῷ λευκῷ τὸ μέλαν καὶ τὸ λευκὸν τῷ μέλανι. τὸ αὐτὸ δὲ ἐπὶ τῶν ῥοπῶν ἐτίθει, τῷ βαρεῖ τὸ κοῦφον σύμμικτον εἶναι δοξάζων καὶ τοῦτο αὖθις ἐκείνῳ. "Anaxagoras, having discovered an ancient doctrine, that nothing comes to be out of what in no way is, eliminated coming-to-be, and introduced segregation instead of coming-to-be. He had the insane idea that all things are mixed with each other, but undergo segregation during the process of growth. For in the same seed, he said, there are hairs, nails, veins, arteries, sinews, and bones: they are non-evident because of their small-partedness, but in the process of growing they are gradually segregated. 'For how' he asks 'could hair come to be from not-hair, and flesh from not-flesh?' He predicates this not just of bodies, but also of colors. For, he says, black is present in white and white in black; and he posited the same for weights, thinking that light is mixed in with heavy and vice versa."

fact *not* that of nutrition, where Anaxagoras might have been explaining why bread must already contain flesh and hair, but one concerning the constitution of animal seed. The seed from which a human being is generated, he argued, must already contain minute portions of hair, flesh, bone etc., in order to be causally capable of leading to the birth of a complete human being constituted out of these stuffs. Clearly the fact that Anaxagoras held this causal thesis about seeds does not in itself commit him to such stuffs as flesh being ultimate and irreducible constituents of the world. But the remark may have misled Aristotle into thinking so, just as it has misled a long series of Anaxagoras's modern interpreters.

If instead we turn to the surviving verbatim passages of Anaxagoras, we find that the ingredients to which he constantly refers are not these stuffs, but opposites like the hot and the cold, the wet and the dry, the bright and the dark.[72] And there is a very strong case for going along with a minority of interpreters (Tannery 1886, Cornford 1930, Vlastos 1950, Schofield 1980) who take these opposites alone to be the basic ingredients. One strong piece of evidence in their support is B 15, where Anaxagoras explains how the earth formed during the cosmic separation: "Dense, wet, cold, and dark came together here, where there is now earth." Earth, it seems from this way of putting it, is not a basic ingredient in the mix, but is itself a product of the partial separation of opposites engineered by *nous*.[73] The same impression is confirmed by the entire set of verbatim quotations preserved by Simplicius, where opposites are again and again listed as ingredients. Indeed, Simplicius himself, despite starting his commentary on Aristotle, *Physics* 1 chapter 4, with the interpretative assumptions about Anaxagoras that he has inherited from Aristotle and Alexander of Aphrodisias, by the end (178.28–179.12) is expressing his strong suspicion that in fact it is the opposites alone that are Anaxagoras's real ingredients.

On such an interpretation the thesis that there is a portion of everything in everything turns out to be, not a wild extravagance, but a metaphysical axiom, and a direct ancestor of Plato's principle of the compresence of opposites. With very few apparent exceptions, every phenomenal stuff in the world does indeed always have some temperature, some color, some weight, some luminosity, some density, some flavor, and so on for Anaxagoras's other pairs of perceptible opposites. Moreover, the principle that separation is never total incorporates the further fact that the scales of temperature, flavor etc.

72. Indeed, not only in the verbatim fragments, but also in the source text from which "How could hair come to be from not-hair . . . ?" is drawn; see previous note.

73. See further, p. 10 above.

seem indefinitely extendible. Nothing is so hot that it could not be hotter, for example: that is, all hot things contain some cold too. As Anaxagoras put it (B 8), ". . . nor has the hot been chopped apart with an axe from the cold or the cold from the hot."

Secondly, the assumption makes much better sense of the principle that each thing's evident character is determined by what predominates in it: ". . . no other thing [than *nous*] is like anything else, but the things that it has got most of in it, those are what each single thing most evidently is and was" (end of B 12).[74] On Aristotle's reading, the competition for predominance can in each case have only one outright winner. If the item on a supermarket shelf has even fractionally more bread than beer in it, it is bread and not beer. Yet obviously bread can vary in flavor, density, darkness, and weight too. And Aristotle is unable to deny the obvious fact that the sweet and the savory, the rare and the dense, the dark and the bright, and the light and the heavy are also ingredients in the mixture. But this now means that the law of predominance breaks up into two radically different clauses. What makes the loaf bread is that the bread component is the outright winner of a competition between all comparable stuffs, including oil, mud, hair, water, urine, leather, iron etc. as well as bread. What gives the loaf its precise flavor, color, and density, on the other hand, is a series of separate competitions, each of them between just one pair of opposites—respectively the sweet and the savory, the black and the white, and the dense and the rare. And these competitions have no outright winners, since nothing is so heavy that it could not be heavier, or so sweet that it could not be sweeter. Thus these secondary competitions will establish nothing more than the *proportion* of hot to cold, heavy to light etc. It is unlikely that the principle of predominance was formulated to cover simultaneously both of these utterly different types of competition. And if we have to choose just one of the two, the competition between opposites is not only the one with the greater explanatory power, but also so powerful as apparently to leave no explanatory work for the other competition to do, as should become clear by the end of the next paragraph.

Anaxagoras's theory of perception similarly makes it hard to find a place for ingredient stuffs like flesh and gold. According to his perceptual theory

---

74. ἕτερον δὲ οὐδέν ἐστιν ὅμοιον οὐδενί, ἀλλ᾽ ὅτων πλεῖστα ἔνι, ταῦτα ἐνδηλό- τατα ἓν ἕκαστόν ἐστι καὶ ἦν. Although Simplicius found ὅτῳ, not ὅτων, in his copy of Anaxagoras, the simple emendation not only yields a far more credible text, but also corresponds to the paraphrases of it in Aristotle and Theophrastus (see Sider 2005, p. 141, although he himself favors the unemended text).

(A 92), perception is an interaction between pairs of opposites. We perceive an external opposite by its contrast with the matching opposite in us. You perceive the heat of the bathwater by the coldness in your toe, the coldness of the seawater by the heat in your legs. Dark-eyed animals such as ourselves perceive bright objects, whereas nocturnal animals have bright eyes with which they can see dark objects. And so on. Thus the theory is specifically set up to explain how we perceive opposites, and it meshes perfectly with the thesis that every external object contains some blend of more or less every pair of opposites.[75] When Anaxagoras writes ". . . the things that it has got most of in it, those are what each single thing most evidently is and was," we can find a comfortable fit with this same perceptual theory. Note the plural: each thing's evident properties (plural) are determined by predominance—hardly a natural way to refer to a single characteristic like that of being bread. Worse, it is not even clear how bread, or flesh, could as such be perceptible, since these stuffs do not have opposites. All that we can perceive of bread should be specific degrees of whiteness, weight, density etc.; and that brings us back to the opposites as the real components.

How about Anaxagoras's famous dictum that "In everything there is a portion of everything"? A criterion of interpretation that is sometimes invoked insists that the word "everything" here must have the same reference at both occurrences.[76] Thus, on the prevailing interpretation in terms of ingredient stuffs, "everything" would refer at both occurrences to the homogeneous stuffs such as flesh and gold: there is a portion of gold in every bit of flesh, and vice versa.[77] How about on the "opposites" interpretation that I am favoring? One could if one wished preserve the same principle by saying that, for example, every bit of hot has got in it not only some cold but also some heavy and some light, some sweet and some bitter, etc. But I do not find that the natural way to understand the dictum, which it will be far simpler to read as saying that every phenomenal thing, for example a horse or a rock, contains every opposite. That may offend against the crite-

75. I say "more or less," not to allow for e.g. odorless objects, since for these a perfectly good explanation would be that they have exactly the same balance of smell-opposites as we have in our own noses, but particularly to cater for auditory opposites. Anaxagoras could well believe that objects themselves have no sound-pitch, low or high, so that at least this pair of opposites belongs not to objects themselves but to something else, e.g. the intervening air.

76. E.g. Guthrie 1969, pp. 284–85, who cites Bailey and Raven as previous proponents of the same argument.

77. I leave aside the problems that modern interpreters have acknowledged in interpreting "gold," "flesh" etc. here: phenomenal (impure) gold and flesh, or ingredient (pure) gold and flesh? See especially Strang 1963.

rion, but I do not believe that the criterion should ever have been invoked in the first place. Here are two reasons.

First, it is easy to devise informal contexts in which the two occurrences of "everything" would not be co-referential. If on seeing an array of food someone with a nut allergy asked which dishes have which ingredients, they might quite intelligibly be told "Sorry, there's a bit of everything in everything," where the first "everything" refers to ingredients, the second to dishes. Second, with regard to Anaxagoras's dictum, he usually does *not* use the same word at both occurrences. Thus in B 4, there are "many things of all kinds" (πολλά τε καὶ παντοῖα) in "all the things that are being combined" (ἐν πᾶσι τοῖς συνκρινομένοις), and "in the universe" (ἐν τῷ σύμπαντι) there are "all things" (πάντα χρήματα). In B6 there are "in everything" (ἐν παντί, singular) "all things" (πάντα, plural); "all things" (πάντα, plural) have a bit of "everything" (παντός, singular), and "in all things" (ἐν πᾶσι) there are "many things" (πολλά). Finally, in B12, "the other things" (τὰ ἄλλα) have a share of "everything" (παντός). In none of these six cases does the phraseology emphasize symmetry between the two items thus connected. Indeed, symmetry is even more absent from the Greek than from these English renditions, in which the inevitability of our adding some form of the word "thing" gives a misleading impression.

Against these six cases, there are just two where Anaxagoras uses the same word: B 11, "In everything there is a portion of everything" (ἐν παντὶ παντὸς μοῖρα ἔνεστι), repeated with an explicit back reference in B 12. And even here he cannot possibly mean the two terms to be co-referential, for the following reason. In B 11 he writes, "In everything there is a portion of everything, and in some there is *nous* too." The things in which *nous* is additionally present must be living beings, so for consistency the first "everything" (ἐν παντί) must refer to the genus of compound beings of which living beings are a sub-genus: he means that in everything, i.e. in every compound entity, there is a portion of everything, and in some, i.e. in some compound entities, there is *nous* too. And the "everything" that is in every compound entity cannot itself be every compound entity, or he would be saying, nonsensically, that every compound being contains a portion of every compound being. So even here the two occurrences of "everything" cannot be co-referential.

In the light of all this, it seems overwhelmingly probable that Aristotle misunderstood the theory—as well he might, given Anaxagoras's anything but lucid exposition.

II   Empedocles

1. THE COSMIC CYCLE

In my first chapter, I identified in the writings of Anaxagoras what I take to be the first Greek manifesto of rational creationism. I concluded by suggesting that Anaxagoras's own agenda was not essentially religious in motivation, but scientific: to exhibit the power of intelligence when it operates on matter to create the world is to uncover the irreducible dualism of mind and matter that constitutes nature itself. As we pursue the story in this second chapter,[1] we will move into more overtly religious territory, in which named divinities take on the key roles. But, above all with the chapter's protagonist, Empedocles (mid-fifth century B.C.), it will be vital not to assume that religion and science were mutually exclusive modes of thought.

Sicilian poet, healer, and wonder-worker, Empedocles described in his poem *On nature* two cycles, a cosmic one and a daimonic one. The cosmic cycle is one of alternating world phases, governed alternately by two divine powers called Love and Strife, each phase apparently containing its own creation of life forms. The daimonic cycle is also governed by Love and Strife. A superior race of daimons, after living in blissful peace during the days of Love's dominance, committed under the pernicious influence of Strife the cardinal sins of animal slaughter, meat eating, and oath breaking. For these sins they have been banished from bliss for ten thousand years ("thirty thousand seasons"),[2] condemned to be reborn as all manner of living things, until their

---

1. Large parts of this chapter are drawn from Sedley 2005a.
2. See O'Brien 1969, pp. 85–88, for this equivalence, based on the Homeric division of the year into three seasons.

eventual return to bliss, a return which Empedocles at the beginning of his poem the *Purifications* announced he had himself finally achieved.

It was once the policy of scholars to keep these two cycles firmly segregated, certainly in different poems, and if possible in separate and irreconcilable areas of Empedocles' thought, the one scientific, the other religious. That old separatist policy was already all but extinct when in 1999 a newly identified papyrus from Strasbourg containing portions of Empedocles' *On nature* was published,[3] putting the final nail in its coffin. For there the daimonic cycle was to be found in the immediate context of Empedocles' physics. If we are to make adequate sense of Empedocles' zoogony—that is, his theory of the origins of life[4]—it must include the creation of these daimons. For, contrary to a common scholarly assumption, the daimons are themselves flesh-and-blood organisms, not mere transmigrating souls or spirits. Indeed, their sin of meat eating would have been quite hard to perform if they had not been.

Empedocles, like Anaxagoras, was working in the aftermath of Parmenides' challenge to cosmology. Parmenides had bequeathed a notorious dilemma: are we to follow mere appearances and accept the existence of the familiar variable cosmos bounded by the spherical heaven, or are we to follow reason, according to which the sphere that constitutes reality must in truth be an undifferentiated and changeless one?[5] Empedocles' solution to the dilemma is to interpret these alternatives diachronically, as each therefore capable of realization in its own turn.[6] The world, he suggests, undergoes an everlasting cycle of change under the alternating government of two divine forces, Love and Strife. Love, alias Aphrodite, is the divine power that strives to maximize harmony and blending, while Strife's aim is the opposite, maximum separation. Periodically Love gains total dominance, and when that happens the world does indeed become the changeless and blissful sphere which Parmenides had described. In most phases of the cycle, how-

---

3. Martin and Primavesi 1999.

4. "Zoogony" should be understood to mean the generation of *life* ($\zeta\omega\acute{\eta}$), not specifically of animals ($\zeta\tilde{\omega}\alpha$), because plants are included too, alongside humans, beasts, and gods.

5. In interpreting Parmenides' reality as literally spherical I am entering a realm of controversy. I defend the interpretation elsewhere (Sedley 1999c), but for present purposes it should be enough to remark (a) that the onus of proof is on anyone who wishes to deny the literal reading, and (b) Empedocles, like Plato (*Sph.* 244e2–8), must have assumed the literal reading himself, if his *sphairos* is, as widely believed, of Parmenidean inspiration.

6. Cf. Plato, *Sph.* 242d4–243a1 for recognition of Empedocles' diachronic model as one available way of dealing with Eleatic monism.

ever, Strife's influence is sufficient to prevent any such pure Parmenidean outcome. It is on those periods of conflict between Love and Strife that we will have to concentrate in the present chapter, because they are the periods during which Empedocles posits the creation and proliferation of living organisms, ourselves included.

The divine players in this drama are in fact not two but six. For Love and Strife exercise their competing powers on the four elements earth, water, air, and fire.[7] These four are themselves divinities, immortal to the extent that they endure through successive processes of mixture and separation. When Strife is at its zenith, the four elemental stuffs stand apart from each other in their familiar stratification with earth at the bottom and fire up at the top, to constitute an entirely unoccupied world. As Love's power returns, she blends portions of the elements to construct living things. In due time, Strife takes over, and as Strife's power grows a new generation of living things is generated. This dual generation of life, once by Love, once by Strife, is the notorious double zoogony of Empedocles, over which controversy has long raged.

2. THE DOUBLE ZOOGONY

The following view, and variants of it, are widely held about this double zoogony.[8] One zoogonic phase is governed by Love, the other by Strife. The zoogony of Love occurs in a phase of increasing Love, culminating in the world's conversion into the perfectly homogeneous sphere *(sphairos)*. The zoogony of Strife occurs in a phase of increasing Strife, culminating

---

7. Because at 31 B 6.1 Empedocles calls the four elements "roots," or more literally "rootings" (ῥιζώματα), but nowhere in his surviving fragments "elements" (στοιχεῖα), it has long been considered more proper to use the former term and always speak of Empedocles' four "roots." I am abandoning this practice, which risks being even more misleading. There is no evidence that "root(ing)s" was Empedocles' regular term, and it would in fact be uncharacteristic of him to use a single technical term for any concept—compare his constantly varying designations of Love, air, water, fire, and earth. (If we happened to have only B 21, would we insist on speaking of "rain" rather than "water"?) To stick to "roots" is to imply that it was his chosen term of art, and from this point of view it is less misleading to use the generic term "elements," especially now that στοιχεῖον has been shown to have already been current in the pre-Platonic period (see Crowley 2005). Eudemus (Simpl. *In Ar. Phys.* 7.10–17 = Eudemus fr. 31 Wehrli) in my view did not, as regularly understood, credit Plato with being the first to use στοιχεῖα for physical elements, but merely with being the first to insist that this term should be restricted to *irreducible* physical principles (τὰς στοιχειώδεις ἀρχάς), as Plato does indeed insist at *Ti.* 48b3–c2.

8. Notably, O'Brien 1969; Guthrie 1969, ch. III; Wright 1981, esp. pp. 53–56; Graham 1988; McKirahan 1994, pp. 269–81; Inwood 2001, esp. pp. 44–49; Martin and Primavesi 1999; Trépanier 2003a.

in the total separation of the four elements. At the culmination of each of these phases, life is inevitably extinguished, and has to be rebuilt from scratch in the next. We ourselves live in an age of increasing Strife. It therefore follows that only the products of Strife's zoogony, and not those of Love's, inhabit our world.

A major obstacle to this last assumption lies in the fact that the extant material concentrates on Love's zoogony, to the almost total exclusion of Strife's. When it comes to the emergence of species, our evidence refers again and again to the zoogony of increasing Love, as we shall see amply confirmed below (pp. 42–43). If this evidence is statistically representative of the original poem in its complete state, the widespread interpretation that makes our own era one of increasing Strife faces an anomaly: Empedocles will have spent far more time on accounting for the origin of life forms which he could do no more than conjecture to have existed in a remote part of cosmic history, and which can have left no descendants in the world we ourselves inhabit, than he did on accounting for life as we know it.[9]

It seems to me vastly more credible that Empedocles' aetiology of life, like everybody else's, was focused on discovering the origin of life as we know it. Some have obtained this desired result by limiting Empedocles' cycle to a single (though endlessly recurrent) cosmic process under increasing Love, with a single zoogony,[10] but this has to face the difficulty that he explicitly, if enigmatically, speaks of two zoogonies, one under Love and the other under Strife. Here is the much-debated B 17. 1–8, which thanks to the new Strasbourg papyrus we now know to be lines 233–40 of the poem:

9. Although it is by no means obvious why Empedocles should have assumed the reverse cosmic process, in the supposed counterworld, to have thrown up the very same life forms that we find in our own world, it is widely held that he did, for whatever reasons, commit himself to this view. But the evidence is, on inspection, vanishingly weak. It consists mainly in Aristotle's assertion (GC II 6, 334a5–7 = A 42) that Empedocles "also says that the world is in the same state now, under Strife, as previously under Love." Aristotle is trying to uncover contradictions between Empedocles' various assertions about the respective motive powers of Love and Strife, and his question here is how, if Love and Strife differ from each other in their motive powers, Empedocles can hold that the world has the same basic arrangement and motions of the four simple bodies in an age dominated by Strife as it previously had in one dominated by Love, i.e. in ages in which it is Love and Strife, respectively, that govern cosmic processes. The obvious way to interpret this previous era governed by Love is, it seems to me, as the golden age enjoyed by our own world before the fall of the daimons, the age when Kypris (= Love) exercised monarchical power to the total exclusion of Ares (= Strife), as described in B 128 (quoted n. 23 below).

10. Hölscher 1965; Bollack 1965–69; Solmsen 1965; Long 1974a; Kirk, Raven, and Schofield 1983, ch. X.

I shall tell a double tale: at one time it grew to be just one from many,
at another it grew apart again to be many from one.
There is a double coming-to-be of mortals, and a double ceasing.
One of them the coming-together *(synodos)* of all things brings
    to birth and destroys,
whereas the other was nurtured, and vanished, when they were
    growing apart again.
And these things never cease their continual change,
    at some times all coming together because of Love into one,
    at other times being severally borne apart again because of Strife's
    hostility.[11]

There is, we are here told, one coming-to-be of mortals at the time when everything is coming together under Love, another when everything is growing apart again under Strife. The same double-zoogony thesis is repeated elsewhere (B 26.4–6, quoted below p. 39), and the occasional attempts that have been made to reinterpret it as describing something other than the creation of life forms now face an additional obstacle in the Strasbourg papyrus.

In the newly discovered lines 291–300 Empedocles goes on to promise, programmatically, that he will start by telling his addressee Pausanias about "the coming together *(synodos)*[12] and the unfolding *(diaptyxis)* of birth," emphasizing the significance of this phrase by repeating it at the close of the passage. I here offer what I hope will be found a plausible reconstruction of the text:

Make sure that my account does not reach only as far as your ears.
If, as you listen to me, you look unerringly upon the things around
    you,
I will show you to your eyes too, so that you may get a greater than
    equal trade,[13]

11. δίπλ᾽ ἐρέω· τοτὲ μὲν γὰρ ἓν ηὐξήθη μόνον εἶναι
ἐκ πλεόνων, τοτὲ δ᾽ αὖ διέφυ πλέον᾽ ἐξ ἑνὸς εἶναι.
δοιὴ δὲ θνητῶν γένεσις, δοιὴ δ᾽ ἀπόλειψις·   235
τὴν μὲν γὰρ πάντων σύνοδος τίκτει τ᾽ ὀλέκει τε,
ἡ δὲ πάλιν διαφυομένων θρεφθεῖσα διέπτη.
καὶ ταῦτ᾽ ἀλλάσσοντα διαμπερὲς οὐδαμὰ λήγει,
ἄλλοτε μὲν Φιλότητι συνερχόμεν᾽ εἰς ἓν ἅπαντα,
ἄλλοτε δ᾽ αὖ δίχ᾽ ἕκαστα φορεύμενα Νείκεος ἔχθει.   240

12. 294 and 300: ξύνοδόν τε διάπτυξίν τε γενέθλης. For simplicity, and to avoid the misleading impression that two different words are at stake, I am transliterating the word for "coming together" not as *xynodos* but as *synodos*, the latter being the standard lexical form in which it occurs in our MSS reports of B 17 (see previous note).

13. That is, in recompense for paying due attention, Pausanias will earn a double return. He will not only *hear* Empedocles' account of zoogony, but also *see* its

first of all the coming-together *(synodos)* and the unfolding of birth,
and all that still now remains of this coming-to-birth.   295
This there is in the wild races of mountain-wandering beasts.
This there is in the twin birth of mankind. This there is
in the progeny of the root-bearing flowers and in the vine-climbing
   grape-cluster.
From them convey to your mind unerring proofs of the account.
For you will *see* the coming-together *(synodos)* and the unfolding
   of birth.[14]   300

"The coming-together and the unfolding of birth," emphasized by its framing position in both 294 and 300, seems to encapsulate the double-zoogony
theme introduced some sixty lines earlier,[15] referring jointly to the syn-
thesizing zoogony of Love and the divisive zoogony of Strife. And the ex-

---

truth in the living things around him. I am not sure whether to construe ἴσων as a
genitive of comparison (assumed in my translation) or as a genitive of value, "that
you may trade greater for equal." Either way, there could be an echo of the unequal
exchange of armor between Glaucus and Diomedes at Homer, *Iliad* VI 230–36, where
the same suggested verb, ἐπαμείβειν, is used.

   14. σπεῦ]δε ὅπως μὴ μοῦνον ἀν' οὔατα [μῦθος ἵκηται.
      εἰ δέ] μευ ἀμφὶς ἐόντα κλύων [ν]ημερτ[ὲς ἐπόψει,
      δεί]ξω σοι καὶ ἀν' ὅσσ' ἵνα μείζον' ἴσων [ἐπαμείβης,
      π]ρῶτον μὲν ξύνοδόν τε διάπτυξίν τ[ε γενέθλης,
      ὅς[σ]α τε νῦν ἔτι λοιπὰ πέλει τούτοιο τ[οκοῖο.   295
      τοῦτο μὲν [ἀν] θηρῶν ὀριπλάγκτων ἄγ[ρια φῦλα,
      τοῦτο δ' ἀ[ν' ἀνθρώ]πων δίδυμον φῦμα, [τοῦτο δ' ἀν' ἄνθεων
      ῥιζοφόρων γέννημα καὶ ἀμπελοβάμ[ονα βότρυν.
      ἐκ τῶν ἀψευδῆ κόμισαι φρενὶ δείγματα μ[ύθων·
      ὄψει γὰρ ξύνοδόν τε διάπτυξίν τε γενέθλη[ς.   300

Most of the text is due to Martin and Primavesi 1999. My own innovations are: 292,
εἰ δέ for their ἠδέ (the space required is about the same) and [ν]ημερτ[ὲς ἐπόψει
for their tentative [ν]ημερτ[έα δέρκευ; 293, μείζον' ἴσων [ἐπαμείβης for their μεί-
ζονι σώμ[ατι κύρει. To Janko 2004 I owe ἄγ[ρια φῦλα for Martin and Primavesi's
ἄγ[ρότερ' εἴδη in 296 (the same suggestion has also been made to me independently
by Laura Gemelli Marciano), and ἄνθεων for their ἄγρων in 297. Janko at one stage
proposed the extremely attractive incorporation of fr. g to provide the last group of
letters in each of lines 293–95. If we followed this proposal, it would go a long way
towards confirming the supplements proposed for the end of lines 293 and 294: we
would get ἴσων [ἐπ]αμείβ[ης (293) and διάπτυξίν τ[ε] γενέθ[λης (294). However,
the proposal faces two difficulties. First, Janko reports that he has since become hesitant about the suggested repositioning on grounds of questionable fiber match, and
is happier with a different collocation which places fr. g immediately to the left of
fr. h. Second, if we did accept it, the current ending of line 295 would have to be
changed, although at present the sequence of letters in the corresponding final line
of fr. g is eluding precise decipherment. I have therefore not included fr. g in my text,
although I still wonder if its inclusion may eventually be vindicated.

   15. Cf. Trépanier 2003a, p. 24, for this point.

emplary list of life forms in the intervening lines should be enough to dispel any doubt that what that earlier passage referred to as the "double birth of mortals" really does by "mortals" mean living organic beings.[16]

And there is more to learn. The double zoogony is clearly presented as the origin of life *as we ourselves know it.* In lines 291–93 Empedocles opens by urging his addressee Pausanias to use his own eyes: he will not only hear but also *see* the truth of the zoogonic account. He then promises to tell him not only about the double generation but also about "all that still now remains of this procreation" (294–95). What then follows, by way of further confirmation, is a citation of the *evidence* for the double zoogony, and it is the present range of life forms that is being cited as the evidence for it. I say this because "This there is ... " (τοῦτο μὲν ... τοῦτο δέ)[17] is Empedocles' favored locution for citing empirical evidence from the natural world.[18] Moreover, the Roman poet Lucretius (II 1081–83) translates a list of life forms from Empedocles which, while not identical with our present list at 296–98, is no more than a variant of it; and he renders Empedocles' locution as "Thus you will find ['invenies sic'] the mountain-wandering race of beasts to be, thus ['sic'] the twin progeny of mankind, thus ['sic'] finally ... "[19] Lucretius had an intimate knowledge of Empedocles' poetry,[20]

16. This point is well made by Trépanier 2003a.

17. 296–97, τοῦτο μὲν αὖ ... τοῦτο δ' αὖ' ... τοῦτο δ' αὖ' ...

18. In B 76 he writes, "This there is in [τοῦτο μὲν ἐν] the heavy-backed shells of sea-dwellers, and, moreover, those of stony-skinned tritons and turtles: there *you will see* [ἔνθ' ὄψει] earth dwelling above flesh ... " I believe that the same can well apply to B 20.1 = Strasbourg papyrus c2. Janko 2004 credibly identifies this fragment as lines 301–8, that is, as the immediate sequel to the above passage (291–300). Assuming that placement, I conjecture that the fragment contains the matching "And secondly{ ... }" passage anticipated by the π]ρῶτον μὲν of 294: "[And secondly I will show you the] separative [process of death]. This there is in (τοῦτο μὲν αὖ) the splendid mass of mortal limbs: at one time we come all together through Love into one, as limbs which a body has acquired when its life flourishes, but at another time, on the contrary, split apart by evil strifes, they wander each of them apart along life's shoreline. Likewise for shrubs, water-housed fish, mountain-bedded beasts, and wing-travelling fowls." I thus agree with Janko (whose text I am here translating, other than in the conjectural opening line, by modifying which I relate the passage somewhat differently to what precedes) that these lines are about death in the natural world as we experience it. If so, there is no problem about taking τοῦτο μὲν αὖ (this time however picked up not by τοῦτο δ' αὖ but by ὡς δ' αὔτως, "Likewise ... ") to be pointing once again to familiar evidence—here that of animal and plant life cycles. The programmatic reference is perhaps to a later exposition of the thesis adumbrated by Empedocles in B 8, that the true nature of "death" is separation.

19. "invenies sic montivagum genus esse ferarum,/ sic hominum geminam prolem, sic denique mutas/ squamigerum pecudes et corpora cuncta volantum."

20. I argue this fully in Sedley 1998a, ch. 1.

and his testimony confirms that the Empedoclean linguistic device he is imitating is one for urging his reader to confront the evidence of the natural world around him.

In these new lines, then, Empedocles first tells Pausanias to use the evidence of his own eyes. Next, he announces that he will recount to him his double zoogony, adding that some of its products are still to be seen today. He proceeds to make this latter point explicit by listing *exempli gratia* beasts, humans, and plants—familiar representatives of today's flora and fauna—as his evidence for that double zoogony. He then adds at line 299, "From these convey to your mind unerring proofs of my account," confirming once again that it is currently existing life forms that constitute his evidence.[21] And in finally repeating, at line 300, that Pausanias will himself "see," by using his own eyes, "the coming together *and* the unfolding of birth," he confirms that it is the entire double zoogony for which the present-day organisms constitute his evidence.

But that would scarcely be possible if between the last phase of increasing Love and our present world the homogeneous sphere had intervened to obliterate all Love's products. It is therefore time to reconsider that aspect of Empedocles' cosmic cycle, and the following revision seems to me to have an unassailable basis in the primary evidence. The much-emphasized oscillation between the ascendancy of the two powers is to be understood primarily as an alternating pattern *within a single world*. The sphere will, it is true, eventually return, but only after many rounds of the cycle (just how many rounds is a question discussed below in Appendix 2 to the present chapter). Later still, the sphere will itself be disrupted by Strife's renewed

---

21. 299: ἐκ τῶν ἀψευδῆ κόμισαι φρενὶ δείγματα μ[ύθων. Martin and Primavesi translate, "From these accounts convey to your mind unerring proofs." This, by construing τῶν with μ[ύθων], interprets Empedocles as locating Pausanias's prospective source of certainty, not in the aforementioned empirical evidence, but in Empedocles' own account. However, in both its other occurrences in Empedocles (B 23.5, 98.5) the same expression, ἐκ τῶν, likewise starting a line, refers back to what precedes: "from these" or "from which." Besides, in introducing the theme of the double zoogony, Empedocles has already explicitly urged Pausanias not to rely on his ears alone, but to use his own eyes (291–93), which sits ill with a reading of line 299 that has Empedocles telling Pausanias to secure his proofs simply from the accounts he is hearing. All these considerations unite to recommend the translation adopted above: "From them [i.e. from animals and plants] convey to your mind unerring proofs . . ." If μ[ύθων] is correctly restored at the end of the line, whether thus as a plural or in the singular form μ[ύθου], we can complete the translation with "unerring proofs of the account": the simple noun μῦθοι can easily refer to Empedocles' account, as it does at B 17.14 (ἀλλ' ἄγε μύθων κλῦθι).

activity, resulting in the separation of the four elemental masses.[22] Following this act of cosmogony, Love will begin her comeback, and the prolonged oscillation between rising Love and rising Strife will start afresh. Apart from the widely separated times when the sphere reappears, there is complete continuity between the phases of increasing Love and those of increasing Strife, such that Love's products, including not only ordinary animals and plants but also for that matter the blessed long-lived daimons, survive. This explains, among other things, why the very same daimons that enjoyed bliss during the reign of Love[23] are now condemned to a long exile under the rule of Strife. If the reign of Love had ended in the sphere, they would have been obliterated before they could fall from grace because of Strife's return.

That this is how the cycle works, although unrecognized in the modern literature, is virtually explicit in Empedocles' text. Fragment B 26 includes the following lines:

> In turn they dominate, as the cycle comes round,
> and they perish and grow into each other in their destined turns.
> For in themselves they are the same, but in running through each
> other
> they become human beings and the tribes of other beasts,
> at some times when coming together because of Love into one world-
> order,
> at other times when being severally borne apart again because of
> Strife's hostility,
> until growing together as one they are—the totality—subdued.[24]

5

---

22. I cannot altogether discount the possibility that, as on the traditional reading, this passage from *sphairos* to separated elements will itself constitute a cosmic phase, a counterworld with its own zoogony. But I can no longer see any evidence or putative inhabitants for such a counterworld, and therefore strongly incline to its exclusion, in company with Hölscher, Bollack, Solmsen, Long and KRS (as cited in n. 8 above). When Aristotle (*DC* 301a15–16) says that Empedocles omitted the cosmogony under Love, I read this as confirming that there was just one act of cosmogony in Empedocles' poem, that by Strife, consisting in the disruption of the *sphairos*.

23. B 128: "Nor did they have as a god Ares or Battle-cry,/ nor Zeus as king, nor Cronos nor Poseidon,/ But Kypris was queen. [. . .]/ Her they propitiated with holy images/ and with drawn pictures and many-odored perfumes,/ and with sacrifices of pure myrrh and scented frankincense,/ and with libations of yellow honey which they threw on the ground./ With unspeakable slaughters of oxen the altar was not drenched,/ but this stood as the greatest abomination among men,/ to eat fine limbs, after bereaving them of life."

24. ἐν δὲ μέρει κρατέουσι περιπλομένοιο κύκλοιο,
καὶ φθίνει εἰς ἄλληλα καὶ αὔξεται ἐν μέρει αἴσης.
αὐτὰ γὰρ ἔστιν ταῦτά, δι' ἀλλήλων δὲ θέοντα

The four elements, by their constant interchange (1–3), become the materials of zoogony (4)—more specifically, of one zoogony in the phases of increasing Love (5), another in those of increasing Strife (6). That this "cycle" is not itself punctuated at every round by the sphere becomes clear in line 7—a line whose addition is so inconvenient for the traditional view of the cycle that no less eminent a scholar than Wilamowitz[25] proposed its excision. For the sequence of 5–7 tells us that the roots are formed into living things by alternately (5) coming together through Love in a process of cosmic unification and (6) being forced apart through Strife, *until finally (7) they are altogether unified in the sphere.* If the sphere were simply the culmination of each phase of increasing Love, the sequence of these three lines would make no sense.[26]

Now that we have seen good reason to accept that the world's history is continuous between phases of Love and phases of Strife, so that the zoogonies of past phases can have survivors in our own, we can turn to the question what the double zoogony consists in. This requires highlighting a well-known testimony of Aetius (V 19.5 = A 72):[27]

1. Empedocles says that the first comings-to-be of animals and plants were by no means integral, but disjointed, with limbs not grown together;

γίνοντ' ἄνθρωποί τε καὶ ἄλλων ἔθνεα θηρῶν,
ἄλλοτε μὲν Φιλότητι συνερχόμεν' εἰς ἕνα κόσμον,   5
ἄλλοτε δ' αὖ δίχ' ἕκαστα φορούμενα Νείκεος ἔχθει,
εἰσόκεν ἓν συμφύντα τὸ πᾶν ὑπένερθε γένηται.

25. Wilamowitz 1930.

26. Cf. the discussion by Graham 1988, pp. 310–11, who shows the difficulty of resolving the problem by interpreting B 26 as purely about microcosmic change. Trépanier 2003a, pp. 28–30, following the lead of Stokes 1967, p. 167, offers the alternative solution that Empedocles twice in the course of the fragment *shifts* between macrocosmic and microcosmic description. Quite apart from the considerable strain this puts on the reader, it requires us to understand εἰς ἕνα κόσμον (5) at the level of a single living being *as distinct from* the level of the world, despite the cosmic signification that κόσμος had undoubtedly acquired by this date (cf. also the occurrence of the same phrase in Strasbourg papyrus a(i) 6 = 267). Another solution, by Ritter 1818 and Bignone 1916, of taking line 7 to refer to the total dominance of Strife, not Love, is well refuted by O'Brien 1969, pp. 314–24, in his long note on this fragment, although O'Brien's own explanation of the line's role (p. 321) remains unclear to me.

27. Ἐμπεδοκλῆς τὰς πρώτας γενέσεις τῶν ζῴων καὶ φυτῶν μηδαμῶς ὁλοκλήρους γενέσθαι, ἀσυμφύσι δὲ τοῖς μορίοις διεζευγμένας, τὰς δὲ δευτέρας συμφυομένων τῶν μερῶν εἰδωλοφανεῖς, τὰς δὲ τρίτας τῶν ὁλοφυῶν, τὰς δὲ τετάρτας οὐκέτι ἐκ τῶν ὁμοίων, οἷον ἐκ γῆς καὶ ὕδατος, ἀλλὰ δι' ἀλλήλων ἤδη, τοῖς μὲν πυκνωθείσης [τοῖς δὲ καὶ] τοῖς ζῴοις τῆς τροφῆς, τοῖς δὲ καὶ τῆς εὐμορφίας τῶν γυναικῶν ἐπερεθισμὸν τοῦ σπερματικοῦ κινήματος ἐμποιησάσης. I have, with-

2. the second, when the parts were growing together, were apparition-like [εἰδωλοφανεῖς];

3. the third were those of whole-natured beings [ὁλοφυεῖς];

4. the fourth no longer from homogeneous stuffs, such as earth and water, but by now through copulation, for some because the animals had gone over to solid nourishment, for some also because the beauty of women produced in them the stimulation of spermatic motion.

Like many supporters of the double-zoogony interpretation, I assume that the first two stages (disjointed limbs, followed by joined-up hybrids) are the zoogony under Love, the third and fourth (whole-natured beings, and finally the practitioners and products of sexual intercourse) the zoogony under Strife.[28] Some have tried instead to read all four stages as constituting a single zoogony, whether in the order listed by Aetius, taken as constituting the only zoogony,[29] or in two variant orders which both depart from that of Aetius, one of them representing a zoogony under Strife, the other a zoogony under Love.[30] This latter option and its variants will turn out to face a major objection, namely that human beings emerge both in stage 2 *and* in stage 4, making it very hard to place both stages in a single zoogonic sequence.

Stage 1 started with a preliminary procedure which Aetius does not specifically mention: Love prepared her materials, such as flesh, bone, and blood (B 96, 98), by mixing the four elements in a variety of calculated proportions. At least in the case of flesh, the proportions of the ingredients were subtly further varied so as to generate a range of different types (B 98.4–5). Empedocles also spoke (B 82) of feathers, leaves, and scales, observing that they are functionally equivalent to each other, and we may conjecture that they too were among the sets of variant components created by Love at this preliminary stage.[31]

Having prepared her materials, Love proceeded to construct the genera-

---

out complete confidence, opted for the bracketed excision (as a dittography from the next clause) as the most economical emendation sufficient to repair the grammar, thus departing from the Diels-Kranz reading in keeping τοῖς ζῴοις in the text: these two words do, after all, make the relevant point that the move from liquid to solid nourishment affected animals but not plants.

28. Notably Bignone 1916, pp. 570–85; Guthrie 1969; and Martin and Primavesi 1999, esp. pp. 54–57, 80–82, 95–97.

29. Kirk, Raven, and Schofield 1983, pp. 302–5.

30. O'Brien 1969, pp. 196–236; McKirahan 1994, pp. 278–81.

31. I am assuming, that is, that stage 2 did not include singleton feathers, hairs etc. as "single-limbed" creatures.

tion of creatures which Empedocles called "single-limbed."[32] From their description as "single-limbed," rather than "single limbs," it seems that these products of stage 1 were not so much detached body-parts as very simple organisms, each with just one specialization. Although Empedocles by way of example talks of them (B 57) as heads without necks, arms without shoulders, and eyes without faces, his further assertion that they roamed around on their own confirms that this was not just an inert organ bank, but already a primitive set of autonomous creatures. Since, moreover, Empedocles is reported to have distinguished between the structures of night-sighted and day-sighted eyes,[33] we may be confident that this primitive stock of autonomous eyes included a variety of types with different specializations. Similar assumptions can be added about the variety of wings, paws, and so on. The stock of limbs and organs was therefore an immensely rich one. Even though they were biologically autonomous, it is inconceivable that they were able to prolong their kinds by reproduction, and we would do better to think of these first creatures as prototypes from Love's workshop, designed all along for combination into the complex organisms of stage 2.

That we have here the first stage of *Love's* zoogony is both well attested[34] and widely recognized. Indeed, a key passage of Simplicius (*On Aristotle's De caelo* 529.1–530.11) ought to be enough to put it beyond doubt, not only that this is the zoogony of increasing Love, but also that it is the origin of life as we ourselves know it. Fragment B 35 describes Love, once she has recovered her ascendancy, as using her powers of mixture to generate a wonderful variety of life forms. Simplicius reports that this introduction of Love's zoogony was soon followed by fragments B 86, 87, and 95, all describing her work in constructing eyes of various kinds. (To these we may be reasonably confident that B 84, on the detailed design of the eye, is also to be joined.)[35] He then (529.28) continues by citing B 71, with its reference to "all the forms and colors of mortals which have *now* come to birth, having been fitted together by Aphrodite,"[36] as explicit confirmation that it is the present world that is being described,

---

32. μουνομελῆ, B 58.
33. Theophrastus, *Sens.* 8, and Simpl. *In De caelo* 529.26 = preamble to B 95 DK.
34. E.g. Aristotle, *DC* 300b24–31; Simplicius, *In Ar. Phys.* 371.33.
35. See below, pp. 52–53.
36. I am unconvinced by the attempt of Trépanier 2003a, pp. 43–45, to undo the obvious implication that Love's products exist in the present world. In particular, his translation "as many as have now come into being, *held together* by Aphrodite" does not seem to me to capture the meaning of the aorist συναρμοσθέντα, which must mean rather that these present beings were, at an earlier date, actually constructed by Love.

thereby making it clear that this passage too occurred in the same context, the narrative of Love's zoogony. He adds (530.5–10) that B 73 and 75, also on Love's creative work, followed soon after.[37] We have here, then, clear evidence not only that the creation of these individual limbs and organs belongs to the era of increasing Love, but also that that zoogony's products are still with us today.

What further confirms that this is the start of Love's zoogony is the way in which the second stage builds on the first. Love initially cannot go beyond the creation of simple creatures, owing to the still considerable power of Strife (B 35.8–9). But as Love's ascendancy further advances, she combines the separate, single-function creatures into complex beings, a process of synthesis which evidently represents the integrationist ambitions of Love rather than the divisive ones of Strife.

This second stage is the most famous phase of Empedocles' zoogony, partly because it aroused Aristotle's ire, partly because it is widely admired as an early anticipation of Darwinian survival of the fittest.[38] Thrown together at random (B 59), the complex combinations of body parts in numerous cases prove non-viable, and perish; but some prove capable of long-term survival. Our sources, Aetius included, emphasize the non-viable life forms, the weird hybrids which Empedocles called "apparition-like." We know from fragment B 61 that these were called "double-faced," "double-chested," "man-faced ox-progeny," and "man-natured with ox heads," and that they included human hermaphrodites.

Is this a sheer flight of fancy on Empedocles' part? It is true that the philosophers seem to have paid little heed to Greece's rich fossil records, which could have provided strong confirmation that monstrous species, now extinct, had once existed.[39] But other evidence readily took its place. For one

---

37. That all of these fragments—B 35, 71, 73, 75, 86, 87, 95—occurred in close proximity is further suggested by Simplicius's concluding remark (530.11), "I have read and cited these from a few of the verses that fell immediately to hand."

38. On Empedocles' place in the history of evolutionary theory, cf. Campbell 2000.

39. See Mayor 2000 for a fascinating account of ancient Greek responses to fossils of extinct mammal species. In ch. 5 she discusses the problem why philosophers seem to have more or less ignored their significance. The materials she has compiled would in my view favor the following answer. Because big bones were found underground, they were assumed to have been *buried*, and were therefore regularly identified as the remains of legendary heroes (Orestes, Theseus, etc.), or at most of anthropoid giants such as the Cyclopes, rather than of sub-human species. The one case where this explanation was insufficient was the fossil beds of Samos, where big skeletons were far too abundant for such a misidentification to be credible. As a result, local legend there found an alternative explanation of their being found underground: they were the remains of now extinct creatures called the Neades, which

thing, hermaphroditism was a well-recognized biological reality,[40] and for another, Greek legend preserved apparent memories of an age in which a creature "man-natured with ox face" actually existed, namely the Minotaur, as well as combinations of man and horse, and other cross-species monsters. Furthermore, Aristotle reports Empedocles as indicating that the same production of non-viable monsters still continues today.[41] Empedocles will here have had in mind the phenomenon of defective births, human and other. For elsewhere (*On generation of animals* IV 3, 769b13–16) Aristotle reports, albeit disapprovingly, the common belief that these are freak cases of hybridization: "They say that what is produced has the head of a ram or an ox, and similarly in other cases that of a different animal, a calf with the head of a child or a sheep with an ox's head." This alleged phenomenon was, I imagine, exploited by Empedocles as an indication, not that Love's zoogonic method is still operative today,[42] but that it has left sufficient vestiges to attest its historical reality.[43]

I note in passing that, if the process by which Love threw up an assortment of largely non-viable life forms is remembered in popular myth, and is still vestigially continuing in the phenomenon of freak births, that strongly implies once more that Love's zoogony was itself located in an earlier phase of our own world, not in a counterworld cut off from ours by obliteration in the sphere. In describing the zoogony of Love (B 35.16–17), Empedocles celebrates her successes with the ecstatic description, "tens of thousands of races of mortals, fitted with every kind of form, a wonder to behold." Can there be any serious doubt that he is here hymning nature as we ourselves know it?

These successful products of Love's zoogony undoubtedly included human beings. For since the failed hybrids explicitly included features of men and women, it is hardly open to doubt that the successes included actual

---

had been so noisy that the ground split open and swallowed them up! This *ad hoc* aetiology confirms that more isolated discoveries of buried big bones were not likely to be recognized for what they were.

40. Cf. Brisson 2002a.

41. *Physics* II 8, 198b31, quoted with full context, pp. 189–90 below. If, as seems likely, Simplicius is merely echoing this when he reports, "And it all still happens the same way nowadays" (*In Ar. Phys.* 372.8–9), he will not, as suggested by Campbell 2000, p. 151, be referring merely to Empedocles' embryology, but more explicitly, like Aristotle, to the continued birth and perishing of monsters.

42. See chapter VI, p. 191 below, where I suggest that Aristotle has nevertheless interpreted Empedocles in this way.

43. For Empedocles' views on the various causes of defective births, see Aetius V 8.1 (= A 8, part, DK). Of these, "multiplication of the seed" and "division into more than one" sound the likeliest to cause hybrid births.

men and women, as indeed it is reported that they did.[44] Confirmation is found in the apparent fact (see Appendix 4 to this chapter) that the successful species included dogs, beasts of burden, sheep, and cattle, which already at this initial stage owed their survival to man's protection. The inclusion of man among the successful outcomes of Love's zoogony will in due course confront us with a considerable problem, but for now I merely note it.

We saw earlier how in the new fragments Empedocles draws Pausanias's attention to the empirical evidence provided by present-day animals and plants, and does so in support of both halves of his double zoogony. What is this direct evidence for Love's zoogony? In the case of the first stage of Love's zoogony, the design and construction of single-limbed creatures, we must assume the empirical evidence to lie in the visibly purpose-made functioning of individual body parts, as typified by the eye. Since what is functionally speaking the very same organ or limb can be found repeated with appropriate variations in species after species, Empedocles must see it as a reasonable inference that the individual functions were devised and embodied first, and only subsequently combined into the vast variety of complex beings that, on his story, emerged as the winners in stage 2. For stage 2 itself, the evidence lies largely in the present vast array of viable creatures, which, as I have sought to show, are the surviving products of Love's zoogony. As for the now extinct Minotaur-like hybrids of stage 2, the empirical evidence lies, we have seen, in its vestigial continuation, the occasional birth of (supposedly) hybrid creatures.

The zoogony in ages of increasing Strife, to which I now turn, is a much more muted affair. The "whole-natured forms" that correspond to Aetius's stage 3 are described, in B 62, as having been the prelude to the emergence, not of a wide range of plants, animals, and even gods, but simply of men and women. That these too are men and women whose descendants are still alive today is confirmed, if confirmation were needed, by the new Strasbourg fragments. There (fr. d) Empedocles refers forward[45] to the full account of Strife's

---

44. Simplicius, *In Ar. Phys.* 372.6–7.

45. Prior to Sedley 2005a (from which the content of the present chapter is largely derived) I had made this suggestion only orally, but it had been cited by Osborne 2000, p. 336 n. 9; Inwood 2001, p. 20 n. 43; Laks 2002, p. 129 n. 6; and Trépanier 2003a, p. 15 n. 37; and had even faced refutation by Kingsley 2002, p. 339 n. 10, followed since by Janko 2004, p. 7. The suggestion is that this new fragment is part of the proem, and is referring *forward* to Strife's zoogony in book II (with αὖθις in d10 meaning "later", and, I further propose, a reading such as λυγρῶν, ὥς ποτ]ε δή at the beginning of d11), rather than a late passage referring backwards to it (with αὖθις meaning "again") as in the *editio princeps*, Martin and Primavesi 1999. There is much to be gained by the economical assumption, which this permits, that all the new frag-

products which he will initiate in book II of his poem (B 62),[46] and adds the words "upon whose remnants the daylight still now gazes."

The initial zoogony by Strife seems to be a variant of a widespread Greek tradition according to which the first human generation sprang from the earth (on which see p. 19 above). In Empedocles' variant, what emerged were not yet men and women but sexually undifferentiated beings, not unlike trees, those archetypically earth-born organisms which he in fact held (A 70) also to have been generated by Strife at that same time (see further below). They were concocted as a mere by-product (or so it seems from B 62) by the passage of heat, when Strife, pursuing its agenda of separation, encouraged fire trapped below the earth to travel upwards in a bid to rejoin its own kind in the heaven. There is no reason to see in this any deliberate act of intelligent creation on Strife's part. The model followed is rather that of spontaneous generation, widely assumed in the ancient tradition to be the origin of life forms, and believed by thinkers as diverse as Aristotle and Lucretius to be attested as a present-day reality (pp. 18–19 above).

It was only subsequently, in the fourth stage listed by Aetius, that Strife furthered its divisive ambitions by splitting these creatures into the two sexes—a motif that has rightly reminded many of Aristophanes' fable in Plato's *Symposium* (see below, p. 55). Although one might have been tempted to associate the creation of sexual polarization with Love,[47] that is

---

ments came from a single piece of papyrus. The point of the forward reference is as follows. Empedocles is busy cataloguing the deplorable current state of the world, but one of its worst features, Strife's introduction of wretched human beings, will be fully described later, and therefore gets only five lines here, with a promise to return to it. I am not sure why Kingsley and Janko think that the proposal is contradicted by the (alleged) parallelism of B 35.1, where Empedocles speaks of now returning "again," πάλιν, to a topic. αὖθις differs from πάλιν in having from Homer onwards the alternative sense (LSJ, s.v., II 3) "later," and no reader of a poem's opening section need have any hesitation in taking αὖθις with a future tense that way, as also for example in the more or less contemporary Aesch. *Ag.* 317. No contradiction with B 35 is involved, or with any passage where αὖθις means "again." Indeed Janko's own persuasive argument that all the Strasbourg fragments come from the same early part of the poem makes it most unlikely that Empedocles is already broaching this topic for the second time.

46. For a demonstration that this is the reference, see Martin and Primavesi 1999, pp. 307–8 (although—see previous note—they there take it to be a back reference, not a forward one as I do).

47. I take this to be what is intended in Kirk, Raven, and Schofield 1983, p. 305, by the remark that Love appears to have achieved more in stage 4 than in stage 3. This point is, however, perhaps more germane to ἔρως (cf. B 62.7, ἐρατόν) than to φιλότης; and although the latter's alternative name Aphrodite might have been expected to point to sexual love, it is in fact never so used in Empedocles' fragments.

plainly not Empedocles' view, as is in fact confirmed by the evidence that he advised against marriage, procreation, and heterosexual intercourse, considering these a mode of furthering Strife's creation and hindering Love's.[48] To him, it seems, sexual politics represents division and discord, not love.

Strife's divisive act looks in fact like an Empedoclean development of Hesiod's Pandora myth (*Works and Days* 47–105, partly quoted p. 54 below), according to which women were introduced into the existing male human population as an act of divine spite, with the precise intention of sowing misery and discord. In Hesiod this malicious creative act is an act of retribution that follows upon Prometheus's seditious release, and distribution to men, of the fire which Zeus had hidden away. It seems possible that in Empedocles both stages of Strife's zoogony originated as an allegorical reading of the Hesiodic myth. For in the first stage it is precisely the release of underground fire that generates the unisex creatures, and in the second it is by separating off women from men that Strife's plans are further advanced.

I have already described what Empedocles considers to be the present-day empirical evidence for Love's zoogony. In the new fragments, we have seen, he attaches equal importance to the present-day empirical evidence for Strife's zoogony. In what does this consist?

As regards its initial stage (= Aetius's stage 3), another text of Aetius (V 26, in A 70 DK) provides the materials for a probable answer. Strife's activity, as I have said, seems to have generated not only humans but trees as well. For here too (as in B 62) it is reported to be the separative power of underground heat that pushes the trees up, suggesting once again the work of Strife. We may infer, then, that present-day trees, or at least some of them,[49] continue to represent the generative effects of Strife in its first zoogonic stage, that of earth-born "whole-natured forms." For earth-born whole-natured forms are what trees still are: according to Aetius's report, it is because they are so evenly mixed that no sexual differentiation occurs

---

48. Hippolytus, *Ref.* VII 29.22, 30.3–4; cf. Osborne 1987, p. 123; Inwood 2001, p. 48. Against this interpretation, Mansfeld 1992, pp. 219–20, argues that it is Hippolytus's own imposition, not backed up by anything he found in Empedocles' verses. Mansfeld makes an impressive case based largely on Hippolytus's failure to quote chapter and verse; but I do not share his view (esp. his n. 44) that the prohibition on sex is contrary to Empedocles' teachings, for reasons which I hope the present chapter makes clear.

49. I conjecture that, at the very least, the laurel constitutes an exception. Since Empedocles is said to have judged it the most suitable of all plants to be reincarnated as (see B 127, including its context in Aelian), it is more likely to be a product of Love than Strife.

in them. We can thus see in the continued sprouting of trees from the soil a surviving index of Strife's initial separative power.

In present-day human beings, with their further segregation into male and female, we see a more advanced stage of Strife's peculiar brand of divisive creativity (Aetius's stage 4). According to Aetius's report (pp. 40–41 above), it is solid nourishment and sexual attraction—both alien to plant biology—that constitute the twin reasons why spontaneous generation from the earth has now ceased for these creatures of Strife. Solid nourishment means that they no longer make do with the simple absorption of earth, water, and other nutrients from the soil. And sexual reproduction in any case renders spontaneous generation unnecessary.

Two features of Strife's zoogony are noteworthy in particular. First, there is this time far less sign of biodiversity. Apart from trees, so far as one can tell Strife's work is cited purely as an anthropogony. This restriction incidentally makes immediate sense of the order in which Empedocles twice lists the range of life forms in B 21 and 23 (quoted below, p. 58): (1) trees; (2) men and women; (3) beasts, fowls, and fish; (4) long-lived gods (for these last as including the daimons, see below).[50] The chosen sequence will represent an ascending order, with Strife's progeny as a whole (1–2) placed before Love's (3–4).

Second, unlike any recorded outcome of Love's zoogony, the human products of Strife's ascendancy are portrayed as wretched. In the Strasbourg papyrus, the whole-natured forms are already "a mixture of much woe."[51] And when, in fragment B 62, they are further separated out into the two sexes, these are described as "men and *much-grieving* women," more likely another indication of wretchedness than a casual stock-epithet.[52]

This grim aspect of the zoogony's products,[53] along with the role played by Strife's hallmark activity, separation, in both stages (in the first stage the work is done by "fire as it was *separated*"),[54] gives the impression that the zoogony really is Strife's own handiwork. An alternative approach, however, holds that all creative acts, this one included, are the work of Love,

50. The groupings, which I have marked with semicolons, are conveyed in Empedocles' text either by variant use of connectives, or by line divisions.

51. π[ο]λυπήμ[ον]α κρᾶσιν, d12.

52. Plutarch, *Q. conv.* 683E maintains that Empedocles' epithets are, quite generally, attempts to capture things' essences or powers, rather than merely decorative. For a full discussion of this aspect of Empedocles' poetry, see Gemelli Marciano 1988. See further, pp. 73–74 below.

53. With Empedocles' association between sexual reproduction and misery, cf. Parmenides B 12.3–6.

54. κρινόμενον πῦρ, B 62.2.

and that the progressive division arises because Love's work is increasingly obstructed by Strife. This latter interpretation faces, among other difficulties,[55] the task of explaining what could possibly motivate Love to continue with zoogony in the age of growing Strife,[56] during which, as we have now seen reason to believe, the species generated during her earlier ascendancy continue to exist.[57] I shall nevertheless keep both alternatives in mind in the discussion that now follows.

The biggest puzzle to emerge from the proposed reconstruction is the following. While most plant and animal species, including a race of biologically generated gods, are created just once, mainly under Love, men and women turn out to have a double origin. They emerge first from the zoogony under Love, and then once more from the zoogony under Strife. If I am right to place both anthropogonies in different phases of a continuous world, how are we to explain Empedocles' flagrant breach of explanatory economy? More particularly, if Love had already created human beings, along with the tens of thousands of other kinds, why would a divine agent like Strife have reinvented the wheel by creating this one species all over again?

In addressing that question, let me start with another question. Given that the evidence does point to this double origin for present-day mankind, is it just a coincidence that the new fragments include, at line 297 (= a(ii) 27; p. 36 above), a striking reference to "the twin birth (or 'nature'?) of mankind"?[58] There seems, I confess, to be much to be said for the view that it *is* just a coincidence, and for agreeing with Martin and Primavesi that the reference is simply to men and women. For although it may seem odd to single out humans for their sexual differentiation, when the same could equally well have been applied to most animals, the fact remains that Empe-

---

55. See also note 16 above for evidence that Strife is, in its limited way, a zoogonic agent.

56. Some may respond to this by reading the personification of Love and Strife in a reductive or minimalist way, as representing no more than the nature of certain physical processes, so that talk of their "motives" would be inappropriate. See §3 below for my reasons for pressing a strong creationist reading.

57. One might also hope to use B 22 in support of the former alternative, according to which Strife is the creative agent of its own zoogony. Lines 4–5 describe Love's creations, living in harmony, after which 6–9 seem to turn to Strife's, living in disharmony. If the corrupt νεικεογεννέστησιν in 9 conceals a word or phrase meaning "generated by Strife," as some editors believe (thus e.g. Inwood 2001, pp. 234–35, "due to their birth in strife [νεικεογεννητῆσι], since their births were in anger"), this would be valuable evidence.

58. ἀνθρώπων δίδυμον φῦμα. I choose "birth" in place of Martin and Primavesi's "offspring." The unique short upsilon in φῦμα seems to link it to φύσις; but Empedocles' use of φύσις is itself often, and rightly, linked to "birth," as testified by B 8.

docles' standard lists of species do tend to speak of humans as "men and women" (B 21.10, 23.6), and that B 61, on the hybrids generated in the second stage of Love's zoogony, includes oxen, men, and women as coordinate examples of the kinds that became chaotically mixed up. The ultimate background to this treatment of men and women as virtually distinct species no doubt lies in Hesiod, who had given women a separate and later origin (p. 47 above). But a more immediate explanation perhaps lies in Empedocles' views on reincarnation:[59] he may be conjectured to have anticipated Plato in placing women further down the hierarchy of reincarnation than men. Indeed, Plato introduces this hierarchical relation with the words, "Since human nature is double . . . ,"[60] arguably an echo of Empedocles. Finally, Lucretius, in a passage I have already cited (p. 37), directly translates Empedocles' phrase (*hominum geminam prolem*, II 1082) in the course of one of his own appeals to the evidence of nature, and it is very hard to see what *he* can have understood by this other than men and women.

Despite this strong case, I am not quite ready to discount altogether the possibility that Empedocles' phrase hints rather at the double origin of mankind. But since in line 297 he is, as we have seen, appealing to the evidence of existing species, the only way in which he could invoke the "twin birth [or nature] of mankind" here would be if he intended, in the sequel, to assert as an *empirical fact* that there are two kinds of human being—not male and female, but distinguished on some other basis. This division into two kinds of people would then become the empirical basis for distinguishing two separate anthropogonies. Even if, more prudently, we do not read line 297 this way, the need remains to ask why Empedocles should have given mankind, uniquely among present-day species, a double origin, as it now seems he did.

I offer the following suggestion. Empedocles is himself, in origin, a product of Love. For Love's zoogony included "long-lived gods," and these probably either are, or include, the "daimons that have a share of long life" (B 115.5).[61] Owing to the daimons' fall from grace, Empedocles tells us that he has been condemned to "wander for thirty thousand seasons away

59. This suggestion was first put to me by Myles Burnyeat.

60. *Ti.* 42a1–2, διπλῆς δὲ οὔσης τῆς ἀνθρωπίνης φύσεως (the regular φύσις replacing Empedocles' exotic φῦμα).

61. Cf. B 146: the process of advancement for men culminates in their becoming "gods," just as in the *Purifications* (B 112.4–5) Empedocles has himself done. Humans are in effect the same species as both daimons and created gods. For example, the daimons who fell from grace through the sin of slaughter (B 115) are presumably identifiable with the human beings (ἄνθρωποι) who, in B 128.8–10, had in the

from the blessed ones, becoming over time all kinds of forms of mortals" (B 115.6–7). The reason why he can expect eventually to recover his divinity lies in that origin as a daimon, plus his progress through a long series of reincarnations, at least the later ones of which are reincarnations in human form (a run of a good twenty human lives, at least in Pythagoras's case, Empedocles tells us in B 129).[62] And part of the process of purification which will hasten his return to divinity lies in sexual abstinence. Not all human beings share his status, he makes clear (B 115.13), and we may conjecture that those who do not are the wretched race of men and women generated in the era of Strife, committed to the divisive sexual politics that Strife imposed upon them. These will be the "much-perishing" human beings over whom Empedocles elsewhere declares his superiority (B 113). They do not undergo reincarnation. Their only, surrogate mode of living on from one generation to the next is instead by sexual reproduction, by contrast with daimons, who, being extremely "long-lived" according to Empedocles, did not need to take up sexual reproduction in order to ensure their continuation as a kind.[63]

What was Strife's motive for its own rare creative act? The wretched hu-

---

age of Kypris not yet committed that sin. Cf. Plato, *Crat.* 397e5–398c4 for an interpretation of Hesiod's golden age myth according to which humans (members of the iron race) can, by self-improvement, *become* daimons (members of the golden race), not only after death but even before it. He may well have Empedocles in mind.

62. I must here state, without defense, my allegiance to the interpretation of Empedoclean reincarnation argued by Barnes 1979, vol. II ch. VIII (e). The daimons, identifiable with Empedocles' "long-lived gods," are regular organic beings generated along with other species, and not to be thought of as transmigrating souls (whether these latter be assumed to be incorporeal entities, discrete portions of pure Love, or anything else). When a fallen daimon "becomes" other creatures, there may be no particular metaphysical theory offered as to what constitutes the continuant, which for all we can tell might be nothing more than the subjective consciousness: Empedocles, having hitherto lived as a daimon, suddenly finds himself conscious of now being a fish or a bush (clothed "in a garment of alien flesh," B 126). If the continuant *is* anything more than this, it is likely to be something purely formal, like the "harmony" with which some Pythagoreans identified the soul; cf. Sedley 1995, pp. 11–12 and 22–26, for the probable inclusion of Philolaus among these.

63. What then about the human beings who were created by Love? Could they have survived without sexual reproduction? I suggest that Love's original "human" creations were solely the blissful gods or daimons, so that their resort to sexual reproduction occurred only after their fall (engineered by Strife according to B 115.14), when they were condemned to the familiar relatively short human life span. (For the lack of a sharp species-distinction between humans, daimons, and gods, see n. 61 above.) Originally, on this hypothesis, it was only the lower species among Love's creations, representing a less perfect level of her achievement, that depended on sexual reproduction for survival.

man beings that Strife's division of the "whole-natured forms" brought into the world were not fallen daimons on their way to recovery of divine bliss, but a species condemned to permanent discord, and no doubt to the wanton slaughter of other life forms as well. One might easily think of them as inspired by Hesiod's description of the fifth and final race created by the gods, the "iron" race of men which contrasts so lamentably with the much earlier golden race of daimons (*Works and Days* 109–201). To populate the world with such beings was, if so, part of Strife's strategy for hindering the advance of Love. It is no doubt to this anthropogony by Strife that Empedocles is referring when he writes:[64] "Alas, wretched and miserable race of mortals, it was from such strifes and troubles that you came into being."[65]

3. CREATIONIST DISCOURSE

So strong has been the presumption that teleology plays no significant part in Presocratic philosophy (at least at this date) that Empedocles' vital role in the history of creationist thought has been systematically neglected or downplayed. Let me, then, emphasize just how pronounced the model of divine craftsmanship is. Love is repeatedly represented as the practitioner of a craft. I have already mentioned, in addition, the end of B 35, Love's concoction of tens of thousands of species, "a wonder to behold." This expression, in all eight of its occurrences in Homer, voices praise of an exceptional artifact, and the same implication is unavoidably preserved in Empedocles' use of it.[66]

Where Anaxagoras's creative power is, as I argued in chapter I, a farmer, Empedocles' Love is a carpenter, figuratively portrayed as using "dowels" and "glue" (B 87, 96) in her harmonious constructions. In the first stage of zoogony, her creation of the eye is described in considerable detail (B 84, 86, 87, 95), with the analogy of a lantern-maker constructing a lantern for the preconceived purpose of lighting his way at night.[67] Assuming that fragments B 86 and B 84 are continuous, we read as follows:

---

64. B 124: ὦ πόποι, ὦ δειλὸν θνητῶν γένος, ὦ δυσάνολβον, | τοίων ἔκ τ' ἐρίδων ἔκ τε στοναχῶν ἐγένεσθε.

65. Cf. Trépanier 2003a, p. 13, on the significance of "strifes" in this passage.

66. B 35.17, θαῦμα ἰδέσθαι. (I am grateful to Jennifer Bryan for the point.) The same applies equally to this expression's occurrences in Hesiod's *Theogony* (575, 581) and the Hesiodic *Shield of Heracles* (140, 224). The most significant antecedent of Empedocles' use may be Hesiod fr. 33a, 15 Merkelbach/West, where the expression is used of a divinely bestowed metamorphosis.

67. That Aphrodite is the subject of B 84 I argue in Sedley 1992a, where I also defend the interpretation assumed in the following remarks. For a very similar inter-

(B 86) From these divine Aphrodite made the unfailing eyes.
(B 84) And just as when someone planning a journey through the
    stormy night
prepares a lamp, a flame of blazing fire,
fitting to it lantern-sides as shields against the various winds,
and these scatter the blowing winds' breath,
but the finer part of the light leaps out   5
and shines across the threshold with its unyielding beams;
so at that time did she bring to birth the round-faced eye,
primeval fire wrapped in membranes and delicate garments.
These held back the sea of water that flowed around,
but the finer part of the fire penetrated to the outside.[68]   10

Empedocles shares the widespread early belief that the reflective surface of
the eye is the primary locus of seeing. Its reflectivity is achieved by a pro-
portionate mixture of water and fire, the water ("the sea of water that flowed
around") being the lachrymal fluid on its surface, while the fire travels outwards from the iris at the center of the eye.[69] This is made possible by a
structure in which the inner fire can get out to the surface yet the external
water cannot penetrate inwards to extinguish the source of the fire. The remarkable cornea—presumably the only perfectly transparent solid substance known to the ancient Greek world[70]—was invented by Love to perform this function. It is the ingenuity of the filter system she devised that
is being celebrated in the last three lines.

---

pretation, cf. Inwood 2001, pp. 258–59. I have argued in Sedley 1998a, p. 20, for the
teleological import of the passage.

68. (B 86) ἐξ ὧν ὄμματ' ἔπηξεν ἀτειρέα δι' Ἀφροδίτη.
    (B 84) ὡς δ' ὅτε τις πρόοδον νοέων ὡπλίσσατο λύχνον
    χειμερίην διὰ νύκτα, πυρὸς σέλας αἰθομένοιο,
    ἅψας παντοίων ἀνέμων λαμπτῆρας ἀμοργούς,
    οἵ τ' ἀνέμων μὲν πνεῦμα διασκιδνᾶσιν ἀέντων,
    φῶς δ' ἔξω διαθρῷσκον, ὅσον ταναώτερον ἦεν,   5
    λάμπεσκεν κατὰ βηλὸν ἀτειρέσιν ἀκτίνεσσιν·
    ὡς δὲ τότ' ἐν μήνιγξιν ἐεργμένον ὠγύγιον πῦρ
    λεπτῇσιν <τ'> ὀθόνῃσι λοχεύσατο κύκλοπα κούρην,
    αἳ δ' ὕδατος μὲν βένθος ἀπέστεγον ἀμφιναέντος,
    πῦρ δ' ἔξω δίεσκον, ὅσον ταναώτερον ἦεν.   10

69. More fully, in night-sighted animals *all* the fire is supplied from inside the
eye, which is why their eyes are visibly bright and fiery. In day-sighted animals some
of the fire is supplied from the illuminated environment, which is why their eyes
are less fiery. See Theophrastus, *Sens.* 8.

70. Cf. the Stoic description at Cicero, *ND* II 142: "[Nature] has clothed and
protected the eyes with the most subtle membranes, which she has made so translu-
cent that we can see through them, yet strong enough to be containers."

Regardless of any debatable details of the lantern analogy, the degree of emphasis on intelligent craftsmanship remains hard to explain away as devoid of theoretical content.[71] The complex structure of the eye has continued down to the present day to be cited as the prime exhibit for the creationist case. That Empedocles' description of the eye has a similarly serious creationist motivation becomes clear once we consider the longer tradition of which it forms a part.

Although Hesiod had already made it clear that both men and women originated as products of divine craftsmanship,[72] neither he nor any known author had developed the idea with any of the meticulous technological detail now being deployed by Empedocles. In Hesiod's two major poems (*Works and Days* 47–105, *Theogony* 521–616), the divine creation of woman occurs rather in the context of a fable, specifically Zeus's punishment of men in retaliation for Prometheus's theft of fire. All the emphasis is on the machinations among the gods and lesser divinities, and this persists even during the account of the creative act itself (*Works and Days* 59–68):

> So said the father of men and gods, and laughed out loud.
> And he ordered renowned Hephaestus as quickly as possible
> to mix earth with water, and to implant human voice
> and strength, and to make it in face like the immortal goddesses:
> the lovely and desirable form of a maiden. And Athena
> he told to instruct her in crafts, how to weave the variegated web.
> Golden Aphrodite he told to pour grace upon her head,
> along with painful yearning and limb-wearying cares.
> And to implant in her a doglike cunning and deceitful character
> was his command to Hermes . . .

Although this may well be Empedocles' ultimate archetype for Aphrodite's creative act, there is a palpable shift of genre. Hesiod's story belongs to the genre of aetiological fable, accounting for some present fact about the human predicament in terms of divinely administered punishment. To see this, and how it differs from what Empedocles is doing, we should look forward in time to what was to become of the genre in subsequent philosophical contexts.[73] One affinity among all these stories, Empedocles' included, is their

---

71. Solmsen 1963 defends a highly reductive reading of Empedocles' craft analogy: "There is nothing in his poems to suggest that the crafts were to his mind a model of purposeful or clearly articulated activity" (p. 477, cf. pp. 478–79). This completely neglects the lantern-maker's forward planning and methodical procedure.

72. Cf. pp. 3–4 above.

73. In what follows, I shall pass over the creationist story humorously put into Euripides' mouth at Aristophanes, *Thesm.* 14–18. It is too brief to permit a judg-

two-stage structure: an original prototype is subsequently modified, typically in the light of some sin or deficiency.[74] Nevertheless, there are also generic differences that should not be neglected.

The most celebrated of kindred Just So stories is Aristophanes' wildly funny myth, narrated by him in Plato's *Symposium* (189d5–191d5). Our earliest ancestors were blissfully spherical creatures, whose insurrection Zeus and his subordinates punished by splitting them in two, condemning each half to a lifelong search for its missing partner. This time, by contrast with the Hesiodic model, the account contains a fair amount of pseudo-science,[75] since the anatomy of the spherical creatures, and the divinely engineered series of experimental modifications to it that culminated in the familiar human race, have to be described with some care in order to make it even *prima facie* plausible that their bisection could have produced beings like *us*. But despite this outward resemblance to an Empedoclean zoogony (especially to Strife's divisive creation of sexually differentiated humans), no reader can ever have thought that Aristophanes' story embodied his or anybody else's theory about actual human origins. Its point, which follows the Hesiodic model, is an essentially moral one about transgression and punishment. Both fables take as their explanandum an aspect of human malaise—sexual politics in Hesiod's story, sexual passion in Aristophanes'—and give it an ancestral origin embodied in a tale of divine retribution.

Take, again, the myth told by Protagoras in Plato's *Protagoras* of the origin of man as a moral being. At Zeus's behest Epimetheus equipped the newly created animal kingdom with protective powers, but inadvertently used up all the natural defensive assets on other species before he got to mankind. To compensate for his brother's failing, Prometheus stole fire from the gods and passed it to mankind, in order to give human beings the protective benefits of technology. Later, to counter the growth of civil strife, Zeus's subordinate Hermes endowed human beings with innate social virtues.

This story, too, retains and develops the Hesiodic motif of divine machinations which lead to a progressive redesign of the human race, while differing in its newly optimistic focus on divine benevolence. We also witness, this time, some entirely serious scientific speculation. Whether the speech's

---

ment as to whether what is being mimicked is Presocratic pseudo-science or a creation fable in the Hesiodic tradition.

74. This structure is illuminatingly analyzed by Betegh forthcoming.

75. Note the passing indication at 190a8–b5 that the earth is spherical—a momentary lapse into real science, but not one to which Aristophanes draws attention.

content is to be attributed to Plato, writing in the early decades of the fourth century, or is assumed to go back to Protagoras himself in the later fifth century,[76] we cannot for the purposes of the present book afford to overlook its sophisticated meditation on the systematic causal relation of survival powers to speciation. Although this no doubt had a partial forerunner in the second stage of Empedocles' zoogony, it is here thought out with a precision that has no obvious antecedent (320d8–321c3):

> In his handing out of the powers, Epimetheus assigned to some creatures strength without speed, while those which were weaker he equipped with speed. To some he gave weapons, while others he left naturally unarmed but gave them some other power for their preservation: to those which he equipped with a small size he assigned winged flight or an underground dwelling, whereas the ones that he made large he preserved by that very largeness. His other distributions too evened things out in this way. His reason for such contrivances was to ensure that no kind should become extinct. And when he had supplied them with means for escaping internecine destruction, he contrived for them protection from the seasons sent by Zeus, by clothing them with thick fur and tough skins, adequate for resisting winter but also capable of withstanding heat waves, and with the intention that when they lay down to sleep these same things should serve each creature as its own natural bedding. He also shod them, some with hooves, others with tough and bloodless hair and skin. After this, he supplied each with its individual nourishment: for some, pasturage from the earth, for others the fruit of trees, for others roots, while to some he gave the meat of other animals as their food. And to these last he assigned a low birth-rate, while to those which were their prey he gave a high birth-rate, thus preserving their kind.[77]
>
> Now not being all that bright, Epimetheus failed to notice that he had used up all the powers on the irrational animals. He still had the human race left unequipped, and had no idea what to do.

There is a great deal here that would transpose, *mutatis mutandis*, into a Darwinian setting, and we should be in no doubt that the principles of speciation have been discerningly considered by either Plato or his source. However, the originating role assigned to the divine creators, far from being part of that scientific discourse, is a fanciful fable that provides no more than its

76. I am sympathetic to the arguments for the latter view in Morgan 2000, chapter V.

77. That speculation of this kind can be traced back at least into the sophistic era is shown by Herodotus (writing in the later part of the fifth century B.C.), who at III 108–9 sees it as a sign of divine providence (108.2)—and this partly with reference to ensuring human survival (109.1)—that destructive species have been made such as to produce few offspring, while natural prey, e.g. hares, are prolific breeders.

narrative context. Thus even if the survey of specialist means of survival reads as real science, the concomitant idea that each power could be bestowed only once is less clearly to be taken seriously, and may belong rather to the realm of explanatory fable.[78] Indeed, in introducing his story Protagoras has explicitly (320c2–7) opted to set it out in the form of a "myth" or "fable" (*mythos*), insisting that he could equally well have presented it as a factual account (*logos*). The entire divine drama belongs to its fabulous content, invoked by Protagoras for merely expository purposes, and can easily be distinguished by readers from the hard theoretical content of the discourse, the latter consisting both in the zoological distinction of man from the rest of the animal kingdom, and also, in the sequel, in the ethical interpretation of man's special gifts.

In Plato's later dialogue the *Timaeus*, to which we will turn in chapter IV, the mixture of mythical with scientific exposition is even more complex, and Plato can be suspected of playing games with the conventional boundaries separating the two genres.[79] For the present, however, my point is limited to the following: Hesiod's aetiological device, that of locating our biological origins in divine management decisions, was to have a post-Empedoclean history in which, although sometimes interwoven with scientific discourse, it would retain a recognizable separate identity. The descriptions of divine craftsmanship that we witness in Empedocles himself represent a separate branch of Hesiod's legacy. Although his Love and Strife are adversaries, the human-like quandaries and quarrels of divine beings have receded from their explanatory role, and in their place the detailed operations of Love's superior intelligence and creative powers have taken center stage.

One way in which this difference manifests itself is in Empedocles' complex analogy between divine and human craftsmanship—a clear index that scientific explanation is his primary concern. It is a novel and significant feature of Empedocles' similes, when compared to their Homeric antecedents, that they invariably compare a natural phenomenon to the production or workings of an *artifact* (B 23, 84, 100), thus inaugurating the long history of creationist explanation in terms of divine technology.[80]

---

78. Cf. Philemon (early Hellenistic comic poet) fr. 93 K.-A., where the beast-human contrast is rather that each non-human species was given a single invariable nature by Prometheus, whereas humans vary in character.

79. See esp. ch. IV §7 below.

80. Craft analogies also recur in non-teleological contexts, e.g. Hipp., *De victu* I 12–24, but not with an emphasis comparable to Empedocles' on the role of a divine craftsman in nature.

In another pair of fragments, B 21 and 23,[81] an alternative, less technological craft analogy emerges:

> (B 21) For from these [the four elements] all that was, is, and will be   1
> has grown: trees and men and women
> and beasts and fowls and water-nurtured fish,
> and even long-lived gods, highest in honor.
> For they themselves stay the same, but running through each other   5
> they alter their appearance, so much difference does mixture make.
> (B 23) Just as, when painters decorate votive offerings—   1
> men whose cunning makes both of them well skilled in their
>   expertise—
> and when they take in their hands the many-colored pigments,
> having mixed them harmoniously, some more, some less,
> they prepare from them figures resembling everything,   5
> both of them making trees and men and women
> and beasts and fowls and water-nurtured fish,
> and even long-lived gods, highest in honor,
> in the same way let not deceit overcome your mind and make it think
>   that from any other origin
> is the source of the countless mortals that have come to light,   10
> but know these things clearly, having heard the account from a god.[82]

Zoogony is here compared to the work of painters decorating votive offerings. In the natural world, the four elements are mixed to create all manner
of trees, men, women, beasts, birds, fish, and gods. Likewise, in the craft of
painting, all manner of trees, men, women, beasts, birds, fish, and gods are

81. The textual continuity between these two fragments is convincingly argued
by Bollack 1965–69, vol. III p. 120.

82. ἐκ τούτων γὰρ πάνθ' ὅσα τ' ἦν ὅσα τ' ἔστι καὶ ἔσται,
δένδρεά τ' ἐβλάστησε καὶ ἀνέρες ἠδὲ γυναῖκες,
θῆρές τ' οἰωνοί τε καὶ ὑδατοθρέμμονες ἰχθῦς,   15
καί τε θεοὶ δολιχαίωνες τιμῇσι φέριστοι.
αὐτὰ γὰρ ἔστιν ταῦτά, δι' ἀλλήλων δὲ θέοντα
γίγνεται ἀλλοιωπά· τόσον διὰ κρῆσις ἀμείβει.

ὡς δ' ὁπόταν γραφέες ἀναθήματα ποικίλλωσιν   1
ἀνέρες ἀμφὶ τέχνης ὑπὸ μήτιος εὖ δεδαῶτε,
οἵτ' ἐπεὶ οὖν μάρψωσι πολύχροα φάρμακα χερσίν,
ἁρμονίῃ μείξαντε τὰ μὲν πλέω, ἄλλα δ' ἐλάσσω,
ἐκ τῶν εἴδεα πᾶσιν ἀλίγκια πορσύνουσι,   5
δένδρεά τε κτίζοντε καὶ ἀνέρας ἠδὲ γυναῖκας
θῆράς τ' οἰωνούς τε καὶ ὑδατοθρέμμονας ἰχθῦς
καί τε θεοὺς δολιχαίωνας τιμῇσι φερίστους·
οὕτω μή σ' ἀπάτη φρένα καινύτω ἄλλοθεν εἶναι
θνητῶν, ὅσσα γε δῆλα γεγάκασιν ἄσπετα, πηγήν,   10
ἀλλὰ τορῶς ταῦτ' ἴσθι, θεοῦ πάρα μῦθον ἀκούσας.

created by mixing and combining pigments. Much of the focus is on explanatory economy—the mixture of a small set of primary pigments (perhaps four, if Empedocles is assuming what was a common artistic practice in antiquity)[83] is enough to constitute numerous and varied images of living things, and the four elements, analogously, are enough by their mixture to constitute the living originals of those images.[84] However, considerable emphasis is also placed on the artists' skill in performing their creative act: "Just as, when painters decorate votive offerings—men whose cunning makes both of them well skilled in their expertise . . . " (B 23.1–2). Thus by the poet's own choice the message is not that the mixture of elements is *all by itself* sufficient to generate life; vital significance is attached to the role played by intelligent, expert control of those elements' mixture. This aspect reflects accurately the emphasis found elsewhere in Empedocles' fragments, where the generative power of mixture is never mentioned without at least equal stress on the role of Love as its creative agent (B 21, 22, 35, 71, 73, 96, 98).[85]

It is an only rarely noticed fact[86] that *two* painters are presupposed. This is conveyed by three references to the artists in the grammatical dual—too many to be explained as casual[87]—and makes it a near certainty that Empedocles has in mind the zoogonies of both Love and Strife. When the two painters are described as if they were operating alongside each other, that implied synchronicity conveys how (as I argued earlier) both zoogonies have contributed to the flora and fauna in one and the same world, namely ours. That the creative work represented by them, the zoogonies of the two divine agents, occurs consecutively rather than simultaneously, is conveyed instead by a device I noted earlier (p. 48), that of listing, in ascending order, first the products of Strife (trees; men, women), and only thereafter the products of Love (beasts, fowls, fish; long-lived gods).

However unexpectedly, and however inexplicitly, even Strife thus emerges as a craftsman of sorts.[88]

---

83. See Ierodiakonou 2005.

84. Cf. Kirk, Raven, and Schofield 1983, p. 294; Curd 2002, p. 150.

85. I have omitted from this list B 107, which refers to the four elements *and* Love and Strife (cf. B 109) as ingredients in the mixture with which we think and feel.

86. Its significance is well brought out by Trépanier 2003a, pp. 35–36.

87. Although the use of dual for plural occurs occasionally in the epic tradition, note that (a) these are the only duals in the surviving poetry of Empedocles apart from B 137.6, where (see Wright 1981 *ad loc.*) there may well be an implicit reference to a pair of agents; (b) the concentration of three successive duals looks far from casual; and (c) one of them, in line 2, is not even required by metrical considerations.

88. Empedocles' inexplicitness is understandable. On the one hand, the two artists mix their colors, and, correspondingly, Love's and Strife's products are mixtures. On

4. DESIGN AND ACCIDENT

The question remains how we are to explain the curious cocktail of artistic creation and sheer accident that features in Empedocles' counterpart to the Genesis story. Love's creations both of organic materials and of single organs and limbs are emphatically intelligent, purposive acts. They enable her to advance her agenda of harmonizing the world, by bringing the four elements into increasing mixture with each other. Strife's creation of divisive, lower-grade human beings is no doubt the mirror image of this, part of its program for maximum disruption: if Love is an agent of intelligent design, Strife's portfolio is, rather, one of intelligent disruption. Yet the highest achievement is clearly to be found in neither of these, but in Love's second generation of organisms, which include the long-lived gods or daimons, capable of a blissfully harmonious life. And these she generated out of the components she had made earlier, not by further purposive design, but by setting up *random* combinations (B 59), of which just the fittest survived. Why the change of explanatory direction from design to accident? The difference between stages 1 and 2 looks as profound as that between artistically creating your own set of playing cards and casually shuffling the pack once you have made it.

There should be no mystery about Empedocles' emphasis, in stage 1, on the intelligent design of individual components. When we recall that the eye, still today creationism's primary exhibit, is the organ whose invention Empedocles most prominently describes, it seems beyond reasonable doubt that he is here writing as a conscious creationist. The question is rather why he abandoned design in stage 2.

Aristotle[89] is dismissive of Empedocles' appeal to zoogonic accident in stage 2, treating it as emblematic of the anti-teleological wing in physics. In view of what we have seen, this portrayal of Empedocles as an opponent of teleology hardly carries conviction. But, for all that, Empedocles' resort to the creative power of accident cries out for explanation. Is it his way of conceding that, for lack of engineering skills, Love was simply incapable of taking the more direct route of constructing from the start none but the viable complex forms? I doubt it.

Empedocles, I suggest, is here driven less by any preconceived notions

---

the other, Strife's contribution consists in progressive *separation*, and its comparison to an artist, if made entirely explicit, would therefore give undue emphasis to the loosest part of the analogy.

89. Esp. *Physics* II 8, as quoted pp. 189–90 below.

of Love's powers than by the nature of his evidence. The hypothesis of creative trial and error on a grand scale has a number of explanatory merits.

First, it accounts for the incredible biodiversity which Empedocles hymns when he speaks of "tens of thousands of races of mortals, fitted with every kind of form, a wonder to behold" (B 35.16–17). The words *"every* kind of form" may even amount to a declaration that *every possible* species was created, thus anticipating Plato's assertion in the *Timaeus* that the world was created to contain all the species that fall within the intelligible genus Animal (30c7–d1, 39e6–40a2, 69b8–c2). Whereas Plato would be able to found this tenet on his doctrine of eternally existing Forms, to which his Creator looked as a model for the comprehensive biodiversity he sought, Empedocles' equivalent would lie in the method of unrestricted trial and error which he apparently ascribes to Love in her second stage of zoogony.

Second, a past procedure of trying out all available permutations is attested both by the mythical record—the stories of minotaurs, chimaeras, and the like—and (as noted above, p. 44) by its reputed vestiges in present-day hybrid births.

If Empedocles' account is, to this extent, evidence-driven, the question remains whether he has been led by his evidence to compromise the principles of intelligent creation that he allowed to govern Love's opening moves. I don't think so. One may compare the attitude of the convergentist wing among modern evolutionists. The fossil record—much like the mythical record in Empedocles' own culture—persuades them to accept that natural selection has involved the extinction of some species. Nevertheless, they argue, the winners in the evolutionary battle have not been determined by mere accident (as the rival contingency thesis holds). An eventual convergence on more or less the species we now have, man included, was a foregone conclusion. One might also compare, at the more basic level of the laws of physics, the currently fashionable anthropic principle, according to which these laws cannot be understood other than from the point of view of the eventual emergence of man. Similar principles to these are, I take it, consciously or unconsciously endorsed by the innumerable science-fiction writers who populate other planets with a humanoid dominant species.

While not actively requiring it, such models are extremely friendly to theories of God-guided evolution. God was able to set up the evolutionary process, and perhaps even the underlying physical laws, confident of where they would lead, namely to us. Much the same idea may be suspected of underlying Empedocles' zoogonic thought. His own tendency to convergentism is witnessed by his otherwise curious conceit that humans were the final products of two quite different zoogonies, Love's and Strife's.

Regardless of this last speculation, it seems clear to me that Empedocles is, in his biological theorizing, in equal measures a scientific and a religious thinker. It is not just that all six of his major players are construed nonreductively as divinities from the Greek pantheon, and repeatedly named accordingly ("Zeus," "Hera," "Aphrodite," etc.). The origin of the divine or semi-divine race of daimons is itself part of Love's zoogony. Their fall under Strife and redemption during the renewed ascendancy of Love are integral facets of the cosmic cycle. Empedocles' agenda is at once a scientific one, driven by the classic issues of cosmology, and a religious one in the tradition of Hesiod, focused on sin and redemption.

If Empedocles is a scientific as well as religious creationist, how was creation motivated in his view? I find it hard to doubt that Love's harmonizing quest was motivated by beneficence. While her ultimate goal of total unification in the sphere is repeatedly being deferred, she takes advantage of her alternating periods of ascendancy to promote the blissful life of peace and harmony that the daimons enjoy. On our present evidence it may be hard to go beyond this bare observation. But the ground is already being prepared for the more articulated theories of divine beneficence that Empedocles' creationist successors will propound. What Empedocles can add, with an emphasis and clarity that neither Plato nor the Stoics would be able to match, is an independent source of bad in the world, embodied in the disruptive persona of Strife.[90]

APPENDIX 1. THE DOUBLE ZOOGONY REVISITED

I have argued above (§2) that the cosmic cycle does not, in most rounds, culminate in the *sphairos*. But how can such a reading be maintained in the face of B 17, where Empedocles introduces his cycle as an alternation between things becoming "one" and their again becoming "many"? Surely the "one" which features in this regular alternation must be the *sphairos*? It is, demonstrably, just that assumption that led Simplicius to locate the *sphairos* at the beginning of each round of the cycle, because B 17.7–13 (= 239–45 of the poem) are the lines that he quotes in support of this interpretation (*In Ar. De caelo* 293.18–294.3 = A 52 DK).[91] But those lines make no explicit ref-

90. Strife is recognized as Empedocles' principle of bad by Aristotle, *Met.* 984b32–985a10.
91. Aetius II 4.8 is the only other source I have located that unmistakably shares this same interpretative assumption, no doubt on the same evidence.

erence to the *sphairos,* and to establish their exact meaning Empedocles' audience had to wait until they had read further into the poem.

This becomes clear as soon as we focus on B 26, whose significance I have discussed above, pp. 39–40. There we learn that the four elements, by their constant interchange (1–3), become the materials of zoogony (4)—more specifically, of one zoogony in the phases of increasing Love (5), another in those of increasing Strife (6). That this cycle (as it is called in the opening and closing lines of the fragment) is not itself punctuated at every round by the *sphairos* becomes clear in line 7, as we saw. For the sequence of 5–7 tells us that the roots are formed into living things by alternately (5) coming together through Love in a process of cosmic unification and (6) being forced apart through Strife, *until finally* (7) *they are altogether unified in the sphairos.*

Further important lessons can be learnt from the continuation (8–12) of the same fragment:

> Thus, in so far as they have learnt to become one out of many,
> and when the one grows apart again they are rendered many,
> to that extent they come-to-be, and their lifetime is not permanent;   10
> but in so far as these never cease from their constant change,
> to that extent they are forever unmoved in a cycle.[92]

Since the "one"-"many" alternation described in lines 8–9 is explicitly picking up on the immediately preceding description of the cycle, it seems clear that becoming "one" does not in Empedocles' usage refer exclusively to the total unification that is the *sphairos,* but equally to what in line 5 was called "coming together . . . into one world-order (εἰς ἕνα κόσμον)," meaning the world governed by Love (as in B 128), a blissful unity but not yet a homogeneous sphere.

This usage has the vital consequence that, when we return to B 17, Empedocles' introductory sketch of the cycle, we can no longer afford to assume that the alternation of "one" and "many" is intended there as limited to the arrival and destruction of the *sphairos.* We must focus especially on the first five lines of the fragment, which are lines 233–37 of the poem:

δίπλ' ἐρέω· τοτὲ μὲν γὰρ ἓν ηὐξήθη μόνον εἶναι   1
ἐκ πλεόνων, τοτὲ δ' αὖ διέφυ πλέον' ἐξ ἑνὸς εἶναι.

---

92. οὕτως ᾗ μὲν ἓν ἐκ πλεόνων μεμάθηκε φύεσθαι
ἠδὲ πάλιν διαφύντος ἑνὸς πλέον' ἐκτελέθουσι,
τῇ μὲν γίγνονταί τε καὶ οὔ σφισιν ἔμπεδος αἰών·   10
ᾗ δὲ τάδ' ἀλλάσσοντα διαμπερὲς οὐδαμὰ λήγει,
ταύτῃ δ' αἰὲν ἔασιν ἀκίνητοι κατὰ κύκλον.

δοιὴ δὲ θνητῶν γένεσις, δοιὴ δ᾽ ἀπόλειψις·   [235]
τὴν μὲν γὰρ πάντων σύνοδος τίκτει τ᾽ ὀλέκει τε,
ἡ δὲ πάλιν διαφυομένων θρεφθεῖσα διέπτη.   5

In opening here with the celebrated words

> I shall tell a double tale: at one time it grew to be just one from many,
> at another it grew apart again to be many from one,

and in recapitulating this alternation later, at 7–8, with verses almost identical to B 26.5–6,

> at some times when all coming together because of Love into one,
> at other times when being severally borne apart again because of
>   Strife's hostility,[93]

he is describing an alternation between unity and plurality which in his eyes,
as B 26 makes plain, operates no less within the continuous history of a single world than it does between one world and the next. Simplicius's interpretation of this "one" as referring exclusively to an absolute unity such as
the *sphairos* was a natural enough assumption for a reader to make at the
early stage of the poem represented by B 17, but proves, in the light of B 26,
to have been a mistaken one. It is Simplicius's great merit that he regularly
cites his evidence verbatim, and it is the evidence he cites in this case that suggests both that, and how, he came to misconstrue Empedocles' precise point.

The opening two lines of B 17 are directly followed by the notoriously
enigmatic 3–5, in which the double zoogony is first announced:

> There is a double coming-to-be of mortals, and a double ceasing.
> One of them the coming-together of all things brings to birth and
>   destroys,
> whereas the other was nurtured, and vanished, when they were
>   growing apart again.   5

These lines have proved open to too many interpretations[94] to be capable,
by themselves, of determining our reading of Empedocles' cycle. The task
is rather to work out how they can be most satisfactorily read in the light
of the interpretation now independently defended.

First, we can exclude any reading according to which the "double ceasing" (3) is explained as the destruction, first, of Love's zoogonic products

---

93. ἄλλοτε μὲν Φιλότητι συνερχόμεν᾽ εἰς ἓν ἅπαντα,
ἄλλοτε δ᾽ αὖ δίχ᾽ ἕκαστα φορεύμενα Νείκεος ἔχθει.

94. See in particular the discussion of various alternatives by Mansfeld 1972;
also Trépanier 2003a, pp. 26–28.

(4), and then of Strife's (5). These products, we have seen, are *not* normally destroyed in the changeover from increasing Love to increasing Strife and vice versa, but persist from one era to the next.

Second, from the Strasbourg fragments (p. 36 above), where these processes are summed up as "the coming-together and the unfolding of birth" (ξύνοδόν τε διάπτυξίν τε γενέθλης), we can draw the following inference. The "coming-together" (σύνοδος) of all things (4) is a cosmic process that governs the more specific "coming-together of birth" (ξύνοδος γενέθλης), this latter being Love's zoogony. Therefore, symmetrically, the "growing apart" of all things (5) is a cosmic process that governs the more specific "unfolding (διάπτυξις) of birth," which is to be identified with the separative zoogony under increasing Strife. And since both "coming-together" and "unfolding" are nouns which designate creative processes, we should not hesitate to accept, as I observed earlier (p. 36), that the pair of terms supplied by the Strasbourg fragments is to be equated with the "double coming-to-be" announced in B 17.3.

In the light of these two indications, we can turn to the parallel question of the double "ceasing" (ἀπόλειψις) added in line 3. This is evidently picked up by "destroys" in 4 and "vanished" in 5. Since, as we have seen, it cannot refer to the destruction of species, there seems only one viable alternative: what ceases (is destroyed, vanishes) is the coming-to-be itself. There is a coming-to-be of living things in the phase of increasing Love, and it also "ceases" in that same phase, in the sense that it does not continue after the phase's termination. There is another coming-to-be of living things in the phase of increasing Strife, and it too "ceases" in that same way, by not outliving its own era.

If this is right, it follows that line 3 means, not "There is a double coming-to-be of mortals and a double ceasing *of them*," but "There is a double coming-to-be of mortals, and a double ceasing *of it.*" Lines 4–5 then add that the one coming-to-be, and its eventual ceasing, are the outcome of an era of increasing Love, whereas the other coming-to-be, and its eventual ceasing, are the outcome of an era of increasing Strife.[95] In this way, the enigmatic lines can comfortably fit the proposed interpretation of the cycle.

The suggested reading has the disadvantage that γένεσις and ἀπόλειψις turn out not to be as symmetrically paired as might have been expected.[96]

---

95. Trépanier 2003a, pp. 26–27, considers but rejects a reading which corresponds to the first half of this proposal, as applied to line 4, while construing line 5 differently.

96. Cf. Diogenes of Apollonia B 7 *fin.* for such a symmetry. However, the unexpected asymmetry in the present passage has a partial parallel in Empedocles B 8.1–2:

But the asymmetry brings the major compensating advantage of explaining—what is otherwise a considerable exegetical headache—why lines 4–5 should use the singular, τὴν μὲν . . . ἡ δέ—"the one . . . the other"—to pick up the reference of 3, rather than a pair of plurals: line 3 is really about the double history of the "coming-to-be of mortals" (γένεσις θνητῶν) alone, with "ceasing" (ἀπόλειψις) strictly subordinate to this, not coordinate.

Consider also the key requirements set by Daniel Graham,[97] who has shown how the entire literary structure of B 17 is designed to emphasize the symmetrical alternation of cosmic processes: they seem to be at least as well satisfied by this long-term oscillation within a single world as they ever were by the traditional two-world cycle. The model I am proposing is, after all, structurally very similar to the traditional one, the main difference being that the alternating phases do not, most of the time, end either in the *sphairos* or in total separation. That difference, however, is crucial, since it makes it possible, as I have emphasized, for the zoogony of one phase to have products surviving into the opposite phase, and thus for us to respect the very clear evidence of the text.

The same modification to the traditional picture also makes it a great deal easier to secure a suitable correlation between, on the one hand, the rise and fall of the daimons and, on the other, the alternating phases of Love and Strife. The daimons, along with other created beings, can survive as individuals from one phase to the next, and their fortunes can map accurately onto the respective successes of the two cosmic forces. We need, for example, no longer worry that a complete correlation of the daimonic and cosmic cycles would have to identify the daimonic golden age in which Aphrodite alone was worshipped (B 128) with the cosmic dominance of Love during the *sphairos*, thus requiring the daimons to have shed blood in an era before there were even any animals. The daimons are Love's creations, and during her ascendancy they enjoy their full measure of bliss; but when the allotted time comes for Strife to regain power they are induced by it into a sin which in turn brings about their banishment and punishment (B 115). Their 30,000 seasons, or 10,000 years,[98] of punishment very probably correspond to the period of Strife's reign, after which Love returns and the daimons are restored to bliss.

φύσις οὐδενός ἐστιν ἑκάστου | θνητῶν, οὐδέ τις οὐλομένη θανάτοιο γενέθλη. Here Plutarch's γενέθλη, which should probably be preferred as *lectio difficilior* to Aetius's τελευτή, shows Empedocles playing with the idea of destruction itself having a birth, more or less the converse of line 3 on the proposed reading.

97. Graham 1988.
98. See n. 2 above.

APPENDIX 2. THE CHRONOLOGY OF THE CYCLE

The *sphairos,* then, does not recur at the end of every phase of increasing Love. Since there is nevertheless incontrovertible evidence that it does eventually recur, it must come only at longer intervals. Just how long, then, are those intervals? The apparent answer is to be found in the Byzantine scholia on Aristotle's *Physics* and *De generatione et corruptione* recently discovered and published by Marwan Rashed.[99] The task of integrating these exciting finds into the traditional picture of the cycle has faced formidable complications, and support for the revision which I am proposing to that traditional picture lies, I believe, in the relative ease with which it can accommodate the new testimonia. The crucial indications come in Rashed's scholia b and c, which I propose to read in reverse order as follows:

[c] καὶ εὐθὺς μετὰ τὴν παρέλευσιν τῶν ξ′ χρόνων ἐν οἷς ἐ<κρά>τησεν ἡ φιλία γενέσθαι ἀπόσπασμα. [b] παυομένης γὰρ καὶ τῆς φιλίας μετὰ τοὺς ξ′ χρόνους οὐκ εὐθὺς ἤρξατο ποιεῖν ἀπόσπασιν τὸ νεῖκος, ἀλλ' ἠρεμεῖ.[100]

[c] Immediately following the passage of (each of)[101] the sixty time-periods in which Love attained dominance, disruption took place. [b] After the sixty time-periods, when Love too was coming to a halt Strife did *not* immediately begin to cause a disruption but remained at rest.

Thus read, scholion c describes the regular continuity between each phase

---

99. Rashed 2001; see also Primavesi 2001 and 2005. These studies contain a wealth of pioneering discussion of the problems raised by the new scholia, and discuss many more issues than I can address in the present context.

100. The emendation ἐ<κρά>τησεν is due to Rashed. The initial καί of [c] is also emended, to οὐκ, by both Rashed and Primavesi, on which see below. I have not translated the two connectives introducing the two scholia, because each serves the scholiast by linking its sentence, not to any neighboring sentence, but to the Aristotelian lemma itself. Both lemmas are remarks by Aristotle in the *Physics* (scholion b *ad* 250b26–29; scholion c *ad* 252a7–10) to the effect that the cycle includes intervening periods of rest. Scholion b, which comes first, explains this (hence γάρ) by informing us when the period of rest occurs: after sixty complete rounds of the cycle. At the second opportunity, the scholiast adds a further piece of information (hence introduced with scholion c's καί, whether translated "and" or "also"): within the sequence of sixty ages no such period of rest intervenes between the dominance of Love and the return of Strife. If the two scholia are drawn from an original continuous text, it seems to me a good bet that they there occurred in the reverse order, as displayed in my translation.

101. Although this distributive meaning is not made explicit, it seems to me as natural a way as any to interpret the aorist, ἐ<κρά>τησεν, "attained dominance." If the scholiast meant that Love's dominance lasted uninterrupted for an entire stretch of sixty time-periods, the imperfect might have been expected.

of increasing Love and the successive phase of increasing Strife, supply-
ing the information that this happens for a sequence of sixty rounds of the
cycle ("time-periods"—literally just "times," and very probably representing Empedocles' own word αἰῶνες, "aeons" or "ages").[102] Scholion b adds the
information that, *after* the sixty rounds, when Love reaches her peak there
ensues a period during which Strife remains inactive. This last must surely
be the era of the *sphairos*. We thus seem to have our answer: it is after sixty
"ages," or full rounds of the cycle, that the *sphairos* finally recurs.

Return now to scholion c. It so severely contradicts the traditional view
of the cycle that up to now the discussions of it have had no choice but to
assume a corruption, the loss of a negative at the beginning, whose rein-
troduction ("<Not> immediately") restores the traditional interpretation,
albeit at the cost of leaving the scholion with nothing to say that is sufficiently different from scholion b to account very plausibly for its addition
by the scholiast. It is, I hope, a merit of my proposed reinterpretation of the
cycle that it not only saves scholion c from the need for this emendation,
but also gives it an independent informational content.

If, as I am assuming, an "age" is the duration of one complete round of
the cycle, this will presumably also have a numerical value in years. Taking
the period of Strife's dominance as 30,000 seasons (that is, 10,000 years)[103]
it is a fair guess that a full "age," including the matching phase of Love's
dominance, is double that, 20,000 years. As for the duration of the *sphairos*
itself, from scholion g it appears that this sums to no fewer than a hundred
ages (" . . . by separation, when after one hundred time-periods Strife becomes dominant"),[104] which, if so, will be Empedocles' way of indicating a
stretch of two million years.

I therefore propose the following figures for the duration of the cycle:
alternating phases of Love's and Strife's dominance, each of ten thousand
years; and finally, after sixty complete rounds of this cycle, totalling 1.2

102. It seems to me that measurement in terms of cosmic phases, such as I am
proposing, gives clearer significance to the strikingly unusual plural χρόνοι than any
assumption that these "times" are defined simply as some fixed measure of years
understood in human terms, e.g., on Rashed's and Primavesi's suggestion, units of
one century, taken to be the longest human life span. I am persuaded by their idea
that the original word in Empedocles may well have been αἰῶνες (cf. a(ii) 6 = 276
in the Strasbourg papyrus, πολλ]οὶ δ' αἰῶνες πρότεροι), but, if so, these will surely
be enormous cosmic aeons (B 16.2 ἄσπετος αἰών, cf. [Ar.], *De mundo* 397a10–11,
401a16), not to be conflated with the quite distinct use of the term to refer to a biological lifespan (B 17.11, 26.10, 110.3, 129.6, cf. 21.12, 23.8, 115.5).

103. See n. 2 above.

104. διακρίσει, μετὰ ρ' χρόνους νείκους ἐπικρατοῦντος.

million years, a two-million-year period of blissful unity, the *sphairos*.[105]
The choice of these figures by Empedocles is likely to sound suspiciously
fanciful, not to say arbitrary.[106] In particular, even if ten thousand and two
million may sound like conveniently round figures for measuring vast
stretches of time, six hundred thousand is, in such a context, a surprisingly
specific number. But this last figure may nevertheless be explicable. A complete world from *sphairos* to *sphairos* amounts to sixty rounds of the cycle,
each of 20,000 years, making a total duration of 1,200,000 years. Precisely
one tenth of this, 120,000 years, is reported by Censorinus[107] to have been
Orpheus's figure for the Great Year—the astronomical period after which
the heavens return to their exact prior state. It is possible, of course, that
that figure was established later than Empedocles, perhaps under his
influence. It is equally possible that the figure was already in the Orphic
tradition by Empedocles' day, and that he calculated the duration of his
cosmic cycle in order to accommodate it, making the duration of a world exactly ten Great Years. Either way, we have here encouraging independent
evidence that the scholiast's numbers may be authentic.[108] And if we adopt
the second assumption, that the "Orphic" figure was already in circulation

105. Because this makes the two million years of the *sphairos* exceed the total
cosmic time in the larger cycle, it may seem to contradict Aristotle's report at *Phys.*
VIII 1, 252a31, if this latter is read as indicating that Empedocles postulated equal
periods of motion and rest. O'Brien 1969, pp. 59–69, and Rashed 2001, pp. 248–51,
make a good case for such a reading of Aristotle, but the latter rightly does not
discount the possibility that Aristotle means by it simply that the lengths of the
periods of motion and rest do not change from one round of the cycle to the next.
In any case, there remains far too strong a doubt as to whether Aristotle is interpreting Empedocles reliably in this chapter, and the evidence that he offers at
250b26–251a5 for cosmic periods of rest remains in my view deeply suspect, even
after all the efforts at rehabilitation in O'Brien 1969, pp. 252–61.

106. A question helpfully discussed during a meeting of the Southern Association for Ancient Philosophy at Oxford in September 2003 is how much trust we
should place in these testimonia, especially given the undisguisedly Neoplatonist
tendency of scholia a and f (for which see Rashed 2001), and above all, it was wondered how likely Empedocles is to have specified the durations numerically. After
further reflection, I think that the "thrice ten thousand seasons" of B 115, the "seven
times seven" days of the foetus's formation "hinted at" in the *Purifications* according to B 153a, and the parallel (usefully brought up by Catherine Osborne during
the Oxford meeting) of Anaximander's precise numerical figures for relative cosmic distances, are enough to encourage confidence that the information is at bottom
authentic. But no doubt, as in B 115 and 153a, Empedocles conveyed the numbers
periphrastically, leaving at least the possibility that their exact values have been mis-
interpreted by the scholiast's source.

107. *De die natali* 18.11.

108. The "Orphic" figure was kindly brought to my attention by Marwan Rashed
after I had written the remainder of the above. I mention this genetic fact about my

by Empedocles' day, then we gain an additional explanatory handle: his cosmological numbers were, viewed in their historical context, not entirely arbitrary, but on the contrary had a basis in supposed astronomical or astrological authority.[109]

APPENDIX 3. WHERE IN THE CYCLE ARE WE?

In our own world the present state of affairs is as follows. Love was previously in the ascendant, for a golden age of Kypris is said to lie in the past (B 128).[110] Since that era, during which Love created her blessed daimons along with most of the world's other flora and fauna, Strife has regained the ascendancy. It has hit back by engineering both the downfall of the daimons (B 115) and a new, discordant anthropogony.[111]

Do we then ourselves live in an age of still increasing Strife? I doubt if Empedocles made the answer to this question entirely explicit. He was himself, as a fallen daimon, at the point of recovering his lost bliss, but was this because the thirty thousand seasons were at an end, and Love back in control, so that all the other fallen daimons could likewise expect more or less imminent salvation? Or had he, by his success in the arts of purification, found a short cut? I strongly suspect that the letter of his text left the answer to this ambiguous, and that in fact the ancient dispute, attested by the Strasbourg papyrus, between those who favored and those who eliminated a series of controversial first person plurals in his text turned on exactly this question.

---

argument not only in order to express my gratitude to him, but also to emphasize that my numerical reconstruction was not prejudiced by the antecedent aim of securing that figure. The figure, on the contrary, lends the reconstruction a modest amount of independent support. However, if as I assume the number sixty, along with its multiples, implies use of the sexagesimal counting system, a pressing question now becomes whether that originally Babylonian system is a plausible presence in a pre-Hipparchan Greek context. (Its use in Greek astronomy from Hipparchus onwards is not in doubt.) Henry Mendell has helpfully pointed out to me the frequency of sexagesimal numbers in Herodotus (e.g. I 202–3, III 90–95, IV 124), suggesting possible Greek familiarity with the system as early as the fifth century B.C. To go beyond this would require an entire separate investigation.

109. For the possible religious and astronomical background to the "Orphic" figure, see van der Waerden 1952 and 1953.

110. Quoted n. 23 above.

111. Since the species generated in one phase normally survive into the next, it is hard to be sure that a new zoogony need occur in every cosmic phase. Minimally, the two phases directly following the last *sphairos* must each have included a zoogony—one of Love, the other of Strife.

Twice in the short span of these papyrus fragments a corrector has elim-inated a first person plural form according to which "we" are coming to-gether into a unity, by changing the termination to that of a neuter plural participle. It is a reasonable inference that this same divergence of readings recurred elsewhere in the poem too. The corrector was surely seeking to re-move any possible implication that we ourselves live in an age of increas-ing Love, in which all fallen daimons can expect to join Empedocles in an imminent return to bliss.[112] If the "we" is eliminated, as on the variant read-ing, it becomes easier to suppose that we still live in an age of increasing Strife,[113] and that Empedocles' return to divinity represents his own short cut, which we can hope to emulate only if we learn his purificatory arts.[114] Thus important cultic consequences could depend on the presence or ab-sence of the disputed first person plurals. I therefore doubt if it is a coinci-dence that this piece of text, like the Derveni papyrus, was found in a tomb.[115]

112. a(i) 6 (= line 267 of the poem), c 3. For other proposals about this textual question, see Martin and Primavesi 1999 *ad locc.*, Algra and Mansfeld 2001, Laks 2002, Trépanier 2003b, and, for a review, Nucci 2005. My own suggestion is that one party to the dispute—sufficiently dominant to have determined the readings that Simplicius later found in his own copy of Empedocles—systematically edited out any first person plurals that might (rightly or wrongly) be suspected of placing "us" in a phase of increasing Love, and that at d10 the unwarranted correction of $\dot{\epsilon}\pi\iota\beta[\acute{\eta}\sigma o\mu]\epsilon\theta'$ to $\dot{\epsilon}\pi\iota\beta[\eta\sigma\acute{o}\mu]\epsilon\nu'$ (intended thus as the neuter plural participle, in keeping with the other corrections, and not as the rare future active $\dot{\epsilon}\pi\iota\beta[\acute{\eta}\sigma o\mu]\epsilon\nu$) was simply the re-sult of too careless or mechanical an application of this same procedure. Martin and Primavesi 1999, pp. 23–24, 309, importantly note that in this last case the corrector has, by placing points on either side of the substituted nu, indicated good manu-script authority for his correction; but this, rather than proving the correction to be dependable, may merely attest that the mechanically generated change was already present in the corrector's archetype; indeed his indication of MS authority in this case could well have the force of a "sic," acknowledging his surprise at the emended reading.

113. Although the reconstruction of d1–10 of the Strasbourg papyrus is ex-tremely conjectural, and cannot be relied on in detail (for example, the restored δῖνον in line 8 looks to me most unlikely), its apparently pessimistic content seems likely to favor this interpretation, and it may well be no accident (see note 115 below) that a stretch of Empedocles' poem containing this stretch was used for funerary purposes.

114. I take it (Sedley 1998a) to have been in the *Purifications,* not the physical poem, that Empedocles proceeded to expound these purificatory arts, as the former work's title itself tends to confirm. Because I also believe (*ib.* p. 6) that the evidence strongly supports the attribution to the *Purifications* of B 111, in which Empedocles promises to teach certain magical practices, I do not go along with those such as Kings-ley 1995a, pp. 217–32, 2002, and Gemelli Marciano 2005 who lean on this fragment in support of the thesis that attainment of control over nature was a dominant con-cern of the physical poem.

115. The fact that, unlike the Derveni papyrus in mainland Greece, the Empe-docles papyrus was not burnt in order to accompany the deceased into the afterlife

APPENDIX 4. A LUCRETIAN TESTIMONY
FOR EMPEDOCLES' ZOOGONY

The Epicureans, Lucretius included, developed a zoogony which invites direct comparison with Empedocles':[116] see chapter V §3 below. However, the Epicurean version omitted Empedocles' first zoogonic stage, in which the world was populated by isolated limbs and organs, and apparently maintained a studied distance from Empedocles regarding one part of the second stage, the part which concerned the *non*-survival of the *un*fittest. Empedocles had here introduced all kinds of cross-breed fantasy creatures, a postulate which the Epicureans are said to have rejected.[117] Lucretius, consistently with this report, prefers implicitly to limit the failures to ineptly constructed creatures within a single animal kind, since immediately following his own zoogony he is emphatic (V 878–924) that centaurs and other such hybrids—reminiscent of the Minotaur-like freaks postulated in Empedocles' zoogony—can never have existed.[118]

When it comes to the survival of the fittest on the other hand (as distinct from the non-survival of the unfittest), the Epicurean and Empedoclean accounts will turn out to converge. This is hardly surprising, because the nature of the survivors was, obviously enough, determined with hindsight by the actual range of present-day species, leaving much less room for disagreement. My evidence for the convergence is as follows.

The new Empedocles papyrus enabled its editors to recognize in Lucretius II 1091–93 a direct translation of an Empedoclean original, the latter having been a characteristically Empedoclean list of life forms which, while not identifiable with lines 296–98 of Empedocles' poem (= Strasbourg papyrus fr. a(ii) 26–28, quoted p. 36 above), began with what seems to have been identical wording to theirs (p. 37 above). That finding in turn provides welcome new confirmation of a principle I have myself previously advocated[119] for the recognition of Empedoclean passages in Lucretius, namely that these

---

will simply reflect the common burial practices of Egypt. If (see n. 45 above) it was a single piece of papyrus, which moreover included at least some eschatological content, and not, as argued by the editors in the *editio princeps*, a randomly selected assemblage of waste paper, this expectation is further strengthened.

116. This appendix is based on Sedley 2003b.

117. Plutarch, *Col.* 1123B.

118. For the anti-Empedoclean nature of this critique, see Campbell 2003, pp. 139–45.

119. Sedley 1998a, pp. 24–25. The new evidence shows that I was too cautious there in not recognizing II 1091–93 as itself Empedoclean by the same criterion.

passages—typically of Empedocles but untypically of Lucretius—are liable to contain accumulations of compound adjectives. For the lines in question are among the four Lucretian passages that bear this particular fingerprint.[120]

Now a further Lucretian passage bearing this same Empedoclean fingerprint is V 864–70, from his zoogony:

> at *levisomna* canum fido cum pectore corda,
> et genus omne quod est veterino semine partum   865
> *lanigeraeque* simul pecudes et bucera saecla
> omnia sunt hominum tutelae tradita, Memmi;
> nam cupide fugere feras pacemque secuta
> sunt et larga suo sine pabula parta labore,
> quae damus utilitatis eorum praemia causa.   870

> But as for the *light-sleeping* minds of dogs, with their faithful heart,
> and every kind born of the seed of beasts of burden,   865
> and along with them the *wool-bearing* flocks and the horned tribes,
> they have all been entrusted to the care of the human race, Memmius.
> For these, having by their own wish avoided the wild beasts and
>   sought peace,
> have found food in plenty, supplied without any labor on their part:
> it is how we reward them for their usefulness.   870

The fuller Epicurean context of these lines will be found in chapter V §3 below, but my present concern is their apparently Empedoclean origin.

The wool-bearing flocks could easily, in an Empedoclean original, have been the Homeric εἰροπόκων ὄϊων or εἰροπόκοις ὀΐεσσιν ("woolly-fleeced sheep"). I have not been able to identify an attested Greek equivalent for Lucretius's hapax legomenon, *levisomna*, but such a term could certainly have been coined by Empedocles (e.g. κυνῶν ἐλαφρύπνων?). The Greek derivative *bucera*, "horned," in 866 may also reflect an Empedoclean original, again including a compound adjective, for example the genitive form βουκέρω εἴδους. Notice that neither *levisomna* nor *lanigerae* is here introduced merely on the model of Homeric stock epithets, but that each plays a directly explanatory role, picking out the feature for which the species in question commended itself to mankind. This is again perfectly coherent with Empedoclean usage, which, although it regularly uses compound adjectives as stock epithets, does on occasion give them a similarly explanatory role.[121] B 61, with its "man-faced ox-progeny" (βουγενῆ ἀνδρόπρωρα, see p. 43

120. The others are I 3 (which in Sedley 1998a, pp. 24–25, I argue to be part of an extended Empedoclean imitation), V 789 (overlooked in Sedley 1998a, but noted by Campbell 2003, p. 54), and V 864–66, discussed below.
121. Cf. p. 48 n. 52 above.

above), is a closely matching example, the pair of compound adjectives sum-
ming up the cause of these creatures' failure to survive and multiply. A final
feature which may conceivably be Empedoclean is the sudden vocative address to Memmius, the first in some 700 lines. Does this perhaps echo an
address by Empedocles to his own dedicatee Pausanias at the equivalent
point?[122] Regardless of these details, the hypothesis of an Empedoclean origin for the lines seems to me hard to resist.

On some matters Lucretius's zoogony maintains a studied difference
from Empedocles',[123] but we have here a theme, the survival of the fittest,
which we know to have been common to the two poets. If Lucretius has here,
in his own zoogony, chosen to translate an Empedoclean original, there is
every probability that he is acknowledging a substantive doctrinal agreement with his revered poetic forerunner. If so, we acquire evidence that
Empedocles' own full account of the zoogony included the theme of certain
species' survival through their usefulness to man. Note, then, how all the
species listed have a utility to man—guarding, transport, wool, and milk—
independent of their slaughter for meat eating, whereas pigs go without a
mention. Pigs are the only animals whose utility to mankind would have
had to be effectively confined to meat eating, a later development which
Empedocles considered a sinful perversion of man's original way of life.[124]

If the Empedoclean origin of V 864–70 is granted, it becomes likely
enough that the whole of V 855–77, which deals with the natural selection
of wild animals as well as domesticated, shares that same origin. But I can
offer no specific evidence to confirm the attribution.

---

122. The same suggestion is made independently in Sedley 2003b, p. 11, and
Campbell 2003, p. 135.

123. See chapter V §3 below. In Sedley 1998a, chapter 1, I emphasized this doctrinal distance between Lucretius and Empedocles, but I am now happy to allow the
case of domestic animals as a rare and significant exception.

124. B 128, quoted p. 39 n. 23 above.

III Socrates

1. DIOGENES OF APOLLONIA

To clear the way for this chapter's protagonist, Socrates, I must start by explaining briefly why I do not believe that his approximate contemporary Diogenes of Apollonia is of major significance for our story, as has sometimes been thought. For Diogenes has been often credited with the earliest version of (roughly speaking) the Argument from Design, that family of arguments which infer the existence of a providential god from the evidence of intelligent creation in the world.[1] And some of the most important arguments stemming from Socrates have been wrongly, in my view, reassigned to Diogenes.

Diogenes, datable to the late fifth century B.C., was by no means in the first rank of Presocratic superstars. He has nevertheless acquired the reputation of being the first teleological thinker. In the only monograph ever devoted to the history of teleological thought in antiquity, published in 1924 by Willy Theiler, Diogenes is given more space than Plato and Aristotle combined, while Anaxagoras gets a mere five pages and Empedocles none at all. I hope I have by now made it clear why I consider such cursory treatment of these latter two Presocratics an injustice. I must now add my reasons for the converse view, that Diogenes of Apollonia is *not* the important figure in this story that he is widely assumed to be.

Diogenes' reputation as a pioneer of teleology has been cemented by a single fragment (64 B 3), which reads as follows:

> For it would not be possible without intelligence *(noēsis)* for it so to be divided up that it has measures of all things—of winter and summer and

---

1. Even the very judicious Pease 1941 gives Diogenes undue credit in this regard.

night and day and rains and winds and fair weather. The other things too, if one wishes to consider them, one would find disposed in this way, the finest possible.[2]

This announcement that everything is disposed in the finest way possible sounds like an anticipation of the teleology developed later by the Stoics and Leibniz, and satirized in the person of Voltaire's Dr. Pangloss, under the rubric "the best of all possible worlds." But in my view Simplicius, our source for the quotation, tells us enough about its context to rule out any such understanding.

Diogenes was a material monist, who nominated air as the universal underlying stuff. Fortunately we have from Simplicius not just some extensive quotations from the opening part of his treatise, but also an indication of the order in which they occurred there. To establish the primacy of air, Diogenes started his argument by maintaining (64 B 2 DK) that a single material substrate, rather than a plurality of coordinate elements, must be postulated, because of its greater explanatory power. He then turned to identifying this single underlying matter, arguing for his distinctive thesis that it is in fact air. As evidence for its identification with air he cited the exceptional powers of air, not of course in air's guise as concealed substrate of everything, which would have been circular, but as manifested in its most directly observable forms, as the stuff of wind, breath, etc. In particular (B 4), he pointed out, breathing air is the very basis of animals' life and intelligence:

> Furthermore, the following too are major signs. Humans and the other animals are kept alive by the air they breathe. And this is both soul and intelligence for them, as will be clearly shown in the present treatise. And if this departs, they die and their intelligence lapses.[3]

It was only after this (at the beginning of B 5) that he proceeded to firm up his conclusion that air is indeed the divine universal principle of everything:

---

2. οὐ γὰρ ἄν, φησίν, οἷόν τε ἦν οὕτω δεδάσθαι ἄνευ νοήσιος, ὥστε πάντων μέτρα ἔχειν, χειμῶνός τε καὶ θέρους καὶ νυκτὸς καὶ ἡμέρας καὶ ὑετῶν καὶ ἀνέμων καὶ εὐδιῶν· καὶ τὰ ἄλλα, εἴ τις βούλεται ἐννοεῖσθαι, εὑρίσκοι ἂν οὕτω διακείμενα, ὡς ἀνυστὸν κάλλιστα. In thus punctuating and translating the last five words, I follow Laks 1983, ad loc., who points out that the usually favored translation, "disposed in the best possible way," has to treat ὡς simultaneously as the correlative of οὕτως and as the ὡς that combined with a superlative means "the [. . .]est possible."

3. ἔτι δὲ πρὸς τούτοις καὶ τάδε μεγάλα σημεῖα. ἄνθρωποι γὰρ καὶ τὰ ἄλλα ζῷα ἀναπνέοντα ζώει τῷ ἀέρι. καὶ τοῦτο αὐτοῖς καὶ ψυχή ἐστι καὶ νόησις, ὡς δεδηλώσεται ἐν τῇδε τῇ συγγραφῇ ἐμφανῶς, καὶ ἐὰν τοῦτο ἀπαλλαχθῇ, ἀποθνῄσκει καὶ ἡ νόησις ἐπιλείπει.

And it seems to me that the thing that possesses intelligence is what people call air, and that it is by this that everybody is governed, and that it controls everything. For this thing seems to me itself to be a god, to extend everywhere, to dispose everything, and to be present in everything.[4]

The highly teleological-sounding fragment B 3 occurred just before Diogenes' argument that breathed air is the basis of individual intelligence. So what is his point in B 3 when he says, "For it would not be possible without intelligence for it [that is, air] so to be divided up that it has measures of all things—of winter and summer and night and day and rains and winds and fair weather"? Very much the same point as the one about breathing: the functioning of air in the world points to it as the ultimate source of intelligence, and thus establishes its causal primacy. The evidence this time comes not from breathed air, but from the obviously intelligent way in which *atmospheric* air manifests itself. For winter and summer, night and day, and weather, all of which he cites, are states of the atmosphere.[5] If, that is, you ask which of the four supposed elements—earth, water, air, and fire—most directly manifests intelligence, the answer is air, witness its role not only in sustaining intelligent life but also in the beneficial cycles of seasons, weather, and day and night. So when Diogenes adds at the end of B 3, "The other things too, if one wishes to consider them, one would find disposed in this way, the finest possible," he cannot by "the other things" mean everything in the world, including for example biological and geographic structures. If he did, his argument for the primacy of air would be ruined. Rather, he must mean: the other manifestations of atmospheric *air*.

Once this context is reconstructed, we can see that no Panglossian teleology is here being formulated. And that fits with the fact that, when Diogenes later turns to discussing physical details such as the distribution of veins in the human body,[6] he uses a style of discourse which in no degree whatsoever anticipates the teleological descriptions of the human body's internal structure later pioneered by Plato and developed further by Aristotle and Galen.

---

4. καί μοι δοκεῖ τὸ τὴν νόησιν ἔχον εἶναι ὁ ἀὴρ καλούμενος ὑπὸ τῶν ἀνθρώπων, καὶ ὑπὸ τούτου πάντας καὶ κυβερνᾶσθαι καὶ πάντων κρατεῖν· αὐτὸ γάρ μοι τοῦτο θεὸς δοκεῖ εἶναι καὶ ἐπὶ πᾶν ἀφῖχθαι καὶ πάντα διατιθέναι καὶ ἐν παντὶ ἐνεῖναι (κτλ.).

5. Cf. Hippocrates, *On breaths* 3, with the comments of Menn 1995, p. 31. For Diogenes' particular interest in meteorology, cf. Simplicius's report (*In Ar. Phys.* 151.20; not universally accepted, however: cf. Kirk, Raven, and Schofield 1983, pp. 435–36) that he wrote a separate treatise on the subject. For Diogenes in the context of Presocratic meteorology, see Taub 2003, pp. 72–76.

6. See Laks 1983, pp. 42–72.

If Diogenes nevertheless has a part to play in our story, it lies in his making explicit what had been no more than implicit in the preceding cosmological tradition: (a) that the underlying material principle of the universe must be assumed to be intelligent, and (b) that an intelligence manifests itself by its arranging things in the *best* or *finest* available way. The latter was one of the fundamental ideas that Plato's cosmology would be devoted to developing, and I shall return to it later in the chapter.

Diogenes is one of the last representatives of the Presocratic tradition. Another is his contemporary Democritus, the atomist to whose radical contribution I shall turn in chapter V. Our main topic in the present chapter is Socrates himself.

2. SOCRATES IN XENOPHON

In 399 B.C. Socrates, aged seventy, was executed by the Athenians on charges of impiety and corrupting the young. He is conventionally considered the key figure in redirecting philosophy, away from cosmology and towards ethics. I believe that that picture is not only correct, but additionally supported by something that modern evaluations of him mention only rarely, his radical stance on the creation issue. The neglect of his contribution to this topic stems no doubt from the fact that the best evidence for it is to be found, not in Plato, but in the less fashionable and, for most tastes, less exciting pages of Xenophon's *Memorabilia*.

Memorabilia I 4 and IV 3 are two chapters of the utmost importance for our theme, although they have stayed largely out of sight in the modern revival of Socratic studies.[7] Theiler, whom I mentioned in the previous section, did recognize their importance, but implausibly transferred much of their philosophical content from Socrates to Diogenes, as did other scholars in his aftermath, including Werner Jaeger.[8] I say "implausibly" because the arguments of these two chapters are just about as alien as anything could be to the world of Presocratic natural philosophy.

Xenophon's Socrates is a fundamentally anti-scientific creationist.[9] To attempt an intellectual reconstruction of divinely created mechanisms, in the

7. McPherran 1996, esp. pp. 272–91, and Viano 2001 are the main exceptions known to me.

8. Theiler 1924; Jaeger 1947 (this is in essence his 1936 Gifford Lectures), pp. 167–70. For criticism, see Vlastos 1952, p. 115 n. 84; Solmsen 1963, pp. 479–80; Laks 1983, pp. xxvii–xxviii, 250–57.

9. There is a useful discussion of this topic in DeFilippo and Mitsis 1994, although they present Socrates' outlook as friendlier to physics than I do.

style of the natural philosophers, is in his view to overreach one's nature as a human being (*Memorabilia* I 1.11–15). True piety, he holds, lies not in emulating god's achievement, but in appreciating god's gifts to us and thereby coming to understand the unique bond that ties man and god to each other. This construal and advocacy of piety provided, according to Xenophon's portrayal, the immediate context and motivation for Socrates to advance his creationist doctrine.

It cannot be pretended that Xenophon is in this anything remotely like a neutral reporter. His principal agenda in the *Memorabilia* is to defend Socrates against the charges of impiety on which he was convicted. One clue as to the lengths he is prepared to go to can be found in his use of the expression *to daimonion*.

Socrates was charged with dismissing the gods recognized and worshipped by the city of Athens, and of bringing in new gods. In particular (cf. Plato, *Euthyphro* 3b5–9, *Apology* 24c1, 31c7–d6), the latter charge was associated with his personal divine sign, to which he used to refer with such expressions as "the divinity *(to daimonion)* that appears to me" (Plato, *Theaetetus* 151a3–4), and commonly known to us simply as "Socrates' *daimonion*." In order to eliminate any such personal divinity from Socrates' pantheon, Xenophon makes the term *to daimonion*, which in Greek usage can also mean simply "the divine," function instead as Socrates' general term for referring to the gods. Hence when Xenophon's Socrates says that *to daimonion* told him to do this or not to do that, he simply means that "the gods" told him, with the divine "voice" through which they communicate not essentially different from any other divinatory sign recognized by Greek religious practice.[10]

In the two classic chapters on piety with which I am concerned here, Xenophon's Socrates talks about our debt to *to daimonion* (I 4.2, 10; IV 3.15), meaning once again by this simply the gods. The presence of such a tactic should serve as a warning that the chapters are part of the same apologetic agenda. Hence we might well expect to see Socrates' religious outlook be-

---

10. This normalization—for which at its most transparent see Xen. *Mem.* I 1.2–4 and *Apol.* 12–13—explains why in Xenophon the *daimonion* does not, as it does in Plato, limit itself to warning Socrates against this or that action, but, in conformity to mainstream views of divination, also tells him what to do (e.g. IV 3.12, 8.1). Whereas in Xenophon's non-Socratic works (with rare exceptions at *On horsemanship* 11.13 and *Hellenica* VI 4.3) his regular adjective for "divine" is θεῖος, in the Socratic works he again and again uses δαιμόνιος in its place—another symptom of the same strategy. This whole aspect of Xenophon's approach has gone largely unappreciated, but see now the valuable discussion by Dorion in Bandini and Dorion 2000, pp. 50–53.

ing reduced so far as possible to a thoroughly conventional one. But, if so, we are in for a pleasant surprise. The chapters, far from rehearsing religious commonplaces, credit Socrates with a radically unconventional theology. No doubt this theology does serve, in accordance with Xenophon's aims, to vindicate Socrates' piety, but it does so by breathtakingly innovative means.

In both chapters, Socrates is shown urging on his interlocutor a proper respect for divinity, by extolling the gods' gifts to us. And in both chapters the argument takes much the same turn. The interlocutor is impressed by the divine gifts Socrates catalogues, but points out that humans do not seem to be more blessed in these regards than other animals are.[11] Socrates then proceeds to demonstrate respects in which on the contrary we *have* been uniquely favored by the gods.

In I 4, the focus is on natural endowments. Maybe sense organs, teeth, innate instincts etc. are gifts we share with lower species, but we also enjoy a whole set of unique privileges, such as intellect, hands, upright posture, and religious sensibility. In IV 3 the focus moves to the environment. Here likewise, it may be true that the succession of day and night, the cycle of seasons, and the abundance of water are gifts we share with the whole animal kingdom. But this time it is in our *relation to* the animal kingdom, Socrates argues, that our unique privilege is to be found. For a whole range of lower animals exists precisely for man's use, whereas no other species has been similarly honored. By these moves, of a fundamentally religious motivation, Socrates develops a teleology that is far more overtly and explicitly anthropocentric than anything we have met in his predecessors.[12] This is anything but surprising in the philosopher who above all others (although in keeping with the spirit of his age) was perceived as moving the philosophical spotlight from the cosmos to man.

11. Among available English translations of the *Memorabilia*, Marchant 1923, which has unfortunately been influential even in some of the recent scholarly discussion, systematically masks this aspect of the argument (as it does many others), e.g. by under-translating φιλοζῴου (I 4.7) as "loving" instead of "animal-loving." Tredennick and Waterfield 1990 is more reliable, although it too under-translates in this particular case. Bandini and Dorion 2000 is the most accurate translation I have consulted, and their n. 251 (p. 143) can also be consulted with profit on the present topic.

12. For Anaxagoras's teleology as implicitly anthropocentric, see p. 24 above. For Herodotus's hint in the same direction, chapter II n. 77 (p. 56 above). Some have compared the Xenophon chapters to the anthropocentric providentialism voiced by Theseus at Euripides, *Suppl.* 196–210; however, those lines concern not the creation of mankind but god's civilizing and environmental gifts to it—unless γλῶσσαν in 204 refers to the gift of the tongue itself, rather than to "language," implausibly in view of the preceding lines.

Even more striking is the almost complete absence of scientific explanation. Recall how Empedocles drew attention to divine craftsmanship by detailing the anatomy of the eye (pp. 52–53 above). Xenophon's Socrates is equally eloquent in praising the eye, but he limits himself to externally obvious benefits (I 4.6):[13]

> What's more, don't you think this too seems like the work of providence? I mean, because of the eye's vulnerability, to have given it a rampart of eyelids which spread open when we have to use it but close during sleep; and, so that the winds should not harm it either, to have planted lashes as a filter; and to have topped off the region above our eyes with a coping of brows, so that not even sweat from our head should cause the eye any harm.

Nor, when the gods' benevolence is being celebrated, do we do find in these pages as austere a notion of benefit as we might have expected if not Xenophon's but Plato's Socrates were speaking. Xenophon's Socrates, who has rightly been described as a "moderate hedonist,"[14] is here happy to include the bestowal of pleasures among the gods' benefactions. Thus according to him it was out of concern for our comfort, rather than for practical utility, that the channel through which excrement is voided was located as far away from our noses and eyes as could be managed (I 4.6).[15] And in privileging humans over other animals, god bestowed on them not only intelligence, but also another unique blessing, non-seasonal sex (I 4.12).[16] The natural world's provision of pleasure as well as utility is cited elsewhere too (I 4.5, IV 3.5, 6), and even god's own pleasure is invoked, as his motive for arranging the world as he has (I 4.17).

This is recognizably Xenophon's Socrates,[17] and yet the ideas put into his mouth represent radical innovation, owing little if anything to Preso-

---

13. For the full context, see pp. 214–15 below.

14. Gosling and Taylor 1982, §2.2.

15. Cf. the Stoic echo at Cicero, *ND* II 141, where nature is compared in this regard to architects who place the sewage outlet of a house discreetly at the rear.

16. Gigon 1953, p. 137, and Dorion in Bandini and Dorion 2000, pp. 144–45, n. 255, discuss an apparent contradiction with the sexual asceticism recommended by Socrates at *Mem.* I 3.14–15. Against any impression that I 4 for this reason reflects a non-Socratic source, note that in the former passage Socrates recommends minimal indulgence with regard to food and drink as well as sex, and does so on the ground that an equal amount of pleasure can be more safely obtained by such restraint. This accords with his moderate hedonism, and he might well regard non-seasonal sex as making man that much freer to delay sexual activity than if it had to be crammed into short periods within a biological cycle. Cf. also *Mem.* IV 5.9.

17. The hedonist leanings probably count against the identification of Antisthenes as Xenophon's direct source on Socrates here—a suggestion briefly canvassed on

cratic cosmology. Nor is the influence, positive or negative, of Plato's portrayal of Socrates in evidence.[18] Indeed, the only point of similarity with Plato is found in what I shall in chapter VII §3 return to as the "Cosmic Intelligence" argument (I 4.8), which as well as occurring here is placed in Socrates' mouth only in Plato's very late dialogue *Philebus* (29a9–30d9). The *Philebus* may even postdate Xenophon's death, making it if anything more likely that Plato has borrowed from Xenophon than vice versa.[19]

It seems to me that we have here in Xenophon a historical depiction of Socrates' ideas on divine creation which not only is inherently credible, but also represents exactly the reorientation from creationist science to creationist piety that we might expect of him. Whatever Xenophon or his source may have done to shape or adapt the material, its originality and significance make it a natural assumption that its authorship really does in essence belong to Socrates.[20] And it does contain, as we shall see shortly, the first recorded antecedent of the Argument from Design.

There are two plausible ways in which, if taken as historically authentic, this Socrates marks a new beginning, and thus, both symbolically and intellectually, heralds the close of the Presocratic era. One of these lies in the fact that by his day the creative power of accident had, thanks to its advocacy by the atomists,[21] emerged as an explanatory model aspiring to compete with intelligent causation. This would almost certainly be why Socrates

---

theological grounds by Caizzi 1966, pp. 100–101; cf. McPherran 1996, p. 287. For Antisthenes' aversion to hedonism, see Caizzi frr. 108–13 and notes.

18. For Xenophon as in general responding to Plato rather than vice versa, cf. Vander Waerdt 1993, pp. 9–11.

19. Cf. D. Frede 1997, p. 215 n. 183. The presence of a version of it also in Aristotle, *PA* I 1 641b13–15 (quoted and discussed pp. 194–95 below) may merely reflect the fact that Aristotle was himself deeply influenced by *Mem.* I 4 (e.g. compare *Mem.* I 4.6 on the arrangement of teeth with Aristotle, *Ph.* 198b24–26 and *PA* 661b6–9, and, on eyebrows and eyelashes, with *PA* 658b14–26). Cf. Johnson 2005, p. 117, for recognition of Aristotle's debt to this chapter.

20. For conclusions pointing in this same direction, see McPherran 1996, pp. 273–91, and more especially Viano 2001. The fact that in both chapters Xenophon explicitly claims to have been present at the conversation (I 4.2, IV 3.2), something he does in only five other chapters of the *Memorabilia*, does not in itself do much to strengthen the case for historical authenticity (see Kahn 1996, p. 33; Dorion in Bandini and Dorion 2000, pp. xxxix–lii), but is at least fully coherent with it.

21. Or were there other radical materialists in Socrates' day? Probably not. Such figures emerge in Plato mainly in his late works (e.g. *Sph.* 265c1–10, *Laws* X), whereas in the earlier *Phaedo* (§2 below) materialist explanation was typified by Anaxagoras, said there to have tried—although he ultimately failed—to include a role for *nous*. No physicist before the atomists positively excluded intelligent powers from the underlying matter; see chapter I §1 above.

became the first to *argue* for the creationist option against the rival materialist hypothesis. Thus it was that the Argument from Design entered the scene.

A second innovation lies in Socrates' disengagement of religion from physics. These two areas of thought (as they eventually came to be) had remained an integral whole to the end of the Presocratic era. Their fusion is most vividly illustrated in the work of Empedocles, but the same point could be made with regard to Heraclitus, Diogenes of Apollonia, or almost any other figure of the period, with the possible exception of Anaxagoras. In Socrates the two modes of thought—the religious and the scientific—move apart, not in the sense that they become in any way incompatible, but in that Xenophon's Socrates on the one hand advocates the cultivation of proper religious attitudes as morally indispensable, but on the other strongly advises against the study of physics at a theoretical level. Appreciation of god's special care for mankind in no way depends on theorizing about just how his gifts have been engineered.

In so far as the Socrates we meet in the pages of Xenophon permits himself any theoretical speculation in this domain, it is with regard to theology. Once freed of physics, theological theory is permitted to remain on the agenda. Thus Socrates is ready to propound a specific argument that the world possesses intelligence (the "Cosmic Intelligence Argument," to which I shall return in chapter VII §3). And he attributes to the supreme deity not only benevolence, but also powers that make that deity both omniscient and omnipresent (I 4.17–18) when he describes god as "so great and of such a kind as at one and the same time to see everything, to hear everything, to be present everywhere, and to take care of everything." This theology has a Presocratic history, but not in the tradition of physics. What it unmistakably echoes and develops is the radical theology of Xenophanes,[22] who in the late sixth or early fifth century B.C. had satirically denounced the anthropomorphization of gods (21 B 11–16 DK), redescribing the supreme divinity as an unmoved being capable of moving everything by the power of thought alone (B 23–26).

I shall return in the next section to Socrates' radical break with the preceding tradition, and in chapter VII to the seminal later influence of the Socratic arguments reported by Xenophon. But first we must pause to examine an argument that he uses in I 4.2–7 of the *Memorabilia*, this time aimed at demonstrating the presence of intelligent creation in the world. (A full translation of the argument will be found on pp. 214–15 below.)

The interlocutor Aristodemus is invited to name the wisest of human

22. Cf. McPherran 1996, p. 287.

beings, and chooses his favorite poets and artists. Socrates then asks him, "Do you consider more admirable those who make mindless and motionless images, or those who make living beings with minds and activities?" This revives Empedocles' comparison between the divine craftsmanship that generates living, three-dimensional animals and the human artistry involved in painting their two-dimensional counterparts (31 B 21 + 23 DK, see p. 58 above). But unlike Empedocles, Socrates has turned a direct comparison into a contrast, using it to emphasize the vast superiority of divine to human artistry.

Aristodemus in reply confesses a greater admiration for the makers of real living beings, but only, he says, if they have produced them by design,[23] not by mere chance. Socrates then sets out to show that the gods must indeed have produced living beings by design: "Compare things with regard to which there is no sign of what they are for, and things which evidently serve a beneficial purpose. Which ones do you judge to be the products of chance, and which of design?" Aristodemus naturally selects as the products of design those things that serve a visible purpose. And this is Socrates' cue to launch into his catalogue (paraphrased above) of our bodily and other assets, presented as direct evidence that our own construction belongs to this latter category, and that our own original maker is therefore more admirable than the most admirable of human artists.

This Socratic argument, typically of those in Xenophon, is somewhat resistant to formal analysis, but its gist is as follows:

1. Representational artists are admirable creators, even though their products are not living beings.

2. If that which produces living beings does so by mere chance, it is not more admirable than representational artists. (Implicit reason: it manifests less intelligence than they do.)

3. If that which produces living beings does so by design, it is more admirable than representational artists. (Implicit reason: it is an intelligent creative artist, as they are, but a more admirable one, since its products are superior to theirs.)

4. To determine whether that which produces living beings does so by mere chance or by design, we must ask whether its products, living beings, are typical of the products of chance or of those of design.

---

23. Despite my criticism of Marchant 1923 (n. 11 above), I gratefully adopt his translation of γνώμη as "design," which after trying out numerous variants I have concluded fits the passage best. Tony Long suggests to me that it would also work well as a translation in Heraclitus 22 B 41 DK.

5.   Products of chance typically do not serve a manifest purpose, whereas products of design typically do so.

6.   Living beings, here represented by humans, are so structured that their every feature serves some manifest purpose.[24]

7.   Therefore that which originally produced living beings, including humans, did so by design.

8.   Therefore that which originally produced living beings, including humans, is more admirable than the most admirable of human artists.

Here we encounter for the first time the explicit disjunction of accident and design, offered as competing causal origins of life. The evidence of systematically purposive structures in nature is then cited by Socrates to discount the first alternative in favor of the second. And his clear, albeit implicit, conclusion is that the origin of life forms lies in a creator superior to any human creator. Do we not have here the earliest instance, or at least direct forerunner, of the Argument from Design?[25]

That label might be disputed on the ground that the Argument from Design is meant to be an argument for the existence of god. The interlocutor Aristodemus is being rebuked by Socrates for his contemptuous disregard of religious practices (I 4.2), but there is no sign that he is an atheist, and therefore no sign that Socrates' argument against him is meant as a proof of the existence of god.[26] Rather (I 4.9–11), as Aristodemus himself explains, he fails to see god at work in our world, and assumes him to be too far above us to require worship. Socrates' argument, being a response to this position, must therefore have as its aim to demonstrate the existence,

---

24.   At I 4.5 Socrates asks whether ὁ ἐξ ἀρχῆς ποιῶν ἀνθρώπους, "the original maker of human beings," gave us eyes etc. for our benefit. The masculine implicitly prejudges the answer to the dilemma posed at step (4), by already construing our originating cause as a personal maker. This anticipation is, I think, an example of Xenophon's relaxed use of logic, and not an indication that intelligent creation is not even being actively defended in the argument. As for the use of the present rather than aorist participle, it is just possible that Socrates means by this "the one who, from the start, has made human beings," thus implying that divine manufacture persists in every new birth. But there is nothing else in the passage to suggest this notion of continuous creation, and I suppose rather that the present participle is chosen simply to mirror οἱ ἀπεργαζόμενοι in I 4.4, in order to emphasize the direct parallelism between human and divine artists.

25.   D. Frede 2002, p. 86, calls it "a highly refined argument from design." She also (p. 90) makes the important negative point that there is no argument from design in Plato, *Laws* X, where one might most expect it.

26.   I have not been able to find any supporting evidence for the description of Aristodemus as "a notorious atheist" (DeFilippo and Mitsis 1994, p. 255), "a disbe-

not of god as such, but of god understood as a beneficent and providential creator.

But it would be misleading and ultimately self-defeating to insist on this as a significant difference from the Argument from Design. It seems harmless to define the Argument from Design as any argument that purports to demonstrate, by citing evidence of rational design in the natural world, the existence of *a creator god*. Naturally any argument of this kind, if effective at all, is effective not just against atheism *tout court* but equally against any theology (such as the Epicurean one, and probably that of Aristodemus too) that acknowledges the existence of one or more deities but denies that they are creators. We are therefore dealing here with what is in logic and essential structure a single argument-type, one that may or may not function as a refutation of atheism, depending on nothing more than the dialectical context in which it is being deployed.

Not only is this the earliest occurrence of the Argument from Design, but it is presumably no accident that Socrates should be its author. A little reflection on our story so far will reveal that its underlying dilemma, that between accident and design as the origin of life, could not have been formulated before the final years of the Presocratic era. For only then, with the emergence of atomism, was the alternative of a purely accidental origin for life forms even conceived. That alternative will be the topic of chapter V. But we can already glimpse how its arrival was the probable catalyst for the first formal *defense* of the creationist alternative. And it was to Socrates that that task fell.

3. SOCRATES IN PLATO'S *PHAEDO*

It is because Plato's brilliant dialogues have eclipsed all our other sources on Socrates that the vital material in Xenophon has been insufficiently appreciated. But my contention will be that Plato's own independent presentation of Socrates' attitude to physics largely confirms the authenticity of Xenophon's portrayal.

In his middle-period dialogue the *Phaedo*, set in the hours leading up to Socrates' execution, Plato puts into his master's mouth an autobiography which seeks to explain why Socrates turned away from natural science and

---

liever" (Pease 1941, p. 166), or even an "agnostic" and "practical atheist" (O'Connor 1994, pp. 151 and 167; see however *ib.* pp. 165–67 for a useful overview of Aristodemus's role in the discussion).

instead took up his own characteristic mode of inquiry, dialectic. The kind of natural science for which he was an enthusiast in his youth, Socrates explains, concentrated on locating the causation of natural processes in the underlying matter. For example (96b3–9), the investigation of the sources of human thought or wisdom *(phronein)* came down to the question which bodily component of us is responsible for it: the air we inhale, the blood in our veins, or our brain? But this methodology (for complex reasons which I set aside here)[27] proved in the last analysis to be explanatorily incoherent. Then one day, Socrates continues, he heard someone reading from a book by Anaxagoras, and was excited to hear that Anaxagoras had a radically different approach to causation, attributing everything to the causal powers of *nous*—intelligence or mind. At last this seemed to be someone talking sense, the young Socrates thought. Naturally, he goes on, he assumed that Anaxagoras would not stop at describing the arrangement and motions of the world's main components, but, since he considered them the products of intelligence, would go on to explain why this was the intelligent, in other words the *best,* way to have arranged things.

Unfortunately the reality, when Socrates eventually obtained his own copy of Anaxagoras's treatise, was a severe disappointment. Despite paying lip service to intelligent causation, Anaxagoras turned out to have limited his detailed descriptions to the same kind of material or mechanical explanation that dominated the rest of the tradition, nominating as the underlying causes such material factors as "airs, aethers, waters, and many other absurdities" (98c1–2). Take for example the classic cosmological question (pp. 3–4 above) why the earth stays still instead of falling. Where Socrates had expected to read an explanation of how the overall cosmic arrangement, including a stationary earth, was a maximally beneficial one for intelligence to have devised, all that he found in Anaxagoras, it seems, was a reassertion of a standard Presocratic-type thesis, probably[28] that the earth is stationary because of air: it floats, that is, on a cushion of air.

I have already, in chapter I, set out why I think this portrayal of Anaxagoras potentially misleading. Although Anaxagoras did not pause to say why the arrangements set up by *nous* were for the best, even in the fragmentary state of the evidence available to us today we can if we try detect the motivations and goals that governed the decisions of the *nous* he postulated. The standoff between Anaxagoras and Socrates is nevertheless a legitimate one, concerning the question where the emphasis should lie in a proper phys-

---

27. I present an interpretation of them in Sedley 1998b.
28. Cf. 99b8–c1, and Aristotle, *DC* 294b13–17.

ical explanation. To assign the causal role to the matter underlying a natural phenomenon is, as Socrates puts it, to confuse the cause proper with "that without which the cause could never be a cause" (99b2–4). Intelligence is the real cause of everything in the world,[29] a causality to be understood in terms of its reasoning about what is best. The underlying matter is *not* the cause; it is simply that item in the story which permits the dictates of intelligence to be put into effect.

The skewed emphasis that Socrates found in the writings of Anaxagoras is one that he exposes by a brilliant analogy (98c2–99b2). Imagine, he says, someone who, having first said that Socrates does everything because of his intelligence, nevertheless proceeds to explain why Socrates is now sitting in prison by nominating as causes the bones, sinews etc. of which his body is composed, while failing to mention that the bones and sinews have themselves been put into their present sitting position by the operations of Socrates' intelligence. For it is Socrates' intelligence that has worked out that, all things considered, it is better that he remain sitting in his death cell than flout the law by escaping. Bones and sinews may well be needed for the sitting, but bones and sinews are, as such, just as good for escaping with as for sitting in prison, so can hardly be singled out as the cause of his doing the latter rather than the former. Hence explanation in terms of intelligence, and likewise of the good, which is the value governing all the decisions of intelligence, simply cannot be replaced by a description of the operations of matter.

It might be tempting to read this as parodying an avowedly *reductive* account of mental causation—one, specifically, that reduces the operations of intelligence to those of matter, in the way that today we can seek to reduce thoughts to physical changes in the brain. Against such a monistic stance, dualists are liable to ask how an intrinsically intelligent thought-process such as a mathematical computation could ever be causally explained simply by tracking how certain chemical changes in the brain and nervous system make the muscles of the mathematician's right arm expand and contract so as to deposit a particular sequence of ink marks. Socrates' parodic example of pointing to bones and sinews rather than to intelligence might well have been expected to be mounting just such a challenge to materialism, especially since, as mentioned above, his own youthful excursion into natural science had already—to his subsequent regret—engaged him in such questions as what is the bodily cause of thinking.

---

29. This must in Socrates' eyes refer to the overall cosmic structure, and not to individual actions and events taken in isolation, bad ones included; cf. *Rep.* II 379c2–7, and chapter IV §5, below.

However, not only does this fail to fit the example very comfortably,[30] but the obvious target for any such attack on reductive psychology would hardly have been the avowed dualist Anaxagoras. Reductionism is the hallmark, rather, of the ultra-materialist atomists (see p. 7 above, and chapter V §1 below). Socrates' attack is on someone who on the one hand gives intelligence a dominant causal role separate from that played by matter, but on the other hand fails to show *how* intelligence is doing its work—in other words, does not explain what is so intelligent—that is, good—about the effects produced.

4. A HISTORICAL SYNTHESIS

This convincingly fits the historical context. The rise to prominence of the atomist theory almost certainly postdated the period of Socrates' youthful studies, which since he was born in 470/469 are presumably datable somewhere towards 450 B.C. Anaxagoras's main work, on the other hand, not only predated them, but also represented the clearest available articulation of a long tradition of Presocratic thought that had from the outset tended towards the assumption that intelligent powers are a primary and non-derivative feature of the material world (chapter I §1 above). If Anaxagoras went further than the rest of that tradition by making intelligence for the first time ontologically distinct from the matter in which it inheres, he was not in any relevant respect rejecting the previous assumption, but adding to it a previously absent demarcation of functions. That is why, as Socrates saw, if even the dualist Anaxagoras, with all his eloquent insistence on the supreme causal power of intelligence, was too focused on the movements of matter to be able to construct credible teleological explanations of phenomena, then *a fortiori* his more materialist colleagues suffered from that failing.

All this, then, rings historically true for Socrates' youthful phase. Note too the absence from the autobiographical passage in the *Phaedo* of any sug-

---

30. Air, blood, and brain (mentioned at 96b3–9 as possible causes of thinking) are not among the material causes mentioned in Socrates' parody. This lack of fit is made even clearer by Socrates' second, or subordinate, parody at 98d6–8: " . . . and again, regarding the fact that I am conversing with you, if he were to state another set of such causal explanations, nominating as causes voices, airs, hearings, and thousands of other such things . . . " This too illustrates the error of omitting intelligence from one's causal account and simply listing the relevant material factors, but there is no possible suspicion that the latter are here envisaged as seeking to *replace* the former.

gestion that the presence of intelligence in cosmic processes or structures was something the young Socrates felt needed to be argued for. Rather, his question was whether anyone in the tradition best represented at that time by Anaxagoras had actually diagnosed *how* intelligence operates. The need, beyond this, to argue against those who would eliminate intelligence altogether from the cosmic process, as we have seen Socrates arguing in the pages of Xenophon, belongs to the period of Socrates' maturity, in the closing decades of the fifth century B.C., after atomism had arrived on the scene.

Equally Socrates' key point in the *Phaedo* passage, that intelligence is an intrinsically good cause which must itself be understood in terms of the good that it aims to realize, was not developed by any Presocratic we know of beyond its bare assertion by Socrates' contemporary Diogenes of Apollonia, who (§1 above) detected the workings of intelligence as being manifested whenever things were done in the best or "finest" possible way. One reason why this link of intelligence to goodness apparently had to await the arrival of Socrates[31] for its full articulation[32] is plain enough. It was from his ethical inquiries, with their concentration on intelligence or wisdom (*phronēsis*) as the very essence of human goodness, that Socrates launched his theoretical account of divine goodness. Divine intelligence, craftsmanship, and power had all been emphasized by the preceding tradition, but it was left to Socrates to give comparable importance to divine goodness. And the essential goodness of god does indeed, unsurprisingly, become a recurrent motif of Plato's Socratic dialogues, as also of Xenophon's theological chapters in the *Memorabilia*.

Thus far, then, nothing historically implausible, and nothing mutually inconsistent, has emerged from the accounts given by Xenophon and Plato.

---

31. Some measure of interaction between Socrates and Diogenes (cf. DL IX 57) would be chronologically possible, since according to Theophrastus (fr. 226A FHS&G = 64 A 5 DK) Diogenes was "more or less the youngest" of the physical philosophers and late enough to be influenced by the atomist Leucippus. Moreover, Socrates and Diogenes may have been to some extent fused in the contemporary public consciousness, since it is well recognized that the "Socrates" of Aristophanes' *Clouds* (423 B.C.) expresses some Diogenian-sounding ideas on physics (see esp. Vander Waerdt 1994b). I am resistant to attempts to extract Socrates' own "physics" from the *Clouds*, and more generally to seeing Diogenes as a major influence on him, for reasons set out in §1 of this chapter and immediately below in the present section, but I would not altogether rule out some influence in the reverse direction.

32. 22 A 102 DK, "Heraclitus says that for god all things are fine and good, and that it is human beings who have taken some to be unjust, others just," could be a partial antecedent, but it is not a verbatim quotation and may well have been filtered through a Stoicizing source. For properly cautious discussion, see Kahn 1979, pp. 183–85.

Moreover, in both authors' accounts Socrates rejects as fundamentally flawed the entire explanatory enterprise undertaken by the Greek cosmological tradition, and advocates appreciation of the creator's goodness as a replacement for his predecessors' misguided attempts to theorize how it has been brought about. There being little evidence of cross-contamination between Plato's and Xenophon's accounts, the extent of common ground between them is most encouraging. Here we really do seem to have the external facts concerning Socrates' rebellion against Presocratic physics.

Where the two interpreters above all differ is regarding the motivation and the consequences of Socrates' abandonment of physics. As regards its motivation, first, Xenophon's Socrates considers the study of cosmological science an act of impiety, a misjudged attempt to replicate god's work, in contravention of man's proper place in the hierarchy. Plato's Socrates, on the other hand, avoids physics for a different reason, one calculated to strike a chord with readers of Plato's *Apology*. In his view, none of those who profess cosmological understanding actually possesses it, not even the great Anaxagoras. Socrates, unlike all the others, at least has the self-awareness to appreciate that he does not understand it. But by contrast with his response in the field of ethics, where he takes his awareness of his own ignorance as a spur to pursue the investigation, in physics he acknowledges his own lack of aptitude for the discipline, and for that reason alone abandons it.

Similarly as regards the consequences of this abandonment, the two authors go their separate ways. For Xenophon the message is simple: his Socrates recognized the moral wisdom of avoiding physics and sticking to the pursuit of virtue. But Plato's agenda was such as to favor a different interpretation. In due course he would write a new dialogue, the *Timaeus*, in which the shelved scientific question how the creator did his work was to be reopened, but this time, by being examined in partnership with the primary theme of god's goodness, to be much more successfully answered than by any predecessor. How was Plato to square this project of creationist science with his Socratic heritage? That Plato was already thinking ahead to the *Timaeus* is revealed by a passing remark contained in Socrates' autobiography in the *Phaedo*. After explaining his abandonment of physics, Socrates adds that he would still be glad to become anyone's pupil if they could teach him the kind of causation that he had hoped in vain to find in Anaxagoras. That is, Plato is signalling to us, Socrates' disillusionment with physics was a response only to the style of physical speculation available down to his own day, and was not meant to exclude a properly reformed and theologized physics such as Plato would indeed himself eventually develop.

In this same passage Socrates' use of the remote future, "I would still most gladly become anybody's pupil . . . " (99c7–8), is curious when one considers that he has, in the dramatic situation depicted in the *Phaedo,* barely an hour to live. But at the authorial level it makes ready sense: in a future Platonic dialogue, the *Timaeus,* Socrates will indeed become the mere auditor of somebody, a presumed Pythagorean named Timaeus, in order to learn how the world arose as the product of a supreme intelligence. By planting this link in his text, Plato legitimates his own lifetime project, portraying his later move into physics not as a betrayal of Socrates but as the very development that Socrates himself would above all else have welcomed.

It is to Plato's own project that we must now turn.

IV Plato

1. THE *PHAEDO* MYTH

At the end of the previous chapter I noted how, long before he came to write the *Timaeus*, a dialogue best dated years, probably decades, after the *Phaedo*, Plato was already planning to vindicate the teleological style of cosmology of which his Socrates had approved but also despaired.[1] I can now add that Plato did not need to wait for the *Timaeus*. For at the end of the *Phaedo* itself Socrates conveys to his audience a myth (107c1–115a8) which, whether or not Socrates himself realizes it (and he almost certainly does not), sketches what Anaxagoras *should* have said.

Socrates, let us recall (chapter III §3), had in his youthful optimism expected Anaxagoras first to state the shape of the earth and its position within the cosmos, then go on to explain why it was *best* for it to be so shaped and positioned. The dialogue's closing myth implicitly answers these very same questions, not only describing the shape and position of the earth but also enabling us to see the good that results from them.

In outline[2] the myth runs as follows. The earth is approximately spherical and located at the center of a spherical surrounding heaven, where it stays motionless thanks to symmetry alone. Below its surface lies a network of underground rivers. At its surface the ground rises to varying levels, so that some regions lie under water, some sit in air, while others rise into the

---

1. For the Socratic origins and inspiration of Plato's teleology, cf. Graham 1991.
2. Although the *Phaedo* myth is too central to my theme to pass over in silence, the interpretation offered here is one that I have already developed at length in Sedley 1990, and my treatment of it will for that reason be somewhat cursory. A fuller defense of the same interpretation can now be found in Karfík 2004, and for important new perspectives on the *Phaedo* myth see Betegh forthcoming.

rarefied upper atmosphere known as the aether. Souls at each stage of their purification are assigned to an appropriate region, ranging from punishment in Tartarus, through incarnation in fish or in air-dwelling creatures like ourselves, all the way up to the privileged inhabitants of the aether, whose life is close in purity and beauty to a totally discarnate one. The density or rarity of the atmosphere—water, air, aether—in each case corresponds to the degree of intellectual purification that the occupying soul has attained. Thus viewed, we are better than fish, but worse than the aether-dwellers. The eventual ideal, no more than hinted at here, is the totally discarnate existence towards which this scale of purification beckons.

On a little reflection it becomes clear that in the myth we can glimpse what it might mean for the earth's shape and position to be designed for the best. Whether or not Plato takes seriously the fantastic geography contained in the myth,[3] he succeeds in conveying his point that the long-term benefit of souls is a good end for the sake of which the earth might credibly have been assigned its shape and position. Meanwhile water, air, and aether, the three explanatory items to which, Socrates earlier complained, Anaxagoras had attached nearly all the explanatory importance, have in the myth been relegated to their proper role: not causes at all, but the materials implicitly *used* by intelligence in constructing its stratified hierarchy of three atmospheres.

Clearly Socrates does not fully see the teleological subtext of the myth, since he has earlier confessed to never having learnt how to do teleological cosmology, and goes to his death without retracting that disavowal. His declared readiness to believe the myth no doubts springs from his belief in divine justice, not from any skill in cosmology. But whoever told him the myth, a person to whom he refers just as "someone," must have had a significantly better understanding of teleological cosmology than he himself did. Who is this anonymous informant? My own candidate is: Plato himself.[4] Plato was notoriously absent from the scene in Socrates' death cell (he was ill), but his authorial presence is unmissable throughout the dialogue. And it is

3. Kingsley 1995a, pp. 71–111, argues that the myth's topography is a Sicilian one of Pythagorean origin.

4. Kingsley 1995a, pp. 89–90, takes the reference to be to a Sicilian Pythagorean informant. In view of the teleological interpretation I propose, this is not to be ruled out, since the eponymous speaker of the *Timaeus*, likewise a proponent of cosmic teleology, is probably—whether real or fictional—a Sicilian Pythagorean. On the other hand, I believe the *Phaedo* to be rather less generous to its Pythagorean antecedents than Kingsley does (Sedley 1995). For a probable concealed self-reference by Plato just after this in the *Phaedo*, cf. Most 1993; for one in the *Theaetetus*, Sedley 2004, p. 37.

Plato's vision of the way forward for teleological science that Socrates unwittingly relays to us in his final minutes of life.

Let us then take note of this new teleology's most striking feature. The immediate beneficiaries of the world's intelligently devised arrangements are *souls*. Unlike Xenophon's Socrates, Plato does not regard nature as in the last analysis anthropocentric. When we are benefited by the structures that divine intelligence has put in place for us, it is not as human beings that we are so benefited, but as souls, whose ultimate reward is indeed to escape human incarnation. A cosmic arrangement centered on enabling the soul to attain virtual divinity is a motif that we will meet, far more fully developed, in the *Timaeus*.

2. INTRODUCING THE *TIMAEUS*

I have spent quite some time sketching the background to the *Timaeus*, and it is high time to enter the dialogue itself, although in the space of one chapter I cannot begin to do justice to this uniquely rich and seminal text.[5] I shall approach it from a specific point of view, that of divine craftsmanship, a notion which it explores more comprehensively than any other text from antiquity. But first a sketch of the whole.

It is both convenient and natural to speak of the *Timaeus* as Plato's "dialogue" on cosmology. Strictly speaking, however, the discourse on cosmology is not that, but a dialogue fragment, consisting in a single speech torn from its larger context. The actual dialogue framing it is, moreover, an uncompleted one, the *Timaeus-Critias*, a truncated series of monologues delivered by members of a small intellectual coterie, one of whom is Socrates.

We learn at the very start that Socrates has already, on the previous day, given his own monologue, portraying an ideal city along lines that were quite familiar to Plato's readers from his *Republic*. In the opening pages of the *Timaeus* itself, Critias undertakes to fulfill a request of Socrates' by describing such an ideal city in action. For the Athens of nine thousand years ago was, it turns out, a city accurately matching Socrates' account, and Critias is by good fortune privy to the long-lost story of its great war with Atlantis. Later still, following Critias's discourse on this theme, another participant, Hermocrates, is due to deliver one of his own, on a theme that is

---

5. Since I cannot engage adequately with the immense wealth of available scholarship on the *Timaeus*, let me at least record my debt to Cornford 1937, Brisson 1992, Zeyl 2000, Harte 2002, Fronterotta 2003, Velásquez 2004, and Johansen 2004, all of which I have consulted regularly while working on this chapter.

unfortunately nowhere indicated. But first, as a prelude to Critias's venture into Athenian prehistory, a Sicilian politician, philosopher, and astronomer named Timaeus agrees to recount the origin of the world itself, down to the creation of man. And it is Timaeus's speech that takes up the rest of the *Timaeus*. The conversation resumes without interruption in the *Critias*, but it then breaks off in the middle of Critias's disquisition, and we never get to hear either the upshot of his story or what Hermocrates was going to tell us after it.

Why is the text in this unsatisfactory state? It is generally held that the *Timaeus* was written towards the end of Plato's life, hence roughly in the 350s B.C. (he died in 347). It seems a good bet that, having for some reason abandoned the larger project, Plato decided to make a cut just before the end of Timaeus's speech and to publish everything that he had written down to there. This was an excellent decision on his part. The resultant text did, after all, prove to be from the start the most influential of all Plato's works, and probably the most seminal philosophical or scientific text to emerge from the whole of antiquity. If it had been withheld from circulation because of the dialogue's incomplete state, the subsequent history of ancient philosophy would have been unrecognizably different. But the price of the compromise was to include material, in the opening pages of the published segment, whose point could not be seen until the remainder was written and made available—which in the event it never was.

I say this because the opening conversation preceding Timaeus's speech had clearly been written as a prelude, not specifically and narrowly to Timaeus's discourse, but to the more extensive and wide-ranging interchange originally planned for the full dialogue, including (but not limited to) Critias's unfinished speech that follows it.[6] We cannot recover Plato's plans for the longer dialogue's architecture, or even afford to assume that they were ever fully drawn up. But in any case we should not expect, simply because Critias's preliminary discourse at 21a7–26e1 and the ensuing speech of Timaeus on the world's origin are juxtaposed, to find any privileged interdependence between them.[7] Any connections we do find between them are

6. I deliberately speak of *Timaeus-Critias-Hermocrates* as a single "dialogue" rather than a "trilogy." *Theaetetus-Sophist-Statesman* is our model of a Platonic trilogy, and its three component conversations are dramatically far more independent of each other than the *Timaeus* and *Critias* are. No one of them would, when published as it stands, have seemed to leave its own business unfinished in the way that the *Timaeus* does.

7. In saying this, my main purpose is to justify my own inattention to the dialogic context of Timaeus's speech, and not to discredit the very skillful work that

condemned to remain provisional and partial, since they would undoubtedly
have had to be rethought in the light of the completed dialogue. It seems to
me on the whole safer simply to treat Timaeus's speech (down to and including its peroration on the first page of the *Critias*) as an autonomous
whole, and to discount or minimize the relevance of its context.

The speech's outward form is largely that of a creation myth, although
the register of its discourse switches repeatedly between myth, fable, prayer,
scientific analysis,[8] and philosophical argument. It is written in formidably
difficult and high-flown Greek, and despite being in prose it follows many
of the conventions of poetry, as no doubt befits a mythical narrative. Here
are its main highlights (not entirely in the order adopted by Timaeus):

- *First principles.* After an opening prayer, Timaeus invokes a
  strong version of the Platonic "two world" metaphysics, which
  separates a realm of intelligible being from one of perceptible
  becoming. The physical world belongs to the latter realm, and
  must be explained with the kind of discourse appropriate to that
  realm, one aiming for "likelihood" rather than the kind of cast-
  iron certainty appropriate to changeless entities.

- *World design.* The product of an intrinsically good "maker" or
  "Demiurge," our world is modelled on an eternal Form, and is
  itself a single, spherical, intelligent entity, consisting of the four
  familiar stuffs, earth, water, air, and fire, plus a soul.

- *Materials.* The Demiurge designed the microscopic structure of
  the four elementary stuffs, imposing beauty and functionality
  on a substrate called the "receptacle" whose motions had prior
  to his intervention been more or less chaotic. The base components are certain primary triangles chosen for their capacity to
  be assembled (and, after dissolution, reassembled) into the plane
  faces of four perfect solids, which in turn serve as the particles
  of earth (the cube), water (the icosahedron), air (the octahedron)
  and fire (the tetrahedron).

- *The world soul* was composed by the Demiurge out of a complex
  mixture of sameness, difference, and being, arranged in two
  strips—the circle of the Same and the circle of the Different—

---

others have done on relating it to that context, for example Osborne 1988 and 1996,
Broadie 2001, and Johansen 2004, chapters 1–2.

8. The classic assessment of the dialogue's scientific content is still Lloyd 1968.

and divided into harmonic intervals. This is the structure that underlies the orderly motions of the heavenly bodies.

- *The human rational soul.* The human rational soul, also constructed by the Demiurge, was modelled by him on the world soul, and was later housed in our approximately spherical heads in imitation of the way the world soul occupies, and rotates through, the spherical heaven. Its incarnation has disrupted its naturally circular motions, but by imitating the world soul it can aspire eventually to restore them.

- *The human body.* Anything the Demiurge makes, including our rational souls, is thereby immortal. To avoid making human beings themselves immortal, the detailed design and construction of the human body, including the mortal soul-parts, had to be delegated to the lesser, created gods. They designed and built the human body as a suitable housing for the rational soul.

- *Other animals.* These were created as deliberately engineered degenerations from the human archetype, designed to imprison ex-human souls for a period of punishment and redemption.

3. AN ACT OF CREATION?

Plato's creator god in the *Timaeus* is billed as a craftsman or *dēmiourgos*, so emphatically, indeed, that the word "Demiurge" has entered our own language to signify a divine craftsman. In the tradition of Empedocles (often and rightly considered an influence on the *Timaeus*), the craft most prominently invoked to support this model is carpentry. At times the assorted craft language employed by Timaeus, of lathes and mixing bowls, is so overt as to demand deliteralization. Readers since Plato's own day have wondered how far to take this deliteralization. Was there really a divine craftsman at all, one who some specific number of years ago constructed the world from preexisting chaotic matter? Or is the building image being employed merely in order to describe the causal role of intelligence in a world which has in reality existed essentially unchanged from infinite time past?

This question has remained an all-time favorite for debate among interpreters of the *Timaeus*.[9] Without entirely upsetting the balance of this book, I cannot give it the space it deserves. On the other hand, from the point of

9. The seminal study of the ancient debate is Baltes 1976–78. For a more succinct overview, see Sorabji 1983, chapter 17.

view of my overall topic I cannot afford to ignore altogether the question whether the divine craftsmanship envisaged by Plato resembled human craftsmanship even to the extent of proceeding through discrete phases of design and progressive construction. I turn therefore to that question, fully aware that my treatment will seem to some provocative, inadequate, or both.

The speaker, Timaeus, tells the story of how a supremely good divine craftsman decided to make a world, prepared his materials, and constructed it as a single spherical living being with its own rational soul, along with a set of less pure rational souls suitable for incarnation in mortal bodies; and how the lesser gods whom he created were then given the task of creating humans and other organisms to house these souls. These phases are not unfailingly described in what would have been their actual chronological order, but in one case Timaeus explains that such a departure from the strict chronological sequence—his choosing to describe the building of the world's body before that of its soul, whereas in fact soul, as ruler, must be senior to what it rules—should not be allowed to mislead us (34b10–35a1).[10] The impression that there *was* a chronological order—that the cosmogony occurred sequentially in phases—is very strong throughout the text.[11]

But is it really credible that Plato believed this? All kinds of difficulties have been raised by interpreters against the literal chronological reading,[12] of which I shall for now mention just one. Such a reading, it is frequently pointed out, appears to contain two flatly incompatible claims: (a) time came into being with the creation of the world, thanks to the building of the great celestial clock (37c6–38c3); (b) *before* the creation of the world there was chaotic motion in the receptacle (51d2–53c3). Impossibly, it seems, the chaotic motion would have to be at a time before time.

At first sight, one might have hoped to be able to give the following unproblematic explanation. The creation story is obviously a myth.[13] And

10. Indeed, the same impression is maintained, without any of the trappings of mythological narrative, at *Laws* 892a2–c8, 896b2–c8, and 967d6–7, where soul is emphatically credited with its own "coming-to-be" (γένεσις) or "birth" (γονή), "having come-to-be before all bodies" (σωμάτων ἔμπροσθεν πάντων γενομένη, 892a5).

11. Baltes 1996, pp. 77–85, displays systematically the difficulties of finding a credible chronological order for the phases of world creation. Although Baltes takes these to confirm that the literal chronological reading is not that intended by Plato, they are just as well taken to explain why Timaeus here does not attempt to describe the actual chronological sequence, which is destined to remain inscrutable to us.

12. Cf. those catalogued by Baltes 1996, pp. 82–85; also Dillon 1997.

13. Timaeus calls his discourse *mythos* (notably at 69b1), but more frequently *logos*. I call it a "myth" here, not because of its self-description, but because it is unmistakably cast in the form of a creation myth.

myths are frequently used by Plato to convey important truths in a non-literal fashion. To take an example briefly mentioned in chapter II (p. 57 above), Plato's character Protagoras undertakes to give his own demonstration that virtue is teachable, indicating to his audience (*Protagoras* 320c2–4) that the very same lesson could be expounded either with a simple discourse *(logos)* or with a myth *(mythos).* Having opted for the latter, he illuminates the nature of our innate moral instincts with an entertaining creation story which on the one hand no one in their right mind would take literally, but which on the other hand leaves the reader a good deal of room for varying *degrees* of deliteralization. For example, few of us will suppose him to mean that, at a time when human beings were still in the planning stage, the often abortive negotiations that he describes as going on between Zeus, Epimetheus, and Prometheus ever actually occurred. On the other hand, some will take away with them, as part of the story's cash value, the implication that our moral instincts are, or at least may be, a divine gift, while others will edit out the entire divine superstructure, and interpret the account in purely naturalistic terms. This interpretative license is not an unfortunate failure of self-expression on Protagoras's part, but an ineradicable feature of mythical exposition. To interrogate Protagoras's myth by asking exactly what it is saying about the origins of human society is just about as pointless as asking, of a hymn, what precisely is the literal reality behind references to God's throne, or to choirs of angels. Mythical discourse has this indeterminacy as an inherent feature, as does most religious discourse. And the *Timaeus* is nothing if not a religious discourse.[14]

In the light of such considerations, we might hope similarly to rest content with the following conclusions about the *Timaeus.* It is cast in narrative form primarily for expository reasons ("for purposes of instruction," as Plato's pupil Xenocrates famously explained it).[15] Not all the details of the narrative— to pick an obvious example, the speech delivered by the Demiurge to the newly created gods at 41a3–d3—*can* credibly be taken as altogether literal truth-claims, any more than can the conversation that Protagoras describes as taking place between Epimetheus and Prometheus. How much, then, are we meant to leave behind, and how much to take away with us? At bottom, if nothing more, Timaeus's cosmogony can be read as expounding for us in fictional narrative form the teleological structure of the world and its princi-

14. Note, among many other religious features, Timaeus's prayers at his speech's opening (27c1–d1) and close (*Critias* 106a3–b6), as well as when embarking on a new and hazardous topic (48d4–e1).

15. Xenocrates frr. 153–57 Isnardi.

pal contents. Most readers, however, will go at least one level beyond this, and take Timaeus to be insisting on the indispensability of divine causation as an explanatory principle. Others will go still further, and suppose him to mean that the divine cause brought the world into being in an original, datable act of creation. At each of these stages, readers will weigh up the pros and cons of the interpretation at issue: does taking this or that feature of the story literally make the account unacceptably naïve, or, worse, self-contradictory? But none need suppose that, with this myth more than with any other, there is a single determinate answer available as to precisely where we should stop.

Why then have readers of the *Timaeus* not rested content to enjoy the license that Plato has bestowed on them by casting his physics in the form of a myth, a license that would leave it quite unproblematic, for those who so wish, to assume that Plato never meant to commit himself to the world's having a temporal beginning?

The obstacle to this easy solution lies in the following passage (28b4–c2):

> Concerning it [the world], then, we must start with the question which is laid down as the question one should ask at the beginning of any topic: whether it always was, having no beginning (*arche*) of coming-to-be, or has come-to-be, beginning from some beginning. It has come-to-be (*gegonen*). For it is visible, tangible, and possessed of body; all such things are perceptible; and perceptible things, grasped by opinion (*doxa*) with the aid of perception, have been shown to be things that come-to-be and have been brought-into-being.[16]

These lines do not treat the world's original creation as an optional feature, belonging to the mythical narrative rather than to the hard science. On the contrary they argue for it. And nowhere else in the *Timaeus* are we likely to doubt that theses for which philosophical argument is supplied are meant seriously—for example, the world's being modelled on an eternal paradigm (28c5–29b1), its uniqueness (31a2–b3), and the existence of Forms (51d3–e6)—whatever doubts we may nurture about the quality of the arguments themselves. How then can we reasonably doubt Plato's seriousness about the thesis that the world had a beginning?

Since antiquity, nonliteralist interpreters have responded to the problem by on the one hand accepting that these lines must be meant seriously, but on the other denying that, when closely scrutinized, they do in fact assert

---

16. σκεπτέον δ᾽ οὖν περὶ αὐτοῦ πρῶτον, ὅπερ ὑπόκειται περὶ παντὸς ἐν ἀρχῇ δεῖν σκοπεῖν, πότερον ἦν ἀεί, γενέσεως ἀρχὴν ἔχων οὐδεμίαν, ἢ γέγονεν, ἀπ᾽ ἀρχῆς τινος ἀρξάμενος. γέγονεν· ὁρατὸς γὰρ ἁπτός τέ ἐστιν καὶ σῶμα ἔχων, πάντα δὲ τὰ τοιαῦτα αἰσθητά, τὰ δ᾽ αἰσθητά, δόξῃ περιληπτὰ μετ᾽ αἰσθήσεως, γιγνόμενα καὶ γεννητὰ ἐφάνη.

that the world had a temporal beginning. The favored alternative is that "it has come-to-be" (gegonen) describes not some past occasion when it first came to exist, but the world's permanent state of change, dependent on its divine cause; and that the word archē refers not to a temporal "beginning" but to a causal "principle" on which the world permanently depends.

Rather than report and dissect the various detailed interpretations developed along these lines, many of them of considerable power and ingenuity, I shall go straight to what remains the obvious objection. This conclusion, that the world "has come-to-be," serves in Timaeus's discourse not only (a) as the formal alternative to holding that it "always was," but also (b) as his formal justification for going on immediately to postulate a "maker" of it, a maker whose actions are from this point on described in language calculated to evoke a datable act of creation. Here is how the text continues from the passage quoted above (28c2–29a1):

> Next, for that which came-to-be we say it is necessary that it came-to-be by the agency of some cause. Now to discover the maker and father of this universe is some task, and to tell everybody about him impossible. The question we should raise about him is the following: by reference to which of two kinds of model did its builder set about making it . . . ?[17]

Timaeus, still here engaged in argument, can be seen, as he will continue to be seen throughout the remainder of the dialogue, to use past tenses in the familiar narrative way appropriate to a single past act of creation. But if any doubt remains, Plato seems determined to eliminate it at the close of Timaeus's speech, a passage too rarely noticed because it is located not at the end of the Timaeus but at the very beginning of the ensuing Critias (106a3–4):

> I utter a prayer to the god [i.e. the world] who previously, at a time long ago, has come-to-be in reality, and just now has come-to-be in words . . . [18]

Timaeus's own very explicit interpretation of what it is for the world to "have come-to-be" (gegonoti, the participial form of the earlier gegonen, "has come-to-be") makes a formidable case for a literal chronological reading of his earlier words.[19]

It seems hard to avoid the conclusion that the divine origin of the world in

---

17. τῷ δ' αὖ γενομένῳ φαμὲν ὑπ' αἰτίου τινὸς ἀνάγκην εἶναι γενέσθαι. τὸν μὲν οὖν ποιητὴν καὶ πατέρα τοῦδε τοῦ παντὸς εὑρεῖν τε ἔργον καὶ εὑρόντα εἰς πάντας ἀδύνατον λέγειν· τόδε δ' οὖν πάλιν ἐπισκεπτέον περὶ αὐτοῦ, πρὸς πότερον τῶν παραδειγμάτων ὁ τεκταινόμενος αὐτὸν ἀπηργάζετο . . .

18. τῷ δὲ πρὶν μὲν πάλαι ποτ' ἔργῳ, νῦν δὲ λόγοις ἄρτι θεῷ γεγονότι προσεύχομαι . . .

19. In support of this conclusion, see also n. 58 below.

a past act of creation is something that Plato makes his main speaker systematically argue for, and which for that reason must be taken seriously despite
the broadly mythical context in which it is showcased. Even Protagoras's speech
develops (*Protagoras* 323a5–328c2) into a manifestly serious ethical exposition which no reader will hesitate to take at face value, despite the mythical
framing. True, in Protagoras's case this philosophically serious discourse does
not include his opening story of our morality's divine origins. But that is only
to be expected, because Protagoras was a religious agnostic, whom an appeal
to divine origins should be expected to serve more effectively as a convenient
fiction than as a theoretical postulate. In Plato's case, the divine origin of the
world is, by contrast, doctrinally of absolute philosophical centrality.

The anti-literalist side of the debate has admittedly been bolstered by
some very impressive arguments based on inconsistencies that it is alleged
would arise from the assumption that the creation was a datable past event.
Some of the inconsistencies are with other dialogues, some—such as the
creation of time, mentioned above—internal to the *Timaeus* itself. It is not
my intention to pursue these here, beyond the following remark. Countless apparent incoherences have been detected by readers in every part of
the Platonic corpus. Normally the Principle of Charity leads us to seek interpretations that will eliminate or minimize them.[20] But as an alternative tactic scholars hoping to absolve Plato of commitment to some specific argument in a specific dialogue have at times resorted to the suggestion that the
argument's self-evident inconsistency, fallaciousness, or implausibility is
Plato's own way of disowning it. Its ubiquitous availability in my view makes
it extremely hazardous ever to invoke this escape clause, which if rigorously
applied would leave Plato virtually without any argument to his name.[21]

---

20. In this spirit, consider Timaeus's inference at 28c1–2 (quoted above), which,
understood literally, can arouse suspicion: the world is perceptible; perceptible things
"have been shown to be things that *come-to-be and have been brought-into-be-
ing*"; therefore the world has come-to-be. The emphasized words refer back to
27d5–28a4, where, however, perceptibles were equated only with things that "come-
to-be" (present tense), without the addition that all such things have at some past
time come-into-being. Is this meant to alert us to a conscious sleight of hand? (I
owe the question to Richard Patterson.) The Principle of Charity suggests rather
that at 27d6 Plato must have intended the two-world contrast between "what always is" (ὂν ἀεί) and "what comes-to-be (γιγνόμενον) and never is" as one between
what *in every respect* is and what *in every respect* comes to be—in which case the
latter would indeed have to include not just qualitative, quantitative etc. coming-to-
be but also substantial coming-to-be.

21. Cf. Scott 2006, pp. 3–5, who points out that in the *Meno*, if this principle
were applied to all the passages for which it has been advocated, not much would be
left to be credited to Plato.

Besides, Plato has taken care to indicate that the presence of some residual inconsistency in his account is unavoidable. At 29c4–d3 Timaeus says:

> So if, Socrates, there are many aspects of many questions, concerning the gods and the coming-to-be of the universe, on which we prove unable to render accounts which are in every respect entirely self-consistent and accurate, do not be surprised. Rather, if we manage to give accounts which are no less likely than someone else's,[22] we should be content, remembering that I the speaker and you the judges possess a human nature, so that on these matters it is fitting for us to accept the likely story and look for nothing further beyond it.

Inconsistencies, Timaeus here indicates, may arise simply because physical discourse can aspire to be no better than "likely" (more on this below, pp. 110–13). Even so, he adds significantly, a discourse like his could prove to be the best account of the world's origin that is humanly available. If so, Plato can hardly be inviting us to construct for ourselves a nongenetic interpretation of the world's "coming-to-be" that will be more accurate than the genetic narrative he has bequeathed us. Rather, he is alerting us that any inconsistencies we may find should be tolerated, and *not* be taken as fatal to his cosmogonic story.

Besides, the actual amount of inconsistency that we have to tolerate need not, on close inspection, prove unacceptably great. Leaving aside the separate issue of the *Timaeus*'s consistency with other dialogues, which I do not believe to be a fully attainable goal for *any* interpreter,[23] the internal consistency of Timaeus's creation account has proved more resilient and defensible than might have been expected, thanks in particular to a classic study by Gregory Vlastos.[24] To revert once more to the example of the creation of time, Vlastos was able to show how time can plausibly here be taken to mean *measured* time, whose creation along with the great celestial clock would not rule out coherent talk of simple "before" and "after" even in the

---

22. In taking μηδενός at 29c7 as masculine I follow Burnyeat 2005, p. 148 n. 13 (also Taylor 1928 *ad loc.*).

23. For example, anti-literalists often cite the principle, first formulated in the *Phaedrus*, that soul is the cause of all motion, as conflicting with the idea in the *Timaeus*, read literally, that there was chaotic motion before the Demiurge had created the world soul. True, this is inconsistent with Socrates' second speech in the *Phaedrus* (245c5–246a2). But that speech is in any case likely to remain inconsistent with the *Timaeus*: (a) in view of 52d4–53a8 it may be hard on *any* reading to absolve Timaeus of positing motions, inherent to the receptacle, that are not dependent on causation by soul; (b) the *Phaedrus* speech makes all three soul-parts survive death, whereas Timaeus attributes survival to the rational part alone.

24. Vlastos 1939, supplemented by Vlastos 1965.

pre-cosmic state of things.[25] What is worth adding to Vlastos's argument is that, as we shall see in chapter V (pp. 144–46 below), the Epicurean critique of Plato's creationism shows that this very same way of understanding "time" in the *Timaeus* was already being assumed at an early stage of the ancient debate.[26] Indeed, quite apart from its merits as an interpretation of Plato, the literally chronological reading of the Timaean creation story was the one generally assumed by the protagonists of the debate reconstructed in this book. For both reasons, it will prove the best one to work with.

An important question remains. *Why* should Plato have chosen to label his temporalized account of the world's divine origin in this way as a non-optional part of his cosmology? After all, one might have thought that his depiction of divine craftsmanship need not be seriously damaged if the account were instead read as nongenetic. Even on the assumption that the original building operation never actually took place, few readers are likely to doubt that divine intelligence is being portrayed as causally responsible for the world's structures, and the possibility that these structures were not at some past time put together in some serial order should make relatively little difference to that. Compare those who hold that moral relations are fundamentally contractual: they need not feel seriously threatened by historical doubts as to whether any such contract was ever actually formulated and entered into.

To see why Plato is not attracted to this alternative path, we need to return to 28b4–29a1 (quoted above, pp. 101–2). The argument for the world's having a genetic origin has the function there of demonstrating the existence of a world-maker, which in turn permits the question whether or not this maker was a good craftsman. And it is no exaggeration to say that the affirmative answer to that question becomes the indispensable basis for the entire cosmogony that follows.

Does Timaeus, in inferring here from the world's having a beginning to its having a maker, intend the former as a merely *sufficient* condition of the latter, or as a *necessary* one too? The text at 28c2–3 leaves the answer underdetermined: "Next, for that which came-to-be we say it is necessary that it came-to-be by the agency of some cause." Here he at least means that whatever comes-to-be has a causal agent. He may or may not be implying in addition that *only* what comes-to-be has a causal agent. If we take him to

25. This is different from Timaeus's implication that there was no "was" or "will be" before the creation of the ordered world (37e3–38a2). Although he gives no reason, he may mean that these locutions presuppose a determinable present, which total disorder could not supply.

26. On this and other occurrences of the interpretation in the ancient debate, see Sorabji 1983, pp. 270–71, 274.

mean the second, then he is assuming that *only* on the premise that the world had a genetic origin can we go on to infer that it is the product of craftsmanship. But even if we take him to mean no more than the first, his premise that the world had a genetic origin still retains an indispensable role in his argument for the all-important conclusion that the world is the product of craftsmanship: take away the premise, and that conclusion—although it might of course still be true—is no longer supported by any argument. On either reading, the premise that the world had a genetic origin is needed by Timaeus in order to ground his conception of divine craftsmanship.

If, then, I have been right to argue that the passage under examination cannot, given its broader context, be credibly deliteralized into the postulation of a nontemporal or eternal cause of the cosmic order, it by now seems clear that Plato himself did not share the view held by many of his successors that divine craftsmanship can be reduced to an unchanging causal relation that has existed from infinite time past. His creationist analogy between human and divine craftsmanship requires, in his eyes, that there should have been at some determinate past time a discrete process of cosmic creation.

Why so? Plato after all did not lack the concept of a cause which is operative without having started causing at some past time, for according to *Republic* VI the Form of the Good is such a cause—of, for example, truth (508e2–3). Rather, he must think that kind of causal relation inadequate to account for the divine design of the world.[27] The Demiurge's contemporaneous effect upon our world seems to be limited to keeping it in existence. For (32c2–4) only the world's creator is capable of either keeping it permanently in existence or destroying it; being good, he naturally chooses the former, and the endless deferral of its demise depends on his enduring good will. That benevolent maintenance need not require any action by the Demiurge, and even if it did, it could at most involve his keeping all the beneficial structures operative, from the world-soul downwards. Any such capacity to maintain an existing structure, well exemplified in the ancient world by medicine, is of a different order from the capacity to bring a structure into being in the first place, the latter being better exemplified by such crafts as lawmaking, architecture, building, and carpentry. And these constructive crafts are the kinds of expertise that do indeed underlie Timaeus's portrayal of the Demiurge.[28] Thus, I suggest, it is precisely the seductive explanatory

---

27. Cf. Broadie 2007 for further difficulties, beyond those considered below, that would confront Plato's explanatory scheme if the world were taken to be eternal.

28. For lawmaking, see 42d2–3. Cf. also the *Gorgias*'s division of *technai*, which contrasts gymnastics and lawmaking on the one side with medicine and juridical

power of his craft analogy that has impelled Plato to insist on a genetic, rather than a static, account of the world's divine causation.

Plato's own pupil Aristotle was quick to point out difficulties of temporal creation. Among other things, it committed Plato to the puzzlingly asymmetric thesis that the world had a beginning but will have no end, and Aristotle, who was joined in this by the Epicureans,[29] found the asymmetry deeply objectionable. The alternative, nontemporal rereading of Plato's account was at this same time being developed by committed Platonists, who, as Aristotle saw them, in doing so were "coming to their own rescue" (*De caelo* 279b32–280a2). Yet even among the Platonists there were plenty who did not feel that they needed rescuing in this particular way.[30] And outside their ranks there was to all appearances *no one* who adopted it.[31] The protagonists of my next three chapters and my epilogue—Aristotle, the Epicureans,[32] the Stoics[33] and Galen[34]—all seem to have concurred in favoring the literal reading of the Platonic creation.

4. DIVINE CRAFTSMANSHIP

What then are the fundamental features of divine craftsmanship? According to Plato's earlier dialogue the *Gorgias*,[35] a true craft or expertise *(technē)*

---

science on the other (464b2–c3). The former pair are evidently singled out as disciplines which initiate new and beneficial states of affairs (in the body and the soul respectively), whereas the latter maintain and restore existing ones.

29. Aristotle, *DC* I 10–11. For the Epicureans, see Cicero *ND* I 20 = Long and Sedley 1987, 13G 2.

30. The impression is sometimes given that there were scarcely more than two literalist Platonists, namely Plutarch and Atticus, because they alone are named by Proclus at *In Plat. Tim.* I 276.30–277.1. But Proclus in fact says there that the same view was held by "many other Platonists." These probably included Polemo (as argued in Sedley 2002), Antiochus (as source of Cicero, *Academica* II 118), Cicero (*Timaeus* 5, *Tusc.* I 70), the contemporary Platonists paraphrased by Seneca at *Ep.* 58.27–29, Severus (Proclus, *op. cit.* I 289.7–9, II 95.28–96.1, III 212.6–9), and Harpocration (schol. *in* Proclus, *In Remp.* II 377.15 Kroll; see Dillon 1971, pp. 142–43).

31. Theophrastus, who was aware of the division of opinion in the contemporary Academy, allowed the nongenetic reading as a *possible* one, frr. 241A–B FHS&G.

32. For Epicurus, see chapter V §2 below.

33. For the Stoics I have in mind my findings in Sedley 2002 (cf. also Dillon 2003, pp. 166–74) that Stoic cosmology arose out of Polemo's interpretation of the *Timaeus*, which was itself literalist in this regard. The late-Hellenistic Stoics Panaetius and Boethus abandoned belief in cosmogony, but it is unclear whether or not they connected this revision to a reading of the *Timaeus*.

34. Galen *ap.* Philoponus, *Aet.* 599.22–601.19; *Compendium Timaei* 39.13 (ed. R. Waltzer and P. Kraus). Cf. Donini 1992, pp. 3497–98.

35. *Gorgias* 500e3–501c1, 503d5–504a5.

has three hallmarks. The expert in any craft (a) looks to an ideal model, form, or standard, (b) understands the nature of his subject matter and can give an account of the causes leading to his eventual product, and (c) aims for what is best, namely for the proper *ordering* of his craft's materials or objects. Thus, for example, a doctor (a) looks to what health is and uses it as a model or standard, (b) knows enough about the nature of the human body to understand how his treatments lead causally to the outcome sought, and (c) aims for a good end, specifically the proper ordering of the body and its components.

The first criterion, that of looking to a model, is one that Plato after writing the *Gorgias* developed in terms of his celebrated theory of Forms. The model to which a craftsman looks is a separated Form, an ideal standard which can at best be embodied, or imitated, in matter only imperfectly. When a carpenter makes a table (as in a familiar passage of *Republic* X, 596a10–b8), we might think of the Form of Table to which he looks as being, as it were, the ideal *function* of a table, one that the actual wooden table he produces could never discharge to perfection in every aspect. Nevertheless, in going back to first principles in this way and looking to the ideal standard, rather than copying some other manufactured table, the expert carpenter may bring his product as near to perfection as a mere copy could ever be. Likewise, according to Timaeus, the divine craftsman undoubtedly looked to an eternal Form, rather than settle for copying some existing, generated entity (28c5–29b1).

Then *what* Form did he look to? According to Timaeus, it was the Form of the genus Animal.[36] And why Animal? For reasons conveyed by the fol-

---

36. I stick with the straightforward translation of ζῷον as "animal," although most translators and commentators prefer "living creature" or its like. In Plato's view the world really is an animal. (It is true that at 76e7–77c5 plants are counted as ζῷα, but even there it means "animals," because their inclusion in the class is established partly by attributing to them perception, pleasure, and pain; see further, n. 74 below.) Moreover, I take the "intelligible animal" to mean the Form of the genus Animal, and not—as on an alternative reading often still invoked, probably in fact by the majority of commentators—to designate the entire intelligible realm, possibly viewed as itself somehow alive. (The two options are well summarized by Zeyl 2000, pp. xxxvii–xxxviii, n. 66.) To my mind the former, more restricted meaning is made abundantly clear throughout. Compare another craftsman's model, the Form of Couch in *Rep.* X. It is called both a Couch (κλίνη, 597b4–6, c2, d1–2) and the essence of Couch (ὃ ἔστιν κλίνη, 597a2, 4, c3, 9). Likewise the Demiurge's model is called both an Animal (ζῷον, 30c2–3, 31b1, 37d1, 3, 69c2) and the essence of Animal (ὃ ἔστιν ζῷον, 39e8). It is said to contain the four subgenera of animals (39e3–40a2), and in addition to these all the individual animal species (30c5–8, 31a4–5, 69c2–3), but never anything *other* than animal species. It is explicitly generic; and although

lowing complex argument (29d7–31a1).[37] First, by the familiar principles governing any craft, the world's creator must have been aiming for the best possible product; everything intelligent is better than its non-intelligent alternatives;[38] so the world had to be made intelligent; intelligence, he reasoned, can come to be only in a soul; therefore he must have chosen to endow the world with soul; only animals can have souls; so he concluded that the world had to be an animal; a real expert, in making any product, looks to the relevant Form; the relevant Form for constructing an animal is the genus Animal; therefore he modelled the world on the Form of Animal. There remained two ways in which he might in principle achieve this: (a) imitate the genus Animal via one of its species, by making the world, for example, a rabbit or a dolphin; (b) imitate the genus Animal directly, by making a generic animal without any of the specializations that mark off its constituent species. Of these, he chose (b), on the ground that completeness is itself a kind of perfection, and that the genus is complete while its species are partial.

This reconstructed chain of reasoning by the Demiurge exemplifies a methodology recurrent in the *Timaeus*. That the world's structure and functioning manifest intelligence was in reality a conviction that Plato had developed out of his Socratic and Presocratic background, with a strong empirical basis. But Timaeus's discourse is not an exercise in interpreting the empirical data; it is presented as an *a priori* attempt to reconstruct the reasoning that would be bound to go into the construction of any world by a good divinity.[39] That the world is the finest of all generated things, and that its creator was the best of causes, are premises baldly stated at the outset (29a2–6), and nowhere treated as in need of defense—it would, after all, be a sacrilege to think otherwise (29a3–4). If by good fortune the unfolding story of how the world was devised and built in fact proves to tally with the data of our own experience, that is something the reader is no doubt expected to note in its favor, but is no part of the actual argument for it. Similar strategies will be used in due course to determine, for example, that the

---

the same point is not made explicitly for Couch in *Rep.*, the Form of Shuttle in the parallel passage of the *Cratylus*, 389a5–390e5, is distinguished from its various species, so is clearly likewise a genus Form. In short, for anyone who accepts that the Couch of *Rep.* X is the Form of Couch, it should follow that the Animal in *Ti.* is the generic Form of Animal. See further, Cornford 1937, pp. 40–41, whose arguments seem to me more than adequate to counter e.g. Taylor 1928, pp. 80–82.

37. For full text and translation of 30b1–c1, see p. 227 below.

38. For the precise interpretation of this, see p. 228 below.

39. Cf. Lennox 1985a.

world had to be given a spherical shape (33b1–7), and had to consist of precisely four elements (31b4–32c4); both of these are demonstrated by Timaeus from first principles, without reference to the consideration that they were already widely accepted as empirical facts.

We may explain this strategy by observing that the physical world can easily seem, especially to a rationalist like Plato, a realm of merely contingent facts. Part of his job in spotlighting its orderliness lies in showing that it exemplifies the principles that rationality itself imposes. In reorientating physics away from predominantly empirical science and towards the exercise of pure thought, Plato is narrowing the gap between it and his preferred method, dialectic. This narrowing contributes to his agenda for rescuing physics from the abandonment to which Socrates appeared to have condemned it. And it is the new focus on reconstructing the creator's *reasoning* that helps with that project of intellectualizing physics.

It is in this context that we can also make the best sense of Timaeus's methodological reservations about cosmology (29b1–c3). Because the world is a mere "likeness" *(eikōn)* of an eternal model, the kind of discourse appropriate for it to aspire to is, he says, a "likely" *(eikōs)* one, as distinct from the entirely stable discourse that is possible when the unchangeable model itself is at issue. Why so?[40] He might have been thought to mean that a mere likeness of X can never give you a completely secure knowledge of X itself, in much the same way as you can never gain accurate knowledge of a person from their portrait. But that cannot in fact be what he means, because its equivalent in physical inquiry would be trying to find out about the model, here the Form of Animal, by studying its mere likenesses, whether these latter be individual dogs and horses, or the world-animal itself.

No doubt such an indirect way of finding out about a Form *would* be more or less doomed to inaccuracy. But it is not the enterprise of the *Timaeus*, and does not correspond to what cosmologists do. They, on the contrary, try to find out about the likeness—that is, the world—in its own right. So what Timaeus must have in mind is the kind of inaccuracy that will arise when reasoning proceeds, not from likeness to model, but from model to likeness. And the latter is indeed how he seems to conceive the enterprise of cosmology. This discipline, as he seeks to practice it, reconstructs the creative reasoning by which the Demiurge worked out how best to make a likeness

---

40. What follows was written before I saw Burnyeat 2005, and has been only slightly adjusted in the light of it. Our views, while different, are not in direct conflict. But the interpretation that I propose is more successful, or so I believe, in explaining why an *eikōs* account is appropriate to an *eikōn*.

of his model in matter. Although the model is singular—for the dialectician there is only one Form of Animal, for example, and presumably only one entirely proper account to give of it—it can spawn a plurality of competing likenesses. Deciding which likeness is, all things considered, the best, and was therefore the one chosen by the Demiurge, cannot for a human observer be an exact science, there being so many competing considerations at stake, many of them inscrutable to us.[41] This explains among other things why, as we saw above (p. 104), Timaeus's methodological preface includes an appeal to our human cognitive inadequacy (29c4–d3, addressed explicitly, and hardly by accident, to Socrates, for whom the limits of human wisdom were a special theme).[42]

To see why this is a relevant consideration, take two apparently unrelated questions. How are the four elements constructed, and how many worlds did the Demiurge make?

The four elements are taken by Timaeus to consist of particles, corresponding in shape to four of the five perfect solids: fire particles are pyramids, earth particles cubes, and so on (p. 97 above). These choices in themselves have some modest empirical basis: pyramids are sharp, cubes are stable, and in a simple way these properties do match those of fire and earth respectively. But many aspects, including the Demiurge's preference for perfect rather than irregular solids, do not invite any such empirical explanation, and at least some of the motivation for the choice is likely to lie in the intrinsic beauty and perfection of regularity by comparison with irregularity. Indeed, the reason why the Demiurge chose the sphere as the shape of the world itself is reported initially (33b1–7) in similarly aesthetic[43] terms: the sphere is the most perfect, beautiful, and comprehensive of all shapes. In both cases there were in fact practical reasons as well, as we will learn in due course, but at least in the case of the world's shape it is the intrinsic perfection of sphericity that is announced as the primary motive.

---

41. Cf. Hankinson 1998, p. 109.

42. The problem now arises whether god, at least, does possess a stable account of the cosmos, since he must be perfectly well aware how he made it. Timaeus is pointedly evasive on the question: in advising without further specification that, being human, we should seek "nothing beyond" the likely story (29d1–3), he leaves unspecified the cognitive status that the implied divine account might have. To judge from 37b8 and 72d4–8, however, a divine account of the physical world would in fact be both "stable" and straightforwardly true. This confirms that the dichotomous analysis of accounts at 29b3–c3 is restricted to human ones.

43. I have found no better word that "aesthetic" for such cases, but in using it I do not mean to imply that for Plato "beautiful" ($\kappa\alpha\lambda\acute{o}\varsigma$) excludes either practical or moral goodness.

That four perfect solids are assigned to the four elementary bodies is something to keep in mind as we turn to the second and apparently unrelated question, how many worlds there are. Here again there were no empirical data to help determine the choice. So the question in Plato's mind had to be the *a priori* one, what number of worlds would reason itself judge *best*? The initial answer (31a2–b3) is the confident "only one," and it is supported by a dazzling variety of reasons. First, the craftsman would want his product to be as like its model as possible, and since there is only a single comprehensive Form of Animal he will have preferred the greater likeness attained by making just one copy of it. Some[44] have thought this a bizarre piece of reasoning on the creator's part, but we should bear in mind that *all* the properties of Forms, unity included, are in Plato's eyes intrinsically good properties, and indeed it later (37c6–38c3) becomes explicit that the Demiurge did his best to embody in his world at least one further property that belonged to the model *qua* Form, namely its eternity. A second pair of reasons for the choice of a single world is that the world's everlastingness would itself be enhanced if there were nothing left outside it to pose a threat, and that its completeness would be enhanced if it consisted of the entire stock of matter, both considerations uniting to confirm that the creator used up all the available matter on the one world he was engaged in making (32c5–33b1). This conclusion in turn feeds into the stipulation that the world was made spherical. For (33b7–34b3) since, by the creator's wise decision, there is nothing outside the world, it has no need of any organs or limbs for external perception, travel, self-defense, or ingestion of food;[45] and this obviates the need for a mouth, arms, legs etc., or for any other appendage or orifice that would give it an asymmetric shape. Thus the world was permitted the perfect sphericity which lesser, asymmetric animal kinds unavoidably lack. This is one way in which a property initially assigned to the world for what we can loosely call aesthetic reasons turns out to be confirmed in addition by practical considerations. In addition, the same complete lack of all external organs and other marks of biological specialization is what ultimately legitimizes the bizarre-sounding concept of a world which is a generic animal, because modelled on the generic Form of Animal, without belonging to any animal species (30c2–31a1). Once again, even though the original ground for the choice was not practical but aesthetic—the need for maximum completeness—it is in due course confirmed by the Demiurge's practical reasoning.

---

44. Esp. Keyt 1971.
45. Nor did it need to create anything external to itself by excretion, since it was designed to be self-sufficient through recycling: 33c4–d3.

We find, then, attributed to the creator an elaborate mixture of reasons for his decisions concerning the world's design, combining the aesthetic and the practical in roughly equal measure. But in the absence of any empirical data on the specific point, the grounds for positing just *one* such world inevitably look more provisional and open to reconsideration than they would have done with even tacit empirical support. Hence much later (55c4–d6), after Timaeus has correlated the four elementary bodies to four perfect solids, we get a glimpse of Plato worrying about an aesthetic drawback of this scheme. What about the fifth, unused perfect solid, the dodecahedron? After a perfunctory and inadequately articulated attempt to assign the dodecahedron to the shape of the whole world (the very shape to which the sphere has previously been assigned),[46] he comes up with the following further possibility. Perhaps there are five worlds, each of them corresponding in shape to one of the perfect solids. If that were to prove correct, the principle of the copy's maximal likeness to one particular model would be replaced by one of complex correlation to a chosen set of models. The new idea is neither altogether discounted, nor further pursued. But the brief hesitation speaks eloquently both about the *a priori* nature of Plato's teleological enterprise, and about its limitations when it purports to reconstruct the creator's thoughts. Imitating an eternal model is no simple matter, and we can never be sure of rediscovering the creator's choices among competing alternative likenesses, and the reasoning that underlay them. That is why discourse about a mere likeness will never result in more than likelihood.

5. IS THE WORLD PERFECT?

The cases I have picked out illustrate the complex character of Plato's attempt to interpret divine craftsmanship in terms of two of the three principles listed on pp. 107–8: that a good craftsman (a) necessarily looks to an eternal model, and (c) aims to impose the best possible order on his materials.

The remaining Platonic principle of craft, (b), is the one about causes: the craftsman understands the nature of his subject matter, and can therefore explain the causes which will systematically bring about the result he aims for. Plato's point in originally formulating this third principle in the *Gorgias* was to separate real experts from those, such as chefs and rhetoricians, who have learnt by mere trial and error how to secure their desired

---

46. One may for this reason suspect that the dodecahedron was used for the decoration of the world, rather than for its actual shape, much as in the *Phaedo* myth (110b5–7) it is used for the spherical earth's decoration.

result, without the scientific control that an understanding of the causal processes involved would have conferred. The world's creator, as a supreme craftsman, certainly did not rely on trial and error, and must have fully mastered the causal processes which he set up. But what are these causal processes, and how regular are they?

Timaeus is very precise in his answer (46c7–48b3, 68e1–69a5). There are two types of cause operative in the world. The dominant type of cause is intelligent agency.[47] The creator himself may well no longer be present in the world's causal processes, but even if so the direct causal products of his intelligence are still manifest in the structures he himself created, from the heavens all the way down to the primary constituents of matter. Not only that, but his intelligence is also indirectly manifested in the divinities that are part of his creation, above all in the world soul. For the world is an intelligent being with its own soul, an arrangement ensuring that it is intelligently governed all the way down. At a very low level, no doubt even our own human intelligences, themselves likewise the creator's handiwork, discharge an analogous causal role.

Alongside intelligent causes like these stands the second category of cause, the mechanical, unintelligent, "auxiliary causes" that Timaeus calls by such labels as "necessity"[48] and "the wandering cause" (48a7). These consist in matter and its properties. That is, when intelligence operates in the world it has to rely on the intrinsic properties of matter, but matter, having no in-

---

47. In the *Timaeus* intelligence is, to put it in Aristotelian terms, a goal-directed *efficient* cause. Aristotle in *Met.* A is in my view quite right that none of his predecessors, Plato included, had anticipated his discovery of the final cause, i.e. made goals themselves causes. In this I dissent from what is widely assumed in the modern literature, and now skillfully argued by Johansen 2004, pp. 106–10. I understand the complex wording of *Ti.* 47b5–e2 (cf. 76d6–8) as follows: "but let (a) *this* be called by us the cause of (b) *this* for (c) *this* purpose: (a) god (b) discovered and bestowed on us sight, in order that (c) by seeing the revolutions of intelligence in the heaven we might use them . . . " (etc.). On such a reading (but for alternatives see Johansen 2004, pp. 107–8), the actual cause here is god. At all events, if ends were also causes, Timaeus's careful restriction of causes to two types—intelligent agents and the matter they use, 46e2–6—would be compromised.

48. Not all uses in the *Timaeus* of the very common word ἀνάγκη refer to this concept. The only unambiguous occurrences are: 47e4–48a7, 56c5, 68e1–69a5, 75d5–e5. Probable occurrences include 46e2, 53d5, 69d7, 70e5. Importantly 75a7–b1, from the famous passage on the fragility of the human head (see further below, pp. 120–21), is *not* such a usage, as is sometimes assumed: bodily tissue is there described as the kind of thing (φύσις) that "necessarily (ἐξ ἀνάγκης) undergoes generation and growth," using a standard adverbial phrase with a dozen other occurrences in the *Timaeus*. I see no justification for the translation in Zeyl 2000, " . . . anything whose generation and composition are a consequence of Necessity . . . "

herent tendency towards good ends, acts in a purposeless way unless it is directed, or in Timaeus's preferred idiom "persuaded," by intelligence.

To make the best sense of this, we may usefully invoke Plato's second criterion for craftsmanship: that a craftsman understands the nature of his subject matter and can give an account of the causes leading to his eventual product. Now in cosmogony the intelligent cause is itself a "craftsman" (46e4), while the "auxiliary causes" are the subject matter it works with. By applying the second criterion of craftsmanship, Plato has inferred that an intelligent cosmogonic cause, in order to be truly craftsmanlike, must have entirely dependable knowledge of what effects will result from each of the material causes it orchestrates, and conversely of what material causes are required in order to generate each desired effect. In the *Phaedo* (99a4–b6), Socrates had effectively excluded material causes, arguing that the matter involved in a causal process is better called a mere necessary condition than a cause. But the *Timaeus*, by emphasizing the role of a cosmic craftsman, more or less requires Plato to retract that exclusion and to reclassify matter as a cause.[49] The craftsman must know the causes of the results he works to bring about, and since these can hardly be identified with the craftsman himself, there must after all be a second kind of cause, constituted by the materials whose effects he understands and orchestrates to his own ends.[50] It is in that orchestration that the divine craftsman's "persuasion" of necessity is to be found.

The question we now have to address is precisely what this persuasion consists in, and how successful it is. One favored reading of Plato's cosmology makes the intransigence of matter, its resistance to intelligent persuasion, the cause of evil in the world.[51] I shall argue against any such read-

---

49. Johansen 2004, pp. 104–6, is arguably over-cautious in distancing the *Phaedo*'s necessary conditions from the *Timaeus*'s "auxiliary causes." In both contexts the main cause is intelligence, the second item the matter it uses. The one difference is that Socrates in the *Phaedo*, unlike Timaeus, denies the appropriateness of "cause" to the latter.

50. In the *Phaedo*, 99c6–102a1, Forms were recruited as an authentic kind of cause. This doctrine does not reappear in the *Timaeus*, where only the two above kinds of cause are listed. Either Plato has thought better of it, or he deems Forms irrelevant to the kind of causation with which physics is concerned.

51. This interpretation has a long history in ancient readings of Plato, and is very widely accepted among modern interpreters too; see e.g. Cornford 1937, pp. 161–77. My skepticism about it owes much to Lennox 1985a, and I also recommend Morrow 1950 as an excellent account of Timaean teleology which is refreshingly free of the interpretation. Its origin may well lie in the ancient tendency to assimilate Timaean matter to what in Plato's unwritten doctrines was called the Indefinite Dyad, since this latter apparently (cf. Aristotle, *Met.* 988a14–17) was already at an early

ing, but will conclude nonetheless that the *Timaeus* does indeed contain a theodicy—an explanation of why a good god permits bad things to happen.

There are, I think, considerable difficulties in defending a reading according to which matter to some extent successfully resists the Demiurge's persuasion. Would Plato's theology really allow that the best thing in the universe, god, might on occasion be defeated by the lowliest thing, matter? This is such an un-Platonic thought that very clear evidence would be needed before the point could safely be conceded. I believe that there is none.

Firstly, although in its initial contrast with intelligence "necessity" gives the impression of being *absolute* necessity (46e1–2), a mechanical transmission of forces sufficient all by itself to determine an outcome, it turns out that this is only what matter is like *in its own nature*—no doubt as manifested paradigmatically by the pre-cosmic chaos, where there was nothing to determine outcomes but the tendencies of matter. As we read on, we find that in the world ordered by intelligence material "necessity" becomes instead increasingly recognizable as *conditional* necessity—what Socrates in the *Phaedo* had already referred to as "that without which the cause [meaning here intelligence] could never be a cause" (p. 88 above).[52] Thus understood, the persuaded matter of the cosmos is no longer sufficient all by itself to determine outcomes. Instead, outcomes are chosen and attained by intelligence, and the matter that intelligence marshals for the purpose is no more than its "auxiliary cause" in achieving those ends (46c7–d1)—necessary *if* they are to be fulfilled. There is no reason to think that, under such intelligent persuasion, material necessity causes any unintended disruption. (For Aristotle's development of this same theme, see chapter VI §3 below.)

Secondly, according to Timaeus's creation myth, the creator started from a fluid kind of matter more or less devoid of determinate characteristics. Although it manifested fleeting traces of the four elements earth, air, fire, and water (52d2–53b5), these traces had no stable basis. The creator had in effect carte blanche as to how he would organize this stuff in building his cosmos,

---

date being understood as the principle of bad. The interpretation is more often assumed than defended (see e.g. Strange 1985 for a subtle attempt to explain how Necessity resists *nous*, without first demonstrating that it does). But for a rare exception see Reydams-Schils 2003, p. 12. Her argument 1 cites the many occurrences of βία, "force," in the *Timaeus*; but none of these seems to me to refer to force exerted by matter on *nous*. Her other three arguments are, I believe, adequately answered in what follows (for her argument 2, see n. 57 below).

52. Of the unambiguous references, listed in n. 48 above, to necessity in its technical sense, the final two (68e1–69a5, 75d5–e5) both explicitly make it conditional, with further confirmation offered by 70e5.

and there are few obvious ways in which the nature of his materials constrained him at this stage. Indeed, there seems to have been precisely one constraint, namely as I have already mentioned that he deemed it prudent to use up all the available matter, rather than leave any outside as a potential source of harm to his creation (32c5–33b1). That meant that the amount of matter to go into the world was fixed independently of his judgment. But no resultant disadvantage of this constraint is ever indicated by Timaeus, and I doubt if Plato intended one. Timaeus's postulation of preexisting matter, rather than of creation *ex nihilo*, not only reflects the time-honored axiom of Greek cosmology that creation out of nothing is a conceptual impossibility, but also conveniently explains why the Demiurge should have felt impelled to make a world in the first place, namely out of a desire to impose order on this disorderly stuff. The additional need for him to use *all* of the preexisting matter is, as we have already seen, in itself a manifestation of his beneficence, and not any kind of constraint, since he had virtual carte blanche in how he shaped it for his ends.

Again, although the Demiurge is said to have used up all the earth, all the air, all the fire, and all the water, we should not infer that he was saddled for better or worse with precise quantities of each not of his choosing, because, as we later learn, even after he had redesigned them on geometrical principles they remained intertransformable. True, he made earth an exception to this, but that was by his own choice, and it seems in any case likely that, in addition to whatever chaotic earth-stuff was already in the receptacle, he was free to impose the shape of earth particles upon just as much of the receptacle as he chose. Hence nothing appears to tie his hands in any detrimental way.

Having decided, for complex mathematical (or quasi-mathematical) reasons which I shall leave aside (31b4–32c4), that four is the correct number of elements, the creator had next to devise a structure for each of them. Why did he choose, for their constituent particles, four of the five perfect solids? I have mentioned Plato's aesthetic commitment to symmetry as inherently better than asymmetry, but we can infer a practical consideration as well. The more asymmetric the particles of fire, earth, water, and air were, the less dependable they would be when intelligence was using them to do its work. Assigning them four maximally symmetrical shapes was therefore the creator's way of on the one hand preserving the behavioral and causal differences among the four, while on the other hand making them as regular in their behavior as was possible.[53]

---

53. Why, then, did he not include spherical particles? Not having plane faces composed of triangles, spheres could not have been dismantled and rebuilt, as the four

According to the second principle of craftsmanship (p. 108 above), a crafts-man is an intelligent agent who, in order to guarantee himself systemati-cally good results, has mastered the nature of the matter he works on along with the causal processes that govern it. The divine craftsman fulfilled this specification by actually devising the nature of his materials in such a way as to maximize their regularity and causal dependability in achieving his goals. He can the more effectively direct matter's causal processes for hav-ing himself created them.

In what sense, then, has our creator been constrained by his materials? He made them exactly as he wanted them, for maximum dependability. But if so, why does Timaeus call matter "the wandering cause"? What he means by this is simply that matter, if left entirely to its own devices, would move in an utterly purposeless way.[54] Above all, this randomness is represented by the pre-cosmic chaos, before the creator had started the process of per-suading matter by endowing it with the regular geometrical shapes which brought order to it. Indeed, Timaeus's main point in describing the pre-cosmic chaos is undoubtedly to help us understand the benefits that intelligence has bestowed in imposing order, by describing what matter would be like even today *if* it were left entirely to its own devices (cf. 53a7–b5).

There is an apparent complication, however. At 48a3, we are told that intel-ligence *(nous)* persuaded necessity "to bring into the best state *the majority* of the things that undergo becoming." Does this not import a degree of fail-ure on the part of intelligence?[55] No. If, as Timaeus here implies,[56] some parts

---

elements were designed to be. If this were a reason for the exclusion, it would raise the further question why Plato thought the impermanence of elemental particles a desideratum. A more aesthetic reason, again no more than implicit in the text, is that the sphere, being the most complete and beautiful of all shapes (33b1–7), was reserved for the world itself, and derivatively (44d3–6) for the human head, our own best part, being too good to assign to mere particles of matter.

54. This does not imply causal indeterminacy: see Johansen 2004, pp. 93–95.

55. Curiously, I have not found this piece of evidence cited in favor of matter's recalcitrance by the commentators, presumably because they take Plato's adherence to the doctrine not to need arguing. Indeed, A. E. Taylor 1928, p. 303, is interested in the opposite question, why Plato expects us to agree that *as much as* half of all matter has been brought under rational control. Note however that Taylor (pp. 299–303, 491–92) has an idiosyncratic view of what Necessity amounts to: brute facts which *appear* to us not to serve a purpose.

56. This is a different point from two others often cited as manifesting the re-calcitrance of matter (cf. Zeyl 2000, p. liii): (a) the erratic motions of the pre-cosmic chaos (52d4–53a7), and (b) the motions which arise in the cosmos from the unequal sizes of the triangles (57d3–58a2). Of these, (a) is irrelevant to the degree of order in the cosmos, and (b) is the Demiurge's own free choice, presumably because the

of the elemental masses retain a degree of undependability even within the present world, there is no reason not to interpret even this as part of the plan.[57]

Take fire. When persuaded by intelligence, fire provides among other things the bodily matter of most of the gods (40a2–3), and the visual rays and illumination through which sight functions (45b2–46c6); and in these systematically beneficial roles, in which it functions as intelligence's "auxiliary cause" (*synaition*, 46c7–d1), it is anything but undependable. On the other hand, experience teaches us that—and this is surely the kind of thing that Timaeus is referring to when he leaves room for exceptions in intelligence's persuasion of matter—there is also unpersuaded or chaotic fire in our world, the sort that manifests itself in forest fires. Similar points might be made about earthquakes, floods, and tornadoes, each of them a manifestation of one of the other four elements when it gets out of control. But I see no sign that the leeway that permits these elements periodically to run riot was seen by Plato as a failing, oversight, or sign of laziness on the part of cosmic intelligence.

On the contrary, for reasons which are admittedly far from explicit, Plato, followed in this by his pupil Aristotle, became committed in his late work (the *Timaeus* included, see 22c1–e2) to the theory that civilizations are at long, astronomically determined intervals wiped out by cataclysms such as floods and conflagrations, being compelled each time to restart from scratch.[58] Civilization, that is, thanks to celestial regularities combined with

---

advantages of making the primary elements available in a variety of grades (e.g. to produce light as well as flame) outweigh the disadvantages.

57. I also take the opportunity here to discount another apparent piece of evidence (cf. Reydams-Schils 2003, p. 12). At 56c5–6 the mathematical arrangements of elemental particles are said to have been brought about by god ὅπηπερ ἡ τῆς ἀνάγκης ἑκοῦσα πεισθεῖσά τε φύσις ὑπεῖκεν, "in whatever way the nature of necessity yielded under willing persuasion." Here "in whatever way" need indicate no more than that god had to work with the predetermined necessities such as they were, e.g. (55d8–56a1) that among the regular solids the greatest stability is necessarily attained by the cube. Every translation I have consulted renders it with something like "*to the extent that* the nature of necessity yielded . . . ," which conveys the impression, unwarranted by the Greek, that the yielding was incomplete. (However, for an exegesis which then avoids that consequence cf. Brisson 1992, followed by Fronterotta 2003.)

58. For Aristotle there have been infinitely many rounds of the cycle (*DC* I 3, 270b16–25, to be read in conjunction with *Met.* Λ 8, 1074a38–b14), and the theory thus conveniently supports his thesis of the world's eternity by making it compatible with the evident fact that civilization is relatively young and still progressing. In case Plato's adherence to the cataclysm theory should be thought a sign that he too endorsed the world's eternity, contrary to what I have argued in §3, note that the *Ti.* account of cataclysms involves "many," not infinitely many, rounds of the

the residual unruliness of the world's constituent stuffs, has a life cycle comparable in this respect to the finite life cycles of individual organisms. And there is every probability that Plato regarded that cyclicity as beneficial.[59] For according to Critias's speech in the *Timaeus*, the newly created civilization of Athens nine thousand years ago was fully virtuous (23b3–d1), whereas *Laws* III portrays the advance of civilization as bringing with it an inevitable decline into vice, with the result that its periodic renewal due to cataclysms is a welcome restitution of the simple virtues (678a7–679e5). In all probability, then, the world's proneness to periodic cataclysms was seen as no design fault at all, but as yet another index of providential planning.[60] If the rationale of the cataclysm theory was never fully spelt out in writing by Plato, that is likely to be because of his failure ever to finish the *Timaeus-Critias*, whose missing later part might well have proved to be its natural context.

There is, then, no reason to suspect that Plato's Demiurge in any way fell short of achieving the best possible disposition of matter, let alone that matter itself was so resistant to persuasion as itself to limit his success. That is not to say that the world is perfect in every detail, but the important question is what *kind* of imperfections it contains and whether they were even in theory avoidable.

To take up a famous example from the *Timaeus*, the gods who created the human head made it more fragile than it ideally would have been. They could have cushioned our skulls with flesh as luxuriously as they did our thighs, but the gain in durability would have been outweighed by the loss of sensitivity (74e1–75c7).[61] Thanks to their skills, they were able to achieve a partial remedy to this defect by channelling certain residues outwards through the follicles to produce the protective thatch of hair, which provided a considerable measure of padding without diminishing sensitivity as a padding of flesh would have done (76b1–d3). The result was not perfect, but that they made the best possible decision is not left in doubt.

The world's design must, on a little reflection, be full of such compro-

---

cycle (23b3–6), and that in the case of the Athenians these were preceded by their original divine creation (23d4–e2). For further aspects of the cataclysm theory, see esp. Cambiano 2002.

59. Cf. Boys-Stones 2001, pp. 8–14, for a nuanced reading of Plato on primitive man.

60. Cf. *Ti.* 22d7, "When the gods purify the earth by flooding it with water . . . "

61. Aristotle, *PA* II 10, 656a14–27, rejects this explanation, instead attributing the skull's lack of padding to the brain's need for efficient cooling. His explanation is anatomically more correct, but arises from his incorrect belief that the brain's function is cooling, not cognitive control.

mises. But it seems odd, and unsupported by the text, to attribute these to the intransigence of matter. Quite regardless of the compliance or otherwise of matter, *any* rational craftsman has to choose between competing advantages and disadvantages. Suppose, for example, that there had been some advantages to making the head square. If that had been so, the reasons for sacrificing these advantages for the advantages of a round head would have had nothing to do with the nature of matter, just with the impossibility of making something simultaneously round and square, and the consequent need to select whatever shape was, all things considered, the more beneficial. Similarly in the case of the head, the combination of durability and sensitivity is said to be impossible to achieve, not in matter as such, but in living tissue, which has to be subject to generation and growth.[62] Whatever reasons Timaeus may have in mind for this claim, he is presenting the restriction as one caused by the demands of biology, not the nature of matter.

There is one further kind of badness in the world of which Timaeus is deeply conscious: moral badness or vice, exhibited in human beings *par excellence*. We therefore must ask how Plato accounts for its inclusion in the world plan, and whether he regards this, at least, as a failure of the divine creation. Why indeed did there have to be human beings at all?

The initial motive for the creation of human beings is a metaphysical one (39e3–40a2, 41b7–d3). The generic Form of Animal on which the world was modelled contains within itself four subgenera, those of the animals associated with respectively fire (the celestial gods), air, water, and earth; and under each of these three lower kinds fall all the individual avian, aquatic, and terrestrial species. If the world itself had not analogously been made to contain animals of all these innumerable species, it would have failed to embody its model, the genus of Animal, as closely as it might have done, and thus been avoidably incomplete. This was why after creating the fiery stargods the Demiurge assigned them the task of constructing all the remaining animals. (If we think of the preexisting Forms of animal species as including all *possible* animals,[63] then in looking to the Forms the Demiurge was creating, within the terms of Platonic metaphysics, the same comprehensive biodiversity as Empedocles' Love had attained by experimental

---

62. 75a7–b2; see n. 48 above for the correct construal of 75a7–b1.
63. At *Ti.* 39e7–40a2 the Demiurge's instructions single out animal kinds only down to the four genera of dwellers in fire, air, water, and earth. But at 30c6–d1 it has already been made clear that these genera divide up into individual species Forms, and that the world's completeness depends on its including *all* of these latter.

means when she combined body parts in all possible permutations to find out which would survive.)[64]

The lesser gods' instructions were that these lower animals, the inhabitants of air, water, and earth, were to be ordered hierarchically. The structural principle underlying the entire animal kingdom was to be (42b2–d2) that transmigrating immortal souls would inhabit one species after another in a systematic order, starting with incarnation in man, after which they might be demoted or promoted according to the quality of the lives they had led. The first demotion from man is to woman, and from there on down to an appropriate beast. Promotions can bring a soul back up to the level of woman or man, or even, if it has led a truly philosophical life, beyond the cycle of incarnations to dwell perpetually in its own assigned star.

We may say then that on the one hand the requirement that the world be the best and most complete possible embodiment of its model demanded its inclusion of a comprehensive animal kingdom, and on the other hand the Demiurge's supreme capacity for intelligent design led to this creation's being put to the best possible use, the graded improvement of rational souls. While individual souls must necessarily suffer, the overall hierarchical structure within which they are punished and rewarded is in Plato's eyes not the Demiurge's partial remedy for previous shortcomings of his creation, but in itself an ideally good one. The presence of moral badness and unhappiness in individuals is not a mark of the world's imperfection, provided that those defects play a necessary part in the bigger picture of cosmic justice.

To understand how a thinker like Plato could thus hold the world to be a better place for containing imperfect beings, we have to start from the supreme importance he attaches to completeness as an intrinsic value. Indeed, the semantics of the word for "complete," *teleios*, make it indissoluble from the overlapping notion of "perfect." God could, had he so chosen, have interpreted the notion of perfection more narrowly and limited his creation to the best beings. The price would have been to build an intelligent but unoccupied world. It would be like setting out to build the perfect zoo, and as a result deciding that no animal is good enough to live in it. Plato's (and,

---

64. See p. 61 above. There is at least one significant difference. Love's experiment eliminated some animals—those without adequate self-defense, for example—that may have been intrinsically viable but could not coexist with the remainder of the animal kingdom. The Platonic creators appear to operate with no equivalent filter. If Plato has even thought about this difference between possible and compossible animals, he shows no sign of concluding that some species may have been left uninstantiated, and is more likely to regard the preexisting species Forms as already limited to kinds capable of coexistence.

he hopes, god's) notion of completeness or perfection is better satisfied by a world containing the entire natural hierarchy, especially when that hierarchy is itself used as the primary conduit of moral value.

Nevertheless, the question of god's own relation to cosmic evil has by now become acute. On the one hand the world must contain inferior animals, and souls sufficiently degraded to occupy them. On the other, the creator is essentially good and can therefore be the cause only of good things—a causal principle of like causing like to which Plato had persistently held.[65] Hence, although the Demiurge himself, being good, is the cause of the good overall world-order and of many of its constituents, he has to avoid being the cause of individual badness (42d3–4). And individual badness, or vice, will occur exclusively in the animal kingdom—paradigmatically in humans, and derivatively in the lower creatures into which corrupted souls will transmigrate. Thus although he creates the rational souls that are to inhabit human and other animal bodies, the Demiurge cannot take on the further task of their incarnation, that being the source of all the vices they will acquire. It is for this reason that he delegates the task of creating human beings to the lesser gods that he has himself created.[66]

It is possible to feel at this point that Plato's creator has an excessively comfortable moral position, reserving the best jobs for himself, while passing on the dirty work to his subordinates. But the reasons for the division of labor spring from Plato's causal theory, and the uneasy compromise that results does at least help bring out the complex status of cosmic evil in Plato's eyes. On the one hand the existence of vice and suffering, as alternatives to virtue and happiness, is part of an overall ideally good design, but on the

---

65. This principle, for which see Sedley 1998b and p. 178 below (cf. also Makin 1990–91), systematically features in the *Timaeus* as a virtually analytic one, yet is accompanied by synthetic-sounding explications. At 29d7–30b6 the creator, being good, was inevitably going to make the world a good one (to Plato a near-truism; cf. Sedley 1998b), yet this is further explained in terms of his goodness entailing ungrudgingness (29e2), which in turn meant that he would not begrudge his product all the goodness it could get. At 41a7–d3 the creator, being intrinsically immortal, for metaphysical reasons cannot help making his products (contingently) immortal, yet this is also explained in terms of motivation: a good creator would not want to destroy his product when he did not have to. Such explanatory overdetermination is an endemic feature of the *Timaeus*; cf. p. 112 above.

66. We must take it that these, although also good, are contingently rather than essentially good. By analogy with the principle which allows them, because only contingently immortal, to create mortal beings, this is what makes it metaphysically possible for them to create beings who will turn out bad. But even then the primary responsibility for actually becoming bad lies with the human beings themselves (42e3–4).

other hand that does not in itself suffice to make these states good ones. Neither the cosmic nor the personal perspective can be altogether eliminated in favor of the other, and local evil is an integral constituent of overall good.

Human beings play an absolutely pivotal role in the hierarchy of life. For it is uniquely when it reaches human embodiment that the rational soul becomes capable of attaining the purification that can, at least ideally, lead on to its release from incarnation and attainment of discarnate bliss. Both the human body and the world around us have been so constructed as to make this possible, and it is scarcely an exaggeration to say that the entire teleological structure of nature converges on this single purpose. Let me develop the point.

Take once more (cf. pp. 52–54, 81 above) the creationist's prize exhibit, the human eye. Although Timaeus has disappointingly little to say about the internal structure of the eye, he has something both eloquent and surprising to tell us about why human beings have eyes at all (46e6–47c4). It is not, as you or I might have thought, to serve such practical purposes as the pursuit of food and the avoidance of hazards. These are trivial and subordinate functions of eyesight compared with the supreme benefit it bestows, which can be explained as follows.

To create the world soul, the Demiurge first mixed up the stuff of rational soul, then shaped it into a pair of celestial circles, divided up into harmonic intervals. The eternally rotating divine world soul was thus formed, and this god's complex revolutions are quite literally its processes of thought.[67] By making the stars fiery the Demiurge has benevolently illuminated those revolutions, so as to render them directly visible to human observers.[68] We have thus been enabled through the study of mathematical astronomy to understand, and to internalize as our own thoughts, the motions that constitute divine intelligence. To master the mathematics of the celestial rotations is literally to think god's thoughts, and is the gateway both to philosophy and to true happiness. To achieve this is however no simple task, because rational souls have since their first incarnation in our heads been bombarded through the sense organs with input which disrupts their naturally circular motions (42e6–44c4). This is Plato's way of explaining, from the point of view of physics, his classic doctrine that re-

---

67. See Sedley 1999b for the literally locomotive reading of the "rotations" of thought.
68. The teleological point is made fully explicit only with regard to the sun's powers of illumination, 39b2–c1, but cf. 40a2–4, where all the heavenly bodies were likewise made of fire for the sake of their visibility (as well as beauty).

liance on the senses is normally detrimental to the operations of pure thought: the senses physically disrupt the circular motions of rational thought. Astronomy is however the sensory bridge which if properly crossed can lead the rational soul back to its naturally circular motions of pure rationality. And both the heavens and human beings have been so structured as to make this transition a possible one.

In insisting that the eye is for astronomy, Plato is revealing the distinctive nature of his hierarchical teleology. Each thing's purpose is the *highest* good whose attainment it facilitates.[69] What applies here to eyes applies equally, in the immediate sequel, to ears too. These, by enabling us both to engage in spoken argument and to study harmonics, likewise confer on human beings the means of developing their philosophical capabilities.[70]

It would be easy to extend this principle of teleological explanation[71] to other features of our bodies and the world. Even lower animals, after all, have the function of rewarding and punishing the souls that transmigrate into them, with a view to those souls' eventual attainment of intellectual purification in a human life. Similarly, since the human body has in its entirety been designed to support the housing of the rational soul in its head (44d3–8), it seems that even our mundane biological functions, whose design and construction are explained in minute detail in the *Timaeus* (69a6–81e5), are conceived by Plato as ultimately for the sake of maintaining the rational soul's incarnate residence.[72] That residence is itself designed to last long enough, at least ideally, to enable the rational soul to master philosophy, yet within the confines of a mortal life span that at a suitable point will release it to move on to its next residence in the hierarchy.

This is a good moment to remind ourselves of the *Phaedo* myth. There, as I pointed out earlier (p. 95), it is implied that the direct beneficiary of a good cosmic arrangement is the soul. First implicitly in the *Phaedo* myth, then explicitly in the *Timaeus*, the world has been structured to provide

---

69. See e.g. Burnyeat 1999, p. 246 n. 63; Johansen 2004, p. 108.

70. Cf. also 75e3–5, where similar value is attributed to speech.

71. For Plato's application of this principle to the function of names in the *Cratylus*, cf. Sedley 2003a, p. 62.

72. At 71a3–72d3, the liver's purpose is to enable even our irrational nature, through divination, to attain some truth. Here the attainment of truth may be being treated as an intrinsic value independently of any good passed on to the rational soul, but there is no need to assume any such restriction, since in various other dialogues Plato regards divinatory communication with the divine as morally valuable, including Socrates' use of his divine sign. Cf. pp. 232–33 below for a plausible Stoic interpretation of Plato's *Crito* which makes Socrates' use of divination pivotal to his moral probity.

souls, through a system of punishments and rewards, with the possibility of self-purification, divinization, and eternal discarnate bliss. Plato's world is not anthropocentric but, as we might rather say, psychocentric. This persistent theme highlights the continuity that extends through a significant part of Plato's career, starting from the *Phaedo*'s cautious progression beyond Socrates' negative response to physics, and culminating in Plato's own eventual full-scale redesign and rehabilitation of that same discipline.

I earlier asked, why did there have to be human beings at all? Timaeus's answer can now be summarized as follows. For metaphysical reasons of completeness the world had to include a comprehensive animal kingdom, humans included. To structure this for the systematic improvement of souls was a beneficent decision on the creator's part. The price which the Demiurge knowingly paid for that structure was the creation of beings prone to moral and intellectual badness (42d2–5)—a result achieved, according to Timaeus, by using less pure ingredients for their souls than he had previously mixed together in making the world soul,[73] and incarnating them into appropriately unruly bodies. Evidently, once the zoological hierarchy had been planned, the rational souls inserted into it *had* to be impure ones, or they would have immediately qualified for release from incarnation and return to their own stars. Importantly though, their degree of impurity was not so great as to make their eventual purification and release an unrealistic aspiration.

We can now finally return to the question, did Plato's creator devise and build a perfect world? Admittedly in one sense the answer must be no. For it is fundamental to Plato's metaphysics that all generated objects are mere copies of Forms, and that no copy can ever fully match its original. This is partly for reasons which have now become clearer. All attempts by a craftsman to realize a Form in matter—whether the product be a table or a world—will involve compromises, well exemplified by the way that skull design had to put sensitivity before durability. Undoubtedly the need to create impure

---

73. At 41d6–7, "mixing them to some extent in the same way, but no longer with the same degree or kind of purity, but producing second- and third-rate specimens," it is unclear whether "the same" means both times "the same as when he was making the world soul" (as standardly understood), or "the same as each other." I prefer the latter, which could be taken to hint that *three* grades of human rational soul were produced (the inclusion of first-rate ones being implicit): that would map satisfyingly onto the tripartition of classes in *Republic*, on the reasonable assumption that the higher the grade of rational soul the better the balance of the whole soul. Be that as it may, the main reason for including inferior souls was, rather than human diversity as such, to ensure that there would be no shortage of demotions, so as to keep the lower ranks of the animal kingdom supplied with souls.

souls was as regrettable a part of the overall design as the need to make skulls fragile. Both, nevertheless, were the best of all the competing options, and both contributed to making ours the best physical world that could possibly have been created. In this latter sense Plato's world is indeed perfect.

6. THE ORIGIN OF SPECIES

We have already seen the reason for the existence of the entire animal kingdom: the world is a better creation for being the most complete possible copy of its model. That model, being the genus Animal, contains within itself all— that is, I have suggested, all *possible*—animal species. The nearest the created world could come to mimicking this structure was by containing within itself instantiations of all those same species. They include both gods, which are immortal fiery animals, and the mortal species associated with air, earth, and water.[74]

If there were already eternal Forms of all these species, the Form of Man included, how much credit is due to their divine creators? Did they have to do any more than mechanically copy a preexisting blueprint? It seems that they did. The creation of the human body, described in minute detail at 69a6–81e5, is presented throughout as displaying a series of brilliant engineering decisions. The temptation to think otherwise arises only if we misunderstand what a Form is. The Form of a table is neither a table nor a diagram or set of instructions for making a table, but rather the ideal *function* of a table, which it is left to the carpenter to embody in the materials at his disposal in whatever way he judges best. Likewise the Form of Man, to which the creator gods undoubtedly looked,[75] should be assumed to specify no more than the function of man: very approximately, that the function of man is to accommodate a rational soul for a suitable number of years in conditions

74. The lower "animals" also include plants, which according to Timaeus are immobile animals. Unlike the beasts, plants have been created, not to house fallen rational souls, but for our utility (76e7–77b1, cf. 41d1–3). On the justification for classing plants as animals, see n. 36 above. I suspect Plato's real motivation for this taxonomic decision to arise from his thesis that the world is modelled on the Form of Animal. If animals and plants were coordinate members of a yet higher genus, it would become unclear why the Demiurge did not model the world on that instead.

75. They must have looked to an eternal Form as their model, since the alternative of looking to a generated model is uncraftsmanlike (28a6–b2). Moreover, it is only by assuming an eternal model that we can absolve them of the faulty workmanship otherwise implied by their copying a created entity when, at 44d3–4, they model the human head on the shape of the (created) world (cf. Burnyeat 2005, p. 158). And it is hard to see *what* Form they could be looking to if not Man, given that there is such a Form.

where it is able to develop and exploit its innate intellectual capacities. All the gods' decisions about how to achieve this—such as locating the rational soul in a spherical head, perched on top of a body equipped with arms, legs, and all the faculties necessary for its transport and survival, but so far as possible insulated by the narrow neck from the harmful influence of the bodily appetites—all these are practical solutions devised in the course of applying their craft. *Mutatis mutandis*, the same kind of craftsmanship will recur in their design of the lower species, to which I now turn.

Most of Timaeus's account of anatomy is admittedly devoted to the human body. But this emphasis partly reflects his assumption that the animal kingdom is to be understood hierarchically from the top down.[76] Plato recognizes, not unlike modern evolutionary theory, that species have not arisen independently but one out of another. He differs, however, in taking that process to have been one of devolution, not evolution. As the rational souls degenerated intellectually and morally, the prototype human body that the gods had designed was progressively refashioned so as to adapt it to its degraded occupants (90e1–92c3): first the female body (90e6–91d5), followed by birds (91d6–e1), footed beasts (91e2–92a4), snakes (92a4–7), and finally fish and shellfish (92a7–c1).

Here, once human incarnation has been left behind, the subsequent incarnations follow a principle of stratification already exploited in the *Phaedo* myth (§1 above). The more unphilosophical the soul, the lower the geographical location to which it is assigned. Thus snakes are lower than quadrupeds, fish lower even than snakes. Along with these appropriate relocations, the head is reshaped from round to elongated, to mirror the fact that the rational soul housed in it is no longer, in this subhuman condition, undergoing its natural circular revolutions of reasoning (91e2–92a2). Instead, these beasts are driven by the irrational soul alone.

The pattern described here is a mirror image of Platonic teleology, discussed earlier (pp. 125–26). Just as the purpose of virtually everything in creation turned out to be that of enabling rational souls to progress, through the study of astronomy, to philosophy, so too the criterion for demotion to the lower reaches of the animal kingdom now proves to lie in a failure to pursue these very same disciplines. Those who have practiced astronomy but in an entirely unphilosophical spirit become birds (more on this below), while those who have abstained altogether from the pursuit of astronomy and philosophy become quadrupeds (91e2–92a4), or worse.

76. For what follows, and the relation of Plato's zoogony to both its predecessors and its successors, cf. esp. the enlightening study of Campbell 2000.

Is this science or fable? No clear cut answer is forthcoming. Here, in his speech's closing crescendo, Timaeus is playing games with his subject matter, constantly crossing and recrossing familiar generic boundaries.

It is hard to mistake a light-hearted element of aetiological fable. The most obvious case of this is the explanation of birds (91d6–e1):

> The race of birds, growing feathers instead of hair, was metamorphosed out of harmless but lightweight men: they were students of things in the heaven who, however, out of naïveté thought the firmest proofs concerning this subject to be achieved through eyesight.

In this Just So story, a highly Platonic one in its detail, we encounter a case of wittily appropriate punishment. It resembles the equally amusing idea in the *Phaedo* (81d6–82b9, not, incidentally, part of the relatively theorized closing myth) that for example tyrants will be reborn as wolves, while people who have lived virtuously by habituation rather than understanding will come back as ants or bees. But for present purposes the motif has been adapted to a dominant theme of the *Timaeus* (pp. 124–25 above), that astronomy, practiced according to the *Republic*'s recommendations (VII 530a4–c2) as a branch of higher mathematics rather than as an empirical discipline, is the privileged route to philosophical enlightenment. The joke is that those Presocratic-type thinkers who have concentrated instead on celestial phenomena (not unlike the heaven-watching "Socrates" mischievously portrayed in Aristophanes' *Clouds* as suspended high up in a basket) will be rewarded by reincarnation as birds: they can fly up to take a closer look, and see what good it does them!

The light-heartedness of this exquisite image seems to be strengthened by its lack of fit with the immediate context: if birds' natural habitat is higher than ours, how can they represent demotion from a human incarnation? But one of the most important lessons to learn from the *Timaeus* is that the presence of humor does not entail the absence of seriousness.[77] The detail that birds have exchanged hair for feathers signals one of the important con-

---

77. This is why I am reluctant to go along with the arguments of Steel 2001 for a reading of the physiology at 69c5–73a8 as comic and *therefore* nonscientific in intention. Take Timaeus's explanation (72e2–73a8) of the windings of the lower gut as designed to save us from extinction through gluttony. Steel remarks (p. 119): "No scholar will deny the ironical character of this remark on the moral finality of the bowels. But why should the previous sections be taken more seriously?" Whatever humor we may sense in the passage, it cannot for this reason be dismissed as nonserious, for its entirely straight-faced and scientific descendant in Aristotle, *PA* III 14, 675a31–b28, includes the following (675b22–28): "Hence those animals that need to be more temperate (σωφρονέστερα) about feeding do not have much space in their lower gut, but many convolutions, and are not straight-gutted. For spaciousness

tributions of the *Timaeus* to biological theory. Empedocles had already introduced the notion that hair, feathers, and scales are functionally equivalent (p. 4 above), but what Plato adds is the idea of hair *becoming* feathers in the course of evolution—or, more strictly in his case, devolution.

The prize example of this is human fingernails and toenails. In familiar theories of progressive evolution these have typically come to be seen as vestigial claws, which, whatever their residual utility may be, no longer serve the vital locomotive and defensive functions they did in the species that originally developed them. Plato's devolutionary theory shares the underlying insight of this, but stands it on its head. Thus earlier, in his account of the gods' original design of the human body, we read the following highly theorized explanation of nails' origin (76d3–e4):

> The triple mixture of sinew, skin, and bone in the plaiting that occurred at the ends of the fingers and toes has dried into a single combined hard skin. These were the auxiliary causes by which it was crafted. But the main cause, the thought with which they have been manufactured, is for the sake of future beings. For those who constructed us knew that women and the beasts would be produced from men, and were aware too that for many purposes many creatures would need the use of claws. Hence right at the time of creating human beings they built in a matrix for the production of claws.

If beasts are descended from humans and not vice versa, then what we today think of as more or less obsolete features, only vestigially remaining in man and therefore evidence *against* our having been directly created, must, on the contrary, have originated in man as markers for future developments,[78] and therefore be signs of divine foresight.

How the degeneration proceeded is well illustrated with regard to the creation of animals with four or more legs, and altogether legless reptiles (91e6–92a7):

> As a result of these [unphilosophical] pursuits, they leant their front limbs and their heads down towards the ground, drawn there by their kinship to it, and acquired heads which were oblong and all kinds of other shapes, corresponding to the way in which each one's revolutions [of thought] had been squashed flat through inactivity. This is the cause of their kind's being

---

produces an appetite for a large quantity of food, and straightness speeds up the appetite. That is the reason why those animals with simple or spacious receptacles are gluttonous, some of them regarding quantity, others regarding speed."

78. This applies more readily to toenails. As regards fingernails, Galen, *UP* III 16.7–17 rebukes Plato for grossly underestimating their utility in this passage, and Aristotle (*PA* 687b21–24) for treating them as no more than protection for the fingertips.

made four-footed—and many-footed too, because under those who were more mindless god placed a larger number of feet, so that they should all the more creep along the ground. And for the most mindless even of these, which spread out their entire body on the ground because they no longer found any use for feet, these they created as footless creatures slithering along the ground.

This has obvious affinities with the genre of aetiological fable. Although it inevitably reminds us of the serpent's punishment in Genesis, a closer affinity is with the later, highly articulated aetiologies in Ovid's *Metamorphoses*, where the origin of a species is repeatedly tied to the story of a mythical man or woman, assigned an appropriate form as a divinely imposed penalty—such as the origin of the spider in Arachne, metamorphosed for competing with Athena at weaving (VI 1–145). The main elements for such an aetiology were already familiar to Plato before the date of the *Timaeus*, for example in Empedocles' story of the daimon whose punishment is to be reincarnated as all manner of creatures, in Plato's own eschatological myths of rebirth as a morally appropriate animal,[79] and in his earlier story, put into the mouth of Aristophanes in the *Symposium* (p. 55 above), of the origin of men and women in Zeus's punitive modifications to an earlier biological archetype.

One might well think the change of register here to signal a deliberate departure from scientific discourse on Plato's part. But a powerful antidote to that reaction is to read the following remarkably similar passage from Aristotle's *On parts of animals* (IV 10, 686a24–b2):

Animals' front limbs and chest are adjacent to their neck and head. Man, instead of the front legs and feet, has arms and the so-called hands. For he alone of the animals is upright, because his nature and essence are divine. The function of what is most divine is thought and understanding, and this is not easy if the upper body is large and pressing downwards, since the weight obstructs the movement of the intellect and of the common sensorium. This is why bodies, when they get too heavy and corporeal, are forced to lean down towards the ground, with the result that, for their protection, nature has placed the front feet under quadrupeds instead of arms and hands. Two hind legs are a necessity for all walking creatures, and such creatures became quadrupeds in cases where their soul could not carry the weight.

This differs in some ways from Plato's zoogony. Reduced intellectual activity is here an integral aspect, not the antecedent cause, of biological de-

---

79. In addition to the *Phaedo*, cited above p. 129, note the *Republic* myth, 620a2–d5, where souls often choose an appropriate animal for their next incarnation.

generacy. And the physiology has been altered to accommodate Aristotle's belief that the seat of thought is in the chest, not in the head as Plato held.[80] Still, the thematic continuity between the two is remarkable. In talking as if humans at some past time degenerated into quadrupeds Aristotle is himself speaking the language of fable, and not expressing the literal belief that these species had a temporal origin;[81] but there can be no doubt that he considers such talk in terms of devolution from the human paradigm to be a scientifically useful way of mapping the natural hierarchy.[82] In doing so, he is according a corresponding scientific seriousness to the passage of the *Timaeus* that has so palpably influenced him here—the passage which above almost all others in this dialogue might have seemed to us no more than playful.

In another way too, Timaeus's zoogony can claim to be more science than myth. Being as it is an eschatology located at the very end of Timaeus's speech, it discharges a function analogous to that of the great eschatological myths, concerning souls' punishment and redemption, that close the *Gorgias, Phaedo,* and *Republic.* Viewed in that light, it is a *scientific* counterpart to the familiar myths, locating afterlife punishment not in a mythical other world, but in the natural kingdom itself.[83]

Timaeus's creation story is a myth, but one subject to constant shifts of register and even of genre. This often leaves his exposition without a determinate cash value in terms of literal truth-claims. Nevertheless, a finding that has repeatedly emerged from the foregoing chapter is that the greatest risks arise from underestimating the serious content of his discourse. Even at its most mythical or its most comic, it is a profound guide to Plato's own views on the world's teleological origin, purpose, and structure.

80. The differences between Plato's and Aristotle's accounts are illuminatingly explored by Gregoric 2005.

81. See the full discussion of this passage and its relation to Aristotle's biology in Lennox 2001b, pp. 317–18.

82. For Aristotle's "anthropocentric" perspective on the natural hierarchy, see Clark 1975, II 2; Lloyd 1983, pp. 26–43. Another affinity with a (supposed) science lies in the resemblance to physiognomic theory, in which beast-like bodily features were interpreted systematically as symptomatic of the corresponding states of character. But this affinity is no greater than that with Aesopic fable, which used animal species to represent human character types. Cf. esp. Sassi 1988 chapter 2.

83. Cf. Saunders 1973.

V   The Atomists

1. DEMOCRITUS

So far in our story the creationists have made all the running, culminating in Plato's *Timaeus*, the ultimate creationist manifesto. Even if one faction of Plato's heirs insisted that he had never meant to say that a discrete act of divine creation had ever taken place, this dialogue's impact on such thinkers as Aristotle, Epicurus, the Stoics, and Galen, with whom my remaining chapters will be mainly concerned, was never diluted or mediated by any such interpretative ploy. They all regarded it as creationist in the literal sense— that is, as describing the world's origin in an intelligent creative act. And they responded accordingly.

In this chapter I turn to the atomist tradition. Epicurus (341–271 B.C.) is for us its most prominent representative, and he was writing at a date when the *Timaeus*, scarcely a generation old, was dominating discussions. But our story must start a century earlier, with the founders of atomism, Leucippus and Democritus. They were among the truly seminal philosophers working at the end of the Presocratic era in the late fifth century B.C. Although Leucippus, the older of the two, is credited with founding the movement, it is Democritus, a much more voluminous and influential writer, who will be our focus here.

Early in chapter I, I advertised atomism as the first Presocratic philosophy to eliminate intelligent causation at the primary level. Instead of making intelligence either an irreducible feature of matter, or, with Anaxagoras, a discrete power acting upon matter, early Greek atomism treats atoms and void alone as the primary realities, and relegates intelligence to a secondary status: intelligence, along with color, flavor, and innumerable other attributes, is among the properties that supervene on complex structures of atoms and void. The atoms themselves are inanimate particles and the void their negative counterpart, possessing only material properties such as size, shape, location, and density. Once atoms have formed a world and its contents, intelligent organisms may well be generated out of these. But it is inconceivable that any world might itself be the product of a *preexisting* intelligence. It should be obvious that the fundamental pattern of causality envisaged here is one which can find innumerable proponents and sympathizers today.

In the hands of Democritus's eventual heir Epicurus, atomism was to become a vital weapon against divine creation, as we shall shortly see. Belief in divine creation brings with it, according to Epicurus, intolerable religious consequences, compelling us to assume that our own lives are under divine surveillance, and to live in terror of the threats this poses. To recognize the truth of atomism, in Epicurus's eyes, has the incalculable merit of freeing us from those consequences by permitting us to account for the world and its contents as the products of mere accident, freed from the specter of divine control.

But was early atomism in its original context, at the end of the fifth century B.C., already motivated by such religious concerns? The chronology would make the hypothesis inherently credible. As emerged in my first three chapters, by the late fifth century there were in the public arena not only the scientific brands of creationism developed by Anaxagoras and Empedocles, but also, more pertinently, the anti-scientific creationism of Socrates, aimed precisely at confirming mankind's utter indebtedness to divinity and the religious obligations imposed by that recognition. The emergence of atomist materialism would make immediate sense as a response to this Socratic theology.

But it is remarkably hard to unearth evidence for any such story.[1] One obstacle to it is that Democritus himself apparently did, within the constraints of his atomism, admit a role for divine beings prone to harm as well as to benefit us, and was later duly criticized by the Epicureans for making the concession.[2] Nor is there any particular reason to assume that Democritus— let alone his predecessor Leucippus—was familiar with the radical ideas of his contemporary Socrates. Socrates published nothing. True, Socrates had a high public profile on the streets of Athens as a philosophical disputant, but

1. Nor is 68 B 5 DK, the story of Democritus's hostility to Anaxagoras over "the cosmic ordering and *nous*," in itself evidence that this disagreement had a specifically religious motivation.

2. See C. C. W. Taylor 1999, pp. 211–16.

Democritus did not spend a significant amount of time at Athens ("I came to Athens and nobody knew me," he was said to have remarked),[3] and the anecdotal tradition maintains that the two never met.[4] Moreover, Socrates himself can be seen in the pages of Xenophon reacting *against* those who deny any divine origin for the world, and partly for this reason I suggested in chapter III (pp. 86, 90 above) that the sequence of cause and effect was in fact the other way round—that the destabilizing influence of Leucippus's atomism was already being felt early enough to have helped shape Socrates' own theology by way of reaction.

It will be safer, then, to think of atomism as motivated by fundamentally nontheological considerations. What were these? Almost certainly the same broad set of considerations as I have suggested prompted the work of Anaxagoras. The great monist Parmenides had argued for the total unity of being, and thus against the reality of the differentiated and changing world we appear to inhabit. In the second half of his poem he had explained that the minimum condition for vindicating the familiar world is to forsake monism for dualism. Somehow—impossibly in his view—there would have to be at least two entities, whose intermixture or interaction would generate change and plurality. Anaxagoras, I suggested in chapter I (p. 11 above), met this challenge by separating *nous*—thought, mind, or intelligence— from the rest of being, and taking mind's action on the raw materials from which it thus stands apart to be what differentiates the latter into a structured world. The atomists, similarly, separated being from a second item, but that second item in their case was "not-being." Where Parmenides had sought to outlaw not-being as a self-contradictory notion, the atomists rehabilitated it by identifying it with void or vacuum.[5] Thus their dualism of being and not-being is a dualism of body and void. Bodies are separated from each other by the intervening void gaps, but since these same bodies themselves contain no void they are atomic particles—incapable of division or other changes, being solid through and through.

Given only the assumption that this stock of atoms is infinite and that they vary sufficiently in shape and size, their mechanical combination into complex structures is all that is required to account for the entire phenomenal world. Thus the truly great claim to fame of early atomism is its explanatory economy. An entire cosmology can be constructed simply by positing two

3. 68 B 116 DK.
4. DL IX 36.
5. How they may have argued for the coherence of their thesis that "there *is* not-being" is discussed in Sedley 1982.

grades of being instead of Parmenides' one. And it is that same concern for economy, we may surmise, that motivates Democritus's austerity about atoms' properties. There is simply no need for atoms to be colored, for example, because the perception of color is adequately explained by appeal to effluences of colorless atoms acting in a certain way on our (likewise atomically composed) eyes and minds. Similarly, there is no need for the atoms and void to be intelligent, because intelligence is adequately explained as a pattern of motion in the complex atomic structure we call a mind or soul. It appears to have been for the sake of explanatory economy, and not out of any anti-religious motivation as such, that atoms and void were shorn of all properties beyond those ineliminably and irreducibly possessed by body *qua* body.

Nevertheless, even if the motivation was not theological, the consequences inevitably were. Since no underlying intelligence is available to organize the atoms,[6] they must be self-organizing. And so they can well be: even obviously inanimate particles, the atomists pointed out, such as pebbles on a beach, have some inherent tendency to group themselves by size and shape, so why not atoms too?[7]

But such primitive self-organization falls immeasurably short of accounting for a magnificently beneficial structure like our world, with its complex life-supporting ecology. Even less does it begin to make it plausible that atoms spontaneously formed themselves into intricately structured organisms like ourselves.

It is here that infinity comes into play. The atomist universe is infinite, consisting of infinite void housing an infinite number of atoms. That in turn means that worlds must form not only where we are but elsewhere too: there could be no explanation of how in infinite space just one region, or even a merely finite plurality of regions, had been specially privileged in this regard. Not only, therefore, is there a plurality of worlds, but the same calculation yields the result that there are infinitely many of them.[8]

---

6. Cf. 68 A 39 DK, Δημόκριτος ὁ Ἀβδηρίτης ὑπεστήσατο τὸ πᾶν ἄπειρον διὰ τὸ μηδαμῶς ὑπό τινος αὐτὸ δεδημιουργῆσθαι, "Democritus of Abdera laid it down that the universe is infinite because it has in no way been crafted by anyone." Our interest here is in the closing explanatory clause, but why is it deemed a ground for the infinity of the universe? I take this to be a version of Melissus 30 B 2 DK, read (cf. Sedley 1999c, pp. 126–27) as follows: if the universe had been generated, it would have to be finite, because any process of generation has to start somewhere and end somewhere; but since it is ungenerated, there is nothing to block the standard Ionian default assumption of its infinite extent.

7. Sextus Empiricus *M* VII 116–18 = 68 B 164 DK = C. C. W. Taylor 1999, D6.

8. See e.g. Philoponus, *In Ar. Phys.* 405.23–27 = C. C. W. Taylor 1999, test. 80d.

But what are these other worlds like? Despite the self-organizing properties of atoms, and also the powers of the vortex, widely agreed to play a key part in cosmic formation,[9] there is such a vast range of shapes and sizes of atoms that the worlds randomly formed out of collections of these will differ dramatically. Some worlds, Democritus predicted, will have no sun or moon, others more than one of each. Some will support no life, and even lack water. And so on. Such accidental variation is inevitable across worlds, in view of their largely random process of formation.[10] This looks like a direct denial of Anaxagoras's confident prediction (chapter I §6 above), based on what can be expected of a world-creating intelligence, that each other world will have one sun and one moon, and will sustain life, just as ours does.

Nevertheless, the fact that there are *infinitely many* worlds ensures that every permutation is to be found somewhere in the universe, Democritus held. Although this last doctrine is not recorded explicitly, it must be what underlies a rarely discussed report in Cicero (*Academica* II 55):

> Democritus, you say, claims that there are infinitely many worlds, some of them not only similar to each other but in every respect so utterly alike that there is no difference whatsoever between them, and indeed that there are infinitely many of *those*, and likewise the people in them.[11]

Democritus has, it seems, calculated as follows: whereas any given accidental world formation is a mere fluke, the larger the number of worlds produced the likelier it becomes that that particular formation will recur; granted, then, that *infinitely* many worlds have been produced, the likelihood of identical-twin worlds becomes a cast-iron certainty—not just twins, in fact, but *infinitely* many identical siblings. And by worlds of the same exact type he means not worlds of the same generic type, but, as our sources make

9. Cf. also Furley 1987, pp. 143–44, for the atomists' additional use of an embryological model in explaining world formation.

10. Hippolytus, *Ref.* I 13.2–3 (= C. C. W. Taylor 1999, test. 78, part), ἀπείρους δ᾽ εἶναι κόσμους καὶ μεγέθει διαφέροντας. ἔν τισι δὲ μὴ εἶναι ἥλιον μηδὲ σελήνην, ἔν τισι δὲ μείζω τῶν παρ᾽ ἡμῖν καὶ ἔν τισι πλείω... εἶναι δὲ ἐνίους κόσμους ἐρήμους ζῴων καὶ φυτῶν καὶ παντὸς ὑγροῦ. "[Democritus said that] there are infinitely many worlds, differing in size; that in some there is no sun or moon, in some a sun and moon bigger than in our world, in some a larger number of them . . . ; and that there are some worlds devoid of animals, plants, and all moisture."

11. "ais Democritum dicere innumerabiles esse mundos et quidem sic quosdam inter sese non solum similes, sed undique perfecte et absolute ita pares, ut inter eos nihil prorsus intersit, et eos quidem innumerabiles, itemque homines." For the reading "et eos quidem innumerabiles," see next note.

clear, worlds resembling each other in the minutest details, including identical inhabitants with the same names and histories.[12]

On the hypothesis favored today by some cosmologists that the universe (or perhaps "multiverse") is indeed infinite, we now have at our disposal a calculation[13] of how far you would have to travel through space before you should expect to find a world in this same degree indistinguishable from our own (I mean one containing *inter alia* another you and another me, with the very same names and biographies): the average distance between identical worlds comes out at 10 to the power of 10 to the power of 28 meters. For Democritus, no actual numerical calculation is historically plausible, and all we can safely say is that he subscribed to a version of the Principle of Plenitude, according to which, given unrestricted opportunity, no possibility goes unrealized. His own way of expressing such calculations was not statistical, but couched in terms of his expression *ou mallon*, "There is no more reason . . . " Of a given range of alternative possibilities, granted (a) that "there is no more reason" for one to be realized than the others, (b) that at least one is realized, and (c) that the opportunity for the others to be realized is unrestricted, then those others must be or become actual at some place and time.[14]

It should, I think, be clear enough how Democritus means to capitalize on this principle in explaining the nature of our own world. Without an intelligent creator, the formation of a world like our own would seem vanishingly unlikely. Even so, for the atoms to come together in this particular arrangement as a result of random motions was still intrinsically possible, and the more worlds there are in the universe the less unlikely that chance result is. Granted, then, the *infinity* of the universe, and the consequent infinity of worlds, it was in fact inevitable that precisely this fluke should occur. Democritus's calculation that every individual world-type must recur repeatedly at suitably vast distances throughout space is

---

12. That according to this text, *Ac.* II 55, there are infinitely many entirely identical worlds and hence a matching infinity of the precise named individuals that inhabit them ("itemque homines") is confirmed both by the sequel in 55 ("in iis quidem innumerabilibus innumerabiles Q. Lutati Catuli") and by *ib.* 125. Hence it is preferable with the majority of editors to read "et eos quidem innumerabiles," simply emending "eo" to "eos," than to delete this phrase with Reid and Rackham. That the identity of worlds extends to named individuals is confirmed by the pseudo-Hippocratic Letter 10 (IX 322 Littré), where Democritus is represented as thinking that there are "numberless Democrituses like himself" in the universe: see Warren 2004b, pp. 356, 358–59.

13. Tegmark 2003.

14. The classic study of these Democritean arguments is Makin 1993.

his way of demonstrating that the providential-seeming features of our world need be no such thing. Worlds exactly like ours necessarily occur in any case. And even if worlds altogether indistinguishable from ours will occur only at mind-bogglingly vast intervals across the universe, worlds sufficiently similar to ours to support intelligent life will no doubt occur with much greater frequency.

How satisfying is this mode of explanation by appeal to accident on an infinite scale? There is a temptation to respond that, since worlds as good as ours could at best occur by sheer accident only once in innumerable billions of instances, it strains credulity to suppose that *we* just happen to have been so lucky as to hit this particular jackpot. It is like winning the lottery: even if it is inevitable that someone will win the lottery this year, it is staggeringly unlikely that it will be you.

But such incredulity should be resisted. First, the system underlying the lottery actually predicts that more or less every week there will be one or more incredulous winners, unable to believe their luck. Second, the incredulous objector is illegitimately assuming that we might, had things not gone so well, be sitting right now in some uninhabitable world, our failed lottery tickets in our hands, envying those more fortunate than ourselves. Just as history is written by the winners, even if they may have won by sheer accident, so too it is inevitable that cosmogony should be written by the intellectually most successful organisms in the universe, regardless of whether their success was achieved by divine benefaction or mere fluke.

2. THE EPICUREAN CRITIQUE OF CREATIONISM

Despite Democritus's discovery of the extraordinary explanatory power wielded by this combination of infinity and accident, the rival conviction according to which we have been divinely selected for our privileged circumstances was so powerfully articulated by his contemporary Socrates, and in the next generation so brilliantly developed into a global physics by Plato in the *Timaeus*, that atomism was compelled to find new weapons. In Epicurus's hands, these were of two kinds. One, to which I shall return at the end, involved strengthening the appeal to the power of accident. The other, on which I shall focus first, was systematic demolition of the supposed evidence for divine benevolence. Although relatively little on this subject survives from Epicurus's own pen, we are fortunate to find many of his arguments eloquently expounded in the Latin verses of his follower Lucretius (mid-first century B.C.). I shall shortly turn to a selection of them.

The main target of attack is clearly the *Timaeus*, either taken on as an unmediated target or, as it seems on occasion, read through the lens of Platonists contemporary with Epicurus.[15] Some of the most direct attacks, in the mouth of Cicero's Epicurean spokesman Velleius in *On the nature of the gods* I 19, focus on the metaphors deployed by Timaeus in his mythical description of divine craftsmanship. Just what set of tools did god use for the construction work he undertook, Velleius wants to know, and how did he manage to get the material elements to *obey* his commands, as Plato implies he did by having divine intelligence "persuade" necessity (see chapter IV §5 above)?[16]

From a literary-critical perspective such an assault can look like insensitive literalism, but from the point of view of Epicurus's anti-vitalist physics the questions remain most pertinent. However inapposite it may seem to demand a precise deliteralization of a mythological narrative (see chapter IV §3 above), it was precisely the job of Plato's heirs to answer these questions if they were going to systematize a Platonic physics. It is perhaps no accident, then, that in this particular critique the finger is being pointed at Plato's original text, and not at its Platonist interpreters.

Another relatively direct engagement with the *Timaeus* is visible when Lucretius puts the following question (V 181–86):

> Also, from where was a model for the creation of the world, and
>   the very
> notion of human beings, first implanted in the gods,
> to enable them to know and see in their mind what they wished
>   to create?
> Or how did they ever come to know the power of the primary
>   particles
> and what they were capable of when their arrangement was altered,   185
> if nature itself did not supply a blueprint of creation?

The first pair of questions here (181–83) is how the gods can have had a "model" or paradigm for the world they created, and how they can already

15. In Sedley 1998a, pp. 75–78, I argue that Lucretius's main arguments against divine creation of the world have as their target not the Stoics, but Platonists more or less contemporary with Epicurus himself, voicing a current interpretation of the *Timaeus*. In Sedley 2002 I explicate this early Academic position in some detail, attributing it to the Academy of Polemo in particular.

16. "By what kind of mental vision could your Plato have envisaged that great building enterprise by which he has god construct the world? What were the building techniques, the tools, the levers, the machines, the laborers, for such an enterprise? How were the air, fire, water, and earth capable of complying with and obeying the architect's wishes?"

have possessed the "notion" or "preconception" (*prolēpsis*, the Epicurean technical term which Lucretius is probably translating here) of a human being. There can be little doubt that this argument originated as a response to the *Timaeus*, where a creator modelled the world on an eternal paradigm, the generic Form of Animal, which itself contained all animal species, man included (pp. 108–9 above). Plato conceived Forms as independently existing objects of pure thought, most straightforwardly exemplified by mathematical entities, although he was equally convinced that value terms shared this same *a priori* status. That there should in addition be Forms of empirical-sounding entities like Animal and Man was a contentious and hesitant further development of the theory, one which did indeed make Plato vulnerable to Lucretius's objection. Animal and man are surely *not* the sorts of items whose nature can be theorized entirely *a priori*, as that of a dodecahedron or a prime number can, even in advance of empirically encountering instances of them. Adventurously, but still fully in keeping with Epicurean epistemology, Lucretius's additional challenge (184–86) extends that same doubt to the laws of physics, maintaining that understanding of these too is necessarily *a posteriori*.

The Epicureans themselves, as the ancient philosophical world's most ardent empiricists, appear to have gone to the opposite extreme from Plato. Not only the preconceptions of biological genera and species but *all* our preconceptions, they assume, have an empirical origin.[17] Even more controversially, but in keeping with their own anthropomorphizing theology, they rely on the further assumption that any divine creator would be subject to the same kinds of epistemological constraints as humans are.

We will later see both these assumptions being put to work. But the present argument does not necessarily depend on them, and raises a difficulty which arises for Plato out of the fundamental metaphysics on which his creationism is founded. Instead of reading it as an anthropomorphist's crude underestimation of the superhuman powers a divine creator would be likely to possess, we can more fruitfully interpret it as turning against itself Plato's own anthropomorphizing account of the divine craftsman.

The first question we have considered was epistemological: how could god have conceived a world ahead of its creation? Next, we find in Lucretius and Cicero a battery of arguments focused on the question, what could possibly have *motivated* this divine act of creation? Sometimes these arguments turn on presuppositions about the nature of god. Like all ancient philosophers, the Epicureans treat god as a paradigm of human happiness, the being most

---

17. DL X 33 = Long and Sedley 1987 (henceforth "LS") 17E.

suitable for us to emulate. The ideal Epicurean lifestyle is one of detached tranquillity, undisturbed by the toils of administration and political competition. The gods are therefore pictured as ideal models of that same detachment, supremely tranquil beings blissfully free from the stresses of world government. Why such beings should voluntarily build themselves a world to run is in the Epicureans' eyes beyond comprehension.[18]

Thus far we have a line of argument directed primarily to those who are already convinced Epicureans, liberated from the prevailing political values of the Greek world and ready to attribute their alternative value system even to the gods. Nevertheless, it represents a vital strand in the ancient debate, as we will see in the next chapter when we find Aristotle likewise restricting god's activities in line with his own highest ideal of human happiness. But I now move to arguments which do not overtly presuppose Epicureanism, and are thus better geared to interschool dispute.

One such group of arguments is focused on a classic question first adumbrated by Parmenides with his appeal to what since Leibniz has been known as the Principle of Sufficient Reason. If the world came into being, why did that event happen *when* it did, and not earlier or later?[19] Parmenides' own point had been not theological but causal: if what there now is came into being from a previous situation in which there was nothing at all, how could there have been a cause[20] already operative to determine that creation should occur at that specific time? The Epicurean attack on creationism differs in not presupposing a pre-cosmic state in which there was nothing at all: according to the Epicureans themselves there was already matter, and according to the creationist theory under their scrutiny there was not only matter but also a god or gods. For this reason the Epicureans transfer Parmenides' question to the specific problem of god's motivation. If god created the world, why did he do it *when* he did?

Lucretius puts the point this way (V 168–73):

18. For the Epicurean *prolēpsis* of god as a detached being not characterized by providence, see e.g. LS 23B–E, 54K.

19. For a rich historical overview of this issue, see Sorabji 1983, chapter 15.

20. Parmenides 28 B8.9–10 DK, τί δ' ἄν μιν καὶ χρέος ὦρσεν | ὕστερον ἢ πρόσθεν, τοῦ μηδενὸς ἀρξάμενον, φῦν. "What thing, also, would have stirred it up to be born later or sooner, having begun from nothing?" I translate τί χρέος "what thing . . . ?", for which see LSJ, s.v. χρέος II 2, and not "what need . . . ?" The latter translation—along with its own variants such as the barely justified "What necessity . . . ?"—has needlessly obstructed discussion of the lines' meaning. The correct meaning is explained by Coxon 1986 in his commentary, p. 198, but curiously he nevertheless translates (p. 64), "what necessity . . . ?"

What novelty could have tempted hitherto tranquil beings, so late on,
to desire a change in their earlier lifestyle?
For those who are obliged to delight in the new are plainly   170
those who are troubled by the old. But where someone had had no ill
befall him up to now, because he had led his life well,
what could have ignited a passion for novelty in such a one?

He here detects an inconsistency between two profiles of god: a supremely
happy being, and a being who initiates new courses of action. If you are
supremely happy, you no doubt have ample motivation to take whatever
steps will maintain your present state, but none to bring about entirely new
states of affairs.

It is clear that some ancient creationist theories could provide a satisfactory answer. Epicurus's younger contemporaries the Stoics, who regarded the
world as having a necessarily limited life span, would reply that god creates
a new world precisely in order to replace the old one that has just expired,
and thus to maintain, rather than replace, his former activity. The argument
preserved by Lucretius was plainly designed not with a Stoic but with a Platonist target in mind,[21] as was natural enough in Epicurus's formative years,
when Stoicism was at best in its early infancy. For Plato's *Timaeus* appears
to describe not a succession of worlds but a single world which, once created,
was to last forever, thanks to divine protection. Lucretius in fact makes it explicit that it is such a theory that he is attacking (V 156–65).

In the passage just quoted, Lucretius asked "what novelty could have
tempted hitherto tranquil beings, *at so late a stage,* to desire a change in
their earlier lifestyle?" Why "at so late a stage"? From Cicero's expansion
of the same Epicurean argument (*On the nature of the gods* I 21),[22] we can
infer that the main point of this expression is the assumption, naturally as-

---

21. Some conflation or even confusion between the two targets was possible. Thus
the second-century A.D. Epicurean Diogenes of Oenoanda, fr. 20 Smith, asks the Stoics, who consider the world a city of gods and humans, why in that case god waited
infinitely many years in the wilderness before building his city.

22. Cicero's spokesman Velleius is here actually addressing both Plato and the
Stoics, but this particular question—although it might in principle be invoked against
the Stoic thesis of long intervals between worlds—seems far more appropriate to
the former. A variant of the same Epicurean argument recorded by Aetius (I 7.8–9)
is addressed to Plato and, this time, Anaxagoras: in the eternity preceding his cosmogonic act, their creator god would have to have been (a) non-existent, (b) asleep,
or (c) awake; but (a) is excluded (god is conceived as eternal), as is (b) (eternal sleep
is death), while (c), combined with the premise of divine blessedness, rules out a cosmogonic act for reasons we have already seen (cf. *ib.* 7).

sociated with the single-creation doctrine, that the act of creation was preceded by an *infinite* span of time in which no creation occurred. This does
indeed pose a problem for the creationists. If god had waited a specific finite
number of years before embarking on world-creation, a reason for the delay might in theory have existed: for example, that was how long it took
him to prepare his plans, his materials, or both. But now try imagining a
single dated act of creation, say in 4004 B.C., preceded by a preparatory
process that took infinitely many years. Why did god not instead create the
world in 4005 B.C.? The answer cannot be that he was not ready yet, because if 4004 B.C. was preceded by infinitely many years of preparation, the
same was already true of 4005 B.C., and indeed of any previous or later year.

Cicero's Epicurean spokesman puts the point by asking "why the world-
builders suddenly appeared on the scene after infinitely many centuries"
(*On the nature of the gods* I 21). He then continues with a most telling explanation of his question:

> For if there was no world, it does not follow that there were no centuries.
> By "centuries" here I don't mean the ones made up by the number of days
> and nights as a result of the annual orbits. Those, I concede, could not have
> been produced without the world's rotation. But there has been a certain
> eternity from infinite time past, which was not measured by any bounding
> of times, but whose extent can be understood, because it is unthinkable that
> there should have been some time at which there was no time.[23]

This enables us to work out that the following exchange had taken place.[24]
Followers of Plato, defending the creation in the *Timaeus* as a literal dated
event, must have already confronted the question why the Demiurge should
have delayed for an infinite time-span before finally acting, and responded
by pointing out that according to the *Timaeus* time came into being only
with the creation of the world—for, as noted in the last chapter (p. 99 above),
that remarkable claim really is to be found in Plato's text (37c6–38c3). Consequently, they could infer, there was no passage of time before the creation,
and therefore *a fortiori* no choice between alternative times at which to set
about the act of creation.

---

23. non enim, si mundus nullus erat, saecla non erant. saecla nunc dico non ea
quae dierum noctiumque numero annuis cursibus conficiuntur; nam fateor ea sine
mundi conversione effici non potuisse; sed fuit quaedam ab infinito tempore aeter-
nitas, quam nulla circumscriptio temporum metiebatur, spatio tamen qualis ea fuerit
intellegi potest, quod ne in cogitationem quidem cadit ut fuerit tempus aliquod, nul-
lum cum tempus esset.

24. For the presence of literalist interpreters of the *Timaeus* in the early Academy, see p. 107 n. 30 above.

The reason why we can infer that this Platonist move must have been made is that Cicero's Epicurean spokesman, in the words I have quoted, is evidently responding to just such a defense. The "time" that did not exist before the cosmos was, he maintains, not time as such, but *measured* time, the sequence of days, months, and years measured by the celestial rotations that came into being only with the heavens. This is not only an intrinsically plausible thesis, but one that has been invoked in the modern era by literalist interpreters of the *Timaeus* as being in all probability Plato's own.[25] For on the literal reading of the *Timaeus*—one, to repeat, which the Epicureans themselves adopted—the cosmos with its celestially measured time was indeed preceded by a state of chaos, in which matter underwent random motions uncontrolled by intelligence. Since this chaos is dated "before" the creation of time, and itself *involved* the before-after sequences that all change necessarily entails, it appears to follow that the creation of what Plato calls "time" along with the cosmos was not the creation of temporal succession as such, but the creation of something more specific, temporal *regularity*, thanks to the construction of the great celestial clock.[26] In the more generic sense of "time," it seems plausible that pre-cosmic change had been going on for infinite time past before the Demiurge got to work. The question thus remains why he permitted disorder to continue for infinite time before rectifying it.[27]

25. See pp. 104–5 above.

26. Sextus Empiricus, M X 181–88 tries to trap the Epicureans into a contradiction similar to that from which Plato was being extricated: they call time a "diurnal and nocturnal appearance" (ἡμεροειδὲς καὶ νυκτοειδὲς φάντασμα), yet hold that there will be *a time at which* our world, and therefore also days and nights, will no longer exist. However, the evidence (Epicurus, *Ep. Hdt.* 72–73, etc.) makes it clear that time was linked by the Epicureans to change and rest in general, with days and nights cited as no more than prominent examples.

27. Despite the plausibility, it is not clear that the *infinity* of pre-cosmic time can be safely inferred in this way. Cicero's Velleius speaks of innumerable "centuries," or perhaps "ages," before the world was created, but from the mere premise that before every moment there was a previous moment nothing follows about an infinitely extended past, since the sequence of moments might for example be set at a diminishing series of intervals, and without absolute measured time there are no coordinates to distinguish such a convergent sequence from one with unvarying intervals. The literalist Platonists could in fact have gone further, and argued that the pre-cosmic chaos must—like everything perceptible, see *Ti.* 28b2–c2—have had a temporal beginning, even if this would have confronted them with difficult questions about what can have preceded *it*. If pressed in either of these ways, the Epicureans might have had to fall back on arguing that within *any* continuum of pre-cosmic time, even one of finite duration, god would have needed a reason to choose this rather than that moment to create the world. But why should there not have been a good reason, for example that the chaotic matter happened just then to be in its most favorable state?

If these Platonists had seriously contemplated the idea of creation out of nothing, as the Judaeo-Christian tradition did, the postulation of pre-cosmic change and temporality might have been deflected: before the creation, there was simply nothing at all over and above god, himself a changeless being. But commitment to the axiom that nothing comes into being out of nothing was pervasive in ancient thought,[28] and in effect blocked off any such escape route by ensuring that the creation was preceded by a state of material disorder. The Epicurean challenge has therefore found a particularly vulnerable spot at which to strike its creationist target.

Another series of questions about divine motivation for creating a world concerns god's relation to *us*. The implication underlying the Epicurean critique is that the opponents—reminiscent here of Xenophon's Socrates (chapter III §2 above)—invoke god's benevolence to mankind as his motive. How is god's benevolence to be understood, the Epicureans ask in reply? They canvass and reject two possibilities.

The first option (Lucretius V 165–67) is that god created the world in order to secure our gratitude. But that falls quickly to the objection that an already supremely happy being could not have need of anything from us, gratitude included. The second, more intriguing option is that our creator was motivated by genuine concern for us, and that the act of bringing us into existence was in itself an altruistic one. But how could that be? As Lucretius says (V 174–80):

> What harm would it have done us never to have been created?
> Did our life lie in darkness and misery   175
> until the world's beginning dawned?
> Although anyone who has been born must wish to remain
> in life so long as the caresses of pleasure hold him there,
> if someone has really never tasted the passion for life
> and was never one of us, what harm does it do them not to have
>   been created?   180

The creationists are, it seems, envisaged as having propounded roughly the following argument:

1. We naturally prefer to prolong our existence, rather than terminate it now.

2. Therefore ceasing to exist now is an intrinsically worse option than continuing to exist into the future by remaining alive.

---

28. According to Galen, *Meth. Med.* I 4.10 the "ancients" regarded this as a fundamental *a priori* axiom. See Hankinson 1991, pp. 126–28; and Sorabji 1983, pp. 245–49.

3. Therefore nonexistence is intrinsically bad.

4. Therefore god, in saving us from our previous nonexistence, was saving us from something intrinsically bad, and to that extent benefiting us.

Although Lucretius here seems to accept (1), he cannot endorse inferences (2) and (3), both of which run directly contrary to his celebrated critique (III 830–1094) of the fear of death.[29] Our familiar and justified preference for staying alive reflects, not the badness of death, but our natural interest in not losing the pleasures we currently enjoy.[30] No such interest is at stake, however, in those who have not yet been born and therefore have no pleasures to prolong. Not yet being individuals, they simply have no interests to consider, and are not possible beneficiaries of divine altruism.

Some of the issues which this raises, and which I cannot adequately address here,[31] are bound up with the celebrated Epicurean symmetry argument, according to which death, being a future state of nonexistence, will not be any worse than our past nonexistence was in all the centuries before we were born. But in the argument we are examining this symmetry between the harmlessness of past nonexistence and that of future nonexistence may threaten to rebound. If (1) is understood as implicitly conceding that death brings a deprivation of pleasures, the symmetry thesis may seem to require that failure to be born in the first place likewise entails a deprivation of pleasures. To defend his case, Lucretius needs to establish a relevant asymmetry. This is, I take it, an asymmetry about *desires*. Death, even if not in itself a bad thing, can frustrate certain preexisting desires, whereas the unborn have no preexisting desires that their continued failure to be born will frustrate. It is for this reason that you can, without considering death an evil, make sense of pitying someone for their future death. You cannot, in the same way, even make sense of pitying some hypothetical individual for not having existed in the first place.

What the argument still fails to address is its opponents' very different understanding of divine goodness. The main moral characteristic of the Epicurean god is, as we have seen, his own tranquillity. But Plato had regarded the creator as an essentially good being who by his very nature wanted to make everything as good as possible. Likewise the god of

29. For a comprehensive study, see Warren 2004b.

30. Cf. Philodemus, *De Epicuro* XVIII 10–17 (Tepedino Guerra 1994), where Epicurus questions whether life is worth prolonging if all hope of pleasure has gone.

31. For the symmetry argument in its full Epicurean context, see Warren 2004a, including p. 209 for the relevance of the present argument.

Socrates and the Stoics is by nature providential, and therefore committed to beneficent activity. A creator of this kind evidently *needed* to create our world and its inhabitants, not out of pity, but in order to be able to exercise his own other-regarding virtues. On this question of god's moral nature Socrates, Plato, and the Stoics were in the opposite camp to Epicurus, as also to Aristotle, both of these latter denying god any other-regarding virtues. This lack of common ground regarding god's nature is often, as in the present case, an obstacle to genuine theological debate between the schools.

I now turn to another argument deployed by Lucretius. Allow for the sake of argument that the gods did make the world from motives of benevolence. Still, he argues, the question remains, who are the beneficiaries? The prevailing assumption, thanks above all to Socrates, was that divine benevolence is aimed at mankind. After all, argues Xenophon's Socrates (*Mem.* I 4, IV 3; cf. chapter III §2 above), not only are we better equipped than any other animal, but the entire natural world, lower species included, functions for our benefit. Lucretius's reply is withering (V 187–234; cf. II 167–81). If you do believe in divine benevolence, one look at the natural world should be enough to dispel the assumption that human beings are its intended beneficiaries. Most of the earth is uninhabitable, and even those parts which we manage to cultivate fight back in every way they can, with brambles, vermin, and pestilence. When a newborn baby takes its first look at the world and bursts into tears it is showing remarkable prescience, given all the troubles that lie ahead for it. It is other animal species that appear to have it easy from birth, without the slightest need for such artifices as education, food production, clothing, and defense. This is consummate mockery of anthropocentric creationism and its presuppositions. We will have to wait for Stoicism in order to see how such objections could be addressed.

For completeness, let us briefly take note of one further argument, in which Lucretius (II 1090–1104) leans on the atomist demonstration of the infinite plurality of worlds, to question god's *capacity* to govern them all.[32] As it comes across, this argument appears to invite at least two replies.

The first is that each of the infinitely many worlds might be governed by its own discrete divinity, there being at least as many gods as there are worlds. Against this, the assumption Lucretius is evidently attributing to

32. Cf. Warren 2004b, pp. 362–64 for a critique of this passage.

his opponents is that, whatever devolution of duties there may be to lesser gods, one supreme god necessarily holds sway over them all. This monarchical (or "henotheist") view of the divine hierarchy was a well-established one.[33] Although it is not adopted by the Epicureans in their own theology,[34] Lucretius is entitled for dialectical purposes to assume that his opponents are committed to it: the kinds of gods who are imagined as exerting power over a human world would indeed be, as their adherents have always thought them to be, related to each other by a hierarchical chain of command. On the other hand, since this assumption of a divine hierarchy had always been applied to the plurality of gods within a single world, it is hard to believe that its proponents would have felt committed to extending it to a universe containing a set of independent worlds, which might, after all, be governed as independently of each other as two autonomous cities.

The alternative reply that Lucretius's argument invites is that a single deity *might*, after all, have the power to govern an infinite set of worlds. What is the ground for doubting this? If we could recover the original Epicurean context in which the argument occurred, we would probably find that it turned on the impossibility of a living being that is infinitely extended in space—as this hypothetical universe-governing god would have to be. At any rate, from some condensed Epicurean critiques of earlier philosophers preserved in Cicero (*On the nature of the gods* I 26–28) we learn that this was a recurrent theme, for they accused Anaximenes, Anaxagoras, and Xenophanes[35] all of incoherently making their god infinite in extent. The ostensible objection to an infinitely extended deity was that sensation is an essential feature of life, that sensation is necessarily performed by means of bodily extremities, and that an infinite being (meaning presumably a being infinitely extended in all directions) has no bodily extremities. This move would no doubt in turn invite the retort that it unnecessarily assumes—as the Epicureans certainly did assume—an anthropomorphizing view of god. And we would be facing once more the recurrent problem

---

33. For a particularly clear statement of it, cf. Xenophon's Socrates at *Mem.* IV 3.13. Its origins as a theological position can be traced to Xenophanes, whose influence Xenophon's Socrates plainly shows (see p. 83 above).

34. A point made by Warren 2004b, p. 363 n. 27.

35. In Xenophanes' case, this reading was no doubt the outcome of combining 21 B 28 DK, on the infinite depth of the earth and hence implicitly the infinite size of our cosmos, with B 25–26, on god's ability to control everything without moving from place to place, implying his omnipresence.

of each party to the debate working from its own preconceived notion of divinity. We have perhaps reached a good moment to move on to our next topic.

3. THE EPICUREAN ALTERNATIVE TO CREATIONISM

I turn now to the positive side of the Epicurean case, which lies in a series of attempts to show how accident is fully capable of accounting for even the most purposive-seeming features of the world.

The natural place to start is with the origin of species, whose adaptedness to their specific biological functions seemed to provide such overwhelming evidence of divine providence. In the pages of Plato, even the religious agnostic Protagoras had found it natural to talk mythically of biological specializations as divinely assigned (p. 56 above).

The rival Epicurean account preserved by Lucretius is as follows. The young earth, being far more fertile than it is today, spontaneously and at random sprouted all kinds of life forms. (As we have already seen in Anaxagoras and Empedocles, pp. 18–19 and 46 above, the earth's inherent capacity to generate life, whether spontaneously or from seed, is more often taken for granted as an agreed starting point than treated as itself in need of explanation.) The vast majority of these primeval organisms were unable to survive and reproduce (V 837–56):

> At that time the earth tried to create many monsters
> with weird appearance and anatomy—
> androgynous, of neither one sex nor the other but somewhere in
>   between;
> some footless, or handless;   840
> many even without mouths, or without eyes and blind;
> some with their limbs stuck together all along their body,
> and thus disabled from doing anything or going anywhere,
> from avoiding harm or obtaining anything they needed.
> These and other such monsters the earth created.   845
> But to no avail, since nature prohibited their development.
> They were unable to reach the goal of their maturity,
> to find sustenance, or to copulate.
> For we see that creatures need the concurrence of many things
> in order to be able to reproduce and to spread their progeny.   850
> First, there must be food. Second, a way for the procreative
> seeds in their bodies to flow out, released from their limbs.
> And third, in order that male and female can have intercourse, they
>   must both possess
> the equipment for indulging in the shared pleasure.

Many animal species must have become extinct at that time,   855
unable to reproduce and to spread their progeny.

But as chance would have it, some kinds turned out to possess all the necessary means to survive, prosper, and perpetuate themselves (V 857–77):

> For whatever creatures you see breathing the air of life,
> it is cunning, courage, or speed
> that has from the start preserved and protected their kind.
> There are many, too, which thanks to their usefulness to us   860
> have survived by being commended to our protection.
> First, the fierce and savage lion species
> has been protected by its courage, foxes by cunning, deer by speed of
>   flight.
> But as for the light-sleeping minds of dogs, with their faithful heart,
> and every kind born of the seed of beasts of burden,   865
> and along with them the wool-bearing flocks and the horned tribes,
> they have all been entrusted to the care of the human race, Memmius.
> For these, having by their own wish avoided the wild beasts and
>   sought peace,
> have found food in plenty, supplied without any labor on their part:
> it is how we reward them for their usefulness.   870
> But those which nature did not endow with any of these advantages,
>   and which
> were thus unable either to live on their own resources or to perform
>   for us
> some service in return for which we might allow
> their species to feed under our protection and be safe,
> these you may be sure lay as the prey and picking of other creatures, 875
> all of them hampered by their fateful handicaps,
> until nature reduced the kind to extinction.

In some cases speed, courage, or cunning was the secret of their success, and
in yet others it was their utility to man and the consequent protection that
this brought. There is no suggestion that any one species evolved into another, or that gradual anatomical adaptation played any part either, so we are
still a long way from Lamarck and Darwin.[36] But the fundamental insight of
natural selection, that accident on a sufficiently vast scale accompanied by
the systematic survival of the fittest could account for the presence of apparently purposive structures in nature, is put to excellent use.

How original was the theory? When Lucretius describes how their utility to man ensured the survival of domestic species (V 864–70), so promi-

---

36. Cf. Campbell 2000, and 2003, pp. 5–6, on reasons for not calling the Epicurean
theory "evolutionist" in the Darwinian sense.

nent are the Empedoclean poetic echoes as to leave little doubt that he is here, as sometimes elsewhere, imitating or even translating a lost passage of Empedocles.[37] This indirect acknowledgment of a philosophical continuity between Empedocles and Epicureanism serves as a reminder that the principle of the survival of the fittest had indeed already been invoked by Empedocles in his own zoogony (pp. 43, 60–61 above). He had described in fantastic terms the second generation of Love's products, randomly fitted together out of previously designed discrete body parts, but in numerous cases hopelessly hybridized and unable to survive. Cross-species freaks such as centaurs and minotaurs stayed around long enough to leave their mark on the historical record, but did not survive in the longer term. (They are, if one disregards the relative brevity of their survival, the dinosaurs of Empedocles' world.) Others, the human race included, were sufficiently successful to survive, proliferate, and prosper.

Despite his recognition that survival of the fittest constitutes common ground with Empedocles, regarding other aspects Lucretius maintains a studied distance. That there should ever, even briefly, have been centaurs, minotaurs, and the like is something that in the immediate sequel (V 878–924) he vehemently denies, on the ground that the metabolisms of different species such as man and horse are too discrepant ever to have functioned in unison in the first place.

More important for our present purposes, Lucretius argues explicitly against the idea, characteristic of Empedocles' first zoogonic stage, that individual body parts such as eyes, hands, and legs were initially designed for their functions. Although this argument need not have Empedocles as its specific target, to the exclusion of Socrates and Plato,[38] it does serve to remind us that Empedocles belonged broadly speaking in the creationist camp. Lucretius's argument against anatomical design is ingenious and audacious in equal measure.

You may be tempted, he warns his reader, to treat organic body parts as artifacts, designed and built for their current functions (IV 823–31):

> One mistake in this context, which I am determined
> you should shun and take precautions to avoid,
> is that of supposing the clear lights of the eyes to have been created   825

---

37. For defense of this claim, see above, chapter II, appendix 4.

38. It is widely held that Lucretius has the Stoics as his primary target, both here and often. Against this, see Furley 1966, and Sedley 1998a chapter 3, where I argue that Lucretius regularly takes over the arguments of Epicurus complete with their original pre-Stoic targets.

in order that we might see what lies before us; that it is in order that
  we might be able to take
lengthy strides that the knees and hips
can be flexed about their base of feet;
and again that the forearms were jointed to the powerful upper arms,
and hands supplied on either side, as our servants,   830
in order that we could perform whatever acts were needed for living.

But, he continues, any such assimilation of natural limbs and organs to artifacts relies on a false analogy between craft and nature (IV 832–57):

All other explanations of this type which they offer
are back to front, due to distorted reasoning.
For nothing has been engendered in our body in order that we might
  be able to use it.
It is the fact of its being engendered that creates its use.   835
Seeing did not exist before the lights of the eyes were engendered,
nor was there pleading with words before the tongue was created.
Rather, the origin of the tongue came long before
speech, ears were created long before
its sound was heard, and all our limbs,   840
in my view, existed in advance of their use.
Therefore they cannot have grown for the sake of their use.
By contrast, fighting out battles with bare hands,
mutilating limbs, and staining bodies with blood,
existed long before shining weapons began to fly.   845
Nature compelled men to avoid wounds before
the time when, thanks to craftsmanship, the left arm held up the
  obstructing shield.
Undoubtedly too the practice of resting the tired body
is much more ancient than the spreading of soft beds;
and the quenching of thirst came into being before cups.   850
Hence that these were devised for the sake of their use
is credible, because they were invented as a result of life's experiences.
Quite different from these are all the things which were first
actually engendered, and gave rise to the preconception of their
  usefulness later.
Primary in this class are, we can see, the senses and the limbs.   855
Hence, I repeat, there is no way you can believe
that they were created for their function of utility.

Craft takes its lead from nature, and therefore presupposes it (843–52). Cups
for example were invented because there was already the natural activity
of drinking, which human contrivance then stepped in to facilitate. Weapons
were devised to improve the preexisting activity of combat, beds to facili-

tate the natural process of sleeping, and so on. Invariably, craftsmanship improves on a process or activity already present in nature. To treat natural entities themselves as divine artifacts is to overlook this feature of craft (836–42). Before there were eyes, there simply was no such thing as seeing, before ears no such thing as hearing, and before legs no such thing as walking. Consequently there was no activity for craft to set about improving. Thus the seductive equation of nature with divine craft collapses, and we must conclude instead that the limbs and organs came into being before their use was discovered or even existed (835, 853–55).

What Lucretius has in mind is clear enough when we compare his lengthy account of the progress of civilization (V 925–1457). Again and again, some cultural institution originated by accident, and its use was only subsequently recognized. No one would ever have devised language in the first place unless our natural vocal noises had turned out to serve a labelling function. No one could have sought a way of creating fire before an accidental blaze caused by, for example, lightning made human beings aware of its powers. No one could have thought of systematically smelting metals before a fire accidentally brought their utility to human attention. And so on. This is no chance pattern in human cognitive history, but an application of the Epicureans' thoroughgoing commitment to empiricism: all notions or "preconceptions" (the term probably rendered by Lucretius at IV 854; cf. p. 141 above) are first acquired through sensory input from outside. In so far as gods are viewed as having cognitive functions, these too are assumed to fall under the same empiricist law.[39] So if no human being could have devised a cultural innovation before nature gave the lead, no god could either.

Epicureanism makes no strong distinction in this regard between the origin of cultural functions and that of biological ones. And that is where the strain starts to show. *Some* uses of body parts are no doubt easily enough explained on the model provided by cultural history, for example the fact that fingers turned out to be useful for counting on, and (to adapt an example from Voltaire's Dr. Pangloss) that ears proved useful for holding spectacles. But it is much less credible that so complex and specialized a structure as the eye—that favorite standby of the creationist—came into being first and was found useful for seeing only thereupon. Lucretius's account could not have acquired the missing plausibility without adopting a gradualist approach to the evolu-

---

39. Compare the Epicurean assumptions, pp. 140–41 above, that the gods could not have had the *prolēpsis* of a world before a world existed, and, p. 149 above, that even for the gods life entails possessing the familiar kind of sensory faculties.

tion of the eye, starting from (say) an accidentally light-sensitive depression in the epidermis, which conferred on its possessor a mildly advantageous awareness of predators, and progressing by minute steps all the way to a stratified mechanism that focuses images of distant objects onto the retina.[40] Without some such gradualist conception, he is forced to imagine instead a range of accidental permutations so vast that even an organ capable of seeing in the way we now see was originally formed by sheer luck, its serendipitous utility then being discovered by its first possessors.

4. EPICUREAN INFINITY

This need for the Epicureans to postulate accident on a staggeringly vast scale brings us back to our starting point, atomism's reliance on the extraordinary power of infinity. So long as the range of accidental permutations is finite, constrained by the spatial and temporal dimensions of a single world, it takes either a sophisticated theory of evolution or a considerable act of faith, if indeed not both, to suppose that mere accident is enough to explain the origin of the eye. But when the atomists stand back and generalize across the entire infinity of worlds, the true power of their explanatory principles becomes evident.[41]

The Epicureans spoke explicitly of the *vis infinitatis*, the "power of

40. I am here loosely paraphrasing Dawkins 1986, pp. 102–4. It is common to read that Darwin despaired of explaining the eye in terms of natural selection, with the following remark quoted as evidence: "To suppose that the eye, with all its inimitable contrivances for adjusting the focus to different distances, for admitting different amounts of light, and for the correction of spherical and chromatic aberration, could have been formed by natural selection, seems, I freely confess, absurd in the highest possible degree." Darwin's continuation, however, is less often cited: "Yet reason tells me, that if numerous gradations from a perfect and complex eye to one very imperfect and simple, each grade being useful to its possessor, can be shown to exist; if further, the eye does vary ever so slightly, and the variations be inherited, which is certainly the case; and if any variation or modification in the organ be ever useful to an animal under changing conditions of life, then the difficulty of believing that a perfect and complex eye could be formed by natural selection, though insuperable by our imagination, can hardly be considered real. How a nerve comes to be sensitive to light, hardly concerns us more than how life itself first originated; but I may remark that several facts make me suspect that any sensitive nerve may be rendered sensitive to light, and likewise to those coarser vibrations of the air which produce sound" (Darwin 1859, pp. 186–87). I am grateful to John Van Wyhe for this reference.

41. Cf. Dawkins 1986, "The odds against [the spontaneous formation of an eye in a single step] are many billions of times greater than the number of atoms in the universe." The Epicurean postulation of a universe with infinitely many atoms makes such odds not just shorter, but altogether powerless.

infinity." What is that? As reported by Cicero (*ND* I 50,[42] 109[43]), Epicurus associated the power of infinity with what he called *isonomia*, "distributive equality." Although, regrettably, the actual term *isonomia* occurs only in one uniquely problematic theological context, where the Epicureans quoted as invoking it appear to be doing so ineptly,[44] the same principle is clearly put to work, and more illuminatingly, elsewhere in our Epicurean sources. According to Cicero's report of this principle of *isonomia*, the power of infinity is such "that all like things match all like things." That is, in an infinite universe, if two types of thing have coordinate status, they exist in equal quantities. As the name *isonomia*, "*distributive* equality," implies, this is not a question of the mere fact that the sum totals of the two items will be equal. For since the Epicurean universe is infinite, even when it comes to comparing atoms themselves with the worlds that they combine in vast numbers to constitute, their sum totals will be identical, in the sense that both atoms and worlds will alike have infinitely many exemplars. Consider an arithmetical analogy: in the series of natural numbers, there is an infinity not only of those numbers themselves, but also of cubic numbers, despite the fact that these latter constitute only a minute proportion of the total. *Isonomia* is to be found, not in the compared items' sum totals, but in their distribution. In the arithmetical case, *isonomia* is satisfied by the equal distribution of odd and even numbers. In Epicurean cosmology, *isonomia* is satisfied at the phenomenal level by the equal distribution of opposite pairs of qualities such as hot and cold, and of coordinate species, for example of elephants and horses; and at the atomic level, by the equal distribution of atoms of different types.

42. The Epicurean Velleius: "summa vero vis infinitatis et magna ac diligenti contemplatione dignissima est. in qua intellegi necesse est eam esse naturam, ut omnia omnibus paribus paria respondeant; hanc isonomian appellat Epicurus, id est aequabilem tributionem . . . " "Moreover, the supreme power of infinity fully deserves long and careful reflection. You must understand that in it there lies a nature such that all like things match all like things. Epicurus calls this *isonomia*, that is, 'distribution in equal proportions' . . . "

43. The Academic Cotta: "confugis ad aequilibritatem (sic enim isonomian, si placet, appellemus) et ais, quoniam sit natura mortalis, inmortalem etiam esse oportere." "You take refuge in 'equal balance' (if you like, let's use that as a translation of *isonomia*), and you say that since there is a mortal nature there must be an immortal one too . . . "

44. For present purposes I am doing my best to avoid the thorniest controversies about Epicurean theology. *ND* I 50 returns to *oratio recta* after a long report of Epicurus himself which was formulated in *oratio obliqua*. I take this (cf. LS II, p. 149) to signal that Velleius now ceases reporting Epicurus and adds his own (that is, a later Epicurean) attempt to support Epicurus's postulation of immortal beings, based on Epicurus's principle of *isonomia*.

The example of elephants is cited by Lucretius (II 532–40) as providing an analogue to the atomic case:[45]

> For to the extent that you see some animals to be rarer,
> and notice nature to be less abundant in them,
> elsewhere in distant lands on the other hand   535
> there may be a great many of their kind, so that their number is
>   made up.
> For example, in the genus of four-footed animals we see pride of place
> to be taken by snake-handed elephants: India
> is fortified by a wall of ivory made from countless thousands of them,
> a virtually impenetrable one, so huge is
> its stock of the beasts, of which we ourselves get to see a mere
>   handful of specimens.   540

From too localized a perspective, he is saying, you might think that elephants are rarer than other animal species; but if you broaden your perspective to take in the whole world, including India, where there are millions upon millions of elephants, you will quickly correct this impression of imbalance. The lesson seems clear. If you choose too small a sample, or too narrow a perspective, you may not find distributive equality. The larger the sample, or the broader the perspective, the more balanced the distribution will turn out to be. Hence, in the case of unrestrictedly large samples, such as an infinite universe provides, you should expect the distribution to display perfect equilibrium.

This, it seems, is what is meant by the "power of infinity." It does not follow that *all* things exist in equal distribution: obviously enough, for example, the numerical distribution of elephants (that is, the average number

---

45. The transition from II 522–31 to 532–40 is puzzling. The former passage is meant to establish merely that there are infinitely many atoms of each type—as the reprise at 541–68 confirms—and not that they are equally distributed. Yet 532–40 is clearly making a point about equal distribution. I assume the full sequence of thought to be: (1) [522–31] That every atomic type has infinitely many exemplars follows from the previously established (I 1008–51) infinity of matter, combined with the newly established (II 478–521) finitude of atomic types. <(2) This applies to *every* atomic type, because if a given atomic type differed from the others in having only finitely many exemplars, it would be rarer than those others, in violation of the principle of *isonomia*; > (3) [532–40] . . . yet at least in the presumably analogous case of natural species (cf. II 333–80) any impression of relative rarity proves to be misleading, and this tends to confirm the principle of *isonomia*. (4) [541–68] Besides, even if (3) were false, its analogue could not be false in the case of atoms, since in an infinite universe even a species of compound with one member could exist only if every type of atom required for constituting it had infinitely many tokens. (5) [569–80] The principle of *isonomia* is also confirmed by the long-term persistence of our world.

of elephants occupying some given unit of space), while identical to the numerical distribution of elephants' trunks, cannot be equal to the numerical distribution of elephants' feet. Likewise, and for the same reasons, the numerical distribution of worlds obviously will not be identical to the numerical distribution of the atoms that constitute them. Just as for every one elephant there are four elephant feet, so for every world there are an uncountably large number of atoms. It is in the case of things of coordinate status, where there is no reason for inequality to occur, that the principle of *isonomia* requires an equal distribution. In this way, *isonomia* is the Epicurean counterpart of Democritus's *ou mallon* principle: it is when there is no more reason for X to occur than for Y to occur that we can expect an equal distribution of X and Y across the universe. We have seen that *isonomia* governs the distribution of animal species and of types of atom. It will also govern the distribution across space of types of world, a point to which I shall return at the end.

With *isonomia* in mind, let us turn to a classic criticism of the Epicurean position. Cicero's Stoic spokesman derides it in the following words (*On the nature of the gods* II 93):

> Does it not deserve amazement on my part that there should be anyone who can persuade himself that certain solid and indivisible bodies travel through the force of their own weight, and that by an accidental combination of those bodies a world of the utmost beauty and splendor is created? I do not see why the person who supposes this can happen does not also believe it possible that if infinitely many exemplars of the twenty-one letters of the alphabet, in gold or any other material you like, were thrown into a container then shaken onto the ground, they might form a readable copy of the *Annals* of Ennius. I'm not sure that luck could manage this even to the extent of a single line.

This is the best ancient antecedent I know for the modern cliché of a monkey with a typewriter which, given unlimited time, will (according to some) eventually type out the plays of Shakespeare. Its origin is frequently attributed to Thomas Huxley in his 1860 debate with the Bishop of Oxford; but that debate predated by some years the invention of the typewriter, and the actual originator, albeit without the Shakespeare example, seems to have been the Swiss mathematician Emile Borel in 1913.

The monkey paradigm, in various forms and at various times, has been favored by evolutionists when defending the possibility of an accidental origin of living cells, on the premise that our planet had a prehistory which, although finite, was long enough to make such an accident credible. The Epicureans, with their doctrine of the actual *infinity* of space, matter, and time, are even better placed to take on an explanatory task of the kind.

To find out how they exploit their infinity doctrine to this end, a useful point at which to start is their modal doctrine, one based not on possible worlds, but on actual worlds. Anything that is necessary, for example a mathematical truth, is actual in *all* the infinitely many worlds.[46] Analogously to this, anything that is possible is also actual in at least *some* of the infinitely many existing worlds.[47] Why so? If something is intrinsically possible, the more numerous the opportunities for its realization, the more probable its realization becomes. If, then, the number of opportunities is infinite, the probability of its realization somewhere appears to become an absolute certainty.

One of the many consequences of this calculation must concern types of world: every possible world is, somewhere in the universe, an actual world. The atomist universe is comparable, less to the proverbial monkey with a typewriter which, given infinite time, will write the plays of Shakespeare, than to an infinite line of monkeys with typewriters. As you work along the line you will find, once in every *n* monkeys, a draft of Shakespeare's plays already completed. Here *n* may be a very large number indeed,[48] but it is finite.

Grant then the mere possibility, however remote or abstract, that a world like ours should form by sheer accident, thanks to the right atoms coming together and organizing themselves into an appropriate structure, even down to the level of individual animal parts. Once the possibility is granted, its realization is no longer a miracle, but a modal certainty. Never mind that the emergence of such worlds may be incredibly rare, say only one time in a trillion to the power of a trillion. Even on such a hypothesis, it is beyond doubt that worlds like ours form and will continue to form. Hence Lucretius seems justified in insisting, as he does,[49] that in an infinite universe a world like ours was bound to occur through mere atomic accident.

---

46. Cf. Philodemus, *Sign.* XV 28–XVI 1.

47. Lucretius V 526–33 = LS 18D 8.

48. The website http://user.tninet.se/~ecf599g/aardasnails/java/Monkey/web pages/ used to run high-speed monkey simulators alongside a Shakespeare concordance. An 18-word stretch from *Henry IV Part II* took two and three-quarter million billion billion billion billion monkey-years to generate.

49. Lucretius I 1021–28, cf. V 419–31. Cf. Epicurus fr. 266 Usener (ps.-Plutarch, *Strom.* 8), "Epicurus . . . says . . . that nothing unfamiliar (ξένον) is realized in the universe, thanks to the infinity of time that has already passed."

This quasi-statistical application of infinity was among the doctrines that Epicurus inherited from his atomist forerunner Democritus. But we must now go back and ask how *successful* Democritus had been in that anticipation. For Democritus invoked his *ou mallon* principle not only to establish the infinity of worlds, but also to demonstrate, by parity of reasoning, that the number of different types of atom is infinite.[50] Atoms are differentiated by shape and size alone. He recognized it as a geometrical fact that, even within a limited size-range, there are infinitely many shapes. If the infinite stock of atoms in a given size range were deemed to manifest some shapes but not others, that would be arbitrary and inexplicable, there being "no more reason" why atoms of this shape than atoms of that shape should exist.

But in thus following out the implications of his *ou mallon* principle, Democritus brought trouble upon himself. If there are infinitely many types of atom, even in an infinite set of worlds there can, it seems, be no certainty that a given arrangement of atoms will recur. On the assumption that all the infinitely many worlds are formed from a reservoir of atoms whose variety is equally infinite, no predictions about recurrence will be possible. It remains a real possibility that, among the infinity of worlds, no two are composed of exactly the same types of atoms in the same numerical proportions.

If it is not guaranteed that our world formation recurs elsewhere in the infinite universe, it follows that its occurrence somewhere even once was not after all inevitable, but fortuitous. The concession is not ruinous, because the lucky fluke was still physically *possible.* But it immediately invites back in the explanatory hypothesis of a divine creator who, against the odds, turned that mere possibility into reality. To put it another way, if atomistic physics cannot furnish physical conditions sufficient for our world to come about, it risks leaving a vacuum for some nonphysical cosmogonic cause to fill.

Thus the admission that there are infinitely many types of atom appears to endanger Democritus's inference from his own principles that there must be worlds altogether identical to each other. Such a consequence may not matter in itself, but its implications do. What applies to minutely defined types of world applies, *mutatis mutandis,* to broadly defined types as well, including, crucially, types of worlds so structured as to be capable of sustaining life with the degree of success that our own world manifests. Democritus previously seemed in a position to argue that the emergence of such worlds does not depend on an almighty fluke, as Cicero's Stoic spokesman joked with his example of accidentally writing the *Annals* of Ennius, but is

50. 67 A 8 DK = C. C. W. Taylor 1999, test. 45.

rather, in an infinite universe, an inevitability. Democritus's universe has now, however, proved to be like an infinitely long row of monkeys writing on typewriters each of which has an infinite number of different keys. Even assuming just twenty-six letter keys, you would have to work through an unimaginably vast number of the monkeys before you found a completed script of *Hamlet;* with infinitely many keys on each typewriter, although you could in theory be so lucky as to find one, there is no reason to predict that you will ever come to a monkey who has typed the play's first line, or even its first letter.

The Epicurean universe, by contrast, seems to have been redesigned to exclude any such danger. For we know that Epicurus went to considerable lengths to argue against Democritus's thesis that there are infinitely many types of atom. To cut a long story short,[51] Epicurus arrived at this result by maintaining that there is a mathematically smallest magnitude. Each atom must consist of a precise number of these smallest magnitudes, and, because each of the constituent magnitudes is so small as to be partless, nothing more than a vanishingly small dot of magnitude, there is only a finite number of arrangements in which any given set of magnitudes can stand. In the diagram on p. 162, take each square to be a smallest magnitude. (This would be easier to imagine if you held the sheet so far away that each square became a mere dot, so small that at any greater distance it would become invisible.)

In the very simple two-dimensional[52] example illustrated in figure 3, atoms consisting of four minimal magnitudes can come in only five possible shapes, as shown. The sixth shape is impossible, because it would involve one smallest magnitude overlapping with *half* of another. But smallest magnitudes do not have halves: if they did, they would not be smallest magnitudes, because their half would be smaller. For simplicity, the diagram has reduced atoms to two dimensions. Converting back into three dimensions, you would find that the number of possible atoms increases, but still stands at only eight.

It follows, by parity of reasoning, that for atoms consisting of *any* finite number of minimal magnitudes there are only a finite number of possible shapes. The Epicurean conclusion is that, since there is also some upper limit to the sizes of atoms, there are only finitely many types of atom in the uni-

---

51. For the longer version, see LS, sections 8–12, esp. 9.
52. More accurately, I am picturing the atoms as three-dimensional but flat, so that the third and fifth shapes can themselves be flipped over to be seen in reverse. Alternatively, these two reversed shapes could be added as a sixth and seventh.

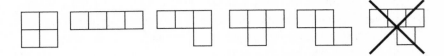

Figure 3

verse. Although the number of atomic types is "unimaginably" large,[53] it is not actually infinite.

The preserved Epicurean arguments for minimal magnitudes are based on the paradoxes of Zeno of Elea, which had exhibited the apparent absurdities entailed by the simple supposition that the process of division can continue without limit. For example, said Zeno, it will be impossible to traverse any distance, however small, because before getting to the end you must get halfway, and, before that, halfway to the halfway point, thus decomposing every movement into an unattainable infinity of sub-movements. Although they invoked this and other arguments for their thesis, I find it incredible that the Epicureans should have felt *compelled* by Zeno's paradoxes of motion to posit a minimal and partless magnitude. It was easy, if they needed to, for them to class Zeno's paradoxes as sophisms, and according to Epicurus a sophism does not need a painstaking solution: it is enough to recognize the evident falsity of its conclusion.[54] Zeno's puzzles supplied the arguments for the theory of minima, but surely not its main motivation.

Similarly, as regards the finite number of atomic types, one finds the Epicureans citing empirical evidence for it which, while not without credibility, can hardly have been enough to motivate let alone enforce the doctrine. According to Lucretius,[55] the doctrine is confirmed by the visible existence of limits in nature. If, he argues, there were an infinite variety of atomic types at the microscopic level, at the macroscopic level qualitative scales would stretch endlessly in both directions: it would in principle be possible to do what we in fact cannot do—to discover further colors, odors etc. beyond the termini of the existing scales. While one can understand the corroborative force of this empirical argument, it is hard to doubt that, had they wanted to defend instead the Democritean thesis of infinitely many atomic

53. Epicurus, *Ep. Hdt.* 43.
54. For Epicurus's treatment of sophisms, see the fragments of *On nature* XXVIII, ed. Sedley 1973, fr. 13 cols. IX–X.
55. Lucretius II 500–21 = LS 12C 3–4.

types, they could have easily found a way to reconcile it with the same empirical data. They might, for example, have maintained that the infinite variety of atomic types is needed to explain why *within* each finitely bounded qualitative continuum there appears to be unlimited scope for variation.

I infer that Epicurus's finitist conclusions—that analysis of a magnitude into its parts cannot continue ad infinitum, and that for this reason the number of atomic types is finite—had for him an importance over and above the Zenonian and empirical arguments used in their defense. And my suggestion is that that importance lay in the need to rescue Democritean atomism from its damaging commitment to an infinite range of atomic types.

To understand how Epicurus's innovation can help, we need to combine three premises. The first premise is that, as we have seen, the number of atomic types is finite. The second is that there is a largest possible size for a world.[56] The third is that, because atoms, and probably space too, are constituted of minimal magnitudes which do not admit of subdivision, the number of different spatial relations in which any two atoms can stand to each other within the compass of a single world is also finite.

Even for two atoms the number of such spatial relations is going to be large, and much larger if one adds the huge, but still finite, range of possible trajectories for one atom's *motion* relative to the other's.[57] For all the massive proliferation of alternatives, within the bounds of any determinate portion of space—say, the space that the largest possible world would fill—

---

56. At Lucretius II 1116–17 a world is said to have a maximum size that it can grow to. Although we are not given a reason for this, it seems likely to have been based on the common Epicurean analogy between worlds and animals. In addition, the following argument seems available as a last resort. By the principle of *isonomia* there is at least some degree of regularity to the distribution of worlds across space. Call the average distance between worlds n miles. Typically, then, a world could not be as big as, say, $3n$ miles in diameter without the likelihood of jostling against another world and breaking up. Given the variability of this distance, there might be the occasional world far enough from any other to survive despite having a significantly larger diameter, say $10n$, $20n$, or even $100n$. But clearly there must be *some* maximum beyond which a world would have no chance of forming and surviving. Hence there is a maximum size for a world. (If there seems something strangely contingent about the existence of a specific size limit, we may note that the weakly defended but nevertheless well-attested Epicurean thesis that there is a maximum size for atoms [LS 12A–C] seems no less arbitrary.)

57. For atomic motion, see LS section 11. Fortunately there are no intrinsic speed variations, because atoms are held all to move through space at a single uniform speed. The range of trajectories likewise comes out as finite, provided that space is assumed to be granular in structure—that is, to consist of minimal magnitudes as body does. For evidence that space was so viewed by the Epicureans, see LS 11F and vol. 1, pp. 51–52.

the number of permutations for these two atoms' spatial and kinetic relations to each other remains finite. If, next, one allows each of the two atoms
to be replaced, in turn, by atoms of every other existing type, the number
of permutations becomes mind-boggling, but remains finite. Finally, instead
of just two atoms apply the same principles of variation to a stock of atoms
large enough to constitute a world, up to the assumed maximum size that
a world can have. The number of available permutations is by now beyond
any human capacity for calculation, but it must still be finite. It follows that
the number of possible world types is finite.

Indeed, the number of possible world types is *de facto* a great deal smaller
than the total number of permutations envisaged by my calculation, because
vast collections of atoms have a propensity to organize themselves mechanically into certain patterns of motion, and thus in many cases to take
on at least the outline structure of a world automatically.

If even one world-type in that unimaginably vast set of permutations is
capable of sustaining life as beneficially as ours does, it is—as we ourselves
might choose to put it—a statistical certainty that worlds of that type exist not only here but also elsewhere in the universe, and will continue to
form in the future. The existence of our world is therefore neither a bizarre
fluke nor an act of god, but a simple working out of distributive inevitabil-
ities on an infinite scale.

It is important to notice here that, by contrast with Democritus and, in
due course, the Stoics as well (p. 208 below), Epicurus seems not to have spoken of two worlds being perfect doublets of each other, down to the minute
detail of containing identical inhabitants with the same names, histories etc.[58]
This is no coincidence.[59] Both Democritus and the Stoics were favorable to
determinism,[60] a doctrine which holds that given the same initial circumstances the very same events, human actions included, will inevitably follow. The postulation of indistinguishable worlds with identical histories is a
large-scale projection of just that thesis. Epicurus, as is well known, coun-

---

58. Epicurus fr. 307 Usener, from Jerome, is unique in attributing to Epicurus
something approaching this, a theory of exact historical repetition. It is probably
just his over-interpretation of Lucretius III 854–58.

59. For other ethical aspects of the atomists' many-world hypothesis, cf. Warren
2004b.

60. Epicurus certainly thought Democritus a determinist, albeit one who failed
to see the ethical consequences of his doctrine (LS 20C 13). It is not universally agreed
that Democritus was in fact committed to any kind of universal physical necessitation (see esp. Hirsch 1990 for doubts on this). I do not wish to argue the point here,
beyond observing that his strong identical-worlds thesis is itself neglected evidence
that he *was* a conscious determinist.

tered the deterministic tendency by incorporating a small degree of genuine indeterminacy into the motions of atoms, the "swerve," sufficient to prevent human action from being fully predetermined by the antecedent physical or psychological conditions. This means that for him, even if world A at some given moment were atomically indistinguishable from world B at some given moment, nothing would follow about those two worlds and their inhabitants also having identical histories. For the same reason, there simply are *no* specifiable atomic conditions sufficient to produce a world containing a human history identical to that in the present world.[61]

Given this indeterminacy, it was only to be expected that his postulation of matching worlds should limit itself to exact repetition of the overall cosmological, ecological, and biological conditions by which those worlds are constituted. For his purposes, our world's twin need not be one in which your perfect double is reading a book containing this precise English sentence. It is enough that the matching world should share with ours the entire set of physical conditions sufficient to produce and sustain life as we know it. This more permissive expectation not only saves Epicurus from both paradox and determinism, but also ensures that the recurrence of the "same" world-type will be statistically much more frequent and less astonishing than in its Democritean equivalent.

My talk of statistical frequencies and certainties easily invites the charge of anachronism. Certainly no actual mathematical calculation of probabilities should be assumed. Nevertheless, in a culture where the throwing of dice was among the favorite games it is hardly conceivable that the relative likelihood of different permutations was an altogether unfamiliar concept. The game of dice was admittedly proverbial more for blind luck than for anything like statistical likelihood.[62] But Aristotle, at least, can be seen invoking an analogy between runs of success in dice-throwing and those in

61. Epicurus *could*, it is true, have gone on to argue as follows: there are only a finite number of possible atomic swerves in the lifetime of a world; so within any infinite set of worlds which are indistinguishable from each other at some given moment in their respective histories there must be a tiny proportion which by sheer accident are also indistinguishable from each other at all other times in their respective histories. However, it may be questioned whether even that coincidence would in his eyes suffice to generate worlds which were perfect doublets of each other. For Epicurus is not a Democritean reductionist (as I argue in Sedley 1988), and in his eyes the atomic constitution of one's body and soul may not be sufficient to determine the entire state of one's consciousness. Hence even two worlds with identical atomic histories might not contain psychologically indistinguishable people.

62. Similarly the game of knucklebones was proverbial for fate. For both games see Kurke 1999, pp. 283–95.

practical activity: the longer the run, the harder its attainment (*De caelo* 292a28–34).

Most directly relevant, however, is the Epicureans' attested commitment to the explanatory power of *isonomia*, "equal distribution" within infinite sets. Given only the premises that there are a finite number of possible world-types, and that across an infinite universe these will be distributed in a more or less regular and endlessly repeated pattern,[63] the case appears to go through: even in the absence of intelligent creation, there had to be worlds like ours.

63. For simplicity I have been assuming arithmetical equality: all world types have equal frequency. But the point would not be endangered if this were replaced by proportional equality. Maybe some world-types are n times rarer than others, e.g. because they depend on a more uneven distribution of their constituent atoms. The requirement that they recur at certain specific intervals will not be endangered: it is only the size of the intervals that will need to be revised.

VI Aristotle

1. GOD AS PARADIGM

Aristotle (384–322 B.C.) was Plato's student for two decades before founding his own school. Is it more fruitful to think of his mature work as anti-Platonist, or as that of an independent Platonist? Although this age-old question does not admit of final resolution, I am convinced with regard to my present topic, the explanation of purposive structures in the world, that most can be learnt by emphasizing, rather than minimizing, Aristotle's Platonic background and training.[1]

Aristotle is the greatest teleological thinker of antiquity, probably of all time, and his teleology takes us to the very heart of his physics, his biology, his metaphysics, and his ethics.[2] It is no part of my purpose, in the single chapter I shall devote to him, to cover all these aspects of his work. Instead I want to defend a portrayal of Aristotle's teleological worldview as a reasoned modification of Plato's creationism. Of course, in this field he was doing much more than modifying Plato. For one thing, he happened to be the ancient world's greatest zoologist, and his zoological research enabled him to develop his teleological thinking to a level Plato could not easily have envisaged. But my focus will not be on Aristotle's biological writings. The chapter will be largely directed at a single book, book II of his *Physics*, which is his systematic defense of the teleological worldview against its competitors.

---

1. Gerson 2005, provocatively entitled *Aristotle and Other Platonists,* appeared only after I had drafted this chapter. It should be consulted for a much more ambitious, and more Neoplatonic, assimilation of the two than I have contemplated, including chapter 4 on issues relating to causation.

2. I must here leave untouched many of the major issues in Aristotle's teleology, on which see esp. Gotthelf 1997.

Plato, like nearly every other thinker in and well after antiquity, associated teleology with conscious purpose. To make the world a purposive structure just is to posit an intelligent mind as its cause. True, the intelligent mind could have created the world and then left it to run itself mechanically, but no ancient thinker—after at any rate Anaxagoras, whose position on the point is open to dispute—was ready to contemplate a split-level theory of that kind. Either the world was intelligently created and is intelligently run, or it originated from non-intelligent causes and is still, with the possible exception of human action, governed by causes of that same kind. We have seen at length how, while the atomists defended the latter view, Plato developed the former: his Demiurge, who created the world, has left it under the overall control of the intelligent and divine world soul.[3]

In conformity to this background, Aristotle too treats the twin issues of creation and administration in strict parallel to each other. The world, along with its resident species, is not the product of an intelligent act of creation, for the simple reason that it had no beginning at all but has always existed—a thesis he defends by appeal to the essential eternity of the heaven's circular motion. And likewise when it comes to the world's continued functioning, there is no divine oversight, planning, or enforcement.[4] So far he may seem to tend closer to the atomist camp, since no divine interest in our world is invoked at any stage. But like Plato, and unlike the atomists, he nevertheless holds that throughout the natural world there are irreducibly purposive structures. Pretty well everything in nature has a purpose, despite the fact that no intelligence either conceived that purpose or administers it.

This restrained teleology has won Aristotle innumerable admirers. For, it is rightly said, purposive structures are indeed basic to nature, quite regardless of the question of divine control or its absence. Never mind whether you are a creationist or the most hardened of Darwinians: you cannot avoid saying that the heart is for pumping blood, the eyelid for protecting the eye, the teeth for cutting and grinding food. Nor, for the Darwinian, are these

---

3. It is admittedly hard to establish how much more the Platonic world soul governs than the celestial rotations. But *Ti.* 37a4–c5 (on which cf. Reydams-Schils 1997) makes it clear that it has true "opinions" (δόξαι) about the sensible world of becoming, and hence does not concentrate its thought exclusively on pure being.

4. True, Aristotle does occasionally talk as if god can be credited with some providential action, e.g. GC II 10 336b27–34, but I join the consensus that regards such locutions as merely figurative (see esp. Solmsen 1963, pp. 485–95, but cf. Bodéüs 2000 for a less dismissive reading).

locutions just a shorthand for some more accurate mode of biological explanation: adequate non-teleological explanations of the parts of the eye are simply not available.

Now it is one thing to commend Aristotle for the refreshing modernity of his teleological thinking, and to contrast it with the antiquated creationism of a Plato. It is quite another thing to suppose that the outlook's appearance of modernity is the key to Aristotle's own rationale in developing the theory in this particular way. Ancient atomism likewise resulted in a great many modern-looking theses, yet started from premises utterly unlike those of modern or even early-modern physics. Similarly, or so I shall argue, Aristotle's minimalist approach to purpose in nature is very far from being a sign of his modernity. Such a recognition should not, however, lessen our appreciation of the light that his ideas can be used to shed.

Where did the motivation for Aristotle's revised teleology come from? From an unexpected quarter, it seems. Plato had famously conceded in book VII of the *Republic* that for a philosopher government ranks second best to the life of pure contemplation. And correspondingly in the *Timaeus,* where he maintains that the entire world has been so structured as to enable the rational human soul to imitate the divine mind through the study of astronomy and philosophy, this imitation of god is located in pure mathematical and philosophical contemplation, rather than in the exercise of moral or political virtues.[5] Yet the divine creator and divine world soul of Plato's *Timaeus* are themselves viewed as partly engaged in world management. If so they are not, even on Plato's own view, exclusively engaged in the best activity available to them.

Aristotle is in this regard more Platonist than Plato himself. He too (*Nicomachean ethics* X 7–8) holds that the kind of happiness that can come from leading a virtuous civic life, although of great value, is second best to the godlike happiness of pure detached contemplation. But he improves on Plato to the extent that he seeks to make his own theology consistent with that same ranking of different brands of happiness. God's activity can only be the best, he argues in *Metaphysics* Lambda, and if so it must be pure contemplation.[6]

The effect of this minor-looking adjustment to Platonism is breathtak-

---

5. I defend this interpretation of the *Timaeus* in Sedley 1999d.
6. It is entirely possible that this complete insulation of god from practical activity took time to evolve, and is not yet fully worked out in the *De caelo,* although even there note for example 292a22–28 on god as free from *praxis.*

ingly far-reaching. If god must be a pure contemplator, he cannot be an administrator.[7] There can therefore be no Demiurge, and no divine world soul. In which case, the world is uncreated and functions without divine oversight. The outcome is, in short, Aristotle's cosmology.

In positing a detached and self-absorbed god, one who is above any inclination to intervene in our world, Aristotle sounds surprisingly similar to Epicurus. Yet unlike Epicurus he fully shares with Plato the conviction that god is the supreme explanatory principle. And he reconciles these two apparently conflicting motifs—god as detached and god as causally supreme—by drawing on another Platonic idea: that god is the supreme object of emulation. The goal of life, as Plato's followers expressed his idea, is "to become as like god as possible."[8] Plato meant this goal mainly as a human aspiration, although in one context (*Symposium* 207c9–208b6) he extended it to the entire animal kingdom by presenting the drive to propagate as mortal organisms' best shot at attaining personal immortality—surrogate immortality, that is, achieved by living on through their descendants—and thereby perhaps also (cf. *Laws* IV 721b6–c8) the perpetuity of their species. Aristotle takes up this cue, and develops the idea still further. The supreme divinity is an unmoved mover, a detached self-contemplator, whose activity is pure actuality, and *everything* else in the world functions by striving, in its own way, to emulate that actuality.[9]

The highest human aspiration, philosophical contemplation, is the most direct imitation of god's own activity (*Nicomachean ethics* X 7, 1177b26–1178a8; X 8, 1178b7–32). Procreation, in humans, lower animals, and plants, is as it had been for Plato a bid for immortality by proxy, another way of imitating god's eternal actuality, namely by perpetuating both oneself and one's species (*De anima* II 4, 415a26–b7; *Politics* I 2 1252a28–30; *On generation of animals* II 1, 731b24–732a1; *Metaphysics* Θ 8, 1050b28–30).[10] Even below the level of plant life, the world's natural cycles, such as the weather cycle whereby the four elementary bodies undergo endlessly repeated intertransformations, are imitations of god's eternal ac-

7. For an especially forthright development of this theology on Aristotle's behalf, cf. the passages of Alexander of Aphrodisias (c. A.D. 200) cited and discussed by Sharples 2003.

8. Annas 1999, chapter 3; Sedley 1999b.

9. Cf. *EE* VII 15, 1249b13–15, "For it is not by giving commands that god is ruler, but as the good towards which practical wisdom gives commands."

10. Cf. Burnyeat 2004, p. 24, for the possibility that in addition the latter cycles are for the sake of the former.

tuality (*Meteorologica* I 9, 346b35–347a10, *On generation and corruption* II 10, 336b34–337a7).

It is, in short, scarcely an exaggeration to say that for Aristotle the entire functioning of the natural world, as also that of the heavens, is ultimately to be understood as a shared striving towards godlike actuality.[11] Admittedly Aristotle does not very often stand back to view the matter panoramically in this way, for his interest is far more often taken up with specific biological structures and processes and their contribution to the organism's success; but he does view it along these lines in *Metaphysics* Lambda 10, the culminating chapter of his theological treatise, to which I shall return in §5.

Even biological structures that might have been accounted for in far more down-to-earth ways are, on occasion, brought by Aristotle under the same explanatory principle of striving for godlikeness. According to Plato in the *Timaeus* (45a3–b2), describing the original creation of the human body, our creators made the face the natural front (here, as in Aristotle's biology, defined by the orientation of the senses), because front is "more honorable" *(τιμιώτερον)* than back, being both of higher ranking and more appropriate to leadership. This evaluative ranking of directions, which the modernizing interpretation would happily have seen Aristotle consign to history, is a doctrine which on the contrary he develops and frequently exploits. According to Aristotle, not only is front more honorable than back, but so are right than left and up than down.

To take the up-down polarity, man's unique uprightness makes him superior, to the extent that his natural up, that is his head, coincides with the cosmos's upward direction (*On parts of animals* II 10, 656a7–13):

> Of this kind is the human race. For it, either alone or most of all among animals known to us, shares in the divine . . . It is alone in having its natural parts in the natural arrangement, and its up is related in the natural way to the universe's up. For alone of the animals, man is upright.[12]

At the other end of the biological spectrum, plants have their natural "up" coinciding with the cosmic down, in that their roots—which are functionally their mouths—are down in the soil. For example (*De anima* II 4, 416a2–5):

11. See esp. Kahn 1985.

12. There are many other relevant passages in Aristotle, but I here limit myself to citing for comparison *HA* I 15, 494a20–b1 (which supplies a good deal more detail), and *De iuv.* 477a21–23. Gregoric 2005 is a valuable comparison of Plato's and Aristotle's explanations of human erect posture, but in my view does not pay sufficient attention to the intrinsic value both attach to our postural kinship with cosmic topography, for which (regarding Plato) cf. Osborne 1988, pp. 107–9.

For up and down are not the same for each and every being, but as the head is in animals so the roots are in plants, if one ought to call organs different or the same by their functions.

Virtually all of this is Platonic in origin. Compare *Timaeus* 90a2–b1:

Concerning the most authoritative kind of soul found in us, we must have the following thought. God has given it to each of us as a daimon—this thing which we say dwells at the topmost part of our body and raises us up from the earth towards what is akin to us in the heaven, because we rightly call ourselves a heavenly plant, not an earthly one. For the divinity keeps our body upright by suspending our head and root from the place out of which our soul was first born.

We can here see how Aristotle's treatment of plants as inverted human beings has its origin in Plato's elevation of human beings to the status of inverted plants. In so far as Aristotle gives "up" and "down" their own specialized biological senses—as Plato had already done in speaking of a "natural front"—Aristotle is no doubt saying something scientifically credible.[13] Try drinking a cup of tea while standing on your head. We might intelligibly ask if you can get the tea to go "down" your throat. Even though its geographical or cosmic direction of flow is up, we understand the expression because in context we assign "down" a meaning determined by biological function alone. Aristotle similarly assigns directions like up and down their own functional biological senses (*De incessu animalium* 4–5).

Nevertheless, the use to which Aristotle puts this mode of expression is hardly so innocuous. When he presents up, front, and right as "better and more honorable" (*On parts of animals* 665a6–26), he does so in the context of explaining why, in human anatomy, nature sometimes favors these orientations even when practical utility alone would not. Thus the heart, as governing organ, occupies the "honorable" front,[14] even though that in turn requires the windpipe, which services it, to be "badly placed" in front of the esophagus; the resultant danger of food going down the wrong hole then requires the remedial provision of the epiglottis.

The reason why, regardless of practical utility, Aristotle attaches an honorable status to the body's sharing the cosmic inclinations up, front, and

13. Thus Lennox 1985b, pp. 266–72, replying to Lloyd 1966, pp. 52–61. It will be evident that my main sympathies are with Lloyd, but Lennox is a valuable guide to the controversy.

14. Unlike Lennox 1985b, pp. 266–69 (cf. Lennox 2001b, p. 254), I understand *PA* 665a19–26 as saying that the reason why the heart must necessarily be at the front is that it is more honorable, and not that it is practically advantageous.

right is his belief, also derived from Plato,[15] that these orientations represent the divine source or direction of motion governing the rotation of the heavens themselves (*De caelo* II 2). The fact that in the anatomy of the best animals, namely humans, inclinations to front, up, and right are repeatedly favored is therefore one expression of our superior likeness to the divine heavens, and through them to god.

If the whole natural world is, in one way or another, pulling itself up by its own bootstraps in the interests of maximum godlikeness, how is that possible? Desire is a faculty that, according to Aristotle, is found only in animals, yet he is explicit that plants too strive for immortality through reproduction, and that in some attenuated way even the four elementary bodies strive for everlasting actuality. Almost certainly the notion of striving will have to be interpreted reductively, as describing an inherent natural tendency. Such psychologizing descriptions of nonpsychological processes, misleading and indispensable in equal measure, have been commonplace in the history of science, from "Nature abhors a vacuum" to Natural Selection and the Selfish Gene. Certainly the *Timaeus* is full of them, including of course intelligence's "persuasion" of the four elementary stuffs (pp. 114–16 above).

But even after effecting such a reduction, we are left with the following result. The reason why in Aristotle's view no directive mind can be at work in natural processes is not any preference on his part for "scientific" over theological modes of explanation. It lies rather in the conviction that the Platonic account gets the theology *wrong*. God's causality in the natural world is omnipresent, as Plato held, but must be such that all the operative drives and impulses belong to the natural entities, leaving god himself eternally detached and self-focused.

2. THE CRAFT ANALOGY

Plato had appealed not merely to divine benevolence in explaining the natural world, but also to divine craft, which was itself in turn to be understood in terms of familiar human craft. It could hardly be denied that Plato had been stunningly successful in explaining the natural world as the product of craftsmanship, and Aristotle must have been loath to throw away those gains. Yet divine craftsmanship was ruled out by his theology, as we have seen. No natural process could be acceptably explained along the lines set

15. In the *Timaeus*, heavenly rotation is both to the right, 36c6, and forwards, 40b1. Cf. also 90a2–b1, quoted above.

by Plato, as decreed by the deliberations of a world soul or of any other immanent deity, let alone a transcendent one. Such then was Aristotle's dilemma. He resolved it, as *Physics* II eloquently attests, by developing his conviction that although nature is not divine craft, it is sufficiently *analogous* to craft in its working for much of the light shed by Plato to remain. So wedded is he to the craft analogy that its characteristic language is ubiquitous in his biological writings, where he frequently for example speaks figuratively of nature as an agent "crafting" (*dēmiourgein*, cognate with "Demiurge") her products.[16]

Aristotle's whole understanding of natural processes relies on his famous distinction between four kinds of cause. And the first way in which the craft model comes to his aid is in enabling him to elucidate that very distinction. His preferred methodology is, as he reminds us at the opening of the *Physics* (I 1, 184a16–21), to start with what is more familiar, or makes more sense, *to us* (that which is *gnōrimōteron hēmin*), and to move from there to what makes more sense *in its own right* (that which is *gnōrimōteron haplōs* or *physei*). The causal processes of nature make more sense in their own right, and exhibit teleology in a higher degree, but the causal processes of craft make more sense to us, because all of us have practiced a craft or witnessed one at close quarters.

Aristotle therefore uses craft examples to demarcate the four causes (*Physics* II 3), before moving on to their application to nature. In a craft, it is normal for the practitioner to impose some form on preexisting matter, for example a sculptor on bronze. Here the *material* cause is the bronze, the *moving* cause (often called the "efficient" cause) is the sculptor, and the *formal* cause is the form he imposes on it, all unmistakably distinct from each other. In addition to these, the sculptor works with a goal in view, perhaps the completion or perfection of the statue, and this too is a distinct motivating factor in the story, the *final* (meaning "end-related") cause. Thus four distinct causes—material, moving, formal, and final—are clearly exhibited by craft, and it is only once we have mastered them and their interrelation in this familiar guise that we are ready to look for them in nature.

In nature, the four causes are much trickier to disentangle from each other. Take the development of a pig, and to begin with, its material cause. The pig's matter—its flesh, bones, and the like—is certainly a causal factor helping to constitute its nature, but is not nearly as readily distinguishable

---

16. Cooper 1982, although to my mind a most penetrating portrayal of Aristotle's teleology, is I think wrong to deny the craft analogy's centrality to Aristotle's physical thought. For a convincing reply on this point, see Broadie 1990, pp. 392–96.

from the pig's form as the bronze was from the shape of the statue it constituted; for one thing, there never was a time in the pig's history or prehistory when all these specific materials existed without already having the
form of pig, in the way that before the statue was made the bronze was there
to be inspected. For an analogous reason the pig's formal cause, that is, its
essential form as a pig, is not at first sight fully distinct from its matter. Third,
take the moving cause of the changes the pig undergoes. This lies initially
(according to Aristotle's theory of animal generation) in its father, and hence
is external to it, as the sculptor was to the bronze, but during its lifetime its
active moving cause becomes an internal one, since this role of mover is taken
over by the pig's own soul, identifiable once more with its essential form.
Nor is the final cause of its growth, that is, the end or goal governing the
process, any more straightforwardly distinguishable from its form, because
that goal really just *is* its fully developed form as a pig, towards which it is
striving.[17]

Nature, then, is difficult. But if we start from the causal distinctions that
craft clarifies we can aspire to understand it. And there is a further reason
why we should hope to progress from craft to nature. A craft, according to
Aristotle, is an extension of what nature already does. (We have already met
this same idea in Epicurus, pp. 153–54 above.)[18] A craft takes over where
nature leaves off, imitating and completing nature's work. For this very reason, he argues (*Physics* II 8, 199a15–20), we can work out that nature already embodies goals or purposes, because that is the only possible source
of the goals which crafts adopt. For instance, since medicine is a craft that
aims to help the body regain its health, that goal of regaining health can be
seen to have already been governing the internal natural healing processes,
which the doctor intervenes merely to facilitate and complete.

In further support of this contention, Aristotle propounds what later
philosophers were to call a "sorites" or "little-by-little" argument (*Physics* II
8, 199a20–30). Take a case from nature in which the presence of purpose is
uncontroversial: a spider weaving its web, or a bird building its nest. These
actions are so obviously goal-directed, he points out, that people have wondered whether spiders and birds might not be exercising intelligence or craft.
Starting from such uncontroversial cases of purposiveness, work down the
natural scale through simpler and simpler processes and structures, until

17. E.g. *Ph.* II 7, 198a24–27; *PA* I 1, 641a25–27.
18. This need not be a sign of Epicurus's knowledge of Aristotle, because both
are likely to have been familiar with the idea from (if nowhere else) Plato *Laws* X
889a4–e1, where it is said to be widely held.

you get to one as basic as plants putting down roots. Since on this natural scale there is no suitable cut-off point at which purpose vanishes, it becomes hard to disbelieve that there is purpose all the way down.

The argument is a seductive one. As a matter of fact, however, sorites arguments are fallacious. Logicians may not agree about where the fallacy lies, but that they must be fallacious seems to follow from the reflection that if they proved anything they would prove far too much, erasing a vast number of indispensable distinctions. For example, if Aristotle's argument proves that there is purpose all the way down in nature, a similar argument would prove that everybody is rich, since as you work dollar by dollar down the scale of bank balances, starting with Bill Gates, you will find no natural cut-off point at which wealth ceases. Even leaving aside that worry, Aristotle's argument faces the objection that it could just as well have been used to prove the opposite: starting from an evidently mechanical and nonpurposive natural process, such as an iron railing rusting, a materialist analysis might plausibly work its way up through more and more purposive-looking items until it reached the bird building its nest, and on from there to human actions, maintaining that the causes remain mechanical all the way up.

Despite any such formal difficulties with the actual argument, the fact remains that for Aristotle, as a practicing biologist, nature really is the continuum that this argument portrays, and that there are virtually no exceptions to his generalization that if anything recurs on a regular basis it must be for the sake of something.

At the top end of the *scala naturae,* likewise, nature forms a near-continuum with craft, it being at times hard to tell where the one stops and the other starts. How, then, does craft still *differ* from nature? This is a vital question. For, once Aristotle has identified the residual differences between craft and nature, his project is to devise perspectives and thought-experiments which will shrink or even erase those differences. Such is his procedure for obtaining illumination from the craft-nature analogy, while stopping short of Plato's position, that of fully identifying nature with divine craft.

The first and most obvious difference between craft and nature, in Aristotle's eyes, is that in craft the moving cause is regularly external to the matter. Carpenters are external to their wood, cooks are external to their ingredients, doctors are external to their patients. It is precisely for this reason that the crafts teach us, more clearly than nature can, that the moving cause acting upon the matter really is a distinct factor in the process. Yet even in craft the moving cause is not *essentially* external, Aristotle points out, and here the gap between craft and nature can be narrowed: if a doctor treats himself, the change in his own body from illness to health results from an internal moving cause. That is *very* much like a natural process. Admittedly in this special case of the self-curing doctor the moving cause is not *essentially* internal, as it would be in nature. It just happens that the doctor is also the patient, and it could easily have been otherwise (II 1, 192b23–27). Still, as Aristotle illuminatingly says, when a doctor cures himself this is just about as near to nature as craft can come (II 8, 199b30–32).

Perhaps Aristotle should have left it at that. But, to take yet a further step in the same direction, he asks us to perform a thought experiment (199b28–30): we are invited to imagine the craft of shipbuilding as being present, not in the shipbuilder, but in the timber itself. If that were so, and the moving cause had become a source of change internal to the matter instead of external to it, we would see ships grow naturally out of piles of planks. This particular image may sound too bizarre to be helpful, and it is a pity that Aristotle did not instead choose for his example a material which could more easily be imagined as shaping itself from inside, such as a lump of clay growing into a pot, the potter's craft having been implanted in it instead of imposed from outside. Even then what such thought experiments reveal, and conceivably are designed to concede, is that the craft-nature gap could never be closed altogether. Provided that they illuminate the continuum of purpose between artificial and natural processes, they have done their job.

But isn't the kind of purposiveness that is present in nature exactly where this analogy fails? The most obvious of objections to Aristotle's reasoning is that purpose is present in craft precisely because of the involvement of a human craftsman with an intellect. And isn't it his most central thesis that this craftsmanship has no analogue in nature, god being entirely detached from the natural world? Without the admission of a creative or productive intellect operative in natural processes, how can purpose exist in nature? And how can the craft analogy be of any assistance?

Here is Aristotle's enigmatic remark on the question (199b26–28):

> It is ridiculous for people not to believe that something is coming about for a purpose if they do not see that the moving cause has deliberated. Yet craft too does not deliberate.[19]

Craft does not deliberate? But of course it does, at least in our everyday experience of crafts on which Aristotle's methodology leans so heavily. Scholars have, in my view, generated unnecessary difficulties over the interpre-

---

19. ἄτοπον δὲ τὸ μὴ οἴεσθαι ἕνεκά του γίγνεσθαι, ἐὰν μὴ ἴδωσι τὸ κινοῦν βουλευσάμενον. καίτοι καὶ ἡ τέχνη οὐ βουλεύεται.

tation of this admittedly dark remark. It is regularly suggested that Aristotle has in mind an idealized picture of the craftsman. This ideal practitioner's skill has developed to such a high degree that he no longer has to ask himself how to perform a particular operation, that is, to deliberate: he just goes ahead and does it.[20]

The trouble is that to the best of my knowledge nowhere else in the Aristotelian corpus has such an idealization of craft yet been found. Quite apart from the fact that few of us would put our lives in the hands of a surgeon who did not deliberate before amputating a leg, or of an airline pilot who did not choose a flight path before takeoff, Aristotle himself again and again depicts the operations of craft precisely in terms of deliberation.[21] Deliberation is how we choose the best means to a given end, and the presence of deliberation in a process is therefore a salient sign that it is end-directed. And yet, for reasons we have yet to discover, Aristotle says in the quoted passage that crafts do not in fact deliberate.

For a more satisfactory understanding of this puzzling remark, I am convinced that we must go back to Aristotle's causal theory. In it, his debt to Plato is greater than is sometimes recognized. For Plato, a fundamental causal process is one which is analytically self-evident.[22] For example, heat makes you hot, and wisdom makes you wise. Such statements are hardly informative, and in modern usage would not normally be deemed causal at all, but at least they seem analytically true, and for Plato that is where their great merit lies. Other, more obviously synthetic causal statements, such as that jogging makes you hot, or that studying geometry makes you wise, are more debatable precisely because they do not keep the cause-effect relation itself transparent.

Now Aristotle's ultimate commitment to this Platonic causal principle is discernible in many contexts, but none more so than *Physics* II 3, the famous chapter in which he formally expounds his theory of four causes, and

---

20. The best defense of this interpretation known to me is Broadie 1990. I am grateful to Sarah Broadie for correspondence on the issue as well.

21. Cf. n. 24 below. True, in his account of deliberation in the *Ethics* (*EN* III 3, 1112a34–b8) Aristotle allows that in certain relatively precise disciplines, such as spelling, deliberation is superfluous. But in that same context he is careful to call these disciplines "sciences" ($\dot{\epsilon}\pi\iota\sigma\tau\hat{\eta}\mu\alpha\iota$), and contrasts them with "crafts" ($\tau\acute{\epsilon}\chi\nu\alpha\iota$), including medicine, in which he insists that deliberation typically *is* required. And medicine, let us recall, is his favored craft in the *Physics* when it comes to the craft-nature analogy. At *Met.* A 1, 981b2–5 acting automatically and unreflectively is the hallmark of menial workers ($\chi\epsilon\iota\rho\sigma\tau\acute{\epsilon}\chi\nu\alpha\iota$), who fall below the level of "craft" ($\tau\acute{\epsilon}\chi\nu\eta$).

22. See further, Sedley 1998b.

which constitutes the immediate background to chapter 8, where the puzzling remark about craft is located. One example that he repeatedly invokes there is that of the moving cause of a building (*oikia*). To answer the question, "What is the moving cause of this building (*oikia*)?" by saying that it is a builder (*oikodomos*) is an excellent answer. Why? Because the causal relationship between builder and building is far from accidental, in that builders and buildings are suitably related much in the way that wisdom, as cause, is suitably related to the effect of someone's being wise. But suppose that the builder is called Jones. To have said, instead, that the moving cause of the building is Jones would, although true, have stated a merely accidental cause. There is nothing about his being Jones that links him causally or explanatorily to the building, in the way that his being a builder manifestly does.

Nevertheless, even to refer to the moving cause of the building as "a builder" falls short of the ideal answer, it turns out. Near the end of chapter 3, Aristotle writes (195b21–25):

> One must always seek the ultimate cause of each thing, as in other matters. For example, a man builds because he is a builder, but the builder builds in virtue of the building craft. This cause, therefore, is prior.[23]

That is, even when we nominate a builder as the cause of the building we have not gone all the way to isolating its immediate moving cause. Strictly speaking the building craft, located in the builder's soul, is the ultimate cause accounting for the building. Jones builds in virtue of being a builder, and the builder builds in virtue of the building craft. We cannot continue this regress, because there is no further thing in virtue of which the building craft causes the building. With the building craft, therefore, we have found the ultimate moving cause.

This admittedly unintuitive refocusing of our causal language serves a vital purpose in Aristotle's metaphysics. Form, he holds, is eternal. In nature, an organism's form preexists it, typically by being already present in its father, who according to Aristotle was the organism's original and external moving cause. (Try substituting the thought that your genetic code in some sense preexisted you in your ancestors.) To throw light on this, Aristotle compares the preexistence of form in nature to the way that in a craft the artifact's form preexists the artifact itself, by being already present in

---

23. δεῖ δ' ἀεὶ τὸ αἴτιον ἑκάστου τὸ ἀκρότατον ζητεῖν, ὥσπερ καὶ ἐπὶ τῶν ἄλλων. οἷον ἄνθρωπος οἰκοδομεῖ ὅτι οἰκοδόμος, ὁ δ' οἰκοδόμος κατὰ τὴν οἰκοδομικήν· τοῦτο τοίνυν πρότερον τὸ αἴτιον.

the mind of the craftsman. The form of some particular building, for example, existed before it was built, namely in the mind of its builder. Thus he writes in *Metaphysics* Zeta 7 (1032b5–14):

> Health is the formula in the soul, and the science. The healthy state comes to be when the doctor has thought as follows: "Since such and such is health, if a healthy state is to be such and such must exist, for example a balanced condition, and if this is going to be, heat." And so he goes on thinking until he brings it down to an end point which he can himself enact. Thereafter, the movement towards a healthy condition which starts from this is already called production. Hence it results that in a way health comes to be from health, and building from building, namely the material building from an immaterial building. For the medical craft and the building craft are, respectively, the form of health and the form of the building. What I am calling immaterial being is the thing's essence.[24]

Vitally, the building craft *is* the immaterial form or essence of the building, resident in the builder's soul before he imposes that same essential form on the bricks and mortar.

In the light of all this, we can return to the enigmatic pronouncement of *Physics* II 8, "It is ridiculous for people not to believe that something is coming about for the sake of something if they do not see that the moving cause has deliberated. Yet craft too does not deliberate." Aristotle does not mean to deny that the craftsman deliberates. But the craftsman is not, in the strictest sense, the moving cause. The ultimate moving cause is, as we have seen, the craft itself, identifiable with the essential form of the product resident all along in the craftsman's soul. And that ultimate moving cause does not do any deliberating.

Seen in this light, Aristotle's strategy is not, as often thought, to deny that deliberation is on the one hand present in crafts but on the other hand absent from nature. His point is rather that, when you strip down to its hard core the causality by which in each of the two domains the moving cause

---

24. ἡ δὲ ὑγίεια ὁ ἐν τῇ ψυχῇ λόγος καὶ ἡ ἐπιστήμη. γίγνεται δὲ τὸ ὑγιὲς νοήσαντος οὕτως· ἐπειδὴ τοδὶ ὑγίεια, ἀνάγκη εἰ ὑγιὲς ἔσται τοδὶ ὑπάρξαι, οἷον ὁμαλότητα, εἰ δὲ τοῦτο, θερμότητα· καὶ οὕτως ἀεὶ νοεῖ, ἕως ἂν ἀγάγῃ εἰς τοῦτο ὃ αὐτὸς δύναται ἔσχατον ποιεῖν. εἶτα ἤδη ἡ ἀπὸ τούτου κίνησις ποίησις καλεῖται, ἡ ἐπὶ τὸ ὑγιαίνειν. ὥστε συμβαίνει τρόπον τινὰ τὴν ὑγίειαν ἐξ ὑγιείας γίγνεσθαι καὶ τὴν οἰκίαν ἐξ οἰκίας, τῆς ἄνευ ὕλης τὴν ἔχουσαν ὕλην· ἡ γὰρ ἰατρική ἐστι καὶ ἡ οἰκοδομικὴ τὸ εἶδος τῆς ὑγιείας καὶ τῆς οἰκίας, λέγω δὲ οὐσίαν ἄνευ ὕλης τὸ τί ἦν εἶναι. Notice how Aristotle develops this point without for a moment wanting to minimize the role of conscious deliberation in the process by which the form is transferred to the external matter. For a builder's deliberation, cf. also PA I 1, 639b25–30.

operates, the deliberation that occurs in craft becomes a strictly ancillary factor. In craft and nature alike, an essential form serves as a moving cause which brings about its own imposition on the relevant matter. The form of the building, present initially in the builder's soul, prompts the movements which end in that same form's being fully present in the bricks and mortar. The form of pig, present originally in the piglet's father and later progressively in the piglet itself, prompts the movements which end in that same form's being fully realized in the mature adult pig.

The use of analogy, such as Aristotle's craft-nature analogy, unavoidably requires that some gap remain between the two compared items. At the same time, however, the greater the number of differences between the analogically related items that can be eliminated or marginalized the more persuasive and informative the analogy becomes. Differences undoubtedly remain between the two processes, and the fact that deliberation plays a part in craft but not in natural processes is one of these. But such differences in Aristotle's eyes should not be allowed to mask the underlying isomorphism between the two causal processes. And pointing out that in neither case does the ultimate moving cause, namely the essential form, do any thinking helps to confirm how deep that isomorphism runs. This is why the causal structure of craft really does enlighten us about the causal structure of nature.

3. NECESSITY

By these and other means, Aristotle defends the presence of non-deliberative but nevertheless purposive structures in nature. The question remains for him to answer, why the kind of explanation pioneered by the early atomists could not account as effectively for the same explananda. And both earlier and later in the same book, book II of the *Physics,* he tries to show why not.

Two explanatory concepts in particular had been invoked by the atomists: necessity and the fortuitous. Although these might sound like antithetical notions, with necessity utterly dependable, the fortuitous utterly undependable, for the atomists they represent two aspects of a single causal story: everything results from the motions and collisions of atoms, and these are necessary in that they follow mechanical sequences of cause and effect, but fortuitous in that they exhibit no systematic or rational, goal-directed structure.[25] Aristotle's project is to show that although necessity and the fortuitous are indeed proper explanatory factors, once we fully understand

---

25. In deference to the prudent warnings of Hirsch 1990, I have avoided talking about unbreakable "laws" here. But I do not share her belief that Democritus, for

what they are we will see that their existence, far from eliminating purpose, confirms its existence.

I shall start with necessity, even though Aristotle himself treats it last (II 9). Those who see necessity at work in nature—he means above all the atomists—make the mistake of assuming that the necessity in question is one whereby the material properties of the world's elements necessitate all outcomes. That, says Aristotle (199b35–200a5) with a characteristic appeal to his craft-nature analogy, is analogous to thinking that, in the building industry, a wall could be the necessary outcome of a pile of stones, as if these might by their mechanical properties alone organize themselves with the heavy ones at the bottom, the lighter ones at the top. Here he no doubt parodies atomist cosmogony, in which the atoms were supposed (p. 136 above) to organize themselves into a world much as the different kinds of pebbles on a beach stratify themselves according to shape and size.

Nevertheless, Aristotle implicitly concedes, these opponents' talk of the "necessary" powers of matter does gesture towards a truth, one they have only half understood. In natural processes matter does manifest necessity, but this is in fact "conditional" or "hypothetical" necessity. *If* a wall is to be built, it is *necessary* that there should be stones. Likewise in nature, the matter underlying any process is necessary *if* the end is to be completed, without in itself necessitating the outcome. Thus natural necessity, once understood, does not replace purpose or render it redundant, but on the contrary presupposes it.

There is, however, a considerable problem as to why Aristotle in this chapter appears to talk as if the *only* necessity operative in nature were conditional necessity. For elsewhere he is quite clear that simple material necessitation occurs too in natural processes, often indeed in partnership with

---

lack of a contemporary teleological target, could not have intended "luck" or "the fortuitous" in an anti-teleological sense: my main thesis in chapters 1 and 2 has been, on the contrary, that the idea of an intelligently structured world was pervasive in Presocratic thought, in which case atomism did indeed pose the earliest challenge to it. I also remain fairly confident that Democritus was a conscious determinist, both for reasons briefly considered on p. 164 above, and because of Epicurus's description of his atomist predecessors as holding "necessity (ἀνάγκη) and the fortuitous (τὸ αὐτόματον) responsible for everything" (LS, 20C 13). Epicurus certainly knew Democritus's work directly, without the intermediacy of Aristotle, and was here writing without great hostility, praising his atomist forerunners and observing that they did not see the harmful implications of the physical determinism that they espoused. I therefore see no reason to suspect distortion, and interpret his remark as important confirmation of Aristotle's. For further pertinent doubts about Hirsch's thesis, cf. Berryman 2002, p. 186.

conditional necessity. The action of breathing, for example, is *necessitated* by the material heating and cooling properties of air, which is why we go on doing it all the time; but it is also *conditionally necessary*, since you cannot maintain your other vital processes unless you breathe (*On parts of animals* I 1, 642a31–b4). But in *Physics* II 9 Aristotle may well be tacitly assuming, rather than eliminating, the simple kind of material necessitation,[26] having chosen to concentrate on the conditional aspect of necessity precisely because this strongly supports the teleological thesis that the book seeks to vindicate.

The way in which simple material necessitation vanishes from view in this chapter, it seems to me, directly and non-accidentally recalls the *Timaeus*. There, as we have seen (p. 116 above), "necessity" initially appears as the simple material necessitation manifested by the mechanical causal properties of the four elementary stuffs. But in the course of Timaeus's speech, it with increasing clarity acquires the profile of conditional necessity. This, I suggested, is because in Plato's eyes what it is for necessity to be "persuaded" by intelligence is precisely for it to stop determining results all by itself and instead to be put at the service of intelligently conceived goals. From a narrow perspective, no doubt, matter does even in an intelligently controlled environment go on necessitating: in my kitchen, for example, a flame lit under the kettle really does necessitate the water's boiling. But from a broader perspective there is no longer any simple necessitation at work: all the material causes in my kitchen put together were insufficient to make the water boil, had not an intelligence—mine—decided that boiling water was needed.

From this broader perspective, we can see why talk of simple necessity is liable to disappear once the subservience of matter to intelligence is stressed. Aristotle's natural world admittedly is not one in which *intelligent* purpose dominates, as it does in Plato's. Nevertheless, he considers *natural* purpose to be omnipresent in that world's structure all the way down, and in *Physics* II 9 points out that natural purpose involves conditional necessity in a way which closely mirrors intelligent purpose. He therefore has much the same reasons as Plato did to treat conditional necessity not simply as coexisting in some kind of equal partnership with simple necessity, but as subsuming it.[27] This is one of numerous cases where reading Aristotle's teleology in the context of its Platonic origins can throw light on it.

26. This is argued by Cooper 1985.
27. At 200a7–10 Aristotle writes "Likewise in everything else that involves purpose, although it cannot happen without the things whose nature is necessary *(τῶν*

The joint project of Plato and Aristotle is to resist Presocratic causal pre-suppositions, viewed as wrongly emphasizing material necessitation at the cost of teleological causation. In attacking misplaced reliance on the explanatory power of necessity, both of them speak of a currently prevailing opinion (*Timaeus* 46d1–3; *Physics* II 9, 199b35–200a1) which considers everything macroscopic to be the result of matter operating, by "necessity," from the bottom up. In my first three chapters I opposed this as an inadequate generalization about Presocratic cosmology, on the ground that before the arrival of atomism body had been regularly treated as if it had vital and even intelligent powers. From this point of view, we may say that the countermove made by Plato and Aristotle is most directly prompted by the atomists, whose explicit restriction of body to possessing purely material properties they see as merely bringing into the open the bottom-up materialism to which the Presocratic physics had been, willy-nilly, committing itself all along.[28]

Aristotle's explanation of how the Presocratic misconception arose can be found in *Physics* II 1, 193a9–30.[29] Aristotle himself, although he associates nature especially with form, thinks that in a certain limited way a thing's matter too can count as its nature. For nature is an internal source or principle of change and rest, and to some extent a thing's matter does function in such a capacity: it would be enough to point out that a thing's tendency to move downwards, to catch fire, or to flow, whenever circumstances permit, is due to its matter.[30] By a thing's matter here Aristotle means its *proximate* matter—for instance, an animal's flesh and bone, or a bed's wood—not its ultimate matter, such as water, earth, or any other primitive constituent. From this entirely proper premise, says Aristotle, some people have made the following further inference: if A's nature is its proximate mat-

---

ἀναγκαίαν ἐχόντων τὴν φύσιν), it does not happen because of these things except as matter [i.e. as material causes], but for a specific purpose." As Cooper 1985 observes, by "the things whose nature is necessary" Aristotle probably means to refer to simple necessity. If so, note how the things in question do necessitate so far as their own nature is concerned, but not as regards the determination of outcomes. This is very close to the *Timaeus* picture as I understand it.

28. In the case of the dualist Anaxagoras, the charge was that he first separated matter from intelligence, then gave all the causal efficacy to mere matter: p. 21 above.

29. Although the authors of the approach in question are not identified here, at *PA* I 1, 640b4–17 very much the same view is attributed to "the ancients."

30. I here pass over the more exotic example (193a12–17, b9–11) of a buried bed which sprouts, not bed, but wood. For its original, very different context in Antiphon, see Pendrick 2002, pp. 126–41, 276–89.

ter, B, and B's nature is *its* proximate matter, C, and so on, then whatever item lies at the end of this chain—a matter so basic that there is nothing more basic that it itself consists of—this last kind of matter constitutes the nature of everything above it in the chain. As Aristotle remarks, this approach results in the typically Presocratic thesis that the nature of everything consists in fire, earth, air, or water, or in some subset of these. Their mistake is to see the relation "being the nature of" as a transitive one, such that if B is the nature of A and C is the nature of B then C is (either uniquely or in a stronger sense) the nature of A. On the contrary, in Aristotle's view, the further you get from A in this chain, the less causal power the matter you identify will have with regard to A's behavior, and therefore the less claim to be its nature.

Aristotle's actual object here, as it happens, is not to attack the Presocratics. He is in the process of demonstrating his own thesis that, as well as form, matter too is in a sense a thing's nature, and he is recruiting the Presocratics to his side. They understood and applied this principle, although unfortunately they went on to *mis*apply it by combining it with their mistaken assumption about transitivity. Typically of Aristotle's use of "standard" (*endoxa*) existing views, his point is not exactly either to vindicate or to condemn his predecessors, but to invoke their indirect support for his own position. Although they were wrong, he means, they must have already half-grasped the Aristotelian principle at issue, because the assumption that they did so explains how they came to make their mistake.

Despite the relatively materialist-friendly context here in *Physics* II 1, the diagnosis is vital background to II 9's attack on materialist "necessity" as being insufficient to replace purpose in nature. Jointly, the two passages explain both the seductive attraction of bottom-up necessitation, and its severe limitations.

From Aristotle's critiques of materialism, however, it should not be inferred that he does not regard material necessitation as a source of imperfection in the world. Plato's world, being the product of an ideally good craftsman, is the best world that could have been manufactured, as I have argued in chapter IV §5. Although it has imperfections, these are not aspects in which the Demiurge failed to get the better of his materials, as many interpreters since antiquity have wrongly supposed. Material "necessity" for Plato is not a source of bad. But where does Aristotle stand on this issue?

So long as the cosmic craftsmanship was vested in a divine craftsman, Plato's religiosity had left him no room for the blasphemy of conceding that the highest being, god, is ever defeated by the lowliest, matter. But once the craft was severed from the craftsman, as it was by Aristotle, and reduced to a heuristically useful analogue for explaining natural structures, the requirement of perfection was lifted. As Aristotle is happy to say (*Physics* II 8, 199a33–b4) without the slightest fear of blasphemy, crafts make occasional mistakes; therefore, by analogy, so can nature.

Moreover, material necessity must take at least some of the blame. The matter with which formal natures work is not prime matter, corresponding to the entirely bland and malleable "receptacle" from which the Demiurge of the *Timaeus* started out. Even if Aristotle is assumed to have sometimes entertained the idea of prime matter (an assumption which is itself controversial), the relevant matter for natural processes is proximate matter, such as flesh and bone in relation to animals, and perhaps earth, water etc. in relation to flesh and bone. These, the material natures of the things in question, are regularly treated by Aristotle in his biological writings as imposing constraints on the powers of formal nature to shape and direct them.[31]

4. FORTUITOUS OUTCOMES

Aristotle's treatment of luck and the fortuitous in chapters 4–6 of *Physics* II has much the same aim as his account of necessity, namely to show that these two items likewise, once properly understood, will turn out not to offer an alternative to explanation in terms of purpose, but on the contrary to entail that there are natural purposes.

I shall use "the fortuitous" to translate Aristotle's *to automaton* (sometimes also rendered "the automatic," "the spontaneous," or "chance"),[32] and "luck" to translate *tychē* (also, confusingly, sometimes rendered "chance"). Luck is, in Aristotle's usage, one species of the fortuitous, namely the fortuitous as manifested in the sphere of human activity. But his account of luck, in chapter 5, is the clearer of the two, and for present purposes I shall focus on it, without always insisting on the distinction between the two terms,[33] especially as Aristotle himself virtually fuses the two in forming his main conclusions at the end of chapter 6.

The following premises about luck are here treated as especially important:

31. For this as a systematic pattern in *De partibus animalium*, see Lennox 1996. It may also be significant that Aristotle tends to explain natural structures and processes in terms of what is "better" rather than "best," whereas the *Timaeus* exhibits the reverse preference.

32. In this I follow the lead of Sharples 1983.

33. Stephen Menn plausibly suggests to me that the two topics are separated for reasons which have more to do with other people's views than with Aristotle's own—

(a) Luck is a matter of "accident" or "coincidence" (*symbebēkos*). It leads to rare or exceptional events, not regular ones.

(b) Lucky events fulfill a purpose.[34]

(c) Luck is considered something "indefinite."

Both (a) and (b) seem intuitively sound: no one would call "lucky" either an entirely regular event, such as the sun's having risen this morning, or some merely random fact, such as there being an odd number of blades of grass in the lawn.

Since (b) lucky events fulfill a purpose, in Aristotle's eyes any adequate analysis of luck must make reference to the final cause—the end or goal served. On the other hand, luck is not itself any kind of final cause: nothing happens for the sake of luck. Aristotle is quite clear (198a1–3) that luck is, on the contrary, a moving cause, since when we describe a happening as "due to luck" we are referring to what brought it about, not its purpose.

Consider, now, Aristotle's specimen case of luck. You go to the market for some purpose, for example to buy bread, but there you meet someone who owes you money, and are thereby enabled to collect your debt. This satisfies premise (a), that lucky events are accidental and hence exceptional rather than the norm: you do not regularly go to the same place as your debtor, and if you did we would hardly say it was lucky you met him there and recovered the debt. It also satisfies premise (b), that lucky events fulfill a purpose: you had an antecedent need or desire to collect the debt, without which we would hardly be inclined to say it was lucky that you succeeded in doing so.

What about premise (c), according to which luck is something "indefinite"? It is at this point that we reenter the technicalities of Aristotle's causal theory, as set out in *Physics* II 3 (pp. 178–79 above). Bearing in mind that luck is classed as a moving cause, remember Jones the builder. To call the moving cause of a building "the building art," or "a builder," is to state its proper cause. To call it Jones, or, worse, "a musician," is to state no more than its accidental moving cause. This is because it is no more than accidental that the building's proper cause, the builder, is also Jones and a musician.

---

with particular reference to those who believe *tychē,* but not *to automaton,* to be divine.

34. Something symmetrical might be said about unlucky events: unless they serve a negative purpose, accidental events would not be called unlucky either. Unlucky events (cf. *Ph.* II 5, 197a25–30) will be either those that serve some negative or malevolent purpose, or those that militate against the fulfillment of some good purpose.

Now take this distinction between proper and accidental causes, and reapply it to the debt-collection case. What is the proper moving cause of collecting the debt? On the same principles we have witnessed in the case of the building, the proper cause can only be *your antecedent desire, or need, to collect the debt*,[35] for that alone among possible moving causes is suitably linked to the outcome, the actual collection of the debt, much as the builder and building art are suitably linked to the building. Yet in this case the desire or need to collect the debt was, in one sense, *not* the active moving cause. What moved you to go to the market was not your desire to recover the debt, but your decision to buy bread. This means that your decision to buy bread was merely the *accidental* moving cause of the debt-collection, analogously to the way that a musician is the accidental moving cause of the building. When you spotted your debtor, your existing desire or need to collect the debt served as the proper cause of your collecting the debt. Your decision to go to the market and buy bread coincided with this— accidentally teamed up with it, we might say—more or less in the way in which Jones's being a musician merely coincided with his being the builder who built the building.

Aristotle holds, then, that in cases of luck there must always be a properly linked moving cause, namely the antecedent aim, desire, or need for precisely *that* outcome. Only when we have isolated this proper cause can we say how the lucky cause comes to be the accidental cause of the very same outcome, namely by coinciding with the proper cause. As for premise (c), that luck is "indefinite," Aristotle now at last feels that he has found the actual philosophical basis for this commonplace intuition. For while there is only one proper cause of the debt-collection, there are an "indefinite" number of accidental causes that may happen to team up with it and produce the desired result: in the example, this was the decision to buy bread, but on other occasions it might be something quite different (197a8–18):

> Therefore the causes from which lucky events might occur are indefinite, and that is why luck too is thought to belong to the indefinite and to be hidden from mankind, and why in a way it might be thought that nothing comes to be from luck. It is reasonable to call all these statements correct. For on the one hand there is a way in which such things do come about from luck, since they come about accidentally, and luck is an accidental cause; on the other hand, in an absolute sense luck is not the cause of anything. For example, a builder is the cause of a building, but accidentally a

---

35. Note that desires etc. are themselves moving causes, even though their objects are likely to function as final causes.

flute-player is. And the causes of someone's arriving and collecting the money when it wasn't for that purpose that they came are infinitely many: the wish to see someone, pursuing someone, avoiding someone, or the intention to go to the theater.[36]

So much, then, for his analysis of luck (for present purposes we can take the broader notion, the fortuitous, to be covered by the same analysis).[37] He invokes the analysis in defense of his teleology by arguing that neither the beneficial structure of an individual organism nor that of the world can be put down to mere luck.

Take individual organisms first. In chapter 8 he reads Empedocles' theory of the survival of the fittest (chapter II §2 and §4 above) as attributing to mere luck such features as the user-friendly arrangement of teeth, which Xenophon's Socrates (chapter III §2 above) had on the contrary cited as an obvious case of divine benevolence. Aristotle's reply to Empedocles is embedded in the following critique of the materialist alternative to teleology (*Physics* II 8, 198b16–199a5):

> There is a puzzle. What prevents nature from producing results not for a purpose or because it is best, but in the way that Zeus rains, not in order to make the crops grow, but of necessity? For what goes up must cool, and what cools must become water and come down; and when this happens, the accidental result is that the crops grow. Similarly if someone's crops rot on the threshing floor, it does not rain *in order that* this should happen, but it is an accident. So what prevents natural parts from being like this— for example that it is of necessity that teeth grow with the front ones sharp and suitable for cutting, the molars flat and useful for grinding food, because of a coincidental outcome, and not because they happened for this purpose? Likewise in the case of other parts in which purpose seems to be present: where everything accidentally turned out as it would have done also if it were coming about for a purpose, these ones were preserved, having been formed in a suitable way fortuitously, whereas those which did not

---

36. ἀόριστα μὲν οὖν τὰ αἴτια ἀνάγκη εἶναι ἀφ' ὧν ἂν γένοιτο τὸ ἀπὸ τύχης. ὅθεν καὶ ἡ τύχη τοῦ ἀορίστου εἶναι δοκεῖ καὶ ἄδηλος ἀνθρώπῳ, καὶ ἔστιν ὡς οὐδὲν ἀπὸ τύχης δόξειεν ἂν γίγνεσθαι. πάντα γὰρ ταῦτα ὀρθῶς λέγεται, εὐλόγως. ἔστιν μὲν γὰρ ὡς γίγνεται ἀπὸ τύχης· κατὰ συμβεβηκὸς γὰρ γίγνεται, καὶ ἔστιν αἴτιον ὡς συμβεβηκὸς ἡ τύχη· ὡς δ' ἁπλῶς οὐδενός· οἷον οἰκίας οἰκοδόμος μὲν αἴτιος, κατὰ συμβεβηκὸς δὲ αὐλητής, καὶ τοῦ ἐλθόντα κομίσασθαι τὸ ἀργύριον, μὴ τούτου ἕνεκα ἐλθόντα, ἄπειρα τὸ πλῆθος· καὶ γὰρ ἰδεῖν τινὰ βουλόμενος καὶ διώκων καὶ φεύγων καὶ θεασόμενος.

37. *Physics* II 6's separate treatment of the broader class "the fortuitous" in the relevant respects follows Aristotle's analysis of luck, except that the goal accidentally fulfilled may in this case be one preexisting in nature rather than in human intentions.

turn out this way perished, and are still perishing, as Empedocles says about the "man-faced ox progeny."

Such is the argument which might lead to puzzlement, and there may be others of the kind. But things cannot be that way. For these things, and all natural things, come about as they do either always or for the most part, whereas none of the things that are due to luck and the fortuitous does that. For it does not seem to be due to luck or coincidence that it rains frequently in winter, but it does if it rains in midsummer. Nor do heat waves in midsummer seem due to luck or coincidence, but heat waves in winter do. If then it seems that things are either due to coincidence or for a purpose, then if it is impossible for these things to be due to coincidence or the fortuitous, they must be for a purpose.[38]

Against Empedocles' explanation of the arrangement of teeth as lucky accident, Aristotle here in the second paragraph invokes premise (a), that luck or the fortuitous leads to rare outcomes, not to regular ones like the disposition of parts in organisms.

Now Aristotle is of course right that no one would consider themselves *lucky* to have their molars at the back rather than in front, any more than they would thank their lucky stars that their hands are at the end of their arms rather than on their legs. But can he have simply overlooked the fact that Empedocles was explaining, not why our bodies continue to be arranged this way today, but how that arrangement originated?

---

38. ἔχει δ' ἀπορίαν τί κωλύει τὴν φύσιν μὴ ἕνεκά του ποιεῖν μηδ' ὅτι βέλτιον, ἀλλ' ὥσπερ ὕει ὁ Ζεὺς οὐχ ὅπως τὸν σῖτον αὐξήσῃ, ἀλλ' ἐξ ἀνάγκης (τὸ γὰρ ἀναχθὲν ψυχθῆναι δεῖ, καὶ τὸ ψυχθὲν ὕδωρ γενόμενον κατελθεῖν· τὸ δ' αὐξάνεσθαι τούτου γενομένου τὸν σῖτον συμβαίνει), ὁμοίως δὲ καὶ εἴ τῳ ἀπόλλυται ὁ σῖτος ἐν τῇ ἅλῳ, οὐ τούτου ἕνεκα ὕει ὅπως ἀπόληται, ἀλλὰ τοῦτο συμβέβηκεν. ὥστε τί κωλύει οὕτω καὶ τὰ μέρη ἔχειν ἐν τῇ φύσει, οἷον τοὺς ὀδόντας ἐξ ἀνάγκης ἀνατεῖλαι τοὺς μὲν ἐμπροσθίους ὀξεῖς, ἐπιτηδείους πρὸς τὸ διαιρεῖν, τοὺς δὲ γομφίους πλατεῖς καὶ χρησίμους πρὸς τὸ λεαίνειν τὴν τροφήν, ἐπεὶ οὐ τούτου ἕνεκα γενέσθαι, ἀλλὰ συμπεσεῖν· ὁμοίως δὲ καὶ περὶ τῶν ἄλλων μερῶν, ἐν ὅσοις δοκεῖ ὑπάρχειν τὸ ἕνεκά του. ὅπου μὲν οὖν ἅπαντα συνέβη ὥσπερ κἂν εἰ ἕνεκά του ἐγίγνετο, ταῦτα μὲν ἐσώθη ἀπὸ τοῦ αὐτομάτου συστάντα ἐπιτηδείως· ὅσα δὲ μὴ οὕτως, ἀπώλετο καὶ ἀπόλλυται, καθάπερ Ἐμπεδοκλῆς λέγει τὰ βουγενῆ ἀνδρόπρωρα. ὁ μὲν οὖν λόγος, ᾧ ἄν τις ἀπορήσειεν, οὗτος, καὶ εἴ τις ἄλλος τοιοῦτός ἐστιν· ἀδύνατον δὲ τοῦτον ἔχειν τὸν τρόπον. ταῦτα μὲν γὰρ καὶ πάντα τὰ φύσει ἢ αἰεὶ οὕτω γίγνεται ἢ ὡς ἐπὶ τὸ πολύ, τῶν δ' ἀπὸ τύχης καὶ τοῦ αὐτομάτου οὐδέν. οὐ γὰρ ἀπὸ τύχης οὐδ' ἀπὸ συμπτώματος δοκεῖ ὕειν πολλάκις τοῦ χειμῶνος, ἀλλ' ἐὰν ὑπὸ κύνα· οὐδὲ καύματα ὑπὸ κύνα, ἀλλ' ἂν χειμῶνος. εἰ οὖν ἢ ἀπὸ συμπτώματος δοκεῖ ἢ ἕνεκά του εἶναι, εἰ μὴ οἷόν τε ταῦτ' εἶναι μήτε ἀπὸ συμπτώματος μήτ' ἀπὸ ταὐτομάτου, ἕνεκά του ἂν εἴη.

Probably not. At the end of the first paragraph, he cites Empedocles as saying that the very same process of natural selection is still going on (198b31–32, " . . . whereas those which did not turn out this way perished, *and are still perishing,* as Empedocles says about the 'man-faced ox progeny'"). If this were right, luck *would* be being invoked even as a present-day cause of biological form. In chapter II §2, I interpreted the Empedoclean claim differently: not that natural selection is still going on, but just that present-day deformed births are vestigial *evidence* of what was once a common natural occurrence. If Empedocles' doctrine were rather that the luck of natural selection is essential to *maintain* present-day biological structures, Aristotle's objection would raise some far more profound questions about whether luck really can permanently continue to underwrite regularity. In the last analysis, however, Aristotle's conviction that what is merely fortuitous cannot be the basis of regularity owes more to his deep teleological convictions than to any technical argument about the true meaning of the terms "luck" and "fortuitous."

I turn now to Aristotle's denial, in response to the atomists, that luck could ever account for the structure of the world taken as a whole. The atomists' position on this has already been set out, with some derision, in chapter 4 (196a24–35):

> Some people consider the fortuitous to be the cause of this heaven and of all the worlds, explaining that it was fortuitously that there arose the vortex and the motion which separated things and set the universe in this arrangement. This is itself pretty amazing. For on the one hand they say that animals and plants neither are nor come to be by luck, but that either nature or intelligence or some other such thing is their cause (it not being just anything that arises from each seed, but an olive tree from this one, a man from that one), yet on the other hand they say that the heaven and the most divine of perceptible things came to be fortuitously, without any cause comparable to that of animals and plants.[39]

---

39. εἰσὶ δέ τινες οἳ καὶ τοὐρανοῦ τοῦδε καὶ τῶν κόσμων πάντων αἰτιῶνται τὸ αὐτόματον· ἀπὸ ταὐτομάτου γὰρ γενέσθαι τὴν δίνην καὶ τὴν κίνησιν τὴν διακρίνασαν καὶ καταστήσασαν εἰς ταύτην τὴν τάξιν τὸ πᾶν. καὶ μάλα τοῦτό γε αὐτὸ θαυμάσαι ἄξιον· λέγοντες γὰρ τὰ μὲν ζῷα καὶ τὰ φυτὰ ἀπὸ τύχης μήτε εἶναι μήτε γίγνεσθαι, ἀλλ' ἤτοι φύσιν ἢ νοῦν ἤ τι τοιοῦτον ἕτερον εἶναι τὸ αἴτιον (οὐ γὰρ ὅ τι ἔτυχεν ἐκ τοῦ σπέρματος ἑκάστου γίγνεται, ἀλλ' ἐκ μὲν τοῦ τοιουδὶ ἐλαία ἐκ δὲ τοῦ τοιουδὶ ἄνθρωπος), τὸν δ' οὐρανὸν καὶ τὰ θειότατα τῶν φανερῶν ἀπὸ τοῦ αὐτομάτου γενέσθαι, τοιαύτην δ' αἰτίαν μηδεμίαν εἶναι οἵαν τῶν ζῴων καὶ τῶν φυτῶν.

Like Xenophon's Socrates, Aristotle here finds it inconsistent of materialists to recognize the role of purposive processes and structures within our
world, yet to deny an analogous cause of the vastly superior and more ordered[40] structure of the world itself. Now when he speaks of the atomists
admitting that animals and plants are the products of "nature or intelligence
or some other such thing," he can hardly be talking about the origin of
species, which he knows they would have vehemently denied to be the work
of a creative intelligence. He must rather be invoking their agreement that
individual animals and plants today come into being, not by luck, but either
through natural propagation, or, as implied by his example of olive trees,
thanks to the intelligent operations of farming.[41] This is meant to show that
they perfectly well understand the notion of luck and correctly avoid applying it to familiar purposive processes, yet misapply it when it comes to
the origin of the cosmos.[42]

At the close of chapter 6, having developed his own account of luck and
the fortuitous, Aristotle returns to this theme of the cosmos itself (198a5–13):

> Since the fortuitous and luck are causes of things of which intelligence or
> nature *could* be the cause, whenever something accidentally becomes the
> cause of these same things, and since nothing accidental is prior to things
> that are *per se*, it is clear that the accidental cause is not prior to the *per se*
> cause either. Hence the fortuitous and luck are posterior to intelligence and
> nature. So however much it might be true that the fortuitous is the cause
> of the heaven, it is necessary that intelligence and nature are prior causes,
> both of many other things and, especially, of this universe.[43]

40. This point about greater orderliness is made explicit in the version of the argument at *PA* I 1, 641b10–23, discussed below.

41. See Wardy 2005 for the complications surrounding the question to what extent Aristotle can comfortably regard olive trees and other cultivated varieties as either "natural" or "artificial." It seems likely, nevertheless, that at least for dialectical purposes he is here treating the propagation of the olive as artificial (and hence
the effect of *nous*), that of man as natural.

42. This way of explaining Aristotle's reference to "intelligence" seems to me
more credible than to suppose, with Morel 2005, pp. 29–30 (where however a footnote allows as possible an alternative reading along the lines I am suggesting), that
the group intended includes such thinkers as Anaxagoras as well as the atomists. It
would be most surprising for Aristotle to associate Anaxagoras's *nous* with zoogony
yet dissociate it from cosmogony, thus virtually reversing his usual criticism of him
(e.g. *Met.* A 4, 985a18–21). Cf. also n. 49 below.

43. ἐπεὶ δ' ἐστὶ τὸ αὐτόματον καὶ ἡ τύχη αἴτια ὧν ἂν ἢ νοῦς γένοιτο αἴτιος
ἢ φύσις, ὅταν κατὰ συμβεβηκὸς αἴτιόν τι γένηται τούτων αὐτῶν, οὐδὲν δὲ
κατὰ συμβεβηκός ἐστι πρότερον τῶν καθ' αὑτό, δῆλον ὅτι οὐδὲ τὸ κατὰ συμβεβηκὸς αἴτιον πρότερον τοῦ καθ' αὑτό. ὕστερον ἄρα τὸ αὐτόματον καὶ ἡ τύχη καὶ νοῦ καὶ φύσεως· ὥστ' εἰ ὅτι μάλιστα τοῦ οὐρανοῦ αἴτιον τὸ αὐτόμα-

Aristotle means the following. Lucky or fortuitous events are, on his analysis, events that lead to the accidental fulfillment of a preexisting natural or psychological goal. Hence, even if our world were assumed to have had an origin, and luck were hypothesized to have played a part in that origin, this would still amount to a concession that the purpose accidentally fulfilled by it was already operative before luck intervened to bring it to fruition.[44]

One might respond that some lucky events produce desirable results that were not either desired or needed in advance. For example, in the Chinese fable recounted by Charles Lamb, when a house complete with its pigsty burnt down and roast pork was accidentally discovered,[45] prior to the lucky event there was neither a desire nor a need for roast pork. Aristotle will have to reply that, if the event is to count as lucky at all, it must have fulfilled an antecedent aim under *some* description: if not the aim of eating roast pork, at least that of eating nutritious or tasty food. Similarly, a farmer who considers himself lucky to have dug up buried treasure (cf. *Metaphysics Δ* 30, 1025a14–19) must have had the antecedent desire, if not to find treasure, at any rate to prosper. If no such goal had existed, under any suitable description, what could be counted lucky about the event? Likewise for the world's origin (assuming for the moment that it had one), we cannot intelligibly invoke the fortuitous or luck as cause without assuming that, under *some* description, an antecedent purpose was being fulfilled by it. And were the atomists to concede that,[46] they would collapse back into the correct position that they were earlier represented as unreasonably resisting. That is, they would be treating the world's origin as on a par with the regular regeneration of life forms within our world, which even hardened materialists such as they are must admit is not purely fortuitous.

τον, ἀνάγκη πρότερον νοῦν αἴτιον καὶ φύσιν εἶναι καὶ ἄλλων πολλῶν καὶ τοῦ δε τοῦ παντός.

44. This may be the one major point on which I part company with the excellent analysis of Aristotelian chance in Judson 1991. As I understand him (esp. p. 92), Judson sees chance events as having no operative *per se* cause at all. This might indeed have been what Aristotle meant, but the concluding argument of II 6 seems to me to exclude it. So when Aristotle writes at 196b21–24 and 198a5–7 that lucky or fortuitous events are ones which *could have been* caused by intelligence or nature, he must mean that the appropriate intelligent or natural *per se* cause, although present, did not as it happens play its full active part in bringing about the result.

45. Lamb 1823. Prior to that they had eaten their pork raw. The humorous twist to the tale is that thereafter, whenever they wanted roast pork, they would burn the house down.

46. No doubt a committed atomist would prefer to challenge Aristotle's analysis of luck, maintaining that the need or aim fortuitously served by an accidental cosmogony did not preexist the event but has been retrojected with the wisdom of

On this hypothesis that the world had a beginning,[47] when Aristotle says that *intelligence and nature* are prior to any luck that might have been involved, he may well mean priority in a temporal sense: an intelligent and natural goal must have already existed at a time before the world's creation. But his own preferred view, outside this adversarial context, is that the world in fact had no beginning. On the latter hypothesis, what does he mean by maintaining nevertheless that intelligence and nature are causes of the world prior to any luck that might be involved?

This time the priority must be causal or explanatory, rather than temporal. The world is an eternal purposive structure, causally dependent on intelligence and nature. The "intelligence" (*nous*) he intends cannot be a Platonic Demiurge: instead, he can only be referring to that detached divine intellect, the Prime Mover, which as the ultimate source of all change he does indeed consider causally prior to the world, and, as the ultimate model for emulation, the *per se* cause of all the changes lower down the scale. But he has also concluded that *nature* is a prior cause in relation to the world. The world taken as a whole, he must mean, is no accidental structure, but manifests natural purpose just as much as individual organisms do.

5. COSMIC TELEOLOGY

The upshot of the last section was that the world, at least as much as its individual contents, is governed by teleological causation. This reading is confirmed by a closely parallel text, taken from a key methodological chapter, *On parts of animals* I 1 (641b10–23):

> Moreover, nothing abstract can be an object studied by physics, because nature does everything for a purpose. For just as in artifacts art is present, in things themselves there appears another such principle and cause, which, like the hot and the cold, we have from the universe. Hence it is more reasonable for the heaven to have come to be by the agency of such a cause, if it has come to be, and to be because of such a cause, than for mortal animals. At any rate, what is ordered and definite is much more evident in celestial things than as belonging to us, whereas what belongs more to mortal beings is variability over time, and the fortuitous. Some

---

hindsight. In the last analysis, Aristotle's argument here is designed to convince Aristotelians, not atomists.

47. For this as a hypothesis that Aristotle takes seriously enough to work with in a context like the present one, cf. *PA* I 1, 641b10–23, quoted at the beginning of the next section.

say that although each animal is and comes to be by nature, the heaven has been formed in the way it is from luck and the fortuitous. Yet nothing whatsoever in the heaven appears the result of luck and disorder.[48]

Here the closing critique of the atomists[49] plainly corresponds to the one we have just met in *Physics* II 4 and 6. It differs in arguing only that the *heaven* cannot be the product of luck or the fortuitous, and not this time explicitly extending that conclusion to the causation of the entire world, but we need not doubt that the two passages share a common agenda and are to be read in the light of each other.

In leading up to his refutation of the atomists, Aristotle's second sentence supplies a premise that was not explicit in the other passage. Final causality, he asserts here, is primarily present in the world as a whole, and in beings like us only derivatively, just as the hot and the cold in us are derivative from cosmic hot and cold. This inference is an unnoticed (as far as I am aware) direct descendant of the argument placed in the mouth of Socrates by Xenophon (*Memorabilia* I 4.8) and Plato (*Philebus* 29a9–30d9), and later (see chapter VII §3 below) elaborately reworked by the Stoics as the very basis of their theology. Just as the water, earth etc. in our bodies are derived from the great cosmic masses of these same stuffs, Socrates had argued, so too our intelligence must be inferred to be derivative from a great cosmic intelligence. Aristotle's version replaces water and earth with two of his own elementary powers, the hot and the cold, and also replaces intelligence with final causality, in conformity with his by now familiar modification of Platonic teleology to remove conscious purpose from na-

48. ἔτι δὲ τῶν ἐξ ἀφαιρέσεως οὐδενὸς οἷόν τ᾽ εἶναι τὴν φυσικὴν θεωρητικήν, ἐπειδὴ ἡ φύσις ἕνεκά του ποιεῖ πάντα. φαίνεται γάρ, ὥσπερ ἐν τοῖς τεχναστοῖς ἐστιν ἡ τέχνη, οὕτως ἐν αὐτοῖς τοῖς πράγμασιν ἄλλη τις ἀρχὴ καὶ αἰτία τοιαύτη, ἣν ἔχομεν καθάπερ τὸ θερμὸν καὶ τὸ ψυχρὸν ἐκ τοῦ παντός. διὸ μᾶλλον εἰκὸς τὸν οὐρανὸν γεγενῆσθαι ὑπὸ τοιαύτης αἰτίας, εἰ γέγονε, καὶ εἶναι διὰ τοιαύτην αἰτίαν μᾶλλον, ἢ τὰ ζῷα τὰ θνητά· τὸ γοῦν τεταγμένον καὶ τὸ ὡρισμένον πολὺ μᾶλλον φαίνεται ἐν τοῖς οὐρανίοις ἢ περὶ ἡμᾶς, τὸ δ᾽ ἄλλοτ᾽ ἄλλως καὶ ὡς ἔτυχε περὶ τὰ θνητὰ μᾶλλον. οἱ δὲ τῶν μὲν ζῴων ἕκαστον φύσει φασὶν εἶναι καὶ γενέσθαι, τὸν δ᾽ οὐρανὸν ἀπὸ τύχης καὶ τοῦ αὐτομάτου τοιοῦτον συστῆναι, ἐν ᾧ ἀπὸ τύχης καὶ ἀταξίας οὐδ᾽ ὁτιοῦν φαίνεται. Cf. Quarantotto 2005, chapters 2–5, on the profound continuity between *Physics* II and *PA* I as regards the articulation of Aristotle's teleology.

49. Although I agree with Lennox 2001b, p. 136, that *PA* I 1, 640b4–17 is not specifically targeted at Democritus, it seems overcautious (*ib.* and p. 145) to extend the same doubt to the present passage or to its doublet in *Ph.* II 4 (cf. n. 42 above). For the causal role of τὸ αὐτόματον in early atomism, cf. n. 25 above, and Morel 1996, pp. 66–75.

ture. But it is unmistakably in the same tradition.[50] Aristotle's prioritiza-tion here of cosmic teleology over that of individual natural processes[51] is a vital but under-appreciated motif, to which I now turn.

Clearly the world as a whole is structured in many ways that are regularly beneficial to life, including the availability of natural resources, and the eter-nally recurrent intertransformation of the four simple bodies that underlies the weather cycle, this latter dependent in turn on the daily and annual cy-cles of the sun. If Aristotle conceded that these everlastingly advantageous cosmic structures require no teleological explanation, he would be playing into the hands of his opponents by implying that, by analogy, regularly advanta-geous structures in individual organisms might equally well be understood as nonpurposive.[52] Worse still from his point of view, he would be making the teleologically governed perpetuation of species in the sublunary world de-pendent on an overall cosmic arrangement whose own eternity was itself not explicable in terms of purpose but just a matter of brute fact. It is easy to see why Aristotle wants to avoid any such dependence of the teleological on the non-teleological, and why instead we have just seen him on the contrary emphasizing that biological teleology depends on a prior cosmic teleology.

Just such a dependence had been a prominent feature of the key back-ground text, Plato's *Timaeus*. There, the world's goodness is the primary explanandum, and the world's comprehensive stocking with organic species, each elaborately engineered to suit its specific function, is in turn explained by its contribution to that goal. Readers of Aristotle have had difficulty in believing that he can have inherited any such prioritization from his teacher, because his zoological treatises rarely mention global teleology[53] and instead

---

50. Johnson 2005, pp. 136–37 with n. 9, translates ἔχομεν . . . ἐκ τοῦ παντός not "we have from the universe" (as I do above, along with all other translators I have consulted, including now Lennox 2001b), but "we ascertain from the universe," de-scribing the sentence as "obscure," as it would indeed be, thus translated.

51. This prioritization reflects Aristotle's pronouncements (*Meteor.* I 1, 338a20–b22, 339a5–9) on the correct order of study, with celestial motion preced-ing zoology and botany. See further, Burnyeat 2004, pp. 13–24; Falcon 2005, pp. 2–13.

52. Indeed, not just equally well, but *a fortiori*, since Aristotle here makes sub-lunary teleology dependent upon its cosmic counterpart. This prioritization does not, however, mean that an organism is so structured as to put its cosmic role before its own self-interest (as Pellegrin 2002 and Johnson 2005 have understood me as as-suming in Sedley 1991; cf. n. 69 below), but that the goal of godlikeness is most fully achieved by the main cosmic structures, from the celestial spheres downwards, and only secondarily and derivatively by organisms like ourselves.

53. Indeed, the one notable exception, widely cited, is *PA* IV 13, 696b25–32, on the inconvenient positioning of the shark's mouth underneath, partly in order to spare other species.

concentrate on the functioning of individual organisms in their own right. But we should not be misled by this emphasis, because it too has its background in Plato. Although the *Timaeus*, taken as a whole, leaves no possible doubt about the subservience of zoological to global teleology, it is its long treatments of anatomy at 69c5–86a8 and 90e1–92c3 that correspond functionally to Aristotelian zoology, and these sections have very little indeed to say about the global perspective. Like Aristotle's biological works, they are squarely focused on individual bodily functioning. Provided that Aristotle's physical and theological writings supply the missing global perspective on teleology—and we will shortly see that they do—the relative restraint shown in the biological treatises should be read as symptomatic, not of his emancipation from Plato, but if anything of a continuing debt to him.[54]

There has been a pronounced reluctance among scholars to attribute to Aristotle any such global teleology, but various further considerations confirm that he intended it. In addition to the above passage from *On parts of animals* I 1 (which as far as I know has not previously been invoked in the debate), and the matching passage from *Physics* II 6 (198a5–13, p. 192 above), in the present section I shall briefly revisit some of the other texts that point to a global teleology. Opponents of an Aristotelian global teleology have had little trouble in picking these passages off one by one, explaining each either as a temporary aberration on Aristotle's part, or as admitting of a more innocuous interpretation.[55] My reply is not that they cannot, at a stretch, be read in these alternative ways, but that their cumulative effect is far more powerful than that of any one taken individually, and sufficient to make such an escape implausible.

To this cumulative evidence, add the remarkable lack of counterevidence. Precisely one passage has been cited as actually contradicting any idea of global teleology. This is *Physics* II 7, 198b8–9, where in a summary of the four causes the final cause is summed up as "because it is better thus, not absolutely (*haplōs*), but relatively to the being of each thing."[56] If "each

---

54. Cf. the valuable remarks in Falcon 2005, pp. 8–9, about the probable dependence of Aristotle's order of exposition on Plato's.

55. I have defended a global-teleology interpretation in Sedley 1991 and 2000, and consider Cooper 1982, Kahn 1985, Code 1997, p. 130, and Matthen 2001 at least broadly in the same camp. The primary critics to whom I am referring here are Wardy 1993, Judson 2005, Bodnár 2005, and Johnson 2005; cf. also Pellegrin 2002, although he does not discuss the passages I rely on (he also seems to be incorrect, in n. 17, to place Sorabji 1980, p. 147 n. 8, in the former camp).

56. διότι βέλτιον οὕτως, οὐχ ἁπλῶς, ἀλλὰ τὸ πρὸς τὴν ἑκάστου οὐσίαν. The interpretation I offer here is largely identical to that in Sedley 1991, p. 190. For Aristotle's own distinction between absolute and relative goods, cf. *EN* 1152b26–27.

thing" means each individual organism taken severally, Aristotle could indeed be denying a global teleology, even if he will at the same time unfortunately be rejecting his own thesis (*On generation of animals* II 1, 731b24–732a1) that animals' drive to reproduce is for the sake of perpetuating their species. But where does his emphasis actually lie? The terminology indicates that he is working with the familiar "absolute-relative" distinction. So when he here asserts that the good served in his teleology is always relative, not absolute, his target could well be Plato's insistence that some decisions, for example that the world should be spherical, were made by the Demiurge on the grounds that certain properties are absolutely or intrinsically better than their alternatives, not because they do anyone or anything any good (chapter IV §4 above). Alternatively, or in addition, he could be extending from ethics to physics his critique of Plato's transcendent and absolute Good, whose alleged unattainability by us in his view makes it teleologically irrelevant (*Nicomachean ethics* 1096b32–35). Either way his emphasis is on denying that his teleology involves any nonrelative good. Hence there is no reason why, when he insists instead that the good served is "relative to the being of each thing," his reference should be assumed to be limited to each discrete individual taken severally, and not more broadly to "everything"—individuals, species, and the world's entire contents alike.[57] This one passage then, in the absence of supporting evidence, falls far short of undermining the considerable weight of testimony in favor of a cosmic teleology, to which I now turn.

To the above-mentioned passages, add next the beginning of *Metaphysics* Lambda 10. This is the vital culminating chapter of his theology, and in it Aristotle speaks fairly explicitly of a global teleology, attributing cosmic goodness to what he calls "the nature of the whole" (1075a11–25):

> We must consider also in which way the nature of the whole possesses the good and the best—whether as something separated and by itself, or as its arrangement. Or is it in both ways, like an army? For an army's goodness is in its ordering, and is also the general. And more the general, since he is not due to the arrangement, but the arrangement is due to him. All things are in some joint-arrangement, but not in the same way—even creatures that swim, creatures that fly, and plants. And the arrangement is not such that one thing has no relation to another. They do have a relation: for all things are jointly arranged in relation to one thing. But it is like in a

---

57. This is, among other things, an answer to the question posed by Judson 2005, p. 360, why on an interpretation such as mine Aristotle would have written "of each thing" rather than "of something." There is no reason to take the former to refer purely internally to individuals' self-benefit.

household, where the free have least license to act as they chance to, but all or most of what they do is arranged, while the slaves and beasts can do a little towards what is communal, but act mostly as they chance to. For that is the kind of principle that nature is of each of them. I mean, for example, that at least each of them must necessarily come to be dissolved; and there are likewise other things in which all share towards the whole.[58]

Just what structures he means to include in this cosmic nature is uncertain, and not a topic on which I plan to dwell at length here, but the broader context leaves no doubt that it starts with the divine unmoved mover and the celestial rotations he inspires, and little doubt that it extends down at least to the cycle of the seasons, the weather, the *scala naturae*, and terrestrial ecology.[59]

But how can the world as a whole have a "nature"? The natures in which Aristotle's chief interest lies are those of individual organisms, and the world is not for him, as it had been for Plato, a living organism.[60] In the above passage, however, when speaking of the world's nature as embodying cosmic good, he compares it not to the nature of an animal, but to the hierarchical structure of an army or household. And in *Politics* I 2 he makes it clear that a city or household—itself a nonorganic structure, despite consisting primarily of organisms—does have a nature, one which is indeed prior to the

58. ἐπισκεπτέον δὲ καὶ ποτέρως ἔχει ἡ τοῦ ὅλου φύσις τὸ ἀγαθὸν καὶ τὸ ἄριστον, πότερον κεχωρισμένον τι καὶ αὐτὸ καθ' αὑτό, ἢ τὴν τάξιν. ἢ ἀμφοτέρως ὥσπερ στράτευμα; καὶ γὰρ ἐν τῇ τάξει τὸ εὖ καὶ ὁ στρατηγός, καὶ μᾶλλον οὗτος· οὐ γὰρ οὗτος διὰ τὴν τάξιν ἀλλ' ἐκείνη διὰ τοῦτόν ἐστιν. πάντα δὲ συντέτακταί πως, ἀλλ' οὐχ ὁμοίως, καὶ πλωτὰ καὶ πτηνὰ καὶ φυτά· καὶ οὐχ οὕτως ἔχει ὥστε μὴ εἶναι θατέρῳ πρὸς θάτερον μηδέν, ἀλλ' ἔστι τι. πρὸς μὲν γὰρ ἓν ἅπαντα συντέτακται, ἀλλ' ὥσπερ ἐν οἰκίᾳ τοῖς ἐλευθέροις ἥκιστα ἔξεστιν ὅ τι ἔτυχε ποιεῖν, ἀλλὰ πάντα ἢ τὰ πλεῖστα τέτακται, τοῖς δὲ ἀνδραπόδοις καὶ τοῖς θηρίοις μικρὸν τὸ εἰς τὸ κοινόν, τὸ δὲ πολὺ ὅ τι ἔτυχεν· τοιαύτη γὰρ ἑκάστου ἀρχὴ αὐτῶν ἡ φύσις ἐστίν. λέγω δ' οἷον εἴς γε τὸ διακριθῆναι ἀνάγκη ἅπασιν ἐλθεῖν, καὶ ἄλλα οὕτως ἔστιν ὧν κοινωνεῖ ἅπαντα εἰς τὸ ὅλον.

59. See fuller discussion in Sedley 2000, where I argue in particular that the second reference to "nature" (retaining unemended the MS reading τοιαύτη γὰρ ἑκάστου ἀρχὴ αὐτῶν ἡ φύσις ἐστίν at 1075a22–23) enables us to recognize a second reference to global nature. Bodnár 2005, pp. 18–19, is right, I think, to reply that the sentence *could* still be read as referring to individual nature. But it becomes much the less natural reading, because "the nature of the whole" is the already announced topic. My preferred reading also gives the ensuing clause (on which Bodnár does not comment) much more point: that each organism is eventually dissolved is hardly an obvious example of the kind of principle *its* nature is, but nicely illustrates the eternal recycling of the elements that is part of the global teleology (above, pp. 170–71), with a distant echo of Plato's assertion that the matter we are made of has been "borrowed" from the world (*Ti.* 42e6–43a1), implying that it must be duly returned.

60. See Nussbaum 1978, p. 97.

natures of its individual human components, since the latter are its parts. Specifically (1252b30–34), this nature is the social or political system's completed form, also identifiable with its final cause.[61] It seems then that any natural collective system composed of discrete natural substances, be it an army, a household, a city, or a world, has as its "nature" its own complex functionality, this being, irreducibly, an end over and above the individual functionality of its various components.[62]

Now consider the passage of *Physics* II 8 quoted in full on pp. 189–90 above.[63] Here Aristotle maintains explicitly that in nature *all* regular events must be for the sake of something, and includes under that generalization the specific case of rainfall. Summer rain, he allows, is rare, and he is ready to treat its occurrence as a mere accident: if a freak summer downpour ruins someone's crops on the threshing floor, that can be accounted an accident, not the purpose for which the rain fell. But winter rain, on which the growth of crops depends, is regular, and this he makes clear does serve a purpose. What purpose? Elsewhere, when considering rainfall in its own right,[64] he is interested only in invoking the material processes of evaporation, condensation etc. But that localized non-teleological perspective is perfectly compatible with another which sees weather as part of an inherently purposive cosmic nature,[65] one which among other things supports agriculture, as the reference to making the crops grow strongly suggests.[66] We might

61. διὸ πᾶσα πόλις φύσει ἔστιν, εἴπερ καὶ αἱ πρῶται κοινωνίαι. τέλος γὰρ αὕτη ἐκείνων, ἡ δὲ φύσις τέλος ἐστίν· οἷον γὰρ ἕκαστόν ἐστι τῆς γενέσεως τελεσθείσης, ταύτην φαμὲν τὴν φύσιν εἶναι ἑκάστου, ὥσπερ ἀνθρώπου ἵππου οἰκίας.

62. For the close analogy between the hierarchical structure of such "systems" and that of an individual organism like man, cf. *EN* IX 8, 1168b31–32, "Just as a city is thought to be above all its most authoritative element, and likewise every other system, so too in the case of man." (ὥσπερ δὲ καὶ πόλις τὸ κυριώτατον μάλιστ᾽ εἶναι δοκεῖ καὶ πᾶν ἄλλο σύστημα, οὕτω καὶ ἄνθρωπος.) For the notion of "nature" in the *Politics,* including the analogy between political and zoological taxonomy, see also Lloyd 1993.

63. Since I have discussed this passage at length in Sedley 1991, I shall here return to it only briefly. Thanks to the seminal study of Furley 1985, there is now widespread, if far from unanimous, agreement that the passage presents rainfall as purposive, but little agreement as to *what* its goal is.

64. *Somn.* 457b31–458a1, *APo* 96a2–6, *PA* 653a2–8, *Meteor.* 346b21–36.

65. Cf. Diogenes of Apollonia B 3, pp. 75–77 above.

66. Cf. chapter I §6 above on Anaxagoras. For the interpretation that the purpose served is water's return to its natural place, see Wardy 1993, pp. 20–21. His primary text for this, *DC* IV 3, 310a34–b16, may indicate no more than that the return of a simple body to its natural place is a return to "form" in the literal sense of "shape," and is therefore probably not associating form with the final cause; but the chapter taken as a whole does I think tend to favor a teleological interpretation (e.g. the com-

think of Aristotelian rain as like human sweat.[67] Viewed in isolation, sweat is a liquid moved by purely material causes such as heating, cooling, evaporation, and weight. Nevertheless, its occurrence is at the same time part of a purposive biological structure within which it serves an obviously beneficial end. In Aristotle's world, rain is very much like that.

A similar dual-perspective explanation accounts for another feature of cosmic teleology, one which Aristotle explicitly advertises in *Politics* I 8, to the incredulity of many of his admirers. Lower species exist for the sake of higher ones (1256b10–22):

> Even at the moment of childbirth, some animals generate at the same time sufficient nutriment to last until the offspring can supply itself—for example all the animals which produce larvae or lay eggs. And those which bear live young have nutriment within themselves for their offspring for a time, the substance called milk. Hence it is equally clear that we should also suppose that, after birth, plants exist for the sake of animals, and the other animals for the sake of mankind—domesticated animals for both usefulness and food, and most if not all wild animals for food and other assistance, as a source of clothing and other utilities. If, then, nature makes nothing incomplete or pointless, it must be that nature has made them all for the sake of mankind.[68]

---

parison to the potentially healthy becoming actually healthy, 310b16–19). Admittedly (cf. *GC* 337a1–15), the result of *all* elements returning to their natural places would be an entirely inactive and thus ungodlike sublunary world, but Aristotle presumably does regard it as better that at any rate most earth is at the center, most water at its surface, most air above that, and most fire at the periphery. Since (cf. *Physics* 252b21–23, 255a10–15, b29–31) water is not a self-mover, it must strictly speaking be moved by one or more external movers. Hence water's regular redistribution by rainfall to its proper place, the surface of the earth, will have as its moving cause the movements in the heavens (cf. *Meteor.* 339a30–31 etc.). This makes rain not an autonomous mover driven by its own ends but part of an overall good cosmic distribution of the simple bodies (to the right places, at the right times, in the right quantities etc.) orchestrated from the top down, and having among its innumerable beneficial outcomes the nourishment of plants.

67. I choose this analogy as easier to illustrate than Aristotle's own example, breathing, *PA* I 1, 642a31–b4, paraphrased p. 183 above.

68. καὶ γὰρ κατὰ τὴν ἐξ ἀρχῆς γένεσιν τὰ μὲν συνεκτίκτει τῶν ζῴων τοσαύτην τροφὴν ὥσθ᾽ ἱκανὴν εἶναι μέχρις οὗ ἂν δύνηται αὐτὸ αὑτῷ πορίζειν τὸ γεννηθέν, οἷον ὅσα σκωληκοτοκεῖ ἢ ᾠοτοκεῖ· ὅσα δὲ ζῳοτοκεῖ, τοῖς γεννωμένοις ἔχει τροφὴν ἐν αὑτοῖς μέχρι τινός, τὴν τοῦ καλουμένου γάλακτος φύσιν. ὥστε ὁμοίως δῆλον ὅτι καὶ γενομένοις οἰητέον τά τε φυτὰ τῶν ζῴων ἕνεκεν εἶναι καὶ τὰ ἄλλα ζῷα τῶν ἀνθρώπων χάριν, τὰ μὲν ἥμερα καὶ διὰ τὴν χρῆσιν καὶ διὰ τὴν τροφήν, τῶν δ᾽ ἀγρίων, εἰ μὴ πάντα, ἀλλὰ τά γε πλεῖστα τῆς τροφῆς καὶ ἄλλης βοηθείας ἕνεκεν, ἵνα καὶ ἐσθὴς καὶ ἄλλα ὄργανα γίνηται ἐξ αὐτῶν. εἰ οὖν ἡ φύσις μηθὲν μήτε ἀτελὲς ποιεῖ μήτε μάτην, ἀναγκαῖον τῶν ἀνθρώπων ἕνεκεν αὐτὰ πάντα πεποιηκέναι τὴν φύσιν.

Here Aristotle follows Xenophon's Socrates in bringing the entire natural hierarchy within the scope of his teleology, which is itself given a manifestly anthropocentric focus. The food chain, and all other cases of interspecies dependence, are cases of nature's purposiveness, with man the ultimate beneficiary standing at the very top of the hierarchy. Once more, the "nature" in question can hardly be identified with the natures of the individual plants and animals, or for that matter with human nature. For Aristotle certainly does not think it is any part of the nature of the plants and lower animals to serve the interests of their predators, human or other;[69] and although it *is* part of human nature to exploit them, Aristotle's point is evidently not that here: for example, plants exist for the sake of animals in general, he is telling us, and that aspect of the hierarchy could hardly be part of human nature. Rather it is the complex cosmic nature that is manifested in the world's interspecies ecology.[70]

The question has been asked[71] how this food-chain teleology can be reconciled with the internal teleology that dominates Aristotle's biological works. If pigs grow and function for slaughter and human consumption, how can they at the same time grow and function for their own well-being? In the next chapter this very same question about pigs will live on as an issue of debate between the Stoics and their critics. But it does seem clear enough to me why it is not ultimately a problem for Aristotle. The natural strivings of living things are for survival, maturation, propagation, and the eternity of their own kind. It is not in the pig's nature to queue up at the slaughterhouse. Nevertheless, the fact that the world actually contains pigs, and

69. On this cf. Pellegrin 2002, p. 312, who cites the case of the camel, pointing out that at *PA* II 14, 674b2–4 its tongue is said to be adapted to dealing with spiny plants, rather than the plants' being adapted to being eaten by the camel. But I see no conflict with the global-teleology interpretation that I advocate, which is about how cosmic nature integrates the natures of individual divine and sublunary substances into a single system, and not about what determines those individual natures in the first place (see esp. Sedley 1991, pp. 190–91).

70. Judson 2005, 357–58, offers a new strategy for disarming the passage. Aristotle's words here are "reflecting the viewpoint of the household manager or statesman: he is simply considering how many animals *can* be used for human ends, and reacting to the thought that some animals are, for example, too fierce to be so used." But this does not sit very comfortably with Aristotle's insistence (however questionable) that nearly all animals are for the benefit of mankind, with no apparent emphasis on the rare exceptions. The concluding inference of the passage, "it must be that nature has made them all for the sake of mankind," also remains in my view a severe obstacle both to this and to two other contemporaneous attempts (Bodnár 2005, pp. 23–24; Johnson 2005, pp. 229–37) to read the passage as describing little more than how we do in fact adapt animals to our own use.

71. Notably Wardy 1993.

potentially contains roast pork,[72] is a systematically beneficial feature of it, which Aristotle could not consistently with his teleological outlook attribute to mere accident. Just as the nature of an animal can be invoked to explain why it has the parts that it does, including some that are at the service of others, so too the nature of the world, including the sublunary realm's complex goal-directed structure with man at its apex, can be invoked to explain why it contains the species, weather-systems, and other amenities that it does. This in no way conflicts with strivings of a quite different kind, those of the pig itself, to perfect and perpetuate its own form rather than sacrifice those aspirations at the human dinner table. Here once more Aristotle's teleology can be best understood by adopting a dual perspective, combining the local and the global levels of explanation.

6. ARISTOTLE'S PLATONISM

We can now return to the question how Aristotle's teleology developed from but also innovated on its background. His man-dominated natural hierar-

72. The preparation of ingredients in cookery would in fact be a good illustration of Aristotle's assertion, "For the crafts too make their material: some of it they make *simpliciter*, some of it they make workable. And we use it on the ground that everything exists for our sake. For we ourselves too are, in one sense, an end ('end' having two senses, as we have said in *On philosophy*)" (*Ph.* II 2, 194a33–36: ἐπεὶ καὶ ποιοῦσιν αἱ τέχναι τὴν ὕλην αἱ μὲν ἁπλῶς αἱ δὲ εὐεργόν, καὶ χρώμεθα ὡς ἡμῶν ἕνεκα πάντων ὑπαρχόντων. ἐσμὲν γάρ πως καὶ ἡμεῖς τέλος (διχῶς γὰρ τὸ οὗ ἕνεκα· εἴρηται δ᾽ ἐν τοῖς περὶ φιλοσοφίας). We human beings are described as being the end for which everything exists, with specific reference to the raw materials we use in our crafts. We are such an end "in a sense," he says, not implying that we are not really or fully an end, but that we are an end in the sense in which "end" refers to the beneficiary for whose sake something exists or comes about, one of Aristotle's two standard senses, as he reminds us in the parenthesis (for a very fine analysis of these two senses, see Johnson 2005, pp. 64–80). Here, then, anthropocentric teleology is present as an assumption right at the heart of Aristotle's exposition of his natural philosophy. There is no warrant for Johnson's reductive exegesis (2005, p. 158): "So, to the extent that the elements are utilized in accordance with art or skill, they *can* of course *be described as* being for the sake of something. But that is beside the point . . . " (emphasis added), a reinterpretation facilitated by his incorrect translation of the passage: " . . . we use everything that exists as for the sake of us [apparently misconstruing the genitives in 34–35 as governed by χρώμεθα]. For we will be [present tense translated as future] in a way an end as well [where 'as well' should go with 'we']" (pp. 76, 158). Elsewhere in the same book (p. 237) the weakening effect of the inserted future tense is achieved by an alternative mistranslation of the last part: " . . . for in that way [added by translator] we *become* [my italics] a kind of end." Others too have been guilty of inaccurate translation here. A sign of the difficulties the passage presents for non-anthropocentrist interpreters?

chy is a direct legacy of Socrates and Plato. In putting all the emphasis on the realization of organic life forms rather than on the purification of detachable souls he is closer to the Socratic than the Platonic component of his heritage.[73] On the other hand, in his detailed scientific investigations of the parts of animals as functionally serving the whole, he is developing the teleological approach to biology which he learnt from Plato.[74]

His momentous innovation on that heritage lies in his theologically motivated decision to insulate god from any requirement to intervene in nature, either as creator or as administrator. The result is that, while Aristotle's world retains all the positive values—both functional and other—that Plato had associated with divine craftsmanship, these are now explained by on the one hand phasing out the divine craftsman as moving cause, and on the other representing nature as so closely isomorphic with craft in its structure as to be capable of producing its results even in the absence of a controlling intelligence. Much of the illuminating brilliance of Aristotle's biology derives from this initial parsimonious decision. And yet even that decision to insulate god's activities was, as I have sought to show, his working out of an essentially Platonic agenda.

Aristotle is no creationist. Nevertheless, his uniquely seminal contribution to the philosophy of biology owes its chief inspiration to the creationist theory that he studied in Plato's school.

73. For Aristotle's echoes of the Socratic teleology at Xen. *Mem.* I 4, see p. 82 n. 19 above.

74. For Aristotle's debts to Plato's biology, in addition to the present chapter see also n. 77, p. 129 above.

VII   The Stoics

1. STOICISM

The Argument from Design has come to be the most celebrated member of a family of arguments aimed at demonstrating the existence of a creator god. Although I have now covered more than a century and a half of debate about creation, from Anaxagoras to Epicurus, extraordinarily we have met only one argument that might merit this title. Having eliminated the minor Presocratic Diogenes of Apollonia from any claim to have articulated a version of it, we were left with Socrates, whom in Xenophon's *Memorabilia* I 4 we saw arguing that living beings are artifacts vastly superior to the inanimate figures created by representational artists. Following that solitary passage, no version of the Argument from Design reappears in the era dominated by Plato and Aristotle,[1] and we have to await the emergence of Stoicism, at the beginning of the third century B.C., before we witness its reappearance. Much the same applies more generally to arguments for the intelligent creation and government of the world. The only other formal or semi-formal arguments for this position in the fifth and fourth centuries are to be found in book X of Plato's *Laws* (c. 350 B.C.), where atheism is combatted by means of a demonstration that soul, at the cosmic as well as the local level, is causally prior to body. It is not my intention to minimize the importance of this classic text, but it seems to me to play a much less overt or direct part in Stoic thought.[2]

---

1. A possible exception is the fragment of Aristotle paraphrased at Cicero, *ND* II 95–96 and usually attributed to the *De philosophia*. However, it is far from clear that this is an argument for the existence of provident gods, rather than (cf. SE *M* IX 20–23) an account of the origin of religious belief.

2. The Platonic text that seems to have carried more weight with the Stoics in this regard is *Phaedrus* 245c5–246a2, if we take SE *M* IX 76 to be Stoic in origin, as

Although virtually every part of Stoic philosophy has a bearing on the theme of this book, the present chapter will focus on what I regard as Stoicism's greatest single contribution to the debate about creationism, namely its systematic engagement in formal argument,[3] of which its version of the Argument from Design is just one manifestation.

Stoicism emerged around 300 B.C., in the immediate aftermath of Epicureanism's arrival on the scene. It is in many ways best understood as an updated version of Socratic philosophy, and the early Stoics were in fact even willing to be known by the title "Socratics."[4] If Stoicism is indebted to Plato as well as to Socrates, that is because the Stoics regarded Plato's dialogues as having developed some of Socrates' ideas in directions that Socrates himself intended or approved. In chapter IV, in fact, I tried to show how Plato's development of a teleological physics was in the *Phaedo* and *Timaeus* advertized by him not as any betrayal of his master but, on the contrary, as an essentially Socratic agenda which Socrates had himself invited. The founder of Stoicism, Zeno of Citium, appears to have accepted this validation, viewing the *Timaeus* as Socratic at least in spirit, so that he and his Stoic successors incorporated a large body of Timaean ideas into their own physics. Zeno had in fact in his youth studied for many years in the Academy, the school originally founded by Plato, and there is strong evidence that the *Timaeus* and its interpretation were high on the school's agenda.[5]

The paradox of Stoicism is that it is, on the one hand, a self-consciously *un*original philosophy, dedicated to recovering, clarifying, and developing its classical antecedents, yet on the other hand the upshot is a highly original approach to philosophical questions, one which for many centuries was able to rival and at times eclipse the work of Plato and Aristotle. Getting the flavor of this transformation, as it applied to the issues surrounding creationism, will be my first task in this chapter.

Indeed, the Argument from Design in various forms features promi-

---

it almost certainly is. I suspect that the fact that there, unlike the *Laws*, Socrates is the speaker led to this preference. However, for a cautious comparison of *Laws* X to Stoic theology, see D. Frede 2002, and for the strikingly Stoic sound of *Laws* X 903b4–d2, see Long 1974b, p. 151.

3. See esp. Dragona-Monachou 1976, Gerson 1990, chapter 4 for useful overviews of Stoic theological argument.

4. Philodemus, *De Stoicis* XIII 3, ed. Dorandi 1982.

5. For the Academy of Polemo, see the evidence assembled in Sedley 2002 and Dillon 2003. That Xenocrates and Crantor were also heavily engaged in Timaean interpretation we know from, *inter alia*, Plutarch's *De gen. an.*

nently in the record of Stoic theology, in a form based not any longer on statues and the like (as in Socrates' original version) but on the Hellenistic world's dazzling feats of engineering. A fine example, a Stoic argument invoking the building of planetary mechanisms by Archimedes and others,[6] is the chief ancient antecedent of William Paley's celebrated comparison of the world to a watch, for which you could not fail to assume that there has been a watchmaker.[7] Where Xenophon's Socrates had compared the artist's manufacture of a statue or painting unfavorably with god's manufacture of a real human being, the Stoics are able to perform a corresponding comparison at the level of the world as a whole. Archimedes' astronomical mechanism was a miniature copy of the world's celestial rotations. Suppose, the Stoics therefore ask, some utterly remote barbarians (the British, for example) were shown one of these sophisticated mechanisms which precisely replicate the motions of sun, moon, and planets: would they doubt for a moment that this was the work of an intelligence? Yet what is the world itself, with its celestial motions, if not a vastly superior and more complex version of that very same machine?[8] The Stoics' appeal to contemporary astronomical mechanisms makes their version of the Argument from Design even more powerful than Paley's watch. In an age of geocentric astronomy, such as theirs, the structural resemblance of state-of-the-art planetary mechanisms to the celestial globe as we see it around us was much greater and more direct than in Paley's heliocentric age.

I shall turn later to other Stoic arguments, but first a little more on Stoic cosmology and its origins. One problem unavoidably faced all sympathetic readers of the *Timaeus:* how to respond to this dialogue's thesis that the

6. Archimedes, named in the version of the Argument from Design at Cicero *ND* II 88 (cf. id. *Tusc.* I 62–63 and SE *M* IX 115) is likely to be the original Stoic example, with Cicero's addition of Posidonius a localizing touch in a Roman context. For evidence of the sophistication of such mechanisms in the Hellenistic period, see Price 1975. For a warning against taking the argument to imply a strictly "mechanistic" view of the world's functioning, see Berryman 2003, p. 362.

7. Paley 1802.

8. Cic. *ND* II 88 (the Stoic spokesman Balbus): "Suppose someone were to bring to Scythia or Britain the armillary sphere recently built by our friend Posidonius, which revolution by revolution brings about in the sun, the moon, and the five planets effects identical to those brought about day by day and night by night in the heavens. Who in those barbarian places would doubt that that sphere was the product of reason? And yet these people [the Epicureans] hesitate as to whether the world, from which all things come into being, is itself the product of some kind of accident or necessity or of a divine mind's reason. And they rate Archimedes' achievement in imitating the revolutions of the heavenly sphere higher than nature's in creating them—and that when the original is a vastly more brilliant creation than the copy."

world had a beginning yet will have no end. This surprising asymmetry shocked critics like Aristotle and the Epicureans,[9] and many Platonists resolved it (see chapter IV §3 above) by saying that in reality Plato thought the world had no beginning, and had described its creation simply in order to elucidate its eternal providential structure. That way of restoring symmetry eliminates any historical act of creation from the story, and requires a corresponding deliteralization of the explanatory appeal to divine craftsmanship. Aristotle indeed, as we saw in chapter VI, went all the way when developing his own alternative, and in denying that the world had a beginning also removed divine design from it altogether.

The Stoics respond in the opposite way. So committed are they to the explanatory power of divine craftsmanship that they prefer to resolve the asymmetry in the converse manner, by giving the world a beginning *and an end*. Fortunately, however, each finite cosmic phase is in their eyes a complete and perfect unity, succeeded by another and yet another world in an endless cycle.[10] Moreover, because of their commitment to our world's being the best possible, they see no reason why any past or future world in the cycle should differ from it in any respect whatsoever. Hence arose their doctrine of eternal recurrence—an endless sequence of identical worlds.

We are back, curiously enough, with a thesis we first met in the early atomists (chapter V, §1 and §4), that of entirely identical worlds with identical inhabitants and identical histories. It is a paradoxical outcome of the debate between creationism and its critics that both sides should have found advantages in postulating identical-twin worlds. But actually there should, on reflection, be no surprise. Both sides have to explain why the world is as it is. The best possible explanation of any state of affairs is a set of conditions jointly sufficient to bring it about. But once those sufficient conditions have been established—whether they take the form of perfect divine beneficence or of random distribution on an infinite scale—it becomes inexplicable *sub specie aeternitatis* that these conditions should produce their result once and only once. The Stoics have been forced to admit that one world does not occupy all the available time; and the early atomists for their part deny that one world uses up all the available time, space, or matter. It is only natural that they should postulate the recurrence, at suitable intervals of time or space, of worlds identical to ours.[11]

9. See p. 107 above.

10. Evidence and analysis in LS, §52.

11. Cf. pp. 164–65 above for the Epicureans' reason for being a partial exception to this.

The single most significant ancestor of Stoic physics is Plato's *Timaeus*.[12] In some cases the Timaean material has been simplified, in others developed and expanded. Various non-Socratic features of Plato's cosmology have been stripped away. For example, the *Timaeus*'s most Pythagorean feature, its appeal to mathematical structure as the basis of rational design all the way down to the geometrical solids used for structuring the four elementary bodies, is omitted. So are the Platonic Forms, cited by Timaeus as the model on which the Demiurge based his act of creation. So again are Plato's division of the soul into rational and irrational parts, with the rational soul treated as immortal, destined to survive its present incarnation and to transmigrate into other human and animal bodies. In all these respects, the Timaean worldview is edited down into a leaner and in some respects more Socratic-looking one. Nevertheless, the radical teleology developed by Plato in the *Timaeus* remains intact, by retention of the core idea that the world is itself a divine living being, governed throughout by an immanent deity. This deity, in Plato the world soul, is by the Stoics simply called "god" or *logos* ("reason").

One case of such Platonizing lies in Zeno's causal theory. The *Timaeus*, although it is the great manifesto of teleology, does not anticipate Aristotle in isolating goals or aims as a distinct class of causes[13]—Aristotle's so-called "final" causes. Instead, it attaches causal preeminence to a specific subset of what Aristotle would call moving or efficient causes (a term more or less corresponding to our modern nontechnical notion of "cause"), namely those among these that are goal-directed and intelligent. They include not only the Demiurge himself but also his lesser agents, in particular the world-soul. Alongside these, Timaeus allows just one other kind of cause, "auxiliary causes" (*synaitia*, 46c7–e2), which he identifies in effect with the matter involved in each causal process. Most if not all changes in the cosmos consist in intelligent causes working on matter, which for its part is "persuaded" by them to do their bidding (chapter IV §5 above). That dual causal scheme is the basic one from which Stoicism also works, with two modifications. First, in line with many interpreters of the *Timaeus* the Stoics treat the Demiurge as not in the last analysis anything over and above the world-soul, so that in their eyes the intelligent cause is nothing but a divinity immanent in the world. Secondly, when it comes to Timaeus's "auxiliary causes," namely the matter involved in the causal process, they faithfully

---

12. Argued in different ways in Reydams-Schils 1999 and Sedley 2002. Another major ancestor is certainly Heraclitus; see Long 1975–76.

13. So I argue, p. 114 n. 47 above.

revert to Socrates' position, declared emphatically in the *Phaedo* (99b2–6), that matter is not in reality a cause at all, just a necessary condition of the workings of intelligence. In this way the underlying causal structure of the Stoic world lies in an entirely passive, causally inert stuff called "matter," imbued by a single, immanent, active, intelligent cause called "god," corresponding respectively to the material substrate and the world soul described in the *Timaeus*.[14] Plato's teleological causal theory is reduced by the Stoics to the action of god on matter.

In Plato's case, the great majority of interpreters have supposed that matter is a partly obstructive force, limiting god's power to make the world ideally good. I argued in chapter IV §5 that this is in fact an incorrect reading. I can now add the indirect endorsement of the Stoics. They, at all events, did not take the kind of matter bequeathed to them in the Timaean tradition to be any kind of obstacle at all to divine control. In our very abundant sources on Stoicism prime matter comes over consistently as purely passive, featureless, and pliable,[15] and the sources of evil are located elsewhere.[16]

2. A WINDOW ON STOIC THEOLOGY

The way in which Stoic cosmology emerged partly by reflection on this partnership of Socratic and Platonic influences is made vividly clear by a passage of the second-century A.D. Skeptic Sextus Empiricus (*M* IX 88–110) which will now become my prime exhibit.[17] Sextus, or more likely his source, sometimes mildly mishandles the material, as we shall see, and it is the material itself that is ultimately to be treasured. The passage preserves, largely intact it would seem, a whole body of early Stoic theological arguments for divine providence.[18] And it gives pride of place to Stoic meditation both on the *Timaeus* and on Xenophon, *Memorabilia* I 4, the latter being the chapter which I have characterized as including the sole occurrence of the Ar-

14. See Seneca *Ep.* 65.2 for this basic causal scheme; cf. further Duhot 1989, pp. 139–52; Reydams-Schils 1999, p. 150. The "swarm of causes" (Alexander, *De fato* 192.18) for which the Stoics came in time to be known is not at this same fundamental physical level.

15. For explicit statements, see Cic. *ND* III 92, Plut. *Comm. not.* 1076C–D. Cf. also Sharples 1994, p. 172 n. 5; Long 1996b, pp. 303–4.

16. The topic of the sources of evil according to Stoicism will not be fully covered in this chapter. For further aspects, see Long 1968, Kerferd 1978, LS § 55.

17. The material which follows in §§ 2–4 is largely identical (other than being in English) to Sedley 2005b.

18. For an overview of Stoic theology, see Algra 2003.

gument from Design before the arrival of Stoicism. That Sextus's source here is Stoic, if not demonstrable, seems entirely credible, especially in view of 102, where the elucidation of an argument propounded by Zeno begins, "And the persuasiveness of the argument is obvious. For . . . " This seems to be the source talking, not Sextus, and the elucidation that follows makes free use of Stoic technicalities.[19]

The passage occurs in a much longer doxography of—predominantly Stoic—theistic doctrines and arguments from which the Skeptic Sextus in *M* IX 60–137 launches his critique of theological doctrine, and within that doxography it is one part of a substantial section (75–122) cataloguing arguments for the existence of god based on the evidence of cosmic order. It stands apart from the surrounding text in bearing all the hallmarks of early Stoicism, referring by name only to the Stoics Zeno and Cleanthes and to their contemporary critic Alexinus, plus Xenophon and Plato as the pre-Hellenistic precursors of their theology. By contrast, the passage which precedes, 75–87, is a synthesis of Stoic argument not tied to individual names; and the passage which follows, 111–18, is likewise a synthesis, attributed this time to "the Stoics *and their sympathizers,*" and focusing, it seems to me, on the sources of motion in a way designed to allow Peripatetics as well as Stoics to be included within its scope. Framed between these two very different sections, our passage stands out as having its own separate origin and internal rationale.

The passage's overall structure is as follows:

A. CLEANTHES

88–91. Cleanthes' argument, based on the concept of a "best nature."

B. XENOPHON, *MEMORABILIA* I 4 AND ITS STOIC DERIVATIVES

92–94. Socrates' argument in Xenophon, *Memorabilia* I 4, including as a component his Cosmic Intelligence Argument.

95.   Paraphrase of the Cosmic Intelligence Argument.

96.   Anonymous parody *(parabolē)* of the Cosmic Intelligence Argument.

97.   Anonymous—presumably Stoic—defense of the Cosmic Intelligence Argument against the parody.

---

19. See further, n. 45 below.

98.   Reformulation of the Cosmic Intelligence Argument.

99–100. An argument presented as equivalent to the Cosmic Intelligence
         Argument, although actually incorporating other elements of the
         original Xenophontic argument.

101.   Zeno's own preferred version, or derivative, of the Cosmic
         Intelligence Argument.

102–3.   The source's explication and defense of Zeno's version.

   C. PLATO, *TIMAEUS* 30B1–C1 AND ITS STOIC DERIVATIVE

104.   Zeno's Rationality Argument.

105–7.   The argument of Plato, *Timaeus* 30b1–c1, presented as equivalent
         to Zeno's Rationality Argument.

108.   Alexinus's parody (*parabolē*) of Zeno's Rationality Argument.

109–10. A Stoic defense of Zeno's Rationality Argument against Alexinus.

My plan is to focus on parts B and C, which I think display both early Stoicism's incorporation of Xenophontic and Platonic material, and the dialectical challenges it faced in the process of digesting and transforming that
material.

3. APPROPRIATING SOCRATES

I shall start with the Xenophon chapter. Sextus's source, whom I shall treat
as being either a Stoic or a Stoic sympathizer, cites the passage not as the
argument of Socrates, but as one put into the mouth of Socrates by
"Xenophon the Socratic." If, as seems probable, this reflects the Stoics' own
way of referring to the argument, they can be seen to avoid the historical
error of assuming Xenophon to be transcribing the unmediated discourses
of the master,[20] but by emphasizing that Xenophon writes as a "Socratic"
they are nevertheless, as self-styled Socratics, no doubt claiming a Socratic
legacy as their own. The implication is much the same as that conveyed by
Cicero's Stoic spokesman at *On the nature of the gods* II 18, who when quot-
ing the same passage attributes it to "Socrates in Xenophon" ("apud
Xenophontem Socrates").

    The source opens section B with what it claims to be a verbatim quota-

---

20. Contrast the tradition, found in DL II 48, that Xenophon's *Memorabilia* is
a virtual transcript of Socrates' conversations.

tion of Socrates' argument in Xenophon. In reality, it can be seen to have been written from memory, without direct transcription from a copy of Xenophon. The Xenophon passage is clearly sufficiently well known for the author to be able to reproduce its phraseology at many points with only minor variations. However, the argument contained in it has been radically reshaped, much more so than the close linguistic echoes might at first seem to suggest. The transformation has all the hallmarks of an appeal to an authoritative text. Although we will witness the Stoics here contending with considerable difficulties in extracting a lucid argument from the passage, it clearly has a sufficiently canonical status for them to require its reinterpretation into a form which on the one hand respects and preserves the most prominent wording but on the other supplies an argument that can credibly be used in defense of Stoic theology. The text's special canonical status is further confirmed by the passage of Cicero mentioned above, where it is again privileged in being quoted verbatim (in Latin translation).

Socrates' argument is one I have already reported in chapter III §2. In a first phase (*Mem.* 1.4.2–6), the interlocutor Aristodemus admits that he admires no one more than the great representational artists, including poets, painters, and sculptors; Socrates gets him to agree that anything that can produce actual living beings is greatly superior to these artists, provided only (as Aristodemus himself insists) that it is producing them by design, and not by mere chance. Socrates then waxes lyrical about the brilliant and benevolent structure of man, in order to persuade Aristodemus that this of all products is least likely to be due to mere chance, manifesting as it does all the hallmarks of rational design. At which point they agree that human anatomy points to the existence of a benevolent creator. It is this first phase that constitutes what I have called the earliest specimen, or at any rate antecedent, of the Argument from Design. But there is more to come.

The transition to the second phase starts at I 4.7. Aristodemus, while expressing partial agreement, emphasizes that every divine gift Socrates has praised is one we share with the entire animal kingdom, and therefore, by implication, not after all a sign of god's special relation to man in particular. This provokes a second phase of Socrates' argument (I 4.8–14), one whose structure is unfortunately anything but clear. Socrates responds by pointing out the many ways in which man *is* uniquely privileged. But initially he does so indirectly, by arguing that just as the earth, water etc. that constitute our bodies are drawn from the great cosmic pools of these stuffs, the same must surely be true of our intelligence: it too must be drawn from cosmic intelligence, whose existence in any case has to be postulated as the ordering factor governing earth, sea, and the other cosmic masses. One incidental upshot of this argument is the conclusion that the world is itself an intelligent being. But in context Socrates' primary point, although if so it is far from pellucid, is probably meant to be that intelligence is yet another gift that comes to us from above, as it were, and that this time the beneficiary is man alone, and not the whole animal kingdom. At any rate, after a few exchanges with Aristodemus, that is the theme which Socrates proceeds to develop, still in response to Aristodemus's implicit denial that man is specially privileged: on the contrary, Socrates' reply continues, man has been uniquely privileged with upright posture, hands, speech, non-seasonal sex, religious sensibility, and technical skills. In all probability, this whole phase of the argument has been conceived to establish the anthropocentric teleology which Aristodemus tried to deny. But it has to be admitted that the place of the Cosmic Intelligence Argument within the whole is far from transparent, leaving more than a little room for variant interpretations.

What becomes of this whole complex argument in the Stoic source reproduced by Sextus? The first phase is slimmed down, as shown by the following juxtaposition:

XENOPHON, *MEM.* I 4.2–7

"Tell me, Aristodemus," said Socrates, "are there people you admire for their skill?"

"Yes," he said.

"Tell us their names," said Socrates.

"Well, for epic poetry I most admire Homer, for dithyramb Melanippides, for tragedy Sophocles, for sculpture Polyclitus, for painting Zeuxis."

"Do you consider more admirable those who make mindless and motionless images, or those who make living beings with minds and activities?"

"Much more those who make living beings, assuming that these come into existence not by a kind of chance but through the agency of some design."

"Compare things with regard to which there is no sign of what they are for, and things which evidently serve a beneficial purpose. Which ones do you judge to be the products of chance, and which of design?"

"It makes sense that the things that come to serve a beneficial function are the products of design."

"Then do you think that it was for a beneficial function that the original maker of human beings equipped them with every means of perception: eyes to see visible things, ears to hear audible things? And what use would smells be to us if we hadn't been equipped with noses? What perception would we have of sweet, spicy, and all the pleasing qualities that enter through the mouth, if a tongue had not been built into us as their arbiter? What's more, don't you think this too seems like the work of providence? I mean, because of the eye's vulnerability, to have given it a rampart of eyelids which spread open when we have to use it but close during sleep; and, so that the winds should not harm it either, to have planted lashes as a filter; and to have topped off the region above our eyes with a coping of brows, so that not even sweat from our head should cause the eye any harm. And the way our hearing receives all sounds without ever getting filled up. And the way all animals' front teeth are suitable for cutting, their molars for taking over what these have cut and grinding it. And the way the mouth, through which animals ingest the objects of their appetites, has been located near the eyes and nose, whereas, because excrement is unpleasant, they have diverted the ducts for this and discharge it as far away as possible from the sense organs. When these things have been done in such a providential fashion, are you in doubt whether they are the products of chance or design?"

"Indeed not," he said, "but when I look at it that way they seem like the contrivance of some wise craftsman who loves animals."

"And to have made a passion for childbearing innate, and also to have made innate in mothers a passion to nurture their offspring, and in their nurslings a huge desire for life and a huge fear of death?"

"These too do indeed look like the contrivances of someone who planned for there to be animals."[21]

SEXTUS EMPIRICUS M IX 92–94

"Tell me, Aristodemus, are there people you admire for their skill?"
"Yes," he said.
"Then who are they?"

21. Εἰπέ μοι, ἔφη, ὦ Ἀριστόδημε, ἔστιν οὕστινας ἀνθρώπους τεθαύμακας ἐπὶ σοφίᾳ; Ἔγωγ᾽, ἔφη. καὶ ὅς, Λέξον ἡμῖν, ἔφη, τὰ ὀνόματα αὐτῶν. Ἐπὶ μὲν τοίνυν ἐπῶν ποιήσει Ὅμηρον ἔγωγε μάλιστα τεθαύμακα, ἐπὶ δὲ διθυράμβῳ Μελανιππίδην, ἐπὶ δὲ τραγῳδίᾳ Σοφοκλέα, ἐπὶ δὲ ἀνδριαντοποιίᾳ Πολύκλειτον, ἐπὶ δὲ ζωγραφίᾳ Ζεῦξιν. Πότερά σοι δοκοῦσιν οἱ ἀπεργαζόμενοι εἴδωλα ἄφρονά τε καὶ ἀκίνητα ἀξιοθαυμαστότεροι εἶναι ἢ οἱ ζῷα ἔμφρονά τε καὶ ἐνεργά; Πολὺ νὴ Δία οἱ ζῷα, εἴπερ γε μὴ τύχῃ τινί, ἀλλ᾽ ὑπὸ γνώμης ταῦτα γίγνεται. Τῶν δὲ ἀτεκμάρτως ἐχόντων ὅτου ἕνεκά ἐστι καὶ τῶν φανερῶς ἐπ᾽ ὠφελείᾳ ὄντων πότερα τύχης καὶ πότερα γνώμης ἔργα κρίνεις; Πρέπει μὲν τὰ ἐπ᾽ ὠφελείᾳ γιγνόμενα γνώμης εἶναι ἔργα. Οὐκοῦν δοκεῖ σοι ὁ ἐξ ἀρχῆς ποιῶν ἀνθρώπους ἐπ᾽ ὠφελείᾳ προσθεῖναι αὐτοῖς δι᾽ ὧν αἰσθάνονται ἕκαστα, ὀφθαλμοὺς μὲν ὥσθ᾽ ὁρᾶν τὰ ὁρατά, ὦτα δὲ ὥστ᾽ ἀκούειν τὰ ἀκουστά; ὀσμῶν γε μήν, εἰ μὴ ῥῖνες προσετέθησαν, τί ἂν ἡμῖν ὄφελος ἦν; τίς δ᾽ ἂν αἴσθησις ἦν γλυκέων καὶ δριμέων καὶ πάντων τῶν διὰ στόματος ἡδέων, εἰ μὴ γλῶττα τούτων γνώμων ἐνειργάσθη; πρὸς δὲ τούτοις οὐ δοκεῖ σοι καὶ τάδε προνοίας ἔργοις ἐοικέναι, τὸ ἐπεὶ ἀσθενὴς μέν ἐστιν

"For poetry I admire Homer, for sculpture Polyclitus, with regard to painting Zeuxis."

"Then isn't it because of their products' exceptional craftsmanship that you approve of them?"

"Yes," he said.

"Then if a Polyclitus statue becomes ensouled too, won't you approve its expert craftsman much more?

"Very much so."

"Haven't you remarked, on seeing a statue, that it is the work of some craftsman? And when you see man, with his fine movement of soul and fine structure of body, don't you think that he has been crafted by some superior intelligence? Also when you see the location and utility of man's parts—that he has made man upright, and given him eyes so as to see what is visible, hearing so as to hear what is audible? And what use would smell be to us, if he hadn't equipped us with noses, and flavors likewise, if the tongue, their arbiter, had not been built into us?"[22]

Apart from a considerable amount of condensation, this differs from its original in two respects. The first is symptomatic of Stoicizing adaptation. In

---

ἡ ὄψις, βλεφάροις αὐτὴν θυρῶσαι, ἅ, ὅταν μὲν αὐτῇ χρῆσθαί τι δέῃ, ἀναπετάννυται, ἐν δὲ τῷ ὕπνῳ συγκλείεται, ὡς δ᾽ ἂν μηδὲ ἄνεμοι βλάπτωσιν, ἠθμὸν βλεφαρίδας ἐμφῦσαι, ὀφρύσι τε ἀπογεισῶσαι τὰ ὑπὲρ τῶν ὀμμάτων, ὡς μηδ᾽ ὁ ἐκ τῆς κεφαλῆς ἱδρὼς κακουργῇ· τὸ δὲ τὴν ἀκοὴν δέχεσθαι μὲν πάσας φωνάς, ἐμπίμπλασθαι δὲ μήποτε· καὶ τοὺς μὲν πρόσθεν ὀδόντας πᾶσι ζῴοις οἵους τέμνειν εἶναι, τοὺς δὲ γομφίους οἵους παρὰ τούτων δεξαμένους λεαίνειν· καὶ στόμα μέν, δι᾽ οὗ ὧν ἐπιθυμεῖ τὰ ζῷα εἰσπέμπεται, πλησίον ὀφθαλμῶν καὶ ῥινῶν καταθεῖναι· ἐπεὶ δὲ τὰ ἀποχωροῦντα δυσχερῆ, ἀποστρέψαι τοὺς τούτων ὀχετοὺς καὶ ἀπενεγκεῖν ᾗ δυνατὸν προσωτάτω ἀπὸ τῶν αἰσθήσεων· ταῦτα οὕτω προνοητικῶς πεπραγμένα ἀπορεῖς πότερα τύχης ἢ γνώμης ἔργα ἐστίν; Οὐ μὰ τὸν Δί᾽, ἔφη, ἀλλ᾽ οὕτω γε σκοπουμένῳ πάνυ ἔοικε ταῦτα σοφοῦ τινος δημιουργοῦ καὶ φιλοζῴου τεχνήμασι. Τὸ δὲ ἐμφῦσαι μὲν ἔρωτα τῆς τεκνοποιίας, ἐμφῦσαι δὲ ταῖς γειναμέναις ἔρωτα τοῦ ἐκτρέφειν, τοῖς δὲ τραφεῖσι μέγιστον μὲν πόθον τοῦ ζῆν, μέγιστον δὲ φόβον τοῦ θανάτου; Ἀμέλει καὶ ταῦτα ἔοικε μηχανήμασί τινος ζῷα εἶναι βουλευσαμένου.

22. Εἰπέ μοι, ὦ Ἀριστόδημε, εἰσὶν οὕς τινας ἐπὶ σοφίᾳ τεθαύμακας; Ἔγωγε, ἔφη. Τίνες οὖν εἰσιν οὗτοι; Ἐπὶ μὲν οὖν ποιητικῇ ἔγωγε Ὅμηρον τεθαύμακα, ἐπὶ δὲ ἀνδριαντοποιίᾳ Πολύκλειτον, ζωγραφίας γε μὴν χάριν Ζεῦξιν. Τούτους οὖν ἀποδέχῃ οὐ διὰ τὸ τὰ ὑπ᾽ αὐτῶν κατεσκευασμένα περισσῶς δεδημιουργῆσθαι; Ἔγωγε, ἔφη. Εἰ οὖν ὁ Πολυκλείτου ἀνδριὰς καὶ ἐμψυχίαν προσλάβῃ, οὐ πολὺ μᾶλλον ἀποδέξῃ τὸν τεχνίτην; Καὶ μάλα. Ἆρ᾽ οὖν ἀνδριάντα μὲν ὁρῶν ἔφης ὑπό τινος τεχνίτου δεδημιουργῆσθαι, ἄνθρωπον δὲ ὁρῶν κατά τε ψυχὴν εὖ κινούμενον καὶ κατὰ τὸ σῶμα εὖ κεκοσμημένον οὐκ οἴει ὑπό τινος νοῦ περιττοῦ δεδημιουργῆσθαι; εἶτα δὲ ὁρῶν θέσιν τε καὶ χρῆσιν μερῶν, πρῶτον μὲν ὅτι διανέστησε τὸν ἄνθρωπον, ὄμματά γε μὴν ἔδωκεν ὥστε ὁρᾶν τὰ ὁρατά, ἀκοὴν δὲ ὥστε ἀκούειν τὰ ἀκουστά. ὀσμῆς γε μὴν τί ἂν ἦν ὄφελος, εἰ μὴ ῥῖνας προσέθηκεν, χυμῶν τε μὴν ὁμοίως, εἰ μὴ γλῶσσα ἡ τούτων ἐπιγνώμων ἐνειργάσθη;

Xenophon, Socrates praises less the practical utility of the sense of taste than its value to us as a source of pleasure; in the revised version that apparent attachment of positive value to pleasure has been edited out, and none of the other references to pleasure in the Xenophon original has been retained. Such omissions no doubt reflect the strongly anti-hedonist inclination of Stoic ethics. Here it looks likely that at least one branch of Stoicism favored Plato's portrayal of Socrates as an anti-hedonist in the *Gorgias* and *Phaedo* over what it found in the pages of Xenophon.[23]

The second difference is that the analogy between the representational arts and divine craftsmanship has been narrowed down to the case of sculpture alone: human beings are in effect living statues, requiring far more brilliant craftsmanship than sculpture in stone or bronze ever could manifest. To maintain this sculptural analogy, the source has omitted elements of Socrates' argument that do not fit it, such as his appeal to innate instincts as evidence of divine benevolence: these, obviously enough, have no direct analogue in a statue, whereas eyes, ears, and the other features emphasized can all be represented one way or another by the sculptor. Indeed, so keen is our source on the sculptural analogy that he has included man's upright posture among the listed features, despite the fact that, in Socrates' argument, upright posture is held over for phase two of the argument, where man's superiority to other animals will become the focus.

A further difference arises at the start of phase 2 of the Xenophon argument. Sextus's Stoic or Stoicizing source manifests an understandable difficulty in working out how it is meant to relate to phase 1. He sticks closely to Xenophon's text, but as a result is unable to display any real continuity within the argument. The Cosmic Intelligence Argument, from phase 2 of Socrates' argument, instead comes over as a virtually autonomous argument that the world is an intelligent being. I place it here alongside the Xenophon version:

XENOPHON, *MEM.* I 4.8	SEXTUS EMPIRICUS, *M* IX 94
Do you think that there is nothing wise anywhere else? And this despite your knowing that there is a lot of earth, of which you have just a little portion in	And this despite your knowing that there is a lot of earth, of which you have just a little portion

23. For the hedonistic tendency of the Xenophon material, see p. 81 above. It seems likely that another branch of the Stoic tradition was faithful to Xenophon in this regard, to judge from DL VII 149: according to the Stoics as reported there, nature "aims for both utility and pleasure, as the construction (δημιουργία) of man clearly shows." The more severe Stoic source used by Sextus could well be drawing on Cleanthes, the most anti-hedonist of the Stoics (cf. Cic. *Fin.* II 69), especially as he is the author of the first Stoic argument the source reports.

your body, and a lot of moisture, of which you have just a tiny bit, and that each of the other things too is huge whereas your body has been fitted together by acquiring a tiny portion of them? Yet intelligence alone, it turns out, you think exists nowhere, and that you laid your hands on it by some stroke of luck? And that it is due to some kind of unintelligence that these vast masses of limitless amount are well arranged?[24]

in your body, a lot of moisture of which you have just a tiny bit, and likewise fire and air. Yet intelligence alone, it turns out, you think exists nowhere, and that you laid your hands on it by some stroke of luck?[25]

Having thus reported Xenophon's text, our author goes on (95) immediately to remark that this is an argument to show that, just like the portions of each of the four elements in you, which are tiny fragments of the cosmic masses of those elements, so too your intelligence can be assumed to be a tiny fragment of a cosmic mass of intelligence; in which case it follows that the world itself has an intelligence, and is itself god.

Although not accurate word for word, and despite omitting the first and last sentences and some elements of the phraseology, the Stoicizing source's purported direct quotation relies on close recall of the Xenophon text, and this once again we can take as a sign that the Xenophon passage possessed canonical status in the Stoic school. As for substantive content, the source's version differs in just one significant aspect. In Xenophon, Socrates starts from the examples of earth and moisture, two traditional components of the human body (cf. Hesiod, p. 54 above), each of which is no more than a minuscule fragment of the world's supply of the same stuffs. He then generalizes the point to "the other things too," without specifying what these are. In taking up and exploiting his argument, Plato (*Philebus* 29a9–30d9) and the Stoics naturally identify them as the remaining two of the four elements, namely air and fire. Whether or not that completion was already in Xenophon's mind, his failure to continue

24. ἄλλοθι δὲ οὐδαμοῦ οὐδὲν οἴει φρόνιμον εἶναι; καὶ ταῦτ᾽ εἰδὼς ὅτι γῆς τε μικρὸν μέρος ἐν τῷ σώματι πολλῆς οὔσης ἔχεις καὶ ὑγροῦ βραχὺ πολλοῦ ὄντος καὶ τῶν ἄλλων δήπου μεγάλων ὄντων ἑκάστου μικρὸν μέρος λαβόντι τὸ σῶμα συνήρμοσταί σοι· νοῦν δὲ μόνον ἄρα οὐδαμοῦ ὄντα σε εὐτυχῶς πως δοκεῖς συναρπάσαι, καὶ τάδε τὰ ὑπερμεγέθη καὶ πλῆθος ἄπειρα δι᾽ ἀφροσύνην τινά, ὡς οἴει, εὐτάκτως ἔχειν;

25. καὶ ταῦτα, φησίν, εἰδώς, ὅτι γῆς τε μέρος μικρὸν ἔχεις ἐν τῷ σώματι πολλῆς οὔσης, ὑγροῦ τε μὴν βραχὺ πολλοῦ ὄντος, πυρὸς ἀέρος τε ὁμοίως· νοῦν δὲ ἄρα μόνον οὐδαμοῦ ὄντα εὐτυχῶς ποθεν δοκεῖς συναρπάσαι;

the list will represent his wish to keep his Socrates as free from physical theory as can reasonably be managed, here sparing him a commitment to the popular but by no means uncontroversial four-element theory. Even his choice of the term "moisture" (ὑγρόν) rather than "water" may be motivated by this consideration. When Socrates' philosophical heirs fill out the list into the traditional foursome, they are in each case also reflecting their own commitment to that theory.

What becomes clear, in the continuation of our Stoicizing report, is that this time the argument had been fully owned and exploited by the Stoics as part of their arsenal. For we find there a debate which has all the hallmarks of others in which we know the Stoics to have engaged with their contemporary critics.[26] Sometimes these debates involve a particularly persistent critic of the early Stoic school called Alexinus, a member either of the Megaric school or of one of its offshoots. And although his name does not occur in this particular part of the report (as it will later, at 108–10) he is more than likely to be implicated. The typical pattern is that a Stoic theological argument is parodied by the critic, who maintains that if their argument proves anything it proves too much. This form of criticism was known as *parabolē*, and the challenge it presented evidently played a key formative role in the development and fine-tuning of Stoic theological argument. Following the *parabolē*, the Stoics typically reply either by reformulating their argument to make it immune to the parody, or by maintaining that the parodic argument is not relevantly parallel to their own.

Here is how Sextus, or his source, sets out the argument and its *parabolē:*

PARAPHRASE OF SOCRATIC ARGUMENT (95)	PARODY (96)
There is a lot of earth in the world, of which you have just a tiny bit.	There is a lot of earth in the world, of which you have just a tiny bit.
And there is a lot of moisture in the world, of which you have just a tiny bit.	And there is a lot of moisture in the world, of which you have just a tiny bit.
<(Likewise for air and fire.)>[27]	(Likewise for air and fire.)
Therefore there is also a lot	Therefore there is also a lot

26. See the pioneering discussion of these arguments in Schofield 1983.
27. The *parabolē* assumes that this line was present in the paraphrase, just as it was in the purported quotation from Xenophon. In adding it I do not mean to suggest necessarily that it has fallen out of the text of Sextus. He or his source may have omitted it out of carelessness.

of intelligence in the world, of which you have just a tiny bit.

Therefore the world is intelligent, and hence is a god.[28]

of bile in the world, of which you have just a tiny bit.

Likewise phlegm and blood.

It will follow that the world is bilious and bloody—which is ridiculous.[29]

If the Socratic argument proves that the world is intelligent, it is equally effective at proving that the world is bilious.

Our source next (97) quotes a response which, although unattributed, is unmistakably a Stoic one: earth, water, air, and fire are simple bodies, the reply goes, whereas bile and its like are compounds; and although the Socratic argument succeeds with regard to the simple bodies, it fails at the level of complex stuffs.[30]

No more is said to defend this claim of disanalogy, but the Stoic reply is indeed a *prima facie* promising one. If you have given me a cake, and I want to establish that the vanilla essence you used in it came from a certain shop, I can reasonably do so by noting that the shop in question is the only local source of the other basic ingredients that you used, and then go on to infer inductively that the vanilla essence, whose source I have not directly established, also came from that same shop. What I would *not* be justified in inferring inductively in the same way is that the raspberry and cream filling came from the same shop, and if I went to that shop in the hope of buying some of it I would be disappointed, because you actually concocted it in your own kitchen *from* the basic ingredients you had bought there. Likewise the bile and other humors in the human body may be made

28. γῆς πολλῆς οὔσης ἐν τῷ κόσμῳ μικρὸν μέρος ἔχεις, καὶ ὑγροῦ πολλοῦ ὄντος ἐν τῷ κόσμῳ μικρὸν μέρος ἔχεις · καὶ νοῦ ἄρα πολλοῦ ὄντος ἐν τῷ κόσμῳ μικρὸν μέρος ἔχεις. νοερὸς ἄρα ὁ κόσμος ἐστίν, καὶ διὰ τοῦτο θεός.

29. γῆς πολλῆς οὔσης ἐν τῷ κόσμῳ μικρὸν μέρος ἔχεις · ἀλλὰ καὶ ὑγροῦ πολλοῦ ὄντος ἐν τῷ κόσμῳ μικρὸν μέρος ἔχεις, καὶ ἤδη ἀέρος καὶ πυρός · καὶ πολλῆς ἄρα χολῆς οὔσης ἐν τῷ κόσμῳ μικρόν τι μέρος ἔχεις, καὶ φλέγματος καὶ αἵματος. ἀκολουθήσει καὶ χολοποιὸν καὶ αἵματος γεννητικὸν εἶναι τὸν κόσμον · ὅπερ ἐστὶν ἄτοπον.

30. "But the argument's defenders say that the parody is not like Xenophon's argument. For he asks the question about simple and primary bodies like earth, water, air, and fire, whereas those who use the parody have switched to compounds. For bile, blood, and the other moisture in our bodies are not primary and simple, but compounded out of the simple elemental bodies." οἱ δὲ ἀπολογούμενοί φασιν ἀνόμοιον εἶναι τὴν παραβολὴν τῷ Ξενοφῶντος λόγῳ. ἐκεῖνος μὲν γὰρ ἐπὶ τῶν ἁπλῶν καὶ πρώτων σωμάτων ποιεῖται τὴν ζήτησιν, ὥσπερ γῆς καὶ ὕδατος ἀέρος τε καὶ πυρός, οἱ δὲ τῇ παραβολῇ χρώμενοι μετεπήδησαν ὡς ἐπὶ τὰ συγκρίματα · χολὴ γὰρ καὶ αἷμα καὶ πᾶν τὸ ἐν τοῖς σώμασιν ὑγρὸν οὐκ ἔστι πρῶτον καὶ ἁπλοῦν, ἀλλ᾽ ἐκ τῶν πρώτων καὶ στοιχειωδῶν σωμάτων· συγκείμενον.

from the earth, water etc. contained in it, without the need to posit an external source of these humors *as such*. Provided that intelligence is agreed to be a simple rather than a compound entity, it can be inferred to be present as an inherent feature of the cosmos, while the same will not have to go for bile and phlegm.

Slightly later, in what looks like an intrusive passage (99–100), the source proceeds to quote an alternative formulation of the argument. It seems plausible[31] that it originated as a variant way of reading the Xenophon argument, one which deemphasizes the Cosmic Intelligence component and thereby offers an alternative means of evading the *parabolē*. Phase 2 is, as a result, paraphrased twice, the first time sticking closely to Xenophon's text, but leaving the linkage between the two phases obscure, the second time departing freely from Xenophon's text and only thereby securing a much closer continuity.[32] The second attempt (99–100) deserves examination in its own right, because it does at least clarify why phase 1 was narrowed down to a straight analogy between the human body and a statue:

> If you saw a well-crafted statue, would you doubt whether a skilled intelligence made it? Wouldn't you, rather, be so far from entertaining any such suspicion that you would actually admire the superiority of the craftsmanship and the skill?[33]

So far this is a brief paraphrase of phase 1 of the argument, but now it continues into phase 2:

> Can it be, then, that although in this example looking at an external shape leads you to testify to its maker, when on the other hand you look at the intelligence within you, vastly more intricate than any statue or painting, you suppose that if it has been brought into being this was the outcome of

---

31. I owe the suggestion to Jason Rheins.

32. The source does not say directly that this second version (99–100) is the completion of the initial argument from design. Instead, having first presented the Cosmic Intelligence Argument as being its completion, it then adds the new argument from sculptural analogy as being equivalent in force to the Cosmic Intelligence Argument, confirming that conflation by adding at the end of the new argument (100 *fin.*, immediately following the portion translated below) "He [the craftsman of human intelligence] would live nowhere but in the world, administering it, and giving both birth and growth to its contents. But that is a god. Therefore there are gods." Although the two arguments are clearly far from equivalent, at least ἀπὸ τύχης in 100 does pointedly pick up εὐτυχῶς at Xen. *Mem.* I 4.8, repeated by our author in his paraphrase at 94 *fin.* This too shows that he is doing his best to represent them as functionally interchangeable.

33. ἀρά γε ἄγαλμα εὖ δεδημιουργημένον θεασάμενος διστάσεις ἂν εἰ τεχνίτης νοῦς τοῦτο ἐποίησεν; ἢ οὕτως ἂν ἀπόσχοις τοῦ ὑπονοεῖν τι τοιοῦτον, ὡς καὶ θαυμάζειν τὴν περιττότητα τῆς δημιουργίας καὶ τὴν τέχνην;

luck, and not due to the agency of some craftsman who possesses superior power and understanding?[34]

Thus understood, the first phase of the Socratic design argument concentrated on the human body, viewed as a work of art immeasurably superior to a mere statue of a human being, and now the second half moves on to a less direct and correspondingly more demanding analogy: that between a statue and a human *intelligence*. Intelligence is an even more intricate entity than the human body, and hence even stronger evidence of divine craftsmanship. The Stoic author has managed to capture one feature of Socrates' argument, namely his move from the human body to human rationality as the ultimate gift from god; but he has done so at the price of virtually abandoning the letter of Xenophon's text.

Note that, in this version of the argument, intelligence is admitted to be a complex entity—not a surprising view to emanate from anyone who, like the early Stoics, had meditated on Plato's *Timaeus* (cf. especially 35a1–37c5, 41d4–7, 43c7–44b7).[35] These anonymous Stoics, it thus seems, dissented from those who responded to the *parabolē* by insisting on the elemental simplicity of intelligence. Instead, they returned to the broader Xenophontic argument and reread it in a way that made a positive virtue of intelligence's complexity: it is precisely intelligence's extreme complexity, they took Socrates to be arguing, that makes it a more admirable artifact than any mere statue could be.

So far the Stoic analysis of the Cosmic Intelligence Argument has not tackled the question how the cosmic supplies of earth, water, air, fire, and intelligence are meant to be explanatorily related to the presence of these items in you and me. But the same Stoicizing source supplies two alternative answers to this very question.[36] The first answer, again unattributed,

---

34. ἆρ' οὖν ἐπὶ μὲν τούτων τὸν ἔξω θεωρῶν τύπον προσμαρτυρεῖς τῷ κατεσκευακότι καὶ φῂς εἶναί τινα τὸν δημιουργόν· τὸν δὲ ἐν σοὶ ὁρῶν νοῦν, τοσαύτῃ ποικιλίᾳ διαφέροντα παντὸς ἀγάλματος καὶ πάσης γραφῆς, γενητὸν ὄντα νομίζεις ἀπὸ τύχης γεγονέναι, οὐχὶ δὲ ὑπό τινος δημιουργοῦ δύναμιν καὶ σύνεσιν ὑπερβάλλουσαν ἔχοντος;

35. The view of intelligence as simple would be the natural outcome of reflection on the *Phaedo* as a canonical Socratic text (cf. *Phd.* 78c1–80c1). Thus the Stoics' dilemma in this matter mirrors the dual—Socratic plus Platonic—origin of their cosmological thought.

36. The first is at 98, the second at 101. That the variant introduced at 99–100 (see above) interrupts the original continuity of these two arguments is, I think, shown by τούτου at the end of 101, which seems to refer back to θεός at the end of 98. (It would not be a natural way to refer back to θεός in the closing line of 100, where the main emphasis is on the plural θεοί.)

satisfies itself with saying that the cosmic supply of X is a *necessary condition* of the local supply of X: "If there were not something earthy in the world, there would not be something earthy in you either . . . " (98).[37] Suitably understood,[38] this secures the desired result with a minimum of commitment (or, less charitably, a maximum of evasion) as to just *how* the cosmic supply underwrites the personal one. It is to this extent the strongest and most resilient interpretation of the Socratic argument, but at the same time the least illuminating about man's relation to the cosmos.

No doubt for this latter reason, the resilient but evasive version of the argument proved unattractive to so forthright a thinker as the Stoic founder Zeno.[39] His own version of the argument,[40] recorded by the same source, postulated a very specific causal relation between macrocosm and microcosm, an explicitly biological one. We may surmise that Zeno was dissatisfied with the impression that cosmic intelligence is, like cosmic earth or water, simply a reservoir of some constituent of human beings. For, in the tradition of the *Timaeus* to which Stoicism belongs, intelligence differs from the four elemental stuffs precisely in being the world's active, moving cause, and to that extent is utterly unlike a mere passive constituent of the human body.[41] Hence we get the following rewrite of the Cosmic Intelligence Argument (101):

37. "It is also possible to pose the same argument like this: 'If there were not something earthy in the world, there would not be something earthy in you either. And if there were not something moist in the world, there would not be something moist in you either. And likewise for air and fire. Therefore also if there were not intelligence in the world there would not be intelligence in you either. But there is intelligence in you. Therefore there is intelligence in the world. And for this reason the world is intelligent, and, being intelligent, is god.'" ἔνεστι δὲ καὶ οὕτως τὸν αὐτὸν συνερωτᾶν λόγον· "εἰ μὴ ἦν τι γεῶδες ἐν κόσμῳ, οὐδὲ ἐν σοί τι ἂν ἦν γεῶδες, καὶ εἰ μὴ ἦν τι ὑγρὸν ἐν κόσμῳ, οὐδ᾽ ἂν ἐν σοὶ ἦν τι ὑγρόν, καὶ ὁμοίως ἐπὶ ἀέρος καὶ πυρός. τοίνυν καὶ εἰ μὴ ἦν τις ἐν κόσμῳ νοῦς, οὐδ᾽ ἂν ἐν σοί τις ἦν νοῦς· ἔστι δέ γε ἐν σοί τις νοῦς· ἔστιν ἄρα καὶ ἐν κόσμῳ. καὶ διὰ τοῦτο νοερός ἐστιν ὁ κόσμος. νοερὸς δὲ ὢν καὶ θεὸς καθέστηκεν."

38. As the conclusion shows (98 *fin.*), this is not meant to be read in such a way that the condition of there being intelligence in the world is satisfied simply by its being present in individual people.

39. Zeno's audacity in the use of argument is a primary theme of Schofield 1983.

40. This is how I am interpreting *ib.* 101, "Zeno of Citium, taking his starting point from Xenophon{ . . . }"

41. In this respect, Zeno may also be influenced by Plato's recasting of the argument at *Phlb.* 29a9–30d9, where despite the analogy between intelligence and earth etc. the former is given causal powers which completely set it apart from the latter. He also has the merit of abandoning the other Stoics' quantitative-sounding talk of "portions" or "bits" of intelligence.

Zeno of Citium, taking his starting point from Xenophon, propounds this argument: "That which emits seed of what is rational is itself rational. But the world emits seed of what is rational. Therefore the world is rational. This brings with it the further conclusion that god[42] exists."[43]

Zeno has thus opted for a very specific interpretation of the way in which cosmic intelligence serves as the source of human intelligence. He has phased out the analogy between cosmic intelligence and the cosmic pools of the four elements, and instead singled out cosmic intelligence as having a unique *causal* relation to the intelligences of individual humans. It is no longer the material reservoir from which our intelligences have been siphoned off, but is instead their quasi-biological parent or progenitor. The way in which the intelligence of the cosmos is manifested in us too is assimilated to genetic transmission through seed. The point is, I take it, more or less as follows. In our human experience, no rational being is or ever could be generated by non-rational beings; rational beings necessarily have rational parents. But if it is true that our own parents generate us, there is a much stronger sense in which the world generates us (or—if the reference is rather to the origin of mankind as a whole[44]—*has* generated us). *A fortiori* it too must be rational. This is indeed more or less the exact content of Zeno's argument as reported by Cicero (*On the nature of the gods* II 22). But in the version we are now considering Zeno makes the parental analogy more explicit and audacious: the world does not merely generate us, but does so by the emission of *seed*. How are we meant to understand this?

The source adds a commentary[45] which does its best to make sense of this extraordinary claim (102–3): yes, the world does emit the seeds from which we grow; however, (a) it "emits" them not by ejaculation, as in familiar biological processes, but by *containing* them in an appropriate way, and (b) the "seeds" it in this sense contains are not biological seeds but "seminal principles" *(spermatikoi logoi)*. In Stoic theory these latter are, as we might say, the biological blueprints of life forms. We should not exclude the possibility

---

42. See n. 36 above for the reference of τούτου here.

43. Ζήνων δὲ ὁ Κιτιεὺς ἀπὸ Ξενοφῶντος τὴν ἀφορμὴν λαβὼν οὑτωσὶ συνερωτᾷ· "τὸ προϊέμενον σπέρμα λογικοῦ καὶ αὐτὸ λογικόν ἐστιν· ὁ δὲ κόσμος προΐεται σπέρμα λογικοῦ· λογικὸν ἄρα ἐστὶν ὁ κόσμος. ᾧ συνεισάγεται καὶ ἡ τούτου ὕπαρξις."

44. I owe this alternative to Stephen Menn.

45. 102–3: "And the persuasiveness of the argument is obvious. For the stimulus of motion in every nature and every soul seems to be from the commanding-faculty, and all the powers sent out to the parts of the whole organism are sent out as from the commanding-faculty as if this were a kind of well-head. Hence every

that it was the need to make the best sense of this particular argument of Zeno's that brought to birth the Stoic notion of "seminal principles."

Regardless of this last speculation, a familiar exegetical pattern has by this stage emerged. Zeno, the founding father of Stoicism, has formulated a breathtakingly audacious argument, notable more for flair than for rigor. Subsequent Stoics have sought to clarify and justify his argument by a formal analysis. But the result is, at least in the present case, a loss of the argument's immediate appeal and vitality, without much additional clarity or cogency emerging. For Stoics, establishing a precise formal analysis and defense of their founder's arguments sometimes proved an uphill task, in ways which mirror the difficulties we have seen them experience with their attempts at formal analysis of the Socratic design argument recorded by Xenophon.

4. APPROPRIATING PLATO

I have now moved the spotlight onto Zeno, and shall keep it there as I turn from Xenophon's influence to that of Plato. The same source as I have already been plundering reports an argument of Zeno's (one known to us from Cicero *On the nature of the gods* II 20 as well), and specifically compares it to a passage from Plato's *Timaeus* (30b1–c1), which once again is quoted verbatim, this time with no deviations other than an announced omission and very minor variations of wording. Actually, though, the announced omission in the middle of the passage is an error, as we shall see, because— although the source does not realize this[46]—the omitted lines are historically speaking the most directly pertinent to the analysis of the argument.

Zeno's own argument is as follows (104):

---

power that belongs to the part also belongs to the whole, because it has been transmitted from the commanding-faculty in the latter. Therefore as the part is in respect of power, so too, much prior to that, is the whole. And for this reason, if the world projects the seed of a rational animal, not by frothy emission as man does, but in the sense that it contains seeds of rational animals, the universe contains these not in the way in which we would say that the vine is a container of grapes, i.e. by inclusion, but because seminal principles of rational animals are contained in it. Hence this is what is meant: 'But the world contains seminal principles of rational animals. Therefore the world is rational.'" Although this commentary might in theory be the continuation of Zeno's own argument, its explanation of σπέρματα as really equivalent to σπερματικοὶ λόγοι, and its consequent rewording of the argument's minor premise and conclusion, read much more like the work of an exegete or apologist.

46. This is visible in the source's bungled attempt, both by excerpting from the full Platonic passage and by means of his commentary at 107, to display precisely what the Platonic and Zenonian arguments have in common. Instead of the actual argument, his commentary concentrates exclusively on the conclusion shared by

The rational is superior to the non-rational; but nothing is superior to a world; therefore the world is rational. And the same goes for "intelligent" and "ensouled": the intelligent is superior to the non-intelligent, and the ensouled to the non-ensouled; but nothing is superior to a world, therefore the world is intelligent and ensouled.[47]

Zeno has given priority to the predicate "rational" (*logikos*), because the world's government by providential reason (*logos*) is among his most fundamental doctrines, and one which had its formal origin primarily in another ancient authority revered by the Stoics, Heraclitus. For Heraclitus had opened his book with a reference to something he called the *"logos,"* and Zeno's Stoic colleague Cleanthes[48] probably became the first interpreter to see in this a reference to the immanent rational principle governing the world, an understanding of Heraclitus which has been widely accepted ever since.[49]

But in acknowledging that the same argument can be run for the predicates "intelligent" and "ensouled" Zeno is making direct reference to the argument's immediate inspiration in the passage of Plato's *Timaeus* quoted alongside it by the Stoicizing source, a text in which "intelligent" and "en-

---

Plato and Zeno, and this among other things brings with it an inept attribution of the quintessentially Timaean κατὰ τὸν εἰκότα λόγον to Zeno as well.

47. [εἰ] τὸ λογικὸν τοῦ μὴ λογικοῦ κρεῖττόν ἐστιν· οὐδὲν δέ γε κόσμου κρεῖττόν ἐστιν· λογικὸν ἄρα ὁ κόσμος. καὶ ὡσαύτως ἐπὶ τοῦ νοεροῦ καὶ ἐμψυχίας μετέχοντος. τὸ γὰρ νοερὸν τοῦ μὴ νοεροῦ καὶ <τὸ> ἔμψυχον τοῦ μὴ ἐμψύχου κρεῖττόν ἐστιν· οὐδὲν δέ γε κόσμου κρεῖττον· νοερὸς ἄρα καὶ ἔμψυχός ἐστιν ὁ κόσμος.

48. For Cleanthes' appropriation of Heraclitus to Stoicism, see Long 1975–76.

49. I share the admittedly controversial view that the interpretation was a Stoic retrojection, based on an anachronistic understanding of the word's various occurrences in Heraclitus's text as reflecting a single technical meaning (for the nature of the anachronism, cf. p. 15 above on "seeds" in Anaxagoras). In fact, as is now increasingly recognized, τοῦ δὲ λόγου τοῦδε in Heraclitus's first sentence (22 B 1 DK) just means "this account," i.e. Heraclitus's own. The fact that he goes on to add that it has always been true, and (in B 2) that it is a common as opposed to a private truth, is not enough to override this, let alone to elevate it to its Stoic status as a divine causal principle. The Stoicizing reading of the passage (probably due to Posidonius) preserved by Sextus Empiricus at *M* VII 132 at least attempts to explain the deictic τοῦ δε, with the admittedly implausible suggestion that while uttering it Heraclitus was somehow or other pointing to the world around him; but even that is preferable to the practice of those modern interpreters who have simply ignored the pronoun. In B 50 the same word λόγου does appear to refer to a divine power or entity, but is a modern editorial emendation which presupposes precisely the Stoicizing interpretation that is here at issue, and so of no evidential value. For the minimalist reading, see further West 1971, pp. 124–29; Barnes 1979, p. 59; Sedley 1992b, p. 32. As West notes, no pre-Stoic source, Plato and Aristotle included, appears to attach any special significance to λόγος in Heraclitus.

souled" are precisely[50] the two predicates at issue. That is, Zeno can be seen as validating Stoicism's Heraclitean heritage by demonstrating that heritage's implicit endorsement in the *Timaeus*.[51] (Compare the foregoing Cosmic Intelligence Argument, where Zeno's own substituted version likewise replaced the supposedly Socratic notion of cosmic intelligence with one of rationality.)

Officially Timaeus, in the passage cited, is not actually giving his own argument for the world's being intelligent and ensouled, but reconstructing the Demiurge's reasoning for making it that way. Here is the Platonic original (*Timaeus* 30b1–c1):

> Upon reasoning he found that, among naturally visible things, nothing non-intelligent will, taking the classes as a whole, ever be a better product than what has intelligence; and that in addition it is impossible for anything to acquire intelligence without soul. As a result of this reasoning he constructed the universe by fitting intelligence into soul and soul into body, in order that he should have made a product which was naturally the finest and best. In this way, according to the likely account, we should say that this world really was made an ensouled, intelligent animal, owing to the god's providence.[52]

The Demiurge, that is, can be conjectured to have reasoned as follows: the world must be the best possible; the intelligent is better than the non-intelligent; intelligence can come to be only in a soul; therefore the world must be made both intelligent and ensouled. And so indeed he proceeded to make it—that is, possessed of soul and intelligence. It should be clear that Zeno has deftly borrowed the Demiurge's reasoning as his own, thus extracting from Plato an argument for divine providence that was never formally there in his text.[53]

---

50. With the trivial difference that "intelligent" is ἐννοῦς in Plato, νοερός in Zeno. This is just a matter of linguistic modernization.

51. For Plato as Heraclitean about the physical world, cf. Aristotle, *Met.* A 6, 987a32–b1, and Irwin 1977.

52. λογισάμενος οὖν ηὕρισκεν ἐκ τῶν κατὰ φύσιν ὁρατῶν οὐδὲν ἀνόητον τοῦ νοῦν ἔχοντος ὅλον ὅλου κάλλιον ἔσεσθαί ποτε ἔργον, νοῦν δ' αὖ χωρὶς ψυχῆς ἀδύνατον παραγενέσθαι τῳ. διὰ δὴ τὸν λογισμὸν τόνδε νοῦν μὲν ἐν ψυχῇ, ψυχὴν δ' ἐν σώματι συνιστὰς τὸ πᾶν συνετεκταίνετο, ὅπως ὅτι κάλλιστον εἴη κατὰ φύσιν ἄριστόν τε ἔργον ἀπειργασμένος. οὕτως οὖν δὴ κατὰ λόγον τὸν εἰκότα δεῖ λέγειν τόνδε τὸν κόσμον ζῷον ἔμψυχον ἔννουν τε τῇ ἀληθείᾳ διὰ τὴν τοῦ θεοῦ γενέσθαι πρόνοιαν.

53. Two formal criticisms. (a) In running the same argument for the predicate "ensouled," Zeno departs from the warrant of Plato's text. The world was made en-

The vital part of Plato's argument, omitted by our source, deserves a closer look. The Demiurge, we learn there, did not reason merely that the intelligent is better than the non-intelligent, but more specifically that "among *naturally visible things* (30b1), nothing non-intelligent will, taking the classes as a whole, ever be a better product than what has intelligence." By adding the qualification "among naturally visible things," Plato has introduced a reference to his two-world metaphysics, which makes a radical separation between on the one hand the sensible or visible realm and on the other the intelligible realm, that of Forms. It is only *within* one of these realms, he apparently means to indicate, that it can be said with confidence that anything intelligent is better than anything non-intelligent. This must apply equally within the intelligible realm: the Demiurge himself, who is intelligent, is after all "the best of intelligibles" (37a1), and therefore better than any of the Forms,[54] which we may assume to be non-intelligent. But if instead one were making a comparison *between* the two realms, it would be scarcely deniable that something non-intelligent in the superior realm, namely a Form, is better than something intelligent in the inferior realm, for example a human being or even a world, both of these being in fact mere copies of Forms and therefore by the principles of Platonic metaphysics *ipso facto* inferior to their originals.

---

souled, according to Timaeus, not because everything ensouled is better than everything non-ensouled, but because, given that it had to be made intelligent, it could not be so made without having a soul. Since in both Platonic and Stoic thought intelligence is naturally good-directed whereas soul as such is not (e.g. the souls of lower animals), this extension might have been considered suspect. However, the principle that everything ensouled is superior to everything non-ensouled did become a Stoic one: witness Marcus Aurelius V 16, τὰ χείρω τῶν κρειττόνων ἕνεκεν, τὰ δὲ κρείττω ἀλλήλων· κρείττω δὲ τῶν μὲν ἀψύχων τὰ ἔμψυχα, τῶν δὲ ἐμψύχων τὰ λογικά. Whether that thesis had been Stoic from the start or arose as a consequence of Zeno's syllogism seems hard to judge. (b) Both Plato and Zeno leave formal gaps in their reasoning. Plato's premise that nothing non-intelligent is better than anything intelligent leaves open the formal possibility that something non-intelligent might be *as good as* (though no better than) something intelligent. Still his argument goes through, so long as we add the assumption that some intelligent things are better than others: it would then follow that the world can be the best thing only if better than at least some intelligent things, which on Plato's premises it could not be without itself being intelligent. Zeno for his part leaves open the possibility that there might be nothing rational, in which case from the fact that nothing is superior to the world it would not follow that it is rational. Naturally this gap is easily closed by pointing out the existence of rational beings such as ourselves.

54. Or, if with Menn 1995 one takes the Demiurge to be a Form, the Demiurge is better than any of the *other* Forms. (Note, incidentally, that the Form of Animal is at 30d2 the "most beautiful" of the intelligibles, though not the "best.")

Zeno has omitted this entire aspect from his version of Plato's argument,[55] reasonably enough given his view that what Plato called Forms are not real entities at all, just our own mental constructs.[56] We have here, then, yet another example of Stoic editing down of the complex scheme presented by the *Timaeus*. For Zeno there is just one ontological realm, the spatio-temporal one, and to this extent the argument can, to its advantage, be drastically simplified.

Zeno's seductively simple argument faced a challenge, however. Alexinus (for this time he is named by the source) parodied it as follows (108):

ZENO'S ORIGINAL (104)	ALEXINUS'S PARODY (108)
The rational is superior to the non-rational;	The poetic is superior to the non-poetic, the grammatical is superior to the non-grammatical (and the objects of study in the other arts are superior to what is not of their kind);
but nothing is superior to a world;	
therefore the world is rational.	
And the same goes for "intelligent" and "ensouled":	
the intelligent is superior to the non-intelligent, and the ensouled to the non-ensouled;	but nothing is superior to a world;
but nothing is superior to a world;	therefore the world is poetic and grammatical.[58]
therefore the world is intelligent and ensouled.[57]	

Once again, in what immediately follows (109–10), the Stoics are reported to have replied to the parody.[59] Their reply is in essence as follows. Zeno's premise is that rational, intelligent, and ensouled are predicates of such positive value that anything possessing any one of them is, regardless of any defects it may have, superior to anything whatsoever that lacks that predicate.

---

55. In fairness I should add that this same point is missed by all the commentaries on the *Timaeus*, ancient and modern, that I have checked.

56. Evidence in LS § 30.

57. For Greek text, see n. 47 above.

58. τὸ ποιητικὸν τοῦ μὴ ποιητικοῦ καὶ τὸ γραμματικὸν τοῦ μὴ γραμματικοῦ κρεῖττόν ἐστι, καὶ τὸ κατὰ τὰς ἄλλας τέχνας θεωρούμενον κρεῖττόν ἐστι τοῦ μὴ τοιούτου· οὐδὲ ἓν δὲ κόσμου κρεῖττόν ἐστιν· ποιητικὸν ἄρα καὶ γραμματικόν ἐστιν ὁ κόσμος.

59. "In reply to this parody, the Stoics say that Zeno means that which is superior *once and for all*, as are the rational to the non-rational, the intelligent to the non-intelligent, and the ensouled to the non-ensouled, whereas Alexinus does not. For in the *once and for all* sense it is not true that the poetic is superior to the non-

Plato had in fact apparently made the same point, but if so he put it ob-
scurely by saying that the non-intelligent "as a whole" could not be better
than the intelligent "as a whole,"[60] or, as I represented it above, "taking the
classes as a whole" (30b2). This might, as a matter of Greek, mean either
that "on the whole" nothing non-intelligent is likely to be better than that
which is intelligent, although there could be exceptions,[61] or that the two
classes are so related that *no* member of the one class is better than *any* member of the other. The Stoics have worked out correctly that Plato's argument
requires the latter, and have found an unambiguous technical way to express it: the rational is "once and for all" (*kathapax*) better than the non-
rational. And fortunately, as they carefully go on to explain, there is no corresponding premise for the predicates "poetic" and "grammatical." For
something non-poetic can perfectly well be better than something poetic,
they remark, as for instance the non-poetic Socrates is better than the poetic Archilochus.[62] Which is why the *parabolē* fails.

This time, then, we have witnessed meticulous Stoic meditation on a classic Platonic text, leading first to the extraction from it of a formal argument
for the world's divine government, then in a second phase to the discovery
in it of materials for defending that argument against its critics.

---

poetic and the grammatical to the non-grammatical. Hence we can see a huge difference in the arguments. After all, Archilochus is poetic but is not superior to
Socrates, who is not poetic; and Aristarchus, who is grammatical, is not superior to
Plato, who is not grammatical." πρὸς ἣν ἀπαντῶντες παραβολὴν οἱ Στωϊκοί φασιν
ὅτι Ζήνων τὸ καθάπαξ κρεῖττον εἴληφεν, τουτέστι τὸ λογικὸν τοῦ μὴ λογικοῦ
καὶ τὸ νοερὸν τοῦ μὴ νοεροῦ καὶ τὸ ἔμψυχον τοῦ μὴ ἐμψύχου, ὁ δὲ Ἀλεξῖνος
οὐκέτι· οὐ γὰρ ἐν τῷ καθάπαξ τὸ ποιητικὸν τοῦ μὴ ποιητικοῦ καὶ τὸ γραμματικὸν τοῦ μὴ γραμματικοῦ κρεῖττον. ὥστε μεγάλην ἐν τοῖς λόγοις θεωρεῖσθαι
διαφοράν· ἰδοὺ γὰρ Ἀρχίλοχος ποιητικὸς ὢν οὐκ ἔστι Σωκράτους τοῦ μὴ ποιητικοῦ κρείττων, καὶ Ἀρίσταρχος γραμματικὸς ὢν οὐκ ἔστι Πλάτωνος τοῦ μὴ
γραμματικοῦ κρείττων.

60. 30b1–3, οὐδὲν ἀνόητον τοῦ νοῦν ἔχοντος ὅλον ὅλου κάλλιον ἔσεσθαί ποτε
ἔργον. I would not want to rule out the further possibility, suggested to me by Alexander Verlinsky, that Plato's dictum refers in fact solely or mainly to particular items,
each taken in its entirety.

61. Cf. *Rep.* 455d, πολὺ κρατεῖται... τὸ γένος τοῦ γένους. γυναῖκες μέντοι
πολλαὶ πολλῶν ἀνδρῶν βελτίους εἰς πολλά.

62. The reported parallel illustration for "grammatical" is that the grammatical
Aristarchus is not better than the non-grammatical Plato. This interprets γραμ-
ματικός as if it meant "grammarian," although it may be doubted whether Alexinus intended it in that sense. But of course the Stoic reply could easily have been
reformulated to allow for the more likely sense "literate," for example that the non-
literate Achilles is better than the literate Cleon.

5. WHOSE BENEFIT?

Up to now I have kept my focus on the process by which Stoic theological argument first emerged out of its Socratic and Platonic heritage and was fine-tuned in an adversarial context. It would be possible to illustrate the same process further.[63] But in the remainder of the chapter I shall turn to a separate question. If the world is the product of divine benevolence, who are the beneficiaries, and how are they benefited?

Since I have already in earlier chapters detected an anthropocentric teleology in Socrates' thought as well as in that of Anaxagoras and Aristotle, it will be no surprise to meet the same feature in Stoicism. That the ultimate beneficiaries of the world's design are its human and divine residents is indeed a prominent feature of Stoic thought.[64] But when, elsewhere in the anonymous source I have been exploiting, the Stoics are found paraphrasing Xenophon's Socrates, I noted (p. 217 above) how his references to human pleasures as gifts from god are studiously omitted. Stoicism, thanks largely to its rivalry with the hedonist Epicureans, tended to minimize the positive value of pleasure, and although it never denied that some kinds of pleasure are natural, one of its adherents, Archedemus, went so far as to classify these pleasures, along with armpit hair, as natural yet devoid of all value.[65]

Pleasure being left to one side, the authentic advantages offered by the world fall instead into two classes. The only genuinely "good" and "beneficial" thing is moral goodness, for this alone can make its possessor happy. And where is moral goodness to be found in the world? Here the *Timaeus* once again provides much of the essential background. Only the world itself, a divine living being, and its resident deities are according to the Stoics already good and happy. Human beings are obliged to work towards these same goals. But the world has at least been designed to lend them systematic support in their quest. All the advantages nature has been designed to provide—such as food, health, and eyesight—are part of that support system. These natural advantages, then, constitute the second tier of nature's benefactions. Although not "good," in that they do not in themselves make

---

63. One example is the arguments the Stoics use in support of Plato's contention that the world's *completeness* makes it superior to any of its parts (e.g. Cic. *ND* II 37–39): here again there is a strong Timaean background.

64. The gods resident in the world are or include its major constituent parts, e.g. earth, sun, moon, stars, and elemental masses (for a brief overview, see Algra 2003, pp. 168–70); this too is a direct heritage from the *Timaeus*.

65. SE *M* XI 73.

their possessor happy, they provide both the context and the means of our journey towards goodness. The way in which we use our reason to negotiate and select among the advantages and disadvantages that nature has laid in our path is a vital part of our progress towards perfect rationality.

To take one key example, divination: it really works. This is not just asserted by the Stoics on the basis of anecdotal evidence, but also argued on *a priori* grounds with a magnificently complex formal syllogism (reported by Cicero, *On divination* I 82–83):

> If the gods exist and they do not indicate in advance to human beings what is going to be, either (a) they do not love human beings, or (b) they are ignorant of what is going to happen, or (c) they think it is not in human beings' interest to know what will be, or (d) they think it beneath their dignity to signal to human beings in advance what will be, or (e) even the gods themselves are incapable of signaling it. But neither (a) do they not love us (for they are benefactors and friends to the human race), nor (b) are they ignorant of the things which they themselves have set up and planned, nor (c) is it not in our interest to know what will be (for we will be more circumspect if we know), nor (d) do they think this beneath their dignity (for there is nothing more admirable than beneficence), nor (e) are they incapable of predicting the future. Therefore it is not the case that the gods both exist and do not signal the future to us. But the gods exist. Therefore they signal the future. And it is not the case that, if they signal the future, they do not give us any means towards understanding those signals (for then their signaling would be pointless). Nor, if they do give means, does divination not exist. Therefore divination exists.

To simplify somewhat: if the gods did not give us signs of future events, this would be due to either their indifference to us, their ignorance of the future, their belief that foreknowledge could be of no help to us, their unwillingness to send signs, or their inability to send signs; each of those options is then separately eliminated as inconceivable, and the conclusion drawn that the gods must then indeed send us signs of the future.

But *what* benefit is this knowledge of the future meant to bring us? The Stoic answer is that knowing what is fated may well guide our moral choices. Chrysippus, the greatest of the Stoics, used the example of Socrates' execution,[66] having discerningly picked up a feature of Plato's *Crito* that has gone virtually unnoticed by its modern readers. At the opening of that dialogue (42d2–44b6), Socrates, waiting on death row, greets his visitor Crito with the news of a prophetic dream which he has interpreted as meaning

---

66. The reconstruction that follows is based on Cicero, *De fato* 30 as interpreted in Sedley 1993, pp. 315–17, to which I refer for a defense. I cannot here reply fully

he will die in three days' time. Socrates nevertheless then proceeds to develop his moral argument that justice requires his staying in prison and accepting execution, rather than take the opportunity to escape, but in the closing line (54e1–2) he reminds Crito of the dream by saying, "Let us act accordingly, since it is the way the god is pointing." To a Stoic eye this meant that Socrates, thanks to his use of divination, already knew what was destined for him, namely an imminent death on a precisely predetermined day, and took this foreknowledge as a cue to develop his moral understanding, by working out *why* accepting his own execution must be the right choice to make. As a result, he was able to die willingly, in the morally exemplary way that history records.

In view of his wisdom and justice,[67] Socrates was bound to make the choice he did, and that is why not only the outcome, his death on that particular day, but also the decisions that led to it were fated and inevitable— as indeed, in Stoicism, everything that happens is. But since, as Chrysippus explicitly insisted (Cicero, *On fate* 30), it was also fated that Socrates would die on that specific day *regardless* of any decisions he took or did not take, we can infer that things were so set up that if, counterfactually, he had *not* been wise and just, and in consequence had tried to escape, he would have died on the same day anyway, albeit unwillingly instead of willingly. For even in a world where the entire course of human history is predetermined, the moral meaning of our actions depends not just on the decisions we do make, but also on what *would* have happened if instead, being different sorts of people, we had decided otherwise.

Going along willingly rather than reluctantly with the divine plan was the hallmark of Socrates' wisdom. You cannot in any case change your destiny, said the Stoics, who were committed fatalists, but you are responsible

---

to the counterarguments of Bobzien 1998, pp. 200–201, 217–21, but note that the interpretation exactly conforms to the saying, attributed to Zeno and Chrysippus and discussed on p. 234 below, about the dog tied to a cart, an attribution which Bobzien's interpretation of Stoic determinism regrettably leads her likewise to reject, pp. 351–54 (cf. also Sharples 2005 for criticism of her in this regard). My view is that, on the contrary, the structure of fate as described by the two passages is central to early Stoic determinism.

67. Although Socrates was the archetype of the Stoic sage, we cannot simply assume that he was agreed to have been wise, given the Stoics' reluctance to recognize any actual sages (Brouwer 2002). However, he was so regarded by, at the very least, Zeno (Tatian, *Oratio ad Graecos* 3.1–2) and Posidonius (DL VII 91). According to the latter as I understand him (differently from Brouwer), Socrates, Diogenes, and Antisthenes must have possessed virtue or they would not have been so successful at promoting moral progress in their pupils.

for the attitude you take to it, and no one could be either good or happy so long as they resisted whatever that fate has ordained for them. In this regard, then, god's provision of divinatory signs is among the most generous benefactions he has bestowed on us.

Indeed, the world and its entire history have an ordained moral structure. As Zeno and Chrysippus both remarked, you should think of yourself as a dog tied to the back of a cart: you can follow willingly, or be dragged, but follow you certainly will.[68] To be good is to understand the world's moral structure and cooperate with it willingly. If we systematically use nature's guidance in ways such as this, we will progress towards authentic moral goodness. We will also learn how what from a narrow perspective look like personal misfortunes are in fact part of an ideally good overall plan. Maybe your illness has been planned in order that someone, your devoted nurse perhaps, can progress towards virtue. To protest at your personal misfortune is, according to Chrysippus,[69] like a foot protesting at its misfortune in having to get muddy. If the foot only understood why it had been put on this earth, namely to help provide a transport system for the rest of the body, it would accept its travails with enthusiasm. To be a Stoic is to think of yourself as a foot.

As in Plato, so too in Stoicism, everything in the natural world has been designed and coordinated to prepare our path of moral self-improvement, providing not just obstacles but also the means to overcome them and thus progress morally.[70] This approach explains not only apparent defects of the world which prove to be in reality no such thing, but also the advantages that nature bestows, from the most basic utilities like provision of food and water to keep us alive, all the way up to our possession of intelligence and eyesight, coupled with the astonishing beauty of the heavens as a divine object of contemplation. All these assets are necessary support for our aspiration to develop our moral understanding of ourselves and the world to the point where we so completely blend our own will with that of divine providence that we become good and happy.

The Stoics' critics naturally enough focused many of their counterarguments on the world's evident faults. The Epicurean Lucretius, we may recall, attacked anthropocentric creationism by bewailing the difficulties the world confronts us with: wild beasts, illness, premature death, and the dif-

---

68. Hippolytus, *Ref.* I 21 = *SVF* II 975 = LS 62A. See note 66 above.
69. Epictetus *Diss.* II 6.9 = *SVF* III 191 = LS 68J.
70. Cf. D. Frede 2002.

ficulty of assembling the resources we need to live (p. 148 above). Obstacles of these very kinds are reinterpreted by the Stoics as being in reality either divine benefactions, or the results of compromises that even a supreme divinity could not avoid.

To take the first category, blessings in disguise, a prominent Stoic example is that the danger presented by an environment containing wild beasts is a natural encouragement to us to develop the virtue of courage.[71] The second category, unavoidable compromises, is illustrated once more with the example made familiar by Plato (pp. 120–21 above), that the human head had to be constructed of delicate materials in the interests of maximum sensitivity, and that its vulnerability to blows was an unavoidable by-product or "concomitant" (*kata parakolouthēsin*) disadvantage of this.[72]

As for the earth's resources, whose inaccessibility and recalcitrance are bewailed by Lucretius, they are as effectively described by the Stoics in terms of their luxurious abundance. The world richly supplies all our needs. Maybe metals are hidden in inaccessible places; nevertheless they are among the assets built into the world's structure which humans alone are capable of using (Cicero, *On the nature of the gods* II 162), so they too are manifestly a component of the anthropocentric design.

Properly understood, in any case, our own individual interests are never self-contained but always inextricably bound up with those of the world as a whole. But how does this work for the rest of nature, especially the lower animals? Here the Stoics run into an apparent difficulty.

On the one hand, they are explicit that lower animals have no autonomous moral rights, because they were brought into existence not for their own sake but for that of mankind. Consider two Stoic examples. First, why does the world contain peahens?[73] They were an unavoidable necessity, if peacocks were to be created. And why were peacocks created? For the sake of their tails, whose beautification of the world is in turn a divine gift to humanity. Thus the hierarchy in this case has four members: the peahen, for the peacock, for the tail, for mankind. The peahen no more exists for her own self-interest than, for that matter, the peacock's tail exists for the tail's self-interest. The second example brings us back to one which featured in my discussion of Aristotle (especially pp. 202–3 above), the pig. According to Chrysippus, the sole reason why god gave the pig a soul was to keep the

---

71. E.g. Porphyry, *Abst.* III 20.1 = *SVF* II 1152, part, = LS 54P(1).
72. Gellius VII 1.10–13 = *SVF* II 1170, part, = LS 54Q(2), part.
73. Plutarch, *SR* 1044D = *SVF* II 1163 = LS 54O.

meat fresh. The pig's soul, he said, has more or less the same preservative function as salt (or, as we might prefer to say, a refrigerator).[74]

On the one hand, then, lower animals are human utilities. On the other, the Stoics wax as eloquent as Aristotle had[75] about the complex structures of organisms, structures manifestly geared to those organisms' own advantage: specialized defense mechanisms such as spines and horns, multiple methods of locomotion by land, water, and air, anatomical adaptations to give access to the appropriate food supply, innate instincts for survival and propagation, and in some cases complex symbiotic relationships between species geared to their mutual advantage. Hence they are committed to some form of Aristotle's doctrine that each animal's endowments function for its own benefit. And here we have the seeds of a contradiction, a cue for Carneades to join the debate.

Leader of the rival Academy, Carneades was the dominant critic of the Stoic school in the mid-second century B.C. In launching an attack on Stoic teleology,[76] Carneades opened with a premise which was certainly of Stoic authorship:

> Every product of nature, when it achieves the natural end for which it was born, is benefited.

He paused here to explain that "benefit" in this context is used by the Stoics to refer to morally neutral natural advantages, not, as in other contexts, to moral benefit. This incidentally confirms that he is indeed borrowing his premise from Stoicism, and I shall offer further confirmation shortly.

He then moved on to the second premise, also of Stoic extraction:

> But the pig has been born for the natural purpose of being slaughtered and eaten.

and thence to his conclusion

> When this happens to it, it achieves its natural end, and is benefited.

If Carneades is right, the Stoics have developed a teleology with comi-

---

74. *Loc. cit.* n. 72 above.

75. In fact the material in Cic. *ND* II 121–29 on this theme purports (125) to be largely Aristotelian in origin.

76. Porphyry, *Abst.* III 20.3 = *SVF* II 1152, part, = LS 54P(2): ὅτῳ δὴ ταῦτα δοκεῖ τι τοῦ πιθανοῦ καὶ θεῷ πρέποντος μετέχειν, σκοπείτω τί πρὸς ἐκεῖνον ἐρεῖ τὸν λόγον ὃν Καρνεάδης ἔλεγεν· ἕκαστον τῶν φύσει γεγονότων ὅταν τοῦ πρὸς ὃ πέφυκε καὶ γέγονε τυγχάνῃ τέλους, ὠφελεῖται. κοινότερον δὲ <τὸ> τῆς ὠφελείας, ἣν εὐχρηστίαν οὗτοι λέγουσιν, ἀκουστέον. ἡ δὲ ὗς φύσει γέγονε πρὸς τὸ σφαγῆναι καὶ καταβρωθῆναι· καὶ τοῦτο πάσχουσα τυγχάνει τοῦ πρὸς ὃ πέφυκε, καὶ ὠφελεῖται.

cally implausible implications. To be eaten by man, if it is indeed the pig's *raison d'être,* has to be in its own interests.

In the previous chapter, when Aristotle ran up against much the same paradox, I provided him with an escape route (pp. 202–3 above). The goal of the pig's being eaten by man is not in any sense part of the pig's nature, but just part of the world's nature. The pig's utility for human nutrition serves simply to help explain why the world, viewed as a complex natural system, contains pigs as well as humans. The resolution required distinguishing two perspectives—a cosmic one and the pig's own individual one. But I do not think the same distinction is going to be quite enough to rescue the Stoics, for whom individual natures are not ultimately intelligible without reference to their place in cosmic nature.

Consider the following part of a Stoic syllogism, preserved by the Roman Stoic (and emperor) Marcus Aurelius (V 16):

> That which is the purpose of each thing's construction and the
>   destination of that construction is the destination of its progress;
> the destination of its progress is that in which its goal lies;
>   where its goal lies is where each thing's advantage and good lie. [77]

This sequence of premises is used by Marcus as part of a more complex argument, aimed at showing that, since we ourselves have been born for the sake of communal relations, communal relations are where our own good lies. That thoroughly Stoic result is derived, in the portion I have quoted, from a demonstration that *everything,* and not just human beings, benefits from serving the end for which it was created. Since the Stoics are also quite explicit that the pig was created for man's use, Carneades' unwelcome conclusion really does beckon, namely that the pig is benefited when eaten by us.

What the Stoics might have said in reply to Carneades is that the pig's advantage is indeed served by its relationship to man, but that just as in the human case addressed by Marcus Aurelius our communal relations are reciprocal—we are born to help each other *and be helped*—so too the end for which the pig is created is a symbiotic relation with man: man feeds the pig, and in due time the pig feeds man. Carneades gained his lethal advantage against them by specifying the pig's goal as that of being slaughtered and

---

77. οὗπερ ἕνεκεν ἕκαστον κατεσκεύασται, πρὸς ὅ τε [δὲ MSS] κατεσκεύασται, πρὸς τοῦτο φέρεται· πρὸς ὃ φέρεται δέ, ἐν τούτῳ τὸ τέλος αὐτοῦ· ὅπου δὲ τὸ τέλος, ἐκεῖ καὶ τὸ συμφέρον καὶ τὸ ἀγαθὸν ἑκάστου. For the final premise, cf. Sen., *Ep.* 61.8, "consummatur itaque bonum eius [sc. man], si id implevit cui nascitur" (= to live in accordance with nature).

eaten, rather than that of supporting and being supported by man. As formulated, the move recalls a salutary warning issued by Aristotle (*Physics* II 2, 194a30–33), against supposing that, just because dying is the *last* thing each living thing is going to do, dying must be the goal of its life. But on the evidence available it is hard not to believe that the Stoics walked right into the trap, by specifying human nutrition as the pig's sole purpose and refusing to interpret the animal's natural relationship to man as in any way a reciprocal one.

It would be wrong to end on a negative note. In almost any dialectical encounter—and we have witnessed many in this chapter—the impression we take away with us is largely determined by which party happens to have made the last recorded contribution to the exchange. On the question of the pig's end, that piece of good fortune may have fallen to the Stoics' most powerful critic, Carneades, but on some other issues of debate we have seen the Stoics edging ahead of their various rivals. What makes the Hellenistic period the true culmination of our story is not the specific successes and failures of any party, but the imposition of a systematic structure on the debate between creationism and its critics. That debate, as I have sought to show throughout this book, had been running since the early fifth century B.C. The joint legacy of the Stoics and their contemporary adversaries is its showcasing in a deftly reasoned network of argument and counterargument.

EPILOGUE   A Galenic Perspective

The most notable absentee from my story so far is Galen, the greatest and most lastingly influential doctor of antiquity, whose voluminous writings have in large part come down to us. I cannot here aspire to do justice to the huge contributions that Galen made to teleological argument.[1] Instead, my main reason for ending up with him is to invoke him as a commentator on what has gone before. Working in the second century A.D., Galen was not only a seminal scientist but also a significant philosophical thinker. He knew his way not just around the medical literature of earlier ages, but also around the scientific and psychological writings of Plato, Aristotle, and the Stoics. Whether or not he also read the Epicurean atomists, he certainly knew about their work, to which he reacts constantly.

Galen is no impartial commentator, and shows little but derision for the attempts of atomism to get by without teleological principles of explanation, just as he has little time for those medical traditions that he associates with the same materialist tendency. His preferences are characteristic of the Roman imperial era in which he lived, and when we survey the classical heritage through his eyes we are in many ways seeing how it looked to nearly all the leading thinkers of late antiquity. Atomist materialism—for all its later glories—had in the end failed to win credence in the culture that gave birth to it, the broad pagan culture of classical antiquity. This was a world stacked sky-high with divinities, in which the Epicureans' unqualified exclusion of divine causation was liable to be perceived as leaving nature stranded and unintelligible. Galen, like all thinkers of later antiquity, looks back with reverence to his classical forebears, and for him these are the doc-

1. For relevant aspects of Galen's work, see especially Hankinson 1989 and 1998, and M. Frede 2003, from all of which I have learnt a great deal.

tor Hippocrates and the philosophers Plato and Aristotle. Plato's worldview is largely appropriated by Galen. He shows exceptional interest in the *Timaeus*, on which he in fact wrote a commentary. And in Aristotle Galen recognizes a fellow scientist, whose detailed anatomical researches often constitute the starting point for his own. What Galen maintains, at enormous length in his monumental teleological treatise *On the usefulness of parts*, is that these researches consistently confirm and illustrate the power of divine craftmanship. Indeed, he goes beyond any of his predecessors in maintaining that the anatomical decisions taken by the Demiurge were not merely intelligent and good, but in every single case, without exception, *the* best possible decision that could have been taken.

Rather than try to survey all of Galen's work in this field, I shall focus briefly on the single example of hair (*On the usefulness of parts* II 154–62).[2] In the *Timaeus* (p. 120 above), head hair was explained as our creators' partial remedy for the unavoidable fragility of the head—with the further specification that they made sure to restrict hair to areas where it would not impede the sense organs. Aristotle, who did not follow Plato in locating the seat of thought in the head and considered the brain primarily a cooling mechanism, explained the extrusion of head hair as a necessitated by-product of the brain's chemistry, even though he also assigned it a certain minor utility in temperature control (*On parts of animals* II 14–15). Galen's explanation of hair takes account of both Platonic and Aristotelian approaches, but develops them beyond anything either predecessor had entertained.[3]

Take facial hair. Galen both explains in Aristotelian fashion what material causes (namely the necessary evacuation of certain bodily residues) result in beard growth, and assigns hair a protective function. But he also makes free with aesthetic features of the arrangement, which among other things contribute to social utility: beards have additional value as a dignified adornment for men, appropriate to the character of their souls. By contrast, beards are unnecessary for women, whose indoor lifestyle does not require this additional layer of padding as a protection against hazards, and, visually, are inappropriate to women's souls. Hence it is provident that women have been spared them.

2. In including here the fascinating topic of Galen on eyelash length, I am mimicking the very apposite "Abschluss" of Theiler 1924, p. 104. Cf. also Hankinson 1989, pp. 218–19, Brisson 2002b, Tieleman 2005.

3. For the teleologist's interest in hair, cf. also Epictetus, *Diss.* I 16.9, on the value of beards as a dignified mark of gender.

Admittedly even Galen, like the Stoic Archedemus (p. 231 above), draws the line at armpit hair, which he concedes is not providentially conferred on us, but rather the bodily analogue of weeds growing alongside the crops in a cultivated field. Nevertheless, his work argues systematically and at length for an even greater degree of divine providence than either Plato or Aristotle had succeeded in cataloguing: whatever *has* been divinely conferred on us reflects the best possible decision on the part of our creator.[4] And what goes for hair goes for every other body part. Nothing, down to the smallest details—for example, the precise number of bones in the hand—could have been varied in the slightest way without the result's being inferior to what now obtains.

As we take our leave of pagan creationism and its pagan critics, we find in Galen some early signs of contact and contrast between the pagan and the Judaeo-Christian tradition about creation.[5] Although in chapter IV I denied that Plato's Demiurge is significantly restricted by his basic materials (since he did after all design them himself), it is certainly nevertheless the case that he has to make numerous practical engineering decisions, often involving compromise. Galen, referring to Moses as the presumed author of Genesis, remarks with some impatience that for Moses God's omnipotence is such that he was able to create the world and its contents by mere fiat, without concern for the properties of matter. Galen's own Platonic Demiurge, by contrast, is a craftsman who works skilfully *with* the properties of his materials. Why is it for example that, whereas our head hair and beards grow, our eyelashes maintain a fixed length? While there are various aesthetic and practical advantages to being free to choose the length of our head hair and beards, it is easy to point out, as Galen proceeds to do, that the protective utility of eyelashes depends vitally on their precise fixed length, and that if they grew longer or thicker they would positively obstruct vision. But the question that interests him more is just what the Demiurge had to do in order to secure this evidently desirable stability of eyelash length. Moses, he suggests, would have contented himself with saying that God ordered the eyelashes not to grow and that they obeyed. In contrast to this, the Platonic tradition's Demiurge is above all else a technician. To ensure the crucial stability of eyelash length, Galen explains, the creator

4. Cf. p. 130 n. 78 n. 28 above for the example of fingernails.
5. Not the earliest, of course, if we count Philo of Alexandria, whose work, however, falls outside the scope of this book. For Galen's contacts with Christianity, see Walzer 1949, Tieleman 2005.

embedded along the rim of the eyelid a hard layer of cartilage (the tarsal plate) specifically to control the ability of these little hairs to grow beyond their appropriate length.

This focus on divine mechanics is emblematic of ancient creationism. In the six centuries from Anaxagoras to Galen, creationism rarely took on an anti-scientific tenor, and when in the hands of Socrates it appeared to do just that, his leading philosophical heirs united in finding a way to circumvent his apparent veto. The atomists, with their faltering anticipations of Darwinism, may for the majority of readers have emerged as today's winners by proxy. On the other hand, the atomists' greatest conceptual contribution, or so I have argued, lay not there, but in harnessing the astonishing powers of infinity to their explanatory task. Nor was the quest to understand the underlying structure of natural processes their exclusive prerogative. In many ways, indeed, what in its historical context emerged as the most scientifically fruitful approach, and the one shared by nearly all the other major thinkers in our story, was to explain cosmic mechanics by reading off the methodology that either was, or might have been, employed by some great cosmic mechanic.

Yet Galen has one last surprise in store for us. Despite his vast battery of arguments for divine craftsmanship, and his detailed use of anatomical research in their support, he declares his real allegiance in the matter to be to Xenophon's Socrates. In the passage I have in mind (*On the doctrines of Hippocrates and Plato* IX 7.9–16), he leaves to the "speculative philosophers" such questions as

> . . . whether this world is self-contained; whether there are more worlds than one; whether there are a huge number of them; and likewise whether this world is created or uncreated; just as also whether, if it had a beginning, some god acted as its craftsman, or no god did, but some irrational and unskilled cause by luck made it as beautiful as *if* a supremely wise and capable god had supervised its construction. But questions like these contribute nothing to running one's own household well or minding out appropriately for the affairs of one's city, or dealing justly and sociably with relatives, fellow-citizens, and foreigners. [. . .]
>
> For it is not, in the way that it is useless to ask whether the world came to be or not, also useless to ask about providence and gods. For that there is something in the world superior in power and wisdom to man is a subject into which it is better for every one of us to inquire. But there is no need to investigate what the gods' essence is like—whether they are altogether incorporeal or have bodies as we do. For these and many other such questions are perfectly useless for "moral and civic" virtues and activities, just as they are for the cure of mental ailments.

The best writings about this are by Xenophon. Not only does he himself condemn the uselessness of these inquiries, he also says that that was what Socrates thought. And his attribution is endorsed not only by the other companions of Socrates, but also by Plato himself: for when Plato links physical theory to philosophy he puts the discourse about it into the mouth of Timaeus, not Socrates.[6]

As Socrates rightly insisted, Galen says here, scientific subjects should be pursued only as far as utility requires. Anything that promotes therapy of body or soul, and anything that convinces us of god's providence, enriches our lives and is therefore justified; and under this latter, theological heading he undoubtedly means to include not only the medical art as such but also his own use of it as evidence for the creationist hypothesis. However, as for the further questions that have occupied me in this book, investigating them serves no practical purpose, and should be shunned, Galen insists. His own example of a useless topic is the question whether the world had a beginning and, if so, whether it was started off by god or by some accident—the question at the very heart of the philosophical debate whose spectators we have been. And in support of this retrenchment Galen is able to invoke the support of the historical Socrates, whose dislike of purely theoretical scientific speculation is proved, he maintains, by the consensus on the point of all the Socratic writers, Plato included. For, as he rightly points out, Plato's decision to put physical speculation into the mouth of Timaeus rather than of Socrates was an acknowledgment that such theorizing was alien to Socratic thought.

Galen knows, exploits, and advances the pagan creationist tradition like no one before him, and does so with all the skill and insight of a practicing scientist. Yet in his reversion to a Socratic aloofness towards theoretical science he is at the same time radically rethinking the true meaning of that tradition.[7] To end, then, let me return for one last overview of the tradition itself.

Throughout this book I have sought to show how the major thinkers of antiquity developed their ideas on our world's origins and causal structure in a context of open-ended debate. It is this complex web of interaction that

6. In translating ὁμολογοῦσι δ᾽ αὐτῷ καὶ οἱ ἄλλοι τοῦ Σωκράτους ἑταῖροι καὶ Πλάτων αὐτός (15) as "And *his attribution* . . . is endorsed by Plato . . . ," I am taking Galen to be citing Plato simply as confirming Xenophon's evidence about Socrates' position, not as agreeing with that position, as some have done.

7. Cf. Epictetus, fr. 1 (quoted and discussed in Long 2002, pp. 149–52), which recommends for Stoicism a remarkably similar reversion to Socratic aloofness regarding speculative science.

makes the uniquely rich cultural phenomenon of ancient philosophy so much more than the sum of its parts, and it has been my overriding priority to illustrate how the discrete episodes that constitute the whole come adequately into focus only when we arrange them into a continuous history. The inspiration we can draw from these seminal thinkers has little to do with right and wrong answers, and everything to do with conceptual and argumentative resources, allied with the power of sheer philosophical imagination. Wherever cosmological science may take us in the future, for these gifts we will always remain in their debt.

Bibliography

Algra, K. 1995. *Concepts of Space in Greek Thought.* Leiden.

———. 2003. "Stoic Theology." In *The Cambridge Companion to the Stoics,* edited by B. Inwood, 153–78. Cambridge.

———, and J. Mansfeld. 2001. "Three Thetas in the 'Empédocle de Strasbourg.'" *Mnemosyne* 54: 78–84.

———, P. van der Horst, and D. Runia eds. 1996. *Polyhistor: Studies in the History and Historiography of Ancient Philosophy.* Leiden.

Allen, R. E., ed. 1965. *Studies in Plato's Metaphysics.* London.

Annas, J. 1999. *Platonic Ethics Old and New.* Ithaca and London.

Baltes, M. 1976–78. *Die Weltentstehung des platonischen Timaios nach der antiken Interpreten.* 2 vols. Leiden.

———. 1996. "Γέγονεν (Platon, Tim. 28 B 7). Ist die Welt real enstanden oder nicht?" In Algra, van der Horst, and Runia 1996: 76–96.

Bandini, M., and L.-A. Dorion, eds. 2000. *Xénophon, Mémorables* I. Paris.

Barnes, J. 1979. *The Presocratic Philosophers.* London.

Berryman, S. 2002. "Democritus and the Explanatory Power of the Void." In *Presocratic Philosophy,* edited by V. Caston and D. W. Graham, 183–91. Aldershot.

———. 2003. "Ancient Automata and Mechanical Explanation." *Phronesis* 48: 344–69.

Betegh, G. 2004. *The Derveni Papyrus.* Cambridge.

———. Forthcoming. "Tale, Theology and Teleology in the *Phaedo.*" In *Plato's Myths,* edited by C. Partenie. Cambridge.

Bignone, E. 1916. *Empedocle. Studio critico, traduzione e commento delle testimonianze e dei frammenti.* Turin.

Blundell, S. 1986. *The Origins of Civilization in Greek and Roman Thought.* London.

Bobzien, S. 1998. *Determinism and Freedom in Stoic Philosophy.* Oxford.

Bodéüs, R. 2000. *Aristotle and the Theology of the Living Immortals.* Albany.

(Original French edition, *Aristote et la théologie des vivants immortels,* Paris and Montreal, 1992.)

Bodnár, I. 1992. "Anaximander on the Stability of the Earth." *Phronesis* 37: 336–42.

———. 2005. "Teleology across Natures." *Rhizai* 2: 9–29.

Bollack, J. 1965–69. *Empédocle.* 4 vols. Paris.

Bonitz, H. 1870. *Index Aristotelicus.* Berlin.

Boys-Stones, G. 2001. *Post-Hellenistic Philosophy.* Oxford.

Brisson, L. 1992. *Platon. Timée/Critias.* Paris.

———. 2002a. *Sexual Ambivalence: Androgyny and Hermaphroditism in Graeco-Roman Antiquity.* (English trans.). Berkeley.

———. 2002b. "Le démiurge du *Timée* et le créateur de la *Genèse.*" In Canto-Sperber and Pellegrin 2002: 25–39.

Broadie, S. 1990. "Nature and Craft in Aristotelian Teleology." In *Biologie, logique et métaphysique chez Aristote,* edited by D. Devereux and P. Pellegrin, 389–403. Paris.

———. 2001. "Theodicy and Pseudo-history in the *Timaeus.*" *Oxford Studies in Ancient Philosophy* 21: 1–28.

———. 2007. "Why no Platonistic Ideas of Artefacts?" In *Maieusis,* edited by D. Scott, 232–53. Oxford.

Brouwer, R. 2002. "Sagehood and the Stoics." *Oxford Studies in Ancient Philosophy* 23: 181–224.

Burnyeat, M. F. 1999. "Culture and Society in Plato's *Republic.*" *The Tanner Lectures on Human Values* 20: 215–324.

———. 2004. "Introduction: Aristotle on the Foundations of Sublunary Physics." In *Aristotle's On Generation and Corruption I,* edited by F. de Haas and J. Mansfeld, 7–24. Oxford.

———. 2005. "Εἰκὼς μῦθος." *Rhizai* 2: 7–29.

Caizzi, F. Decleva. 1966. *Antisthenis Fragmenta.* Milan.

Calvo, T., and L. Brisson, eds. 1997. *Interpreting the Timaeus-Critias.* Sankt Augustin.

Cambiano, G. 2002. "Catastrofi naturali e storia umana in Platone e Aristotele." *Rivista storica italiana* 114: 694–714.

Campbell, G. 2000. "Zoogony and Evolution in Plato's *Timaeus:* The Presocratics, Lucretius and Darwin." In *Reason and Necessity: Essays on Plato's Timaeus,* edited by M. R. Wright, 145–81. London.

———. 2003. *Lucretius on Creation and Evolution. A Commentary on "De Rerum Natura" 5.722–1104.* Oxford.

Canto-Sperber, M., and P. Pellegrin, eds. 2002. *Le Style de la pensée. Receuil de textes en hommage à Jacques Brunschwig.* Paris.

Clark, S. R. L. 1975. *Aristotle's Man.* Oxford.

Clay, J. S. 2003. *Hesiod's Cosmos.* Cambridge.

Code, A. 1997. "The Priority of Final Causes Over Efficient Causes in Aristotle's *PA.*" In *Aristotelische Biologie: Intentionen, Methoden, Ergebnisse,* edited by Wolfgang Kullmann and Sabine Föllinger, 127–43. Stuttgart.

Cooper, J. 1982. "Aristotle on Natural Teleology." In *Language and Logos*, edited by M. Schofield and M. Nussbaum, 197–222. Cambridge. (Reprinted as part of Cooper 1987, and in Cooper 2004: 107–29.)

———. 1985. "Hypothetical Necessity." In Gotthelf 1985: 151–67. (Reprinted as part of Cooper 1987, and in Cooper 2004: 130–47.)

———. 1987. "Hypothetical Necessity and Natural Teleology." In Gotthelf and Lennox 1987: 243–74. (Combines Cooper 1985 and 1982.)

———. 2004. *Knowledge, Nature, and the Good*. Princeton and Oxford.

Cornford, F. M. 1930. "Anaxagoras' Theory of Matter." *Classical Quarterly* 24: 14–30, 83–95. (Reprinted in Furley and Allen 1975: 2.275–322.)

———. 1937. *Plato's Cosmology*. London.

Coxon, A. H. 1986. *The Fragments of Parmenides*. Assen and Maastricht.

Crowley, T. J. 2005. "On the Use of *stoicheion* in the Sense of 'Element.'" *Oxford Studies in Ancient Philosophy* 29: 367–94.

Curd, P. 2002. "The Metaphysics of Physics: Mixture and Separation in Empedocles and Anaxagoras." In *Presocratic Philosophy. Essays in Honour of Alexander Mourelatos*, edited by V. Caston and D. W. Graham, 139–58. Aldershot.

Darwin, C. 1859. *The Origin of Species*. London.

Dawkins, R. 1986. *The Blind Watchmaker*. London.

DeFilippo, J., and P. Mitsis. 1994. "Socrates and Stoic Natural Law." In Vander Waerdt 1994a: 252–71.

Diels, H., revised by W. Kranz. [Abbr. DK]. 1952 (and later editions; original edition 1903). *Die Fragmente der Vorsokratiker*. Berlin.

Dillon, J. 1971. "Harpocration's *Commentary on Plato:* Fragments of a Middle Platonist Commentary." *California Studies in Classical Antiquity* 4: 125–46. (Reprinted in id. 1990, *The Golden Chain. Studies in the Development of Platonism and Christianity*, 125–46. Aldershot.)

———. 1997. "The Riddle of the *Timaeus:* Is Plato Sowing Clues?" In *Studies in Plato and the Platonic Tradition*, edited by M. Joyal, 25–42. Aldershot.

———. 2003. *The Heirs of Plato*. Oxford.

Donini, P. L. 1992. "Galeno e la filosofia." *Aufstieg und Niedergang der Römischen Welt* II 36.5: 3484–3504.

Dorandi, T. 1982. "Filodemo. Gli Stoici (*PHerc.* 155 e 339)." *Cronache Ercolanesi* 12: 91–133.

Dragona-Monachou, M. 1976. *The Stoic Arguments for the Existence and the Providence of the Gods*. Athens.

Duhot, J.-J. 1989. *La Conception stoïcienne de la cause*. Paris.

Falcon, A. 2005. *Aristotle and the Science of Nature*. Cambridge.

Fine, G., ed. 1999. *Plato*. Vol. 1, *Metaphysics and Epistemology;* Vol. 2, *Ethics, Politics, Religion, and the Soul*. Oxford.

Frede, D. 1997. *Platon. Philebos*. Göttingen.

———. 2002. "Theodicy and Providential Care in Stoicism." In Frede and Laks 2002: 85–117.

———, and A. Laks, eds. 2002. *Traditions of Theology. Studies in Hellenistic Theology, its Background and Aftermath*. Leiden.

Frede, M. 2003. "Galen's Theology." In *Galien et la philosophie* (Entretiens sur l'antiquité classique de la Fondation Hardt XLIX): 73–129.

Fronterotta, F. 2003. *Platone, Timeo.* Milan. (2nd edition 2006.)

Furley, D. 1966. "Lucretius and the Stoics." *Bulletin of the Institute of Classical Studies* 13: 13–33. (Reprinted in Furley 1989a: 183–205.)

———. 1976. "Anaxagoras in Response to Parmenides." *Canadian Journal of Philosophy*, suppl. vol. 2: 61–85. (Reprinted in Furley 1989a: 47–65.)

———. 1985. "The Rainfall Example in *Physics* ii.8." In Gotthelf 1985: 177–82. (Reprinted in Furley 1989a: 115–20.)

———. 1987. *The Greek Cosmologists.* Vol. I. Cambridge.

———. 1989a. *Cosmic Problems.* Cambridge.

———. 1989b. "The Dynamics of the Earth: Anaximander, Plato, and the Centrifocal Theory." In Furley 1989a: 14–26.

———, and R. E. Allen, eds. 1970 and 1975. *Studies in Presocratic Philosophy.* 2 vols. London.

Gemelli Marciano, L. 1988. *Le metamorfosi della tradizione: Mutamenti de significato e neologismi nel Peri physeos di Empedocle.* Bari.

———. 2005. "Empedocles' Zoogony and Embryology." In Pierris 2005: 373–404.

Gerson, L. P. 1990. *God and Greek Philosophy.* London.

———. 2005. *Aristotle and Other Platonists.* Ithaca and London.

Gigon, O. 1953. *Kommentar zum ersten Buch von Xenophons Memorabilien.* Basel.

Gosling, J., and C. C. W. Taylor. 1982. *The Greeks on Pleasure.* Oxford.

Gotthelf, A. 1997. "Understanding Aristotle's Teleology." In *Final Causality in Nature and Human Affairs,* edited by R. F. Hassling, 71–85. Washington.

———, ed. 1985. *Aristotle on Nature and Living Things.* Cambridge.

———, and J. Lennox, eds. 1987. *Philosophical Issues in Aristotle's Biology.* Cambridge.

Graham, D. W. 1988. "Symmetry in the Empedoclean Cycle." *Classical Quarterly* 38: 297–312.

———. 1991. "Socrates, the Craft-analogy and Science." *Apeiron* 24: 1–24.

Gregoric, P. 2005. "Plato's and Aristotle's Explanation of Human Posture." *Rhizai* 2: 183–96.

Guthrie, W. K. C. 1969. *A History of Greek Philosophy.* Vol. 2. Cambridge.

Hahn, R. 2002. *Anaximander and the Architects.* Albany.

Hankinson, R. J. 1989. "Galen and the Best of all Possible Worlds." *Classical Quarterly* 39: 206–27.

———. 1991. *Galen, On the Therapeutic Method.* Oxford.

———. 1998. *Cause and Explanation in Ancient Greek Thought.* Oxford.

Harte, V. 2002. *Plato on Parts and Wholes.* Oxford.

Hirsch, U. 1990. "War Demokrits Weltbild mechanistisch und antiteleologisch?" *Phronesis* 35: 225–44.

Hölscher, U. 1965. "Weltzeiten und Lebenszyklus." *Hermes* 93: 7–33.

Ierodiakonou, K. 2005. "Empedocles on Colour and Colour Vision." *Oxford Studies in Ancient Philosophy* 29: 1–37.

Inwood, B. 2001. *The Poem of Empedocles*. 2nd edition. Toronto.

Irwin, T. 1977. "Plato's Heracliteanism." *Philosophical Quarterly* 27: 1–13.

Jaeger, W. 1947. *The Theology of the Early Greek Philosophers*. Oxford.

Janko, R. 2004. "Empedocles, *On nature* I 233–364: A New Reconstruction of *P. Strasb. Gr. Inv.* 1665–6." *Zeitschrift für Papyrologie und Epigraphik* 150: 1–26.

Johansen, T. 2004. *Plato's Natural Philosophy*. Cambridge.

Johnson, M. R. 2005. *Aristotle on Teleology*. Oxford.

Jourdan, F. 2003. *Papyrus Derveni*. Paris.

Judson, L. 1991. "Chance and 'always or for the most part.'" In *Aristotle's Physics*, edited by L. Judson, 73–99. Oxford.

———. 2005. "Aristotelian teleology." *Oxford Studies in Ancient Philosophy* 29: 341–66.

Kahn, C. H. 1960. *Anaximander and the Origins of Greek Cosmology*. New York.

———. 1979. *The Art and Thought of Heraclitus*. Cambridge.

———. 1985. "The Place of the Prime Mover in Aristotle's Teleology." In Gotthelf 1985: 183–205.

———. 1996. *Plato and the Socratic Dialogue*. Cambridge.

———. 2001. *Pythagoras and the Pythagoreans*. Indianapolis and Cambridge.

Karfik, P. 2004. *Die Beseelung des Kosmos: Untersuchungen zur Kosmologie, Seelenlehre und Theologie in Platons Phaidon und Timaios*. Leipzig and Munich.

Kerferd, G. B. 1978. "The Origin of Evil in Stoic Thought." *Bulletin of the John Rylands Library* 55: 177–96.

Keyt, D. 1971. "The Mad Craftsman of Plato's *Timaeus*." *Philosophical Review* 80: 230–35.

Kingsley, P. 1995a. *Ancient Philosophy, Mystery, and Magic*. Oxford.

———. 1995b. "Notes on Air: Four Questions of Meaning in Empedocles and Anaxagoras." *Classical Quarterly* 45: 26–29.

———. 2002. "Empedocles for the New Millennium." *Ancient Philosophy* 22: 333–413.

Kirk, G. S., J. E. Raven, and M. Schofield. 1983. *The Presocratic Philosophers*. 2nd edition. Cambridge.

Kurke, L. 1999. *Coins, Bodies, Games, and Gold: The Politics of Meaning in Archaic Greece*. Princeton.

Laks, A. 1983. *Diogène d'Apollonie*. Lille.

———. 2002. "Reading the Readings: On the First Person Plurals in the Strasburg [sic] Empedocles." In *Presocratic Philosophy: Essays in Honour of Alexander Mourelatos*, edited by V. Caston and D. W. Graham, 127–37. Aldershot.

Lamb, C. 1823. "A Dissertation upon Roast Pig." In *Essays of Elia*. London.

Lennox, J. 1985a. "Plato's Unnatural Teleology." In *Platonic Investigations*, edited by D. O'Meara, 195–218. Washington. (Reprinted in Lennox 2001a: 280–302.)

———. 1985b. "Theophrastus on the Limits of Teleology." In *Theophrastean Studies on Natural Science, Physics and Metaphysics, Ethics, Religion and Rhetoric*: 143–51. New Brunswick. (Reprinted in Lennox 2001a: 259–79.)

———. 1996. "Material and Formal Natures in Aristotle's *De partibus animalium.*" *Proceedings of the Boston Area Colloquium in Ancient Philosophy* 14: 217–40. (Reprinted in *Aristotelische Biologie. Intentionen, Methoden, Ergebnisse*, edited by S. Föllinger and W. Kullmann, 163–81, Stuttgart 1997; and in Lennox 2001a: 182–204.)

———. 2001a. *Aristotle's Philosophy of Biology: Studies in the Origins of Life Science*. New York.

———. 2001b. *Aristotle, On the Parts of Animals*. Oxford.

Lloyd, G. E. R. 1966. *Polarity and Analogy*. Cambridge.

———. 1968. "Plato as a Natural Scientist." *Journal of Hellenic Studies* 88: 78–92.

———. 1983. *Science, Folklore and Ideology*. Cambridge.

———. 1993. "L'idée de la nature dans la *Politique* d'Aristote." In *Aristote, Politique*, edited by P. Aubenque, 135–59, Paris. (English trans. in G. E. R. Lloyd, *Aristotelian Investigations*, 184–204, Cambridge 1996.)

Long, A. A. 1968. "The Stoic Concept of Evil." *Philosophical Quarterly* 18: 329–43.

———. 1974a. "Empedocles' Cosmic Cycle in the 'Sixties." In *The Presocratics*, edited by A. P. D. Mourelatos, 397–425. New York.

———. 1974b. *Hellenistic Philosophy*. London.

———. 1975–76. "Heraclitus and Stoicism." *Φιλοσοφία* 5–6: 133–56. (Reprinted in Long 1996a: 35–57.)

———. 1996a. *Stoic Studies*. Cambridge.

———. 1996b. "On Hierocles Stoicus apud Stobaeum." In *ΟΔΟΙ ΔΙΖΗΣΙΟΣ*. Le vie della ricerca (Studi in onore di Francesco Adorno), edited by M. S. Funghi, 299–309. Florence.

———. 1996c. "Parmenides on Thinking Being." In *Proceedings of the Boston Area Colloquium in Ancient Philosophy* 12: 125–51.

———. 1999. "The Scope of Early Greek Philosophy." In *The Cambridge Companion to Early Greek Philosophy*, 1–21. Cambridge.

———. 2002. *Epictetus: A Stoic and Socratic Guide to Life*. Oxford.

———, and D. N. Sedley. [Abbr. LS]. 1987. *The Hellenistic Philosophers*. 2 vols. Cambridge.

Louguet, C. 2002. "Note sur le fragment B4a d'Anaxagore: Pourquoi les autres mondes doivent-ils être semblables au nôtre?" In *Qu'est ce que c'est la philosophie Présocratique?*, edited by A. Laks and C. Louguet, 497–530. Lille.

Makin, S. 1990–91. "An Ancient Principle about Causation." *Proceedings of the Aristotelian Society* 91: 135–52.

———. 1993. *Indifference Arguments*. Oxford.

Mansfeld, J. 1972. "Ambiguity in Empedocles B 17 3–5: An Interpretation." *Phronesis* 17: 17–39.

———. 1992. *Heresiography in Context*. Leiden.

Marchant, E. C., trans. 1923. *Xenophon. Memorabilia and Oeconomicus.* London and Cambridge, MA.

Martin, A., and O. Primavesi. 1999. *L'Empédocle de Strasbourg.* Berlin and New York.

Matthen, M. 2001. "The Holistic Presuppositions of Aristotle's Cosmology." *Oxford Studies in Ancient Philosophy* 20: 171–99.

Mayor, A. 2000. *The First Fossil Hunters: Paleontology in Greek and Roman Times.* Princeton.

McKirahan, R. D. 1994. *Philosophy before Socrates.* Indianapolis and Cambridge.

McPherran, M. 1996. *The Religion of Socrates.* University Park, PA.

Menn, S. 1995. *Plato on God as Nous.* Carbondale and Edwardsville.

Miller, M. 2001. "'First of all': On the Semantics and Ethics of Hesiod's Cosmogony." *Ancient Philosophy* 21: 251–76.

Morel, P.-M. 1996. *Démocrite et la recherche des causes.* Paris.

———. 2005. "Democrito e il problema del determinismo. A proposito di Aristotele, *Fisica* II, 4." In Natali and Maso 2005: 21–35.

Morgan, K. 2000. *Myth and Philosophy from the Presocratics to Plato.* Cambridge.

Morrow, G. 1950. "Necessity and Persuasion in Plato's *Timaeus.*" *Philosophical Review* 59: 147–63. (Reprinted in Allen 1965: 421–37.)

Most, G. 1993. "A Cock for Asclepius." *Classical Quarterly* 43: 96–111.

Mourelatos, A. P. D. 1973. "Heraclitus, Parmenides, and the Naïve Metaphysics of Things." In *Exegesis and Argument,* edited by E. N. Lee, A. P. D. Mourelatos, and R. Rorty: 16–48. Assen.

Natali, C., and S. Maso, eds. 2005. *La catena delle cause.* Amsterdam.

Nucci, M. 2005. "L'Empedocle di Strasburgo. La questione delle tre *Theta.*" *Elenchos* 26: 379–401.

Nussbaum, M. 1978. *Aristotle's De Motu Animalium.* Princeton.

O'Brien, D. 1969. *Empedocles' Cosmic Cycle.* Cambridge.

O'Connor, D. 1994. "The Erotic Self-sufficiency of Socrates: A Reading of Xenophon's *Memorabilia.*" In Vander Waerdt 1994a: 151–80.

Osborne, C. 1987. *Rethinking Early Greek Philosophy.* London.

———. 1988. "Topography in the *Timaeus:* Plato and Augustine on Mankind's Place in the Natural World." *Proceedings of the Cambridge Philological Society* 214: 104–14.

———. 1996. "Space, Time, Shape and Direction: Creative Discourse in the *Timaeus.*" In *Form and Argument in Late Plato,* edited by C. Gill and M. M. McCabe, 179–211. Cambridge.

———. 2000. "Rummaging in the Recycling Bins of Upper Egypt. A discussion of A. Martin and O. Primavesi, *L'Empédocle de Strasbourg.*" *Oxford Studies in Ancient Philosophy* 18: 329–56.

Paley, W. 1802. *Natural Theology, or Evidences of the Existence and Attributes of the Deity, Collected from the Appearances of Nature.* London.

Panchenko, D. 1994. "*OMOIOΣ* and *OMOIOTHΣ* in Thales and Anaximander." *Hyperboreus* 1: 28–55.

————. 2002. "Eudemus fr. 145 Wehrli and the Ancient Theories of the Lunar Light." In *Eudemus of Rhodes*, edited by I. Bodnár and W. W. Fortenbaugh, 323–36. New Brunswick.

Pease, A. S. 1941. "Caeli enarrant." *Harvard Theological Review* 34: 163–200.

Pellegrin, P. 2002. "Les ruses de la nature et l'éternité du mouvement. Encore quelques remarques sur la finalité chez Aristote." In Canto-Sperber and Pellegrin 2002: 296–323.

Pendrick, G. 2002. *Antiphon the Sophist*. Cambridge.

Pierris, A., ed. 2005. *The Empedoclean Cosmos: Structure, Process and the Question of Cyclicity*. Patras.

Podbielski, H. 1986. "Le Chaos et les confins de l'univers dans la *Théogonie* d'Hésiode." *Les Études Classiques* 54: 253–63.

Price, D. De Solla. 1975. *Gears from the Greeks*. New York.

Primavesi, O. 2001. "La daimonologia della fisica empedoclea." *Aevum Antiquum* n.s. 1: 3–68.

————. 2005. "The Structure of Empedocles' Cosmic Cycle: Aristotle and the Byzantine Anonymous." In Pierris 2005: 245–64.

Quarantotto, D. 2005. *Causa finale, sostanza, essenza in Aristotele*. Naples.

Rashed, M. 2001. "La Chronographie du système d'Empédocle: Documents byzantins inédits." *Aevum Antiquum* n.s. 1: 237–59.

Renehan, R. 1980. "On the Greek Origin of the Concepts Incorporeality and Immateriality." *Greek, Roman, and Byzantine Studies* 21: 105–38.

Reydams-Schils, G. 1997. "Plato's World Soul: Grasping Sensibles without Sense-perception." In *Interpreting the Timaeus-Critias*, edited by T. Calvo and L. Brisson, 261–65. Sankt Augustin.

————. 1999. *Demiurge and Providence. Stoic and Platonist Readings of Plato's Timaeus*. Turnhout.

————, ed. 2003. *Plato's Timaeus as Cultural Icon*. Notre Dame.

Ritter, H. 1818. "Über die philosophische Lehre des Empedokles." In *Analecta litteraria*, edited by F. A. Wolf, 411–60. Berlin.

Sassi, M. M. 1988. *La scienza dell'uomo nella grecia antica*. Torino. (English trans., *The Science of Man in Ancient Greece*. Chicago 2001.)

Saunders, T. 1973. "Penology and Eschatology in Plato's *Timaeus* and *Laws*." *Classical Quarterly* 23: 232–44.

Schofield, M. 1980. *An Essay on Anaxagoras*. Cambridge.

————. 1983. "The syllogisms of Zeno of Citium." *Phronesis* 28: 31–58.

————. 1996. "Anaxagoras' Other World Revisited." In Algra, van der Horst, and Runia 1996: 3–19.

Scott, D. J. 2006. *Plato's Meno*. Cambridge.

Sedley, D. 1973. "Epicurus, *On nature* Book XXVIII." *Cronache Ercolanesi* 3: 5–83.

————. 1982. "Two Conceptions of Vacuum." *Phronesis* 27: 175–93.

————. 1988. "Epicurean Anti-reductionism." In *Matter and Metaphysics*, edited by J. Barnes and M. Mignucci, 295–327. Naples.

————. 1990. "Teleology and Myth in the *Phaedo.*" *Proceedings of the Boston Area Colloquium in Ancient Philosophy* 5: 359–83.

————. 1991. "Is Aristotle's Teleology Anthropocentric?" *Phronesis* 36: 179–96.

————. 1992a. "Empedocles' Theory of Vision in Theophrastus *De sensibus.*" In *Theophrastus: His Psychological, Doxographical and Scientific Writings,* edited by W. W. Fortenbaugh and D. Gutas, 20–31. New Brunswick.

————. 1992b. "Sextus Empiricus and the Atomist Criteria of Truth." *Elenchos* 13: 19–56.

————. 1993. "Chrysippus on Psycho-physical Causality." In *Passions and Perceptions,* edited by J. Brunschwig and M. Nussbaum, 313–31. Cambridge.

————. 1995. "The Dramatis Personae of Plato's *Phaedo.*" In *Philosophical Dialogues: Plato, Hume and Wittgenstein,* edited by T. Smiley, 1–26. Oxford.

————. 1998a. *Lucretius and the Transformation of Greek Wisdom.* Cambridge.

————. 1998b. "Platonic Causes." *Phronesis* 43: 114–32.

————. 1999a. "Parmenides and Melissus." In *The Cambridge Companion to Early Greek Philosophy,* edited by A. A. Long, 113–33. Cambridge.

————. 1999b. "The Ideal of Godlikeness." In Fine 1999, vol. 2, 309–28. (= revised version of "Becoming Like God in the *Timaeus* and Aristotle," in Calvo and Brisson 1997: 327–39.)

————. 2000. "*Metaphysics Λ* 10." In *Aristotle's Metaphysics Lambda,* edited by M. Frede and D. Charles, 327–50. Oxford.

————. 2002. "The Origins of Stoic God." In Frede and Laks 2002: 41–83.

————. 2003a. *Plato's Cratylus.* Cambridge.

————. 2003b. "Lucretius and the new Empedocles." *Leeds International Classical Studies* (http://www.leeds.ac.uk/classics/lics) 2.

————. 2004. *The Midwife of Platonism: Text and Subtext in Plato's Theaetetus.* Oxford.

————. 2005a. "Empedocles' Life Cycles." In Pierris 2005: 331–71.

————. 2005b. "Les Origines des preuves stoïciennes de l'existence de dieu." *Revue de Métaphysique et de Morale* 4: 461–87.

Sharples, R. W. 1983. *Alexander of Aphrodisias on Fate.* London.

————. 1994. "Plato, Plotinus, and Evil." *Bulletin of the Institute of Classical Studies* 39: 171–81.

————. 2003. "Threefold Providence: The History and Background of a Doctrine." In *Ancient Approaches to Plato's Timaeus,* edited by R. W. Sharples and A. Sheppard, 107–27. London.

————. 2005. "Ducunt volentem fata, nolentem trahunt." In Natali and Maso 2005: 197–214.

Sider, D. 2005. *The Fragments of Anaxagoras.* 2nd edition (1st edition 1980). Sankt Augustin.

Solmsen, F. 1963. "Nature as Craftsman in Greek thought." *Journal of the History of Ideas* 24: 473–96.

————. 1965. "Love and Strife in Empedocles' Cosmology." *Phronesis* 10: 109–48.

Sorabji, R. 1980. *Necessity, Cause and Blame: Perspectives on Aristotle's Theory*. London.

———. 1983. *Time, Creation and the Continuum*. London.

Steel, C. 2001. "The Moral Purpose of the Human Body: A reading of *Timaeus* 69–72." *Phronesis* 46: 105–28.

Stokes, M. 1962. "Hesiodic and Milesian Cosmogonies." *Phronesis* 7: 1–37.

———. 1967. *One and Many in Presocratic Philosophy*. Washington.

Strang, C. 1963. "The Physical Theory of Anaxagoras." *Archiv für Geschichte der Philosophie* 45: 101–18. (Reprinted in Furley and Allen 1975: 2.361–80.)

Strange, S. 1985. "The Double Explanation in the *Timaeus*." *Ancient Philosophy* 5: 25–39. (Reprinted in Fine 1999: vol. 1, 397–415.)

Tannery, P. 1886. "La Théorie de la matière d'Anaxagore." *Revue Philosophique de la France et de l'Etranger* 12: 255–77.

Taub, L. 2003. *Ancient Meteorology*. London and New York.

Taylor, A. E. 1928. *A Commentary on Plato's Timaeus*.

Taylor, C. C. W. 1999. *The Atomists: Leucippus and Democritus*. Toronto.

Tegmark, M. 2003. "Parallel Universes." *Scientific American*, May 2003.

Tepedino Guerra, A. 1994. "L'opera filodemea *Su Epicuro* (PHerc. 1232, 1289β)." *Cronache Ercolanesi* 24: 5–54.

Theiler, W. 1924. *Zur Geschichte der teleologischen Naturbetrachtung bis auf Aristoteles*. Zurich. (2nd edition 1965, Berlin.)

Tieleman, T. 2005. "Galen and Genesis." In *The Creation of Heaven and Earth. Re-interpretations of Genesis I in the Context of Judaism, Ancient Philosophy, Christianity, and Modern Physics*, edited by G. H. van Kooten, 125–45. Leiden.

Tredennick, H., and R. Waterfield, trans. 1990. *Xenophon. Conversations of Socrates*. Harmondsworth.

Trépanier, S. 2003a. "Empedocles on the Ultimate Symmetry of the World." *Oxford Studies in Ancient Philosophy* 24: 1–57.

———. 2003b. "'We' and Empedocles' Cosmic Lottery: P.Strasb.Gr. inv. 1665–1666, ensemble a." *Mnemosyne* 56: 385–419.

Vander Waerdt, P. 1993. "Socratic Justice and Self-sufficiency: The Story of the Delphic Oracle in Xenophon's *Apology of Socrates*." *Oxford Studies in Ancient Philosophy* 11: 1–48.

———. 1994a. *The Socratic Movement*. Ithaca and London.

———. 1994b. "Socrates in the *Clouds*." In Vander Waerdt 1994a: 48–86.

Velásquez, O. 2004. *Platon. Timeo*. Santiago.

Viano, C. 2001. "La cosmologie de Socrate dans les *Mémorables* de Xénophon." In *Socrate et les Socratiques*, edited by G. Rhomeyer Dherbey and J.-B. Gourinat, 97–119. Paris.

Vlastos, G. 1939. "The Disorderly Motion in the *Timaeus*." *Classical Quarterly* 33: 71–83. (Revised version in Allen 1965: 379–99; also reprinted in Vlastos 1995, vol. 2: 247–79.)

———. 1950. "The Physical Theory of Anaxagoras." *Philosophical Review* 59: 31–57. (Reprinted in Furley and Allen 1975, vol. 2: 323–53, and in Vlastos 1995, vol. 1: 303–27.)

———. 1952. "Theology and Philosophy in Early Greek Thought." *Philosophical Quarterly* 2: 97–123. (Reprinted in Vlastos 1995, vol. 1: 3–31.)

———. 1965. "Creation in the *Timaeus:* Is it a Fiction?" In Allen 1965: 401–19.

———. 1995. *Studies in Greek Philosophy.* Edited by D. W. Graham. 2 vols. Princeton.

Waerden, B. L. van der. 1952. "Das grosse Jahr und die ewige Wiederkehr." *Hermes* 80: 129–55.

———. 1953. "Das grosse Jahr des Orpheus." *Hermes* 81: 481–83.

Walzer, R. 1949. *Galen on Jews and Christians.* London.

Wardy, R. 1993. "Aristotelian Rainfall or the Lore of Averages." *Phronesis* 38: 18–30.

———. 2005. "The Mysterious Aristotelian Olive." *Science in Context* 18: 69–91.

Warren, J. 2004a. *Facing Death: Epicurus and his Critics.* Oxford.

———. 2004b. "Ancient Atomists on the Plurality of Worlds." *Classical Quarterly* 54: 354–65.

West, M. L. 1966. *Hesiod Theogony.* Oxford.

———. 1971. *Early Greek Philosophy and the Orient.* Oxford.

Wilamowitz, U. von. 1930. "Lesefrüchte." *Hermes* 65: 245–50.

Wright, M. R. 1981. *Empedocles, The Extant Fragments.* London.

Zeyl, D. 2000. *Plato. Timaeus.* Indianapolis and Cambridge.

Index Locorum

Aetius
- I 7.8–9   143n22
- I 7.13   6n19
- II 1.2   16n48
- V 8.1   44n43
- V 19.5   40–41
- V 26   47

Alexander of Aphrodisias
De fato
- 192.18   210n14

Anaxagoras (Diels-Kranz 59)
- A 1 (10)   14n39
- A 11–12   14n39
- A 87   16n49
- A 92   28–29
- A 113   18n51
- A 116   23n65
- A 117   23n65
- B 1   9, 13n37
- B 4   14, 17, 21, 23, 30
- B6   30
- B 8   16, 28
- B10   19, 26
- B 11   10, 11, 23, 30
- B 12   11–12, 20, 22, 23, 28, 29, 30
- B 14   20n58
- B 15   9–10, 13, 17, 27
- B 16   13
- B 17   15

Anaximander (Diels-Kranz 12)
- A 10   5n16
- B 1   6

Anaximenes (Diels-Kranz 13)
- A 7(a)   4n12
- A 20   4n12

Antiphon (orator)
- 6.9   20n58

Aristophanes
Thesmophoriazousae
- 14–18   54n73

Aristotle
De anima
- 404b1–5   23n65
- 404b1–2   24n69
- 415a26–b7   170
- 416a2–5   171–72
De caelo
- 270b16–25   119n58
- I 10–11   107n29
- 279b32–280a2   107
- II 2   173
- 292a22–28   169n6
- 292a28–34   166
- 29318–294.3   62
- 294b13–17   87n28

Aristotle
De caelo (continued)
    295b10   5n14
    300b24–31   42n34
    301a15–16   39n22
    302a28–b5   13n36
    302b4–5   13n36
    310a34–b16   200n66
    310b16–19   201n66
Eudemian ethics
    1215b11–14   24n69
    1216a10–16   24n69
    1249b13–15   170n9
Historia animalium
    494a20–b1   171n12
    569a29–570a3   18n52
Metaphysics
    981b2–5   178n21
    A3–4   1n2
    984a11–13   8n26
    984b15–22   7n22
    984b23–31   3
    984b32–985a10 62n90
    985a18–21   21n60, 192n42
    987a32–b1   227n51
    988a14–17   115n51
    1025a14–19   193
    1032a12–b1   18n52
    1032b5–14   180
    1050b28–30   170
    1074a38–b14   119n58
    Λ 10   171
    1075a11–25   198–99
Meteorologica
    338a20–b22   196n51
    339a5–9   196n51
    339a30–31   201n66
    346b35–347a10 171
Nicomachean ethics
    1096b32–35   198
    1112a34–b8   178n21
    1152b26–27   197n56
    1168b31–32   200n62
    X 7–8   169
    1177b26–1178a8 170
    1178b7–32   170
On generation of animals
    731b24–732a1   170, 198

    761b24–763b16   18n52
    762b28–30   19n54
    769b13–16   44
On generation and corruption
    314a24–b1   13n36
    334a5–7   34n9
    336b27–34   168n4
    336b34–337a7 171
    337a1–15   201n66
On parts of animals
    639b25–30   180n24
    640b4–17   184n29, 195n49
    641a25–27   175n17
    641b10–23   192n40, 194–95
    641b13–15   82n19
    642a31–b4   183, 201n67
    656a7–13   171
    656a14–27   120n61
    II 14–15   240
    658b14–26   82n19
    661b6–9   82n19
    665a19–26   172
    674b2–4   202n69
    675a31–b28   129n77
    675b22–28   129
    686a24–b2   131
    687a8–10   24
    687b21–24   130n78
    696b25–32   196n53
On progression of animals
    4–5   172
On youth and old age
    477a21–23   171n12
Physics
    184a16–21   174
    192b23–27   177
    193a9–30   184
    193a12–17   184n30
    193b9–11   184n30
    194a30–33   238
    194a33–36   203n72
    II 3   174, 178–79
    195b21–25   179
    II 4–6   186–94
    196a24–35   191
    196b21–24   193n44
    197a8–18   188–89
    197a25–30   187n34

198a1–3	187
198a5–13	192, 197
198a5–7	193n44
198a24–27	175n17
198b8–9	197
198b16–199a5	60n89, 189–90
198b24–26	82n19
198b31–32	191
198b31	44n41
199a15–20	175
199a20–30	175
199a33–b4	186
199b26–28	177, 180
199b28–30	177
199b30–32	177
II 9	182–83, 185
199b35–200a5	182
199b35–200a1	184
200a7–10	183n27
203b11–15	6n19
250b26–251a5	69n105
250b26–29	67n100
252a7–10	67n100
252a31	69n105
252b21–23	201n66
255a10–15	201n66
255b29–31	201n66

Politics

1252a28–30	170
1252b30–34	200
1256b10–22	201

Protrepticus (ed. Ross)

fr. 10a	7n22

[Aristotle]
De mundo

397a10–11	68n102
401a16	68n102

Censorinus
De die natali

18.11	69

Cicero
Academica

II 55	137, 138n12
II 118	107n30
II 125	138n12

De divinatione

I 82–83	232

De fato

30	232n66, 233

De finibus

II 69	217n23

De natura deorum

I 19	140
I 20	107n29
I 21	143–44
I 26–28	149
I 26	6n19
I 50	156
I 109	156
II 18	212
II 20	225
II 26	224
II 37–39	231n63
II 88	207
II 93	158
II 95–96	205n1
II 121–29	236n75
II 141	81n15
II 162	235
II 142	52n70
III 92	210n15

Timaeus

5	107n30

Tusculan disputations

I 70	107n30

Democritus (Diels-Kranz 68)

A 39	136n6
B 5	134n1
B 116	135
B 164	136n7

Derveni Papyrus

24	22n61

Diodorus Siculus

I 7.3–6	18n52
I 10.1–7	18n52

Diogenes of Apollonia (Diels-Kranz 64)

A5	90n31
B 2	76
B 3	75–77, 200n65
B 4	76
B 5	76–77
B 7	65n96

Diogenes Laertius
II 8 — 16n49
II 9 — 18n52, 22n64
II 16–17 — 18n52
II 19 — 16n46
II 34 — 212n20
VII 91 — 233n67
VII 149 — 217n23
VIII 5 — 7n22
IX 36 — 135n4
IX 57 — 90n31
X 33 — 141n17

Empedocles (Diels-Kranz 31)
A 8 — 44n43
A 42 — 34n9
A 52 — 62
A 70 — 46, 47
A 72 — *40–41*
B 6 — 33n7
B 8 — 37n18, 49n58
B 8.1–2 — 65n96
B 16.2 — 68n102
B 17 — 66
B 17.1–8 — *34–35*
B 17.1–5 — *63–64*
B 17.3 — 65
B 17.7–13 — 62
B 17.11 — 68n102
B 17.14 — 38n21
B 20.1 — 37n18
B 21 — 48, *58*, 59, 84
B 21.10 — 50
B 21.12 — 68n102
B 22 — 49n57, 59
B 23 — 48, 57, *58*
B 23.5 — 38n21
B 23.6 — 50
B 23.8 — 68n102
B 26 — 63
B 26.1–7 — *39–40*
B 26.4–6 — 35
B 26.5–6 — *63–64*
B 26.10 — 68n102
B 35 — 42–43, 46n45, 52, 59
B 35.16–17 — *44, 61*
B 57 — 42

B 58 — 42n32
B 59 — 43, 60
B 61 — 43, 50
B 62 — 45, 46, 47, 48
B 62.7 — 46n47
B 71 — 42, 43n37, 59
B 73 — 43, 59
B 75 — 43
B 76 — *37n18*
B 82 — 41
B 84 — 42, *52–53*, 57
B 86 — 42, 43n37, *52–53*
B 87 — 42, 43n37, 52
B 95 — 42, 43n37
B 96 — 41, 52, 59
B 98 — 41, 59
B 98.5 — 38n21
B 100 — 57
B 107 — 59n85
B109 — 59n85
B 110.3 — 68n102
B 111 — 71N114
B 112.4–5 — 50n61
B 113 — 51
B 115 — 50–51, 66, 69n106, 70
B 115.5 — 68n102
B 124 — 52
B 126 — 51n62
B 127 — 47n49
B 128 — 34n9, *39n23*, 50n61, 63, 66, 70, 74n124
B 129 — 7n22, 51
B 129.6 — 68n102
B 137.6 — 59n87
B 146 — 50n61
B 153a — 69n106

Empedocles, Strasbourg papyrus
a(i) 6 (= 267) — 40n26, 71n112
a(ii) 6 (= 276) — 68n102
a(ii) 21–30 (= 291–300) — *35–38*
a(ii) 26–28 (= 296–98) — 37, 72

a(ii) 27 (=297)   49–50
c   37n18
c3   71n112
d   45–46
d1–10   71n113
d10   71n112
d12   48n51

Epictetus
Discourses
I 16.9   240n3
II 6.9   234n69
fragments
1   243n7

Epicurus
Letter to Herodotus
43   162n53
72–73   145n26
On nature XXVIII
13 IX-X   162n54
fragments (Usener)
266   159n49
307   164n58

Eudemus (ed. Wehrli)
fr. 31   33n7

Euripides
Supplices
196–210   80n12

Galen
Compendium Timaei
39.12   107n34
De methodo medendi
I 4.10   146n28
De usu partium
II 154–62   240
III 16.7–17   130n78
*On the doctrines of
Hippocrates and Plato*
IX 7.9–16   242–43

Gellius
VII 1.10–13   235n72

Heraclitus (Diels-Kranz 22)
A 102   90n32
B 1   226n49

B 2   226n49
B 30   8n25
B 41   84n23
B 50   226n49

Herodotus
I 202–3   70n108
III 90–95   70n108
III 108–9   56n77
IV 124   70n108

Hesiod
Theogony
116–17   2
521–616   54
535   4n7
575   52n66
581   52n66
Works and Days
47–105   4, 47, 54
59–68   54
60   23
109–201   52
110   4
128   4
144   4
158   4
765–828   22
fragments (Merkelbach/West)
33a, 15   52n66

[Hesiod]
Shield of Heracles
140   52n66
224   52n66

Hippocrates
De flatibus
3   77n5
De victu
I 12–24   57n80

[Hippocrates]
Epistulae
10 (IX 322 Littré)   138n12

Hippolytus
Refutatio
I 8.3   16n49
I 9.5–6   18n52

Hippolytus
Refutatio (continued)

I 13.2–3	137n10
I 21	234n68
VII 29.22	47n48
VII 30.3–4	47n48

Leucippus (Diels-Kranz 67)

A 8	160n50

Lucian
Muscae Encomium

7	7n22

Lucretius

I 3	73n120
I 1008–51	157n45
I 1021–28	159n49
II 167–81	148
II 333–80	157n45
II 478–521	157n45
II 500–21	162n55
II 522–31	157n45
II 532–40	157
II 541–68	157n45
II 569–80	157n45
II 871–73	18n52
II 898–901	18n52
II 926–29	18n52
II 1081–83	37
II 1090–1104	148
II 1091–93	72
II 1116–17	163n56
III 713–40	18n52
III 830–1094	147
IV 823–31	152–53
IV 832–57	153
V 156–65	143
V 165–67	146
V 168–73	142–43
V 174–80	146
V 181–86	140
V 187–234	148
V 419–31	159n49
V 526–33	159n47
V 878–924	152
V 789	73n120
V 795–800	18n52

V 837–56	150–51
V 855–77	74, 151
V 864–70	73, 74, 151
V 864–66	73n120
V 878–924	72
V 925–1457	154

Marcus Aurelius

V 16	228n53, 237

Melissus (Diels-Kranz 30)

B 2	136n6
B 7	5n17

Ovid
Metamorphoses

I 416–37	18n52
VI 1–145	131

Parmenides (Diels-Kranz 28)

A 37	8
B 8.9–10	142n20
B 12–13	8
B 12.3–6	48n53

Pherecydes (Diels-Kranz)

7 B 1A	3n4

Philemon (Kassel/Austin)

fr. 93	57n78

Philo
De aeternitate mundi

57	19n54

Philodemus
De Epicuro

XVIII 10–17	147n30

De signis

XV 28–XVI 1	159n46

De Stoicis

XIII 3	206n4

Philoponus
De aeternitate mundi

599.22–601.19	107n34

In Aristotelis De anima

86.29–30	7n21

In Aristotelis Physica

405.23–27	136n8

Plato
Apology

24c1	79
31c7–d6	79

Crito

42d2–44b6	232
54e1–2	233

Cratylus

389a5–390e5	109n36
397e5–398c4	51n61

Critias

106a3–b6	100n14
106a3–4	102

Euthyphro

3b5–9	79

Gorgias

464b2–c3	106–7n28
500e3–501c1	107–8
503d5–504a5	107–8

Laws

678a7–679e5	120
721b6–c8	170
889a4–e1	175n18
892a2–c8	99n10
896b2–c8	99n10
967d6–7	99n10
903b4–d2	206n2

Phaedo

78c1–80c1	222n35
81d6–82b9	129
96a5–99d2	1n2
96b2–3	18n52
96b3–9	89n30
98c1–2	87
98c2–99b2	88
98d6–8	89n30
99a4–b6	115
99b2–6	210
99b2–4	88
99b8–c1	87n28
99c6–102a1	115n50
99c7–8	91–92
107c1–115a8	93–95
110b5–7	113n46

Phaedrus

245c5–246a2	104n23, 205n2

Philebus

28d5–9	1n2
29a9–30d9	82, 195, 218, 223n41

Protagoras

320c2–7	57
320c2–4	100
320d8–321c3	56
323a5–328c2	103

Republic

379c2–7	88n29
455d	230n61
508e2–3	106
530a4–c2	129
589b1–3	24n68
596a10–b8	108
597a2	108n36
597a4	108n36
597b4–6	108n36
597c2	108n36
597c3	108n36
597c9	108n36
597d1–2	108n36
620a2–d5	131n79

Sophist

242d4–243a1	32n6
244e2–8	32n5
265c1–10	82n21

Symposium

189d5–191d5	55
190a8–b5	55n75

Theaetetus

151a3–4	79

Timaeus

21a7–26e1	96
22c1–e2	119
22d7	120n60
23b3–d1	120
23b3–6	119–20n58
23d4–e2	120n58
27c1–d1	100n14
27d5–28a4	103n20
28a6–b2	127n75
28b2–c2	145n27
28b4–29a1	105
28b4–c2	101
28c1–2	103n20

Timaeus (continued)

28c2–29a1	*102*
28c2–3	*105*
28c5–29b1	101, 108
29a2–6	109
29a3–4	109
29b1–c3	110
29b3–c3	111n42
29c4–d3	*104*, 111
29d1–3	111n42
29d7–31a1	109
29d7–30b6	123n65
29e2	123n65
30b1–c1	212, 225, 227
30b1–3	230n60
30b1	228
30b2	230
30c2–31a1	112
30c2–3	108n36
30c5–8	108n36
30c6–d1	121n63
30c7–d1	61
30d2	228n54
31a2–b3	101, 112
31a4–5	108n36
31b1	108n36
31b4–32c4	110, 117
32c2–4	106
32c5–33b1	112, 117
33b1–7	110, 111, 118n53
33b7–34b3	112
33c4–d3	112n45
34b10–35a1	99
35a1–37c5	222
36c6	173n15
37a4–c5	168n3
37b8	111n42
37c6–38c3	99, 112, 144
37d1	108n36
37d3	108n36
37e3–38a2	105n25
39b2–c1	124n68
39e3–40a2	108n36 121
39e6–40a2	61
39e7–40a2	121n63
39e8	108n36

40a2–4	124n68
40a2–3	119
40b1	173n15
41a3–d3	100
41a7–d3	123n65
41b7–d3	121
41d1–3	127n74
41d4–7	222
41d6–7	*126n73*
42a1–2	50n60
42b2–d2	122
42d2–5	126
42d2–3	106n28
42d3–4	123
42e3–4	123n66
42e6–44c4	124
42e6–43a1	199n59
43c7–44b7	222
44d3–8	125
44d3–6	118n53
44d3–4	127n75
45a3–b2	171
45b2–46c6	119
46c7–48b3	114
46c7–e2	209
46c7–d1	116, 119
46d1–3	184
46e1–2	116
46e2–6	114n47
46e2	114n48
46e4	115
46e6–47c4	124
47b5–e2	*114n47*
47e4–48a7	114n48
48a3	118
48a7	114
48b3–c2	33n7
48d4–e1	100n14
51d2–53c3	99
51d3–e6	101
52d2–53b5	116
52d4–53a8	104n23
52d4–53a7	118n56
53a7–b5	118
53d5	114n48
55c4–d6	113
55d8–56a1	119n57

56c5–6   119n57
56c5   114n48
57d3–58a2   118n56
68e1–69a5   114, 116n52
69a6–81e5   125, 127
69b1   99n13
69b8–c3   61
69c2–3   108n36
69c2   108n36
69c5–86a8   197
69c5–73a8   129n77
69d7   114n48
70e5   114n48
71a3–72d3   125n72
72d4–8   111n42
72e2–73a8   129n77
73d3–e4   130
74e1–75c7   120
75a7–b2   121n62
75a7–b1   114n48, 121n62
75d5–e5   114n48, 116n52
75e3–5   125n70
76b1–d3   120
76d6–8   114n47
76e7–77c5   108n36
76e7–77b1   127n74
90a2–b1   172, 173n15
90e1–92c3   128, 197
90e6–91d5   128
91d6–e1   128, 129
91e2–92a4   128
91e692a7   130–31
91e6–92a7   130
92a4–7   128
92a7–c1   128

Plutarch
Adversus Colotem
1123B   72n117
De communibus notitiisi
210n15
De Stoicorum Repugnantiis
1044D   235n73
Quaestiones convivales
683E   52n52

Porphyry
De abstinentia
III 20.3   236
III 30.1   235n71

Proclus
In Platonis Timaeum
I 276.30–277.1   107n30
I 289.7–9   107n30
II 95.28–96.1   107n30
III 212.6–9   107n30

Scholia on Aristotle
on *Generation and Corruption,* and *Physics*
    67–70

Scholia on Proclus
on *In Plat. Remp.* II
377.15   107n30

Seneca
Letters
58.27–29   107n30
65.2   210n14

Sextus Empiricus
Adversus mathematicos
VII 116–18   136n7
VII 132   226n49
IX 20–23   205n1
IX 60–137   211
IX 75–122   211
IX 75–87   211
IX 76   205n2
IX 88–110   210–30
IX 92–94   215–16
IX 94   217–18, 221n32
IX 95   218, 219–20
IX 96   219–20
IX 97   220
IX 98   222n36, 223n37, 223n38
IX 99–100   221

Sextus Empiricus
Adversus mathematicos
IX 100   221n32, 222n36, 223n40

Sextus Empiricus
Adversus mathematicos (continued)

IX 101	222n36, 223–24
IX 102–3	224n45
IX 102	211
IX 104	225–26, 229
IX 107	225n46
IX 108–10	219
IX 108	229
IX 109–10	229
IX 111–18	211
X 181–88	145n26
XI 73	231n65

Simplicius
In Aristotelis De caelo

529.1–530.11	42
529.26	42n33
529.28	42
530.5–10	43
530.11	43n37

In Aristotelis Physica

7.10–17	33n7
151.20	77n5
157.22–24	14n40
178.25	16n48
178.28–179.12	27
371.33	42n34
372.6–7	45n44
372.8–9	44n41

Tatian
Oratio ad Graecos

3.1–2	233n67

Thales (Diels-Kranz 11)

A 14	4n12
A 22	6, 7

Theophrastus
De causis plantarum

I 5.2	18n53
III 1.4	18n53

De sensibus

8	42n33, 53n69

fragments (Fortenbaugh et al.)

241A-B	107n31
226A	90n31

Xenocrates (fragments, ed. Isnardi Parente)

153–57	100n15

Xenophanes (Diels-Kranz 21)

B 10–16	8n23
B 11–16	83
B 23–26	8n23, 83
B 25–26	149n35
B 28	149n35

Xenophon
Apology

12–13	79n10

De re equestri

11.13	79n10

Hellenica

VI 4.3	79n10

Memorabilia

I 1.2–4	79n10
I 1.11–15	79
I 3.14–15	81n16
I 4	78–86, 148, 204n73, 210–11
I 4.2–7	83–86, 214–15
I 4.2–6	213
I 4.2	79, 82n20, 85
I 4.4	85n24
I 4.5	81, 85n24
I 4.6	81, 82n19
I 4.7	80n11, 213
I 4.8–14	213
I 4.8	82, 195, 221n32
I 4.9–11	85
I 4.12	81
I 4.17–18	83
I 4.17	81
IV 3	78–86, 148
IV 3.2	82n20
IV 3.5	81
IV 3.6	81
IV 3.12	79n10
IV 3.13	149n33
IV 3.15	79
IV 5.9	81n16
IV 8.1	79n10

General Index

Academics, Academy, 140n15, 144n24, 206, 236
aether, 9, 13, 87, 94
Alexander of Aphrodisias, 27, 170n7
Alexinus, 211, 219, 229–30
Anaxagoras, 3n6, 7–31, 75, 80n12, 82n21, 83, 87–91, 93–94, 133, 134n1, 135, 137, 143n22, 149, 168, 184n28, 192n42, 200n66, 226n49
Anaximander, 3n6, 5, 6, 69n106
Anaximenes, 3n6, 149
Antiochus, 107n30
Antiphon the Sophist, 184n30
Antisthenes, 81n17, 233n67
Archelaus, 18n52
Archedemus, 231
Archimedes, 207
Argument from Design, xv, xvii, 75, 82–86, 205–7, 210–11, 213
Aristodemus, 83–86, 213–14
Aristophanes, 54n73, 90n31, 129.
  See also Plato, *Symposium*
Aristotle, xvi-xvii, 1, 18, 77, 119, 133, 143, 148, 167–204, 206, 208, 236, 239–41; on Anaxagoras, 10, 21, 26–28, 30, 192n42; on atomists, 182, 184, 191–93, 195; on Empedocles, 60, 189–91; relation to Plato, 107, 114n47, 167–70, 172–74, 178, 183–84, 197–99, 203–4; *Metaphysics* Lambda, 169, 171, 198–200; *Nico-machean ethics* X, 169; *Parts of*

animals, 186n31, 194–96; *Politics*, 199–200, 201–2
atomism, atomists, xvi, 3n6, 7, 23, 82, 86, 89–90, 133–66, 168–69, 182, 184, 191–93, 195, 239, 242
Atticus, 107n30

Boethus, 107n33
Borel, Emile, 158

cataclysms, 119–20
Carneades, 236–38
cause, 87–89, 91, 94, 98, 101–12, 106–9, 113–16, 123, 133, 142, 168, 173, 174–75, 178–81, 184, 187–88, 209–10
Chaos, 2–3
Chrysippus, 232–35
Cicero, literalist interpreter of *Timaeus*, 107n30
Cleanthes, 211, 217n23, 226
Cosmic Intelligence Argument, 82–83, 211–14, 217–25
craft, craftsmanship, 23, 52–59, 84–85, 98–99, 105–15, 127–28, 140, 141, 153–55, 173–81, 186, 204, 216, 221–22, 240–42
Crantor, 206n5

daimons, 31–32, 34n9, 39, 48, 50–51 60, 62, 66, 70, 131, 172
Darwin (Charles), Darwinism, xv, 43, 56, 151, 155n40, 168, 242

Demiurge. *See* craft
Democritus, 133–39, 158, 160–65
Derveni Papyrus, 71n115
determinism, 164–65, 233–34
Diogenes of Apollonia, 1, 75–78, 83, 90, 200n65, 205
Diogenes of Oenoanda, 143n21
Diogenes of Sinope, 233n67
divination, 79, 125n72, 232–34

earth, stability of, 3–4, 87, 93
Empedocles, 31–74, 75, 83, 84, 121–22, 131, 152, 189–91
Epicureans, Epicurus, 72–73, 107, 133–34, 139–66, 170, 175, 182n25, 206, 207n8, 234, 239
evil, source of, 62, 88n29, 115–27, 148, 185–86, 210, 234–35
eye, 42, 52–54, 60, 81, 124–25, 154–55

final cause, 2n2, 114n47, 174–75, 187, 197, 200
fortuitous, the, 181, 186–94
fossils, 43n39

Galen, xvii, 77, 133, 239–44

hair, 120, 231, 240–42
Harpocration, 107n30
head, 114n48, 118n53, 120–21, 126–28, 130, 235
Heraclitus, 5, 8, 83, 209n12, 226–27
Hermotimus, 7n22, 25n70
Hesiod, 2–4, 8, 22, 47, 54, 57, 62
Hippocrates, 240
Huxley, Thomas, 158

infinity, 136–39, 144–45, 155–66
intelligence, 9–12, 19–25, 27, 30, 31, 75, 82n21, 87–90, 94–95, 109, 114–15, 118–19, 133–35, 137, 140, 145, 168, 175, 183, 184n28, 191–92, 194, 207, 225–30; simple vs complex, 221–22. *See also* Cosmic Intelligence Argument
isonomia, 156–58, 163n56, 166

Kelvin, Lord, 19n57

Lamarck, Jean-Baptiste, 151
Lamb, Charles, 193
Leibniz, Gottfried, 76, 142
Leucippus, 90n31, 133–34, 139–57
Lucretius, 37–38, 50, 72–74, 139–64, 234
luck, 186–94

mind (*nous*). *See* intelligence
moon, 13, 14, 20–22, 25, 137, 207
Moses, 241

necessity, 114–16, 118, 119n57, 140, 181–86, 207n8
noēsis. *See* intelligence
nous. *See* intelligence

Orpheus, 69
ou mallon, 138, 158, 160
Ovid, 131

Paley, William, xv, 207
Panaetius, 107n33
Pandora, 4, 47, 54
Parmenides, 1–2n2, 8, 11, 32–33, 135–36, 142
Philolaus, 51n62
Plato, 1–2, 62, 77–78 147–48, 152, 167–70, 173, 176, 185, 204, 239–41; on Anaxagoras, 21–24, 87–89, 93–94, 218; on Socrates, 78, 82, 86–95, 206; influence on Stoicism, 205, 208–11, 222, 223 225–31, 243; *Apology*, 91; *Cratylus*, 125n71; *Critias*, 95–96; *Crito*, 125n72, 232–33; *Gorgias*, 106–7n26, 107–8, 113–14, 132, 217; *Laws* X, 82n21, 85n25, 205; *Meno*, 103n21; *Phaedo*, 21, 82n21, 86–95, 115, 125–26, 128, 129, 131n79, 132, 217; *Phaedrus*, 104n23; *Protagoras*, 55–57; *Republic*, 95, 126n73, 129, 132, 169; *Symposium*, 46, 55, 131; *Timaeus*, xvi, 4n8, 25, 57, 61, 91–92, 93, 94n4, 95–133, 139–41, 143–45, 169, 171, 173–74, 183–84, 186, 196–

98, 206, 208–11, 222, 223, 226–31, 240, 243; unwritten doctrines, 115n51
Plutarch, on *Timaeus*, 107n30, 206n5
Polemo, 107n30, n32, 140n15, 206n5
Posidonius, 207n8, 226n49, 233n67
Presocratics, 1–2, 75, 78, 81–83, 86, 87, 129, 133, 184–85
Prometheus, 47, 54, 55–56, 100
Protagoras, 55–57, 100, 103
Pythagoras, 7n22, 51
Pythagoreanism, Pythagoreans, 3n6, 92, 94nn3–4

receptacle, 3

seed(s), 13n36, 14–20, 23, 191, 224–25, 226n49
Severus, 107n30
Simplicius, 14, 62, 64
Socrates, 1, 75, 78, 139, 148, 149n33, 152, 204, 209–10; approved by Galen, 242–43; influence on Stoicism, 222n35, 231, 206–7, 212–25; on limits of knowledge, 111; as moral exemplar, 232–33; in Plato, 86–89, 93–95; against physical speculation, 78–79, 110; relation to Democritus, 134–35;

in Xenophon, 78–86, 146, 189, 192, 195, 202, 205, 231
spontaneous generation, 18–19, 46, 48, 150
Stoics, 62, 107, 133, 143, 148, 152n38, 195, 205–38
sun, 13, 14, 20–22, 25, 124n68, 137, 196, 202, 207

Thales, 3, 6–7
Theophrastus, 28n74
time, 67–70, 99, 104–5, 144–45, 159n49, 208

Voltaire, 76, 154
vortex, 3, 5–6, 9, 13, 20–22, 137

worlds, simultaneous plurality of, 15–19, 21, 23n66, 24, 112–13, 136–37, 148–49, 159–66, 191, 242; serial plurality of, 208

Xenocrates, 100, 206n5
Xenophanes, 3n6, 83, 149
Xenophon, 78–86, 90–91, 95, 146, 148, 149n33, 189, 192, 195, 202, 205, 207, 210–25, 231, 242–43

Zeno of Citium, 206, 209, 211–12, 223–29, 233n67
Zeno of Elea, 162–63

Text:	10/13 Aldus
Display:	Aldus
Compositor:	Integrated Composition Systems
Printer and binder:	Maple-Vail Manufacturing Group